A Chronicle
of Jeopardy

—————————————————— *1945–55*

A Chronicle
of Jeopardy

————————————— 1945-55

by REXFORD G. TUGWELL

The University of Chicago Press

Library of Congress Catalog Number: 55-8360

THE UNIVERSITY OF CHICAGO PRESS, CHICAGO 37
Cambridge University Press, London, N.W. 1, England
The University of Toronto Press, Toronto 5, Canada

C. 2

CONTENTS

Our tragedy today is a general and universal physical
fear so long sustained by now that we can even bear it. There
are no longer problems of the spirit. There is only the
question: When will I be blown up? Because of this, the
young man or woman writing today has forgotten the problems
of the human heart in conflict with itself which alone can
make good writing because only that is worth writing about,
worth the agony and the sweat."

—From William Faulkner's speech of acceptance upon the award
  of the Nobel Prize for Literature, Stockholm, December 10, 1950.

THE villain of my ten-year chronicle of jeopardy is the Bomb, the genocidal weapon which first engulfed two Japanese cities in its apocalyptic fire. That early, and, by later measurements, almost miniature, device was able to and did kill in the hundreds of thousands. As I have gone on from year to year, I have had to note, in this one decade, the perfection of that much more efficient killer, the improved A-bomb, and its wide adaptation to tactical as well as strategic uses. Then I have had to record the prospect and the arrival of the dreadful H-bomb, which raised the hundreds of thousands sacrificed at Hiroshima and Nagasaki easily to potential millions. The perfected A-bomb has not been used in anger; and the H-bomb has only bloomed in its preposterous magnitude in the lonely testing grounds of the Pacific. Nevertheless, mankind has been confronted with an imperative. This Bomb did not need to be used in war to be convincing. Its annihilatory power was amply demonstrated when what had been a Pacific island became a large hole at the bottom of the sea.

Altogether there had been, by the end of the decade, perhaps

1

seventy nuclear explosions—the record not being easy to compute because the distinction between small atomic devices (artillery war heads, for instance) and "conventional" weapons tended to become blurred. The testing in Nevada of atomic instruments was only semipublic; and numbers became difficult to distinguish. Also it was not known in the West how many devices had been tested in Russia. It was known from radioactive dust that explosions had taken place, but not how many.

There has been a quite natural confusion about publicity. Because the further actual use of the Bomb must seem, to anyone who contemplates it seriously, to require a moral decision of which no human could be capable, those who determine publicity policies for the government have not really known whether they were dealing with a secret weapon being prepared for use or with a monstrous retaliatory warning against attack. This last is not exactly to be described as bluff; it is more a feeling that it would be unthinkable for hostile statesmen to risk the certain destruction carried by the ever enlarging Bomb. Their nation would receive as well as give. If warning is the utility possessed by nuclear bombs, the more the enemy knows about them the better, because there can be no doubt about their actuality or about American ability to deliver them on target, even after the enemy bombers have left their bases.

So at one time ordinary citizens seem to be taken into the confidence of those who know, because they work with the weapon, what its potentialities are. And at other times they are treated as though they were all security risks likely to betray to the enemy any knowledge they may be allowed to have; they are therefore kept in ignorance. There has been the added complication that the Soviet Union, assumed to be the enemy, has not only built bombs of the same sort as those perfected by the United States and Britain but has surprised our scientists by producing "improvements." There have been times when it was hinted in a kind of panic that, in the race for nuclear supremacy, the Soviets might be ahead.

But the policy respecting publicity has been only a reflection of confusion concerning the weapons themselves—whether or not it was actually intended ever to use them. So statesmen have ended in a kind of wandering inconsistency which is, I am afraid, characteristic of all our reactions during these ten years. Public men, no less than others, have been swayed and called to violence. They have caught themselves on the brink of fatal decision.

Many instances of precipitate response will be found in this chronicle. Statesmen acting thus were responding partly to their own impulses to action when no action was possible and so were exhibiting the typical phenomena of frustration. Partly they were influenced by the heavy load of responsibility they carried which tortured all their decision-making. This last had to be the final governing consideration.

It is more possible to have sympathy for public men so put to cruel ordeal when it is recalled how, as private citizens, we ourselves have been pulled this way and that, have been convinced and then made aware of the foolishness of the conviction, have raged inwardly—and perhaps outwardly—at the frustration enforced by circumstance.

We can forgive ourselves, as well as statesmen, for this childish behavior when we understand how widely it was shared. Even the best intelligences, the most careful and well-balanced minds, have exhibited these tendencies. Perhaps they have been quicker than most to recover balance. But their problem was just as difficult. I have before me, for instance, two letters written by Lord Bertrand Russell in which there is a complete reversal. If such a mental disturbance was possible for him as these letters exhibit, it could happen to anyone. And anyone could, as I believe, follow him in regaining sanity. These letters were published in the *Saturday Review*.[1]

This is a quotation from a letter of 1948:

As soon as Russia rejected the Baruch proposals I urged that all nations favoring international control of atomic energy should form an alliance and threaten Russia with war unless Russia agreed to come in and permit inspection.

If Russia overruns West Europe, the destruction will be such as no subsequent reconquest can undo. Practically the whole educated population will be sent to labor camps in Siberia or on the shores of the White Sea, where most will die of hardships and the survivors will be turned into animals. . . .

Even at such a price I think war would be worthwhile. Communism must be wiped out, and world government must be established. . . .

1. October 16, 1954, p. 25. The second letter resulted from an inquiry about the first which was written to Dr. Walter Marseille in 1948 and which seemed not to agree with later (1954) published views of the distinguished philosopher. The second letter was written to the editor of the *Saturday Review*. Only part of each letter is quoted.

This is a quotation from a letter of 1954:

I should not be wholly sincere if I did not admit that my opinions have undergone a change somewhat deeper than that warranted by strategic considerations. The awful prospect of the extermination of the human race, if not in the next war, then in the next but one or the next but two, is so sobering to any imagination which has seriously contemplated it as to demand very fundamental fresh thought on the whole subject, not only of international relations, but of human life and its capabilities. If you were quarreling with a man about some issue that both you and he had thought important just at the moment when a sudden hurricane threatened to destroy you both and the whole neighborhood you would probably forget the quarrel. I think what is important is to make mankind aware of the hurricane and forgetful of the issues which had been producing strife. I know it is difficult after spending many years and much eloquence on the evils of Communism or Capitalism, as the case may be, to see this issue as one of relative unimportance. But, although this is difficult, it is what both Soviet rulers and the men who shape the policy of the United States will have to achieve if mankind is to survive. . . .

Lord Russell had wanted a preventive war; he was now convinced that one was not possible. In the face of extermination, arguments about social organization seemed trivial, finally, and he now advocated a policy of *rapprochement*. This was a retreat many others had made, not perhaps so lucidly as Lord Russell, but they, like him, had ended inconclusively. *Rapprochement*, like a bargain, requires two parties—also good faith, and guaranties of performance. These were something to work for. But how difficult it was to live with the problem thus posed, everyone knew, because everyone faced it.

I am tempted to refer to the monstrously enlarging Bomb as a political cancer. And indeed the analogy is not a bad one. It has certainly corrupted and confused all our national actions, has eaten at our individual minds with the poisonous fog of fear which emanates from it; and its effects have spread even into our relations with each other—since each of us must have an attitude toward it and since we differ bitterly as to whether that attitude has adequate justification. Because we have within us this gnawing fear, our reactions are abnormal. We seem unable to think about what we ought to do except in frightened calculation of the likelihood—latent, of course, because thrust hurriedly into the unconscious whenever reality obtrudes—that we ourselves and those we love may be dissolved and blown into the high sky, disappearing as the dust and mist of the familiar mushroom (or, as a soldier said of the 1952

H-bomb, "the cauliflower") into which all matter is caught up when fission or fusion happens with the intent to destroy.

The ambivalences, the dilemmas, the confusions, to which humans are prone anyway, have been acerbated and further confused by the presence in our midst of this pervasive malaise. The poison is in the air, and we must deal with it. Our ordinary occupations are no longer more secure than the cautious forays for food of our hairy ancestors who lived, naked and fearful, in an environment dominated by the great carnivores. Our great carnivore is a device created by our scientists but directed by politicians who handle the issues it raises with the awkward clumsiness to be expected from the revolutionary imperatives it has created.

Yet we are moral creatures. We have not loosed our hold on the traditions and beliefs by which we have always lived. We have not because we cannot and remain men. We know in our hearts that this thing in our midst is wrong—utterly wrong—by any test of any ethical system of any time. By Christian standards, for instance, nothing so challengingly wicked has ever appeared to test men's capacity for discerning the right and cleaving to its precepts.

Yet each of us who is critical of the politicians' behavior must ask himself what he would have done in the various crises of the decade if he had been responsible for the decisions that had to be made. What, for instance, would he have done in 1949, when the H-bomb was finally admitted by the scientists to be feasible and when it was realized that, if it could be made by Americans, it would be made by others? Even if he had confidence that the Soviets would not use it once it was made—and not many Americans did— then it had to be considered what the situation would be if another Hitler should come into its possession. Did anyone doubt Hitler's freedom from those moral scruples which would cause withholding of the Bomb?

No, when Harry S. Truman had to decide whether the United States should produce H-bombs, he was acting as our surrogate. We were and are in it with him. That he had to do it for us does not entitle us to blame him—not unless we can honestly say that we would have decided differently.

One of the most disconcerting of all the consequences following on nuclear weaponeering has been the withdrawal of policy from public discussion. President Truman need not have made that decision alone. So good a democrat should have seen the position into which he had been thrust by all the nondemocrats around him and have fortified himself with public consent. For this alone can we really call him to task.

There has been plenty of talk carried on quietly among troubled people. There has even been a good deal of publicity emanating from newsmen in Washington who know well enough the avidity with which every morsel of real information will be received. So the information has leaked out, and has grown and spread through the years, that what the testing of various bombs reveals is that the improved weapons are destructive beyond the most excited forebodings. Description of a muted sort, and even pictures, of the relatively small explosions in 1952 were made available in 1954. That two-year interval, however, spanned several crises provocative enough to have started a war. And obviously the bombs might have been used, although officially the public had not yet been notified of their existence.

This will serve for illustration of the security neurosis which has seized our policy-makers, which they have cynically passed on to us, and which has precluded any democratic participation in decision-making. Even after the whole world knew what had happened in the Pacific, through leaks from those who had been present, frowns of official displeasure were turned on any discussion whatever of the events. Since the potential enemies obviously knew about them, the secrecy could only be intended to keep Americans in ignorance and, where not in ignorance, at least quiet.

If such official attitudes are not intended to prevent discussion of the Bomb's potential and of the consequences which might follow its use, what are they intended for? But protests from the scientists and others have had no effect. The existence of civilization being literally at stake, people are prevented from having the facts which would enable them to decide for themselves what their government ought to be doing. No such antidemocratic demonstration has ever been tolerated before in American history.

The result of this smothering of public participation in the most consequential decision of our history has been just what would have been expected. Gradually those who manage strategy for our survival have committed themselves to reliance on this most powerful —and most doubtful—weapon ever devised. And this in spite of the consideration which would occur to anyone of sense—that its possession by our potential enemies as well as ourselves has made it totally unusable. There is not one strategic air force, poised for momentary action, on widely spaced air fields; there are two. One of them is ours; but the other is the Soviets'. The situation is such that the start of one flight would activate the start of the other. Attack without retaliation is known to be impossible.

What kind of strategy is it, then, which, under the name of "the New Look," brags of a power "to retaliate." Who has any interest in retaliation? What is wanted is survival for ourselves—that, and not the destruction of Russians, is where the national interest lies.

The arrival at the obviously impossible dilemma into which the stifling of discussion and the intrusting of strategy-making to a closed group of policy-makers has landed us is the greatest peril of all our experience as a nation. The decline of democracy into this deepening danger has seemed to paralyze a traditionally free and individualistic people. They have submitted to the discipline of security—a false security, as I believe—as they have never before submitted to any dictation from anyone or any conspiring group.

I have tried to record what has happened in these matters from year to year; especially I have tried to show how the poison of the Bomb has spread through the body politic, how that organism has tried to combat and eject it, and how that effort has gradually failed before a destructive potential beyond comprehension which is yet being used for mortal purposes as though it were mere old-fashioned dynamite.

I have deliberately not rewritten any chapter after leaving it. Theoretically each of the ten was written on the anniversary of Hiroshima. Much of the whole year was devoted to the gathering and collating of the materials necessary to the quick writing in the few summer weeks I allowed for it each year, keeping the period short because my intention was to record, year by year, the situation as it existed on the fatal anniversary.

It will be remarked, I am quite aware, that the early chapters differ from the later ones in proceeding from more obviously personal reactions. This was something I could not seem to help. If I could have managed it, I should have kept the whole chronicle in that vein. I am not a historian in any professional sense and did not want to pretend to be. I set out merely to say how this monstrous intrusion looked to me and how it affected my own reactions to the world; beyond that I intended to make an assessment of its effect on the prospects of the nation, but one which could not be mistaken for a pretentious judgment beyond my range and capacity.

I found myself, as the years passed, less able to feel that my reactions were either private or unique. As I watched the growing volume of expressed opinion being transformed into a considered view of man's prospects in his new circumstances, the labor of making each year's assessment grew more formal, and I was less and less able to keep to the role of speaking only for myself. As I became more concerned—more frightened, if you like—I became more detached. Nothing seemed to matter any more but an almost automatic recording of a degeneration from which there was no relief and no hope of relief.

After a few years, also, there arose the conflict with the great Russian imperium; then there was the entry on the fatal contest with China. Individuals counted less and less as sides were taken; all Westerners—and especially all Americans—were merged in one mass by a kind of polarity. Never in a fairly long life had I ever felt so little an individual and so much part of an entity as in the years after 1947. This did not mean that all of us, me included, shaped our policies automatically or even that we were wise in reaching them. I became more critical than ever, actually, of American policy; but the urgency changed. It no longer mattered what went on within myself or any other self, except as it emerged in collective decision. Because decision, suddenly, was charged with potential destruction or survival.

My later chapters have more or less written themselves. I became a historian—not necessarily a skilful or an adequate one. My account was far less a description of the way I saw it than an attempt to grasp the way we were all seeing it and what that meant for our future. This most difficult of endeavors was one I should not have had the temerity to undertake if I had not been led into rather than freely chosen it.

Perhaps I may be excused some inconsistency. There have been grave shifts in the decade I have written about. I did not always see what was emerging and what was disappearing with the clarity Lord Russell exhibited as he faced the facts he knew about. My excuse is that I have written as a complete layman, not even a historian, a member of the public, with no sources of information not open to any concerned student and no contacts in "informed circles." I was certain that, at one stage, I discerned a conspiracy, or a kind of conspiracy, looking toward a preventive war. This was when the military-industrial clique moved in on President Truman before he had mastered his duties. It was abortive; and the common sense of certain military leaders together with the inertia of public opinion finally dragged the initiative to a stop. But there was much support for such a policy—witness, again, Lord Russell's belief that it was necessary!

The same danger revived again under the leadership of Mac-Arthur, who, if he had been allowed, would have brought on the preventive war by crossing the Yalu. There continued to be echoes of this impulse even into the fifties when the H-bomb made it more illogical and at the same time more dangerous than it had been before MacArthur's temerity was, it is believed, shared by General Clark, Admiral Radford, and Secretary Dulles. When the Russian nuclear explosions took place, the possibility of the conquest of the Communist world vanished; but the possibility did not wholly vanish from reluctant minds—minds involved in determining what the American policy ought to be.

Still it diminished; and it was transformed into all sorts of avoidances of reason. From 1949 the only possible policy for the United States was to reach an arrangement for coexistence. It was the only possible policy for the Soviets too. Their leaders said so repeatedly. But in 1954 the American Secretary of State, if he recognized the hard reality he faced, was still, perhaps in deference to isolationist sentiment, repudiating it. To accept coexistence, he said, was to condemn hundreds of millions of souls to despotism.

This was nonsense. They might be condemned to despotism; but an arrangement for coexistence would not condemn them further. It would not promise rescue; but also it would not promise physical destruction. And surely the first responsibility was to those who still had the freedom Mr. Dulles spoke about. The alternative, as someone remarked, to coexistence was codestruction. Only gradually and reluctantly did we come to accept stalemate as a third possibility.

This danger through which we passed of conspiracy to bring on preventive war was, as I came to believe, frustrated by those who had superior military sense. I credit General Bradley and his colleagues among the Joint Chiefs of Staff with more wisdom than I am able to discover in contemporary statesmen. I was not always aware of the hard strategic logic which characterized these military men. The adventurers were quite another group—the self-conscious capitalists who saw in communism a threat to their system which was intolerable, together with others among the military who regarded themselves as statesmen but who actually were shortsighted chance-takers.

What I am saying is that I do not pretend to have been wiser as I made my annual explorations than I was able to be at the time and with my knowledge. And my self-imposed limitation, which prevented revision, has inevitably revealed some discrepancies, some changes of mind, and some mistakes of emphasis or even fact. But my excuse is that we were all that way, that my representation of the American mind in that year is not too inaccurate; and that my main purpose anyway was to mirror, as faithfully as I could, our passage through a decade of despond. I hoped, of course, that, if holocaust did not come, we should have passed through the ordeal. I did not imagine we should still be in it a decade after Hiroshima. For a long time—throughout the forties—I was convinced that 1952 would be the year of crisis. If we survived that year, it must be because we had come to some arrangement with the Soviets. My timing was wrong; we continued to flounder. And there no longer seemed in prospect any climactic time which, if survived, would allow us to hope for release from tension.

It has not been easy to persist over ten years, especially since what I had to record I came more and more to believe was a chronicle of perils escaped from by miracles which could not be counted on to recur regularly. Our statesmen have been, it seems to me, incorrigibly reckless. But after the fashion of drunken men who are said to be specially protected by Providence, I began to realize, toward the last, that, having survived into what, if we had any intelligence left at the service of restraint, was stalemate, we might, in the years to come, reverse the trend of the first atomic decade. In the new age it might even be that the terror of that decade—the Bomb—might, under another guise, be the blessing of ages yet to come.

CHAPTER I *1945*

ON THE Day of the Bomb, August 6, 1945, and during the following week, I happened to be in New York, staying at the old Algon-
quin Hotel on Forty-fourth Street close to Times Square. This was
a strategic position to experience as well as observe, with whatever
detachment a human being could have whose own atoms were involved, the behavior of a species which had at last contrived an
effective means for its own annihilation without any adequate individual or collective defense. It was obvious that no one could ab-
stract himself from the consequences of this invention or have any
considerable influence on its management. A realization of their
helplessness could be seen to creep gradually over the faces of men
throughout those first days of the atomic era. The human spirit had
withdrawn into the hidden chambers of men's minds, wounded and
frightened. It brooded there in the dark.

There had just been finished a war against gangsters belonging
to two widely separated races. They were, I firmly believed, properly called "gangsters," because they had refused to recognize the
restraints of civilization and had regarded themselves as not only
above law but above morality and religion. They had, indeed, created new moralities and religions for their own purposes and imposed them with frightening facility on their people. Neither nation
had been a backward one; both had been quite otherwise. Their
citizens had been among the most talented, the most industrious,
and the most skilled in the arts of large organization. They had
lacked merely the power and the esteem they had craved; and they
had determined to force its granting if no other way could be found.

Only through the operations of their own hysteria had the gangsters been deprived of the absolute and ultimate power of the Bomb. They had outlawed the Jews; and certain brilliant Jews had been among those who had carried the vital knowledge into exile. There was some inclination at the moment to see in this event one of the wise provisions of a benevolent principle in the affairs of mankind; but this view of the matter was neither lasting nor general. Nor was it widely felt that any such principle was to be trusted in the future. The fact that the direct ancestry of the Bomb involved Jewish intellectuals and that it had been convenient for the Nazis to hold the Jews responsible for German shortcomings and ill luck was considered to be merely an accident. Certainly the Japanese, although they also had fostered a racial myth, had not been kept from succeeding with the Bomb by anything except a slight lateness. The exile of Albert Einstein, Lise Meitner, Niels Bohr, Enrico Fermi, Leo Szilard, Edward Teller, and others was merely a curious quirk in events. It could not be counted on to recur.

There was a much more general conviction that all of us had at last been delivered over to Fate or Chance, that implacable and inscrutable fashioner of events which under so many names has always terrorized mankind. The feeling of being lost in the universe, of not being the object of any special concern by an all-seeing and all-powerful Providence, but rather of being the object of something like hostility, and required to create, out of nothing assured, whatever safety, confidence, security they were ever to have, engulfed even those people who ordinarily had taken life as it came without question as to where it was going or what it meant while it was going there.[1] It had suddenly become a deadly practical business to consider the impractical. Despised theorists suddenly ceased to be comic and became figures of frankensteinian horror.

It was, of course, not true that the Bomb had come upon us suddenly. Like other inventions which have startled the ignorant, it had a long and logical ancestry. Only those were wholly unprepared for it who did not know what had been going on in the chemistry-physics laboratories and in the mathematicians' studies of the universities. That the uninformed included many who ought to have

1. This has never been better expressed than by Sir Arthur Balfour in, for instance, *A Defence of Philosophical Doubt* (London: Macmillan & Co., 1879), as well as in his other works. His, however, was an attitude which ran contrary to the prevailing one of his Edwardian-Georgian time.

known was in fact one of the strangest and most unaccountable phases of the events now taking place. It was one of my most familiar mysteries. I had long ago given up trying to understand why my social science colleagues refused to take account in their professional work of the new discoveries in physical science and the significant applications made of them in industry. Sometimes it seemed as though they recognized no connection between industry, which was based on science, and economics. I had even written a book once in the attempt to furnish elementary knowledge of scientific management and to establish at least the missing connection. The developments I described were of such a nature, I thought, as to make an entirely new approach to social and economic theory imperative; but it was an imperative which went so largely unrecognized that it could almost be said to have been ignored.[2]

That a unitary world would be born was obvious to anyone who did not wear philosophical blinders. That industrialists and bankers preferred to create and run a collective world without interference would not have deterred a generation of genuinely realistic economists. But on the day of reckoning they were almost as obsolete as old-fashioned admirals and generals.

Times Square on the Day of the Bomb, that night, and on subsequent days and nights for a week was the scene of a performance carried out according to required custom with strict but nearly empty fidelity. New Yorkers and their visitors—for any New York crowd is always at least half visitors—were acting under compulsion; but, unless they drank a great deal or in some similar way induced forgetfulness and frenzy, they were always being overcome by the enormity of implications which weighed upon their minds, always stopping with a laugh half-done, a shout half-over, a gesture half-made. Everyone who could read had seen the story of the Bomb's creation. It had been carefully prepared in advance by the science editor of the *New York Times*,[3] and everyone understood it well enough so that its implications were clear. They could not help shuddering, however, at the picture so vividly presented by Mr.

2. This small book of mine, published in 1927, was called *Industry's Coming of Age*. It had caused no furor in its time and was by now long out of print.

3. Mr. William L. Laurence.

Laurence of the assembled scientists who had huddled in a dugout some six miles from the experimental tower at Alamogordo and had waited in the bleak New Mexican dawn for what might happen. There seemed not to have been complete certainty that the fission, once started, would stop short of all the atoms in the universe or at least—what interested people most—our own planet. If there had been the faintest doubt—and that desert dugout was the very picture of doubt—had not an ultimate chance been taken with human kind whose further existence was put in jeopardy? How often on that day did people, peering at each other, wonder that they had not disintegrated and imagine that at almost any time they might—that in the twinkling of an eye they might be destroyed.

Postwar Britishers had been discussing Sir William Beveridge's plan for guaranteed income; here at home we had been having hearings on a full-employment bill; men had intended to have, if they could, an interlude of peace, a respite from eternal strain. The cares and worries of illness, joblessness, family care—all these, they had been thinking, would be eased by turning the immense energies released for the war to the uses of peace. They were in a mood to refuse the bankers' and economists' veto power over production, having been taught that there was nothing sacred about money and nothing necessarily disastrous in a public debt incurred for public purposes. They had been looking forward to a really better world. And here close upon them was a far worse insecurity, a far greater necessity for taking thought.

The night of the Bomb it became, of course, a wild, jostling, riotous crowd beneath the gargantuan overhang of the advertising lights. The rioting was ritualistic in the only manner permissible under such auspices, and it went on and on for days and nights as the Japanese hesitation was prolonged. The first night, with windows open to the street, sleep was impossible in the incredible jangle. On the second night, in a kind of stupor and riding on the almost solid volume of the noise, I seemed to be carried irresistibly into a world of dream.

With a group of companions, evidently serious intellectuals of some sort, I seemed to be engaged in earnestly probing the fate of mankind. We arrived at the conclusion that some secret was still unfound which held the key—the key to happiness, perhaps, or to permanent peace, or to security. It was, at any rate, the key to some fundamental solution for men, something they had sought all through their evolution, lived, worked, and died for. We had come close, in our discussion, to finding it, so close that the great and final satisfaction of salvation was palpable in the air. But we had to have that last secret; lacking it, all the rest—the work, the suffering, the long reflection—would come to nothing, and man's career as a species would end in oblivion. It was a formula we sought, like that which transmuted matter into energy; something, at least, as fundamental as transmutation, without which no further progress was possible. It gradually appeared, either because of the news we heard or from the nature of our reasoning—I could not be sure which— that the situation was even worse than this. We had to find something further not for the sake of peace, happiness, security, but for *survival*. Dissolution waited impatiently.

The discussion among the dream companions, which had begun somewhat casually, had gradually intensified until it reached a state of intolerable tension and urgency. We suddenly became aware that gigantic horns were blowing in the outer darkness; they grew louder, in a strange low register, so that we had to shout thinly if we were to be heard. The dream was vivid. There were not more than a dozen of us in a vast place; it might have been a marble platform in a wide valley or in a great stadium. There was light only where we sat, in thronelike chairs too large for us, and shouted at one another. Nevertheless, although the horns of doom grew louder, we reached agreement. But it was only agreement that we could not sit and discuss matters any longer. We had to go and search.

We started on what seemed to be a long journey of exploration. We went away from a walled place, walking into a countryside which stretched before and around us in far perspective, with innumerable homesteads, meadows, forests, hills, and streams. We went toward it in company at first; but then, as roads branched off, we separated one by one until finally I was all alone at the end of the last road. Ahead of me was an upland meadow with high rich grass; beyond there lay a dark forest, and just visible above the forest, illuminated with an unearthly light, a mountain topped with a city's useful towers. That, I supposed vaguely, was where my part of the search ended. But I was by now overcome with lethargy, and my sense of compulsion was falling away. I left the road, walked out into the waist-high grass, and pushed through it slowly until I had to stop, all purpose gone, feeling empty.

Then I awoke and lay for a long time as dawn came and the clamor from Times Square died away, thinking about my dream, and wondering, as the last of it faded, whether all my companions had similarly stopped in a meadow unable to fight through the tangled hindrances.

Those days were all dreamlike in a way. We did the usual things, ate, talked, walked in the streets, even went to the theater once or twice, but there was a quality of unreality in all we did which could not be denied. I had trouble escaping from the influence of that first night's dream. I never before had carried over into my waking life the atmosphere, much less the scenery, of a dream. I found myself elaborating it, trying to identify my companions and recall the shouted conversation. It would not come clear, of course; but it haunted me until we actually left New York and its milling crowds. All during that week it was hard to concentrate on my affairs or to persuade anyone else to make the effort. Consequently, I had a great deal of time to sit talking with friends, to walk in the streets, to linger over books and papers. This idleness doubtless contributed to the unreal quality of those days and to the vividness of my recollections. These centered about two figures with whom I had been associated, men who had a certain relation to this release of atomic energy—neither, of course, as inventor.

These two were Simon Nelson Patten and Franklin Delano Roosevelt, one a professor in the University of Pennsylvania, more than a quarter of a century dead, and the other the President to whose loss we were hardly yet accommodated.[4]

It will be understood why I should have thought much of President Roosevelt during those days. He had had the imagination to understand that the Bomb was possible and had risked more than any other public man would ever have risked to perfect it. If it had not come off, he would have been set down—a notion his detractors had already been at some pains to foster—as a trier of impossible nostrums, an encourager of unlikely and expensive experiments. Several incidents from the past would have been brought up. It

4. He had, of course, died on April 12 of that same year.

would have been recalled how he had tried to meet the crisis of economic depression in 1933 by changing the weight of gold in the dollar—when gold had long since disappeared from use in domestic exchange. It would have been said that the billions risked in developing the Bomb had been thrown away as recklessly as those spent on dams, homesteads, and other public works to which his enemies had always objected. He had been wrong about gold; and he had been confused and inconsistent about the NRA, the AAA, tariffs, and trust-busting, and, in fact, about most of his economic adventures. But he had never been confused about Hitler or the Japanese warlords. He had never underestimated the strength of their hatred for democracy and democrats, or the fate they had in mind for those who resisted totalitarianism.

On the very day Hitler became chancellor of the Reich, President Roosevelt told me that this meant years of trouble for Americans and perhaps war at the end. Hitler was, he said, a strange, half-mad creature; and yet he possessed an incomparable machine for destruction, which would be run with formidable efficiency. Only a few times in my association with him had I seen the Rooseveltian mask drop and the face appear which the world never saw and no camera or artist ever caught. This was one of those times. I do not exaggerate when I say that the inner Roosevelt was a man utterly different from the one known to his countrymen. I have never heard of another masquerade so long and so successful. Harry Hopkins, Judge Rosenman, perhaps a very few others, might sometime tell of similar experiences with him. This to me was so shocking as to create an impression which will never fade. From that day— indeed, from an earlier one whose date I do not know—I am certain that his main preoccupation was the world struggle between democracy as he conceived it and the totalitarianism that Hitler, Mussolini, and the Samurai proposed to impose. He was convinced not only that the struggle would come but that its violence would be of a kind hitherto unexperienced. He thought that its course would be unorthodox and that we must prepare in unusual and even bizarre ways to take advantage of all the scientific organization we possessed and that we ought to use every means for developing more. It must have seemed to him a providential gift that the Nazis and Fascists should send into exile their best brains and that we should receive the gift.

I recalled vividly the day when we had talked about this over luncheon. I thought it must have been in the spring of 1935, because the table was set on the terrace outside his office, and there were flowers in the garden and a delicate breeze which he praised in order to disparage air-conditioning. Hall Roosevelt, Mrs. Roosevelt's brother, was the other guest. The talk all during lunch, and for some time afterward, was about German applied science, especially developments in metallurgy, in power and energy, and in ersatz commodities. The question in the President's mind was: What could we do to catch up? Hall Roosevelt knew a great deal about metals, and he was quite certain that recent German advances had given them enormous advantages. It was the same, it seemed, in the turning of coal into fuel for motors, in electronics, and in other fields. Round and round the talk went, but the theme was always the same. It was difficult to apply government funds to research, if for no other reason than that a majority of the Congress was implacably unwilling. And the great private corporations whose laboratories were so amply advertised were really far behind their competitors abroad. Even then, as I can see now, the President was determined to meet the challenge to our way of life which was arising in Germany, and he was willing to use any means that would strengthen us for the coming struggle. That day he proposed to Hall Roosevelt an immense project for research; but whether anything came of it I do not know. From then, or thereabouts, I was no longer one of the family and so lost touch with happenings in their circle.

Now the Bomb had been dropped on Hiroshima. And another at Nagasaki had made the first one obsolete—as one of the scientists announced with an air of being himself amazed. We had triumphed this time in the very field with which President Roosevelt had been so preoccupied when Hitler had come to power. It was a matter of controversy—and perhaps always would be—whether he had tried to avoid the conflict or whether, as some said, he had helped to precipitate it. I did not know more than that his intentions were that we should sometime come to grips with the evil thing and that, if he could, he would make us strong against that day. But I was sure that this firm purpose had guided every political event, every international arrangement, even every domestic policy since the earliest days of his presidency.

The Japanese militarists occupied in his regard a lesser plane of opprobrium; but his mind was equally made up that they would have to be dealt with before the outstanding issue could be settled. There was a difference in his attitude toward them. He feared the Nazis, for he felt the issue between them and ourselves was in doubt. He was not certain that we could win, because he was never quite sure that the nation could be brought to take seriously its girding for battle, and he knew the capacity of the Germans for efficiency and ruthlessness. Considering the size of their nation and its resources, they were far ahead of us in all that would count in the test that was to come; and our own size and resources might well be useless if we remained a helpless, divided, and inchoate people. He would try to gain sufficient consent to his policy so that we should do what was necessary to prepare. But I do not think that he was confident of success; and this uneasiness persisted well into the war and perhaps accounted in part for his rapid aging in those years.

The Japanese he did not respect in this way. Perhaps he expected that they would be taken care of promptly by the Navy, in which he had so much faith. The losses at Pearl Harbor must have been a punishing shock, especially since he had personally picked the commander and could almost be said to have built himself the fleet we lost there. The Japanese never seemed to find out how weak we were after Pearl Harbor, but the President's knowledge of our long defenselessness in the Pacific must have been for him an almost intolerable strain.

I had not known anything about the Bomb; but I had suspected a great deal, as I suppose most of those did who had physicist friends. I did not think—who could who was not a physicist?—that we should actually perfect a weapon by way of atomic fission. Had not the Nazis been far ahead of us in all the modern weapons, from rockets to the robot projectiles that had threatened defeat to the British? I wondered how certain the President could have been and whether the risks he had taken for success had borne him down. Even the scientists themselves, when it came to the final test long after theoretical perfection was reached, had crouched uncertain in the New Mexican dawn. I stopped short, one day that week, walking in upper Fifth Avenue and wondered—wondered urgently—if the President had been certain even of the theoretical success of the

Bomb before he died in April. It seemed somehow very important.

Why important? Because, if he had known, he had had a share in our release from strain and terror; and, if he had known, he had also had a sense of triumph over all the forces within and without which he had so long had to combat. If ever there had been a personal victory, this had been it. It seemed incredibly unfair to consider that he might never have known how complete the victory was. But that thought raised a new issue. I found myself thinking that he was one of the few people who, if he had lived to see that day, would have had no uncertainty about a future dominated by the development of atomic energy. He would have said that it had saved us once and that it was obviously destined for permanent good. I thought that he would not have used it in war. He would rather have used its potential to force peace. He had that kind of political ability.

With atomic energy men might someday be released from all their oldest preoccupations. With it food, clothing, and shelter might become things to be had in a not distant future at much less cost in labor. We should no longer have to sacrifice, to save, to compete, to grab from others in order to have the decencies of life and perhaps many of its amenities. So much seemed obvious even on this first day and in my first wonder. Other inventions had put man ahead—sometimes miraculously, as it must have seemed to those who first had the wheel, the lever, electricity, or the radio—but here was one beyond the most fervid imaginings, and it promised an economic utopia. It also promised—or should I say threatened?—to undermine many cherished moral concepts. As for orthodox economic and political principles, their basis had been destroyed, even for the most obtuse, when the haze had cleared from Hiroshima.

On Central Park South, as I turned to go up into the park, I recalled—as I thought I should have done hours before on the instant of first reading about the Bomb—a phrase from Patten, "scarcity or surplus, pleasure or pain," in a book written at least forty years ago. Another incident now came back to me as vividly as had the picture of the President at lunch on the White House Terrace, talking about the dangers of German applied science.

I had met Patten, then approaching retirement, on a walk such as I was taking now. It was in West Philadelphia, and he seemed older than his age, and worn. I thought as I looked at him from some way off that something was troubling him; he seemed agitated. But, when he came closer, I saw that his disturbance came from elation. Indeed, his face seemed to be lit from within. This must have been in 1915, when I was a graduate student at the University of Pennsylvania. It was a winter day, wet and dreary; but Patten had not varied his morning's routine because of the weather. For a longer time than anyone could remember he had gone every day all the way into the city to breakfast at the University Club and walked all the way out again, past Rittenhouse Square, over the Schuylkill bridges, and up to Logan Hall through the West Philadelphia streets. It was a long walk, and obviously to Patten it was something like following a plow or a harrow for part of the morning. He wore great clodhopper shoes and heavy clothes. He looked like the weathered farmer which, at heart, he was. This morning, however, he was transported. As I met him, alone in the middle of a block, I remarked on his obvious euphoria. He laughed and said that he had no doubt that his inner joy showed—this was the greatest day of his life!

I inquired further. He asked if I had not read the morning papers. I said I had but that I had not seen anything remarkable. He said that I ought to look again, for today all the English economists had been destroyed. My face must have registered mystification. He chuckled, cracked the big joints of his fingers, and fairly danced as he said, "Why, didn't you see about this man Einstein, this mathematician whose formula indicates that matter is transmutable into energy?"

"Well," I said feebly, "I really don't see. . . ."

"You will," he said, "you will. In your lifetime mankind will know what it really is to have plenty."

He went on to say what I had heard him hint at before. I now realized that the shackles the economists had tried to put on men's thinking were being broken by the scientists. Pain, scarcity, competition, and greed must now at last give way to pleasure, abundance, and co-operation. For everyone would have enough of everything. "Haven't I been saying so?" he cried. "Haven't I said that men's salvation lay in thought, in invention, in creative work; that there were no limits, that what is most characteristic in nature is her

richness, not her niggardliness? *Their* system was built on scarcity
to protect the British exploiters of labor; mine is built on abundance, the abundance of generous nature. I was right; I am right:
Einstein has at last proved it beyond any doubt. Nature's riches are
endless."[5]

In Patten's voice there was the consciousness I had noticed so
often, of stores of wheat and corn, fat flocks, full barns and grana-
ries, all the wealth of his native Illinois.[6] His was an American
philosophy, shaped by the history of an adventurous people moving
into an environment which yielded to their exploring efforts greater
and greater riches. He had been tormented all his life by the necessity of explaining Americans to themselves, of showing them how
to look forward, to accept and to multiply goods; and also how
very restricting it was *not* to accept and to look only backward.
Most of the other economists of his generation had differed sharply
from this attitude. They had learned from the English classicists
rather than from American experience. They were fearful and withdrawing. They had talked of the need for saving, for cautious conservation, of the dangers of overexpansion, of the rainy day to come.
They had based themselves on the "iron laws" of economics and
on the "Malthusian Doctrine." Patten was the scientific counterpart
of the brawling, roaring, magnificent pioneers, the river- and moun-
tain-men, who subdued the Midwest and sprawled across the plains
and mountains to the Pacific. He saw this pioneering returning now
on itself, going on, in different fashion, into the future. He was
aware that, if we unlocked more of nature's secrets, explored more
of her realms, we should always be opening new storehouses of

5. Although I have the most vivid recollection of this encounter, I cannot recall
at this distance the particular announcement or article to which Patten referred.
It was obviously an account of the relativity theory, published in that year—the
field theory had been published in 1905. There was not then the interest in science
among the laity that there is now; and there was not much more interest among
social scientists. No one but Patten had the faintest idea that the most violent
effect on economics and political science might emanate from an obscure mathematician's thinking; and Patten had never succeeded in transmitting his prescience
to any others. His immediate colleagues were either technicians like Huebner,
Mead, Hess, Rowe, McCray, Smith, and other older professors at the Wharton
School or reformers of immediate abuses like Nearing, King, and a few other
younger instructors. None of them thought of his own work as likely to be profoundly affected by the theory of relativity.

6. Matters of which I made something in writing the only biography he has ever
had, for the *American Economic Review*, some years later.

resources. What limited us was mostly our own minds. We were fearful; we thought small, cautious thoughts. But here—and he laughed in the Philadelphia gloom—was a glorious German Jew who opened the universe to the creature man. "Now let us walk into the kingdom," he sang to the lowering clouds.

It was a biblical phrase; but Patten was a biblical man. I thought he was the picture of an Old Testament prophet, and I knew that he talked of decades or centuries, not of years. But I did see what he meant. I shall not say more of him. I only note here that I thought back, especially, on this Day of the Bomb, to the transfigured face and the shaking voice of an old man heard in a commonplace Philadelphia street thirty years before. I had thought of it many times since. I had never doubted that he had been right; and in my own way I had worked, as he had taught me to do, toward the opening of men's minds and hearts to their own possibilities.

It was ironical that our first amazed consciousness of unleashed power should have come through fear of its limitless destructiveness. It pointed up so clearly the danger—the greatest of all dangers to man—that his inventions may destroy him because he will not acknowledge their nature and shape his society to their requirements, for they are—and long have been—loose among us. We must grasp, not avoid, them or pretend that they are not there and that we need to do nothing about them.

We now had, at once, to acknowledge that individualism, competition, private initiative, and production only for profit were as destructive as tigers loose in a circus crowd. We could only live on in our world if we collectivized, co-operated, produced for use, shared with one another. But, if we conformed to these necessities, we could live as only kings, potentates, and American millionaires have heretofore dared to think of living. We had, in other words, a choice between untold luxury for everyone and the total destruction of everything. And damned if I didn't half-believe that we would choose destruction! For I was very sore and cynical about American intellectuals and academicians. They had never accepted Patten, and everyone since who had attempted his approach had been ignored.

Even with the overwhelmingly powerful argument of the Bomb,

I sadly thought that many of my colleagues might yet try to explain it away. This would be in the tradition of the British admiral whose more realistic brother had told him in exasperation that he expected him to disappear beneath the sea on his own bridge, bombed from the air, while still explaining why battleships were superior to airplanes. And sure enough he had—on a British dreadnaught, sunk by Japanese bombers in the South China Sea. So, I thought, most of the economists will go down extolling individualism and private enterprise, sunk, if not by the superior power of a nationalized collectivism, then by some idiot who has been encouraged by his public relations counsel to think himself a modern Caesar entitled to the exclusive use of the Bomb.

I was, no doubt, angry. It was not because the Bomb had taken the world by surprise. It was because there were those in the world who ought to have expected and prepared for it. True, all the vested interests of our society would have been opposed to the necessary accommodations; but it is one thing to tolerate exploiters when they only require all of us to work for them and quite another when there is involved the immediate ruination of civilization itself. The condition of surviving at all into the future had now for several decades clearly been that we should collectivize and plan. This course, however, had been ridiculed and rejected. Had not the Congress taken the utmost pleasure in abolishing the National Resources Planning Board, the sole pale representative in Washington of calculated foresight, after a few years of parlous support by the President's emergency fund? The planning function ought long ago to have been made co-ordinate with the executive, legislative, and judicial functions. It had not been because it was not yet considered sufficiently important. Indeed, it was considered to be a silly foible of impractical professors, and no one even remotely thought of it as a serious governmental instrument. True, there was the Bureau of the Budget, which had rudimentary advisory duties that approached planning. But it was only an annual budget; and the Congress still maintained the appropriations committees which had been inherited from the Continental Congress of more than a hundred and fifty years before and used them in such ways as to nullify any planning.

Thus we had nothing, in a national sense, with which to meet the crisis which had now indisputably arrived. I recalled the last such crisis, which I had watched with similar amazement—the coming of the war itself. I had thought that called for collectivization. We had, however, got through it with a peculiar and very dangerous substitute: the subsidizing of big business with the establishment of some new central machinery for government. We had been able to support the subsidies by the hidden taxation of inflation, and fortunately the war had not gone on long enough to make the process intolerable. The central machinery had been a series of devices for enlarging the executive and spreading administrative control over the ramifying war agencies.[7] Here again makeshifts had sufficed; a war that we got through by adding its requirements to our ordinary peacetime production—indeed, to an enlarged civilian production—had obviously not called for much sacrifice or discipline.

We had been able to avoid planning because we could afford to be prodigal. We could still afford waste; and, when the new energy was made generally available, we should be able to waste even more if we liked. But we faced a different decision now: whether the new energy should support us or whether it should destroy us. My greatest fear was that even now this fact, which loomed like the sun in the sky today, might by tomorrow be ignored in that protective boredom with which most of us seal ourselves off from unpleasant reality. The Bomb had been in the making for a long time, and we had ignored every intimation of it until it burst over Hiroshima. Today we felt naked to its potential threat. Another day and we might be listening eagerly to soothsayers who would gradually persuade us to forget. Then might come a day of doom.

I was by now deep into Central Park. There were children on the lawns and in the playgrounds. It was cool for August in New York, and all the small folk were agreeably busy with their own affairs. Their elders were gathered in agitated groups in the neighborly habit of park frequenters. The bits of conversation to be overheard in passing indicated the center of their interest. They were well enough aware that the orderly peace of lawns and trees, of ponds and convenient benches, of the guardian apartment homes standing all around, was deceptive. These were not the people who were

7. Worked out by the Committee on Administrative Management, whose report was published in 1938.

raucous in Times Square. They were not hoodlums or thoughtless irresponsibles; they were the solid stuff of America. They were the people who read through the Sunday *Times,* who supported the Citizens Housing Council, the Community Chest, and the Foreign Policy Association. But they had not been ready for this. They were appalled by it. Most of them, I gathered, deplored the event at Hiroshima; they thought that we should have bombed some desert island and advertised it so that the lesson for the Japanese would still be inescapable. We had somehow compromised ourselves by joining to this extent in the *Schrecklichkeit.* Bombings, hitherto, they had not thought wrong; but this one, yes!

More than one person I heard say, as I had said to myself, "The President would not have let the military people use it." I knew who they meant by "the President." It was not the present occupant of the White House; it was *their* President, who was now gone. The conversations ranged on into the future. Now everyone was digging out of his knowledge and his memory what he already knew. He found it extensive when he catalogued it with friends. For the American public—this public—was neither unintelligent nor uninstructed. Many remembered a good deal of the literature that foreshadowed it. But all of them were now wondering how they could have been so blind to its implications. Of course, as I heard one man say, it was all very well to talk about vast changes in the future, but, if they were not to come right away, the old routine could not be broken on account of them. A man must go to his work in the morning, and he must come home at night.

It was, another said, like the story of the amateur who overheard two astronomers speculating about the cooling-off of the earth and was tremendously agitated until he found that they were speaking of a time *billions* instead of *millions* of years in the future. There had been reason for concern so long as "atomic energy" was only a phrase which referred to something which might exist a billion years away; but suddenly it had been reduced to a million, and now we were all excited. I thought he laughed a little uncertainly at his own joke. And, in fact, one of the group to whom he was talking said something obviously sharp, for the laughing stopped at once. The billion had not come down to a million or even a thousand or a hundred but possibly to five or six.

These New Yorkers, confronted like others all over America with both peace and the Bomb in a single day, found themselves unable to take it in their stride. There was urgent need to know, if any hope were to be held for the future world, a hundred things which no one now knew. When the new power should be applied to transportation, to manufacture, to the production and processing of food, clothing, and building materials, to medical experiment and the making of medicines, to temperature control . . . wherever it might be applied, it was bound to be revolutionary. Beyond that all was hazy. There was speculation about the future of utilities. Would all our elaborate system for generating and distributing electricity become obsolete at once? Those people in Central Park thought of that on the first day. Those were the blue-chip investments into which they had put their savings. Similarly, they owned stocks in the coal, oil, and lumber industries, perhaps in cotton mills or automobile concerns. It was hard to think of anything, except perhaps real estate, which would not be cheapened when the new energy was put to work. And if everything was to be dirt cheap, why save—and so why savings banks—why insure—and so why insurance companies—why speculate—and so why brokers and all the paraphernalia of Wall Street? The imagination could range among a thousand possibilities of obsolescence and not seem too fantastic. Obviously, people were saying, this was a more far-reaching discovery than steam or electricity or the vacuum tube or even—to go far back—than those marvels, fire, the wheel, and the lever. Men's spirits as well as their minds, as they confronted all this, were overwhelmed. They had been tired out; they were exhausted from years of war. Now they had to expect a peace which would preclude the relaxation for which they had longed.

My own thoughts became almost lyric as I escaped for the time being from the prevalent exhaustion. I, too, dwelt on the peacetime uses of fission rather than the destructive power which was evidently about to become available. Mankind had been very improvident in the last century and a half. Since the so-called industrial revolution of the eighteenth and nineteenth centuries, multiplication had gone on until the earth held some two billion souls—not more than *could* be well accommodated by known possibilities but many more than *were* supported in some comfort. This squeeze, according to the

English economists, came about because population always tended to outrun its means of support and would always press on its supply of goods. Its periodic reduction by war, famine, and disaster would help some; but there would always be many on the margin of starvation. The operation of this "Malthusian law," it was conceived, had been postponed by advances in techniques of both agriculture and industry, but only postponed! The time would come when these advances would be exhausted. Then the terrible fix into which men had got themselves would become manifest. Instead of local famines, there would be world-wide famine. Universal misery would descend on the improvident species. But now that the illimitable resources of atomic power had been unlocked—to take the place of our inefficient extraction of power from coal, oil, water, and wind—there might result an equally illimitable production of goods. It did seem unlikely that this vast new resource could be monopolized as other sources of power had been—at least if a modicum of common sense should govern its exploitation.

For no private interest, not even any one individual, or company, or university, or nation, could claim exclusive ownership even by right of discovery. It was a joint enterprise of that one-half of 1 per cent of unusual ability, of which more ordinary mortals are the supporting base, that had done the job. It was ours, and all mankind's. They had presented us with it. How was it thinkable that it should not be used for the benefit of all? And, if it was, what would become of the economic system the businessmen had made with the economists' collusion? I thought I could see.

Patten had taught us what to look for. He had told us to expect— and to learn to live with—abundance. If it had seemed a billion years away instead of a practical million, it was not because he had not been explicit. He not only had foreseen the unlocking of atomic energy but had urged the exploitation of other resources to be found in varied technologies so that men could live better. But he had also understood that good living bred better living. A people healthy, sane, educated, responsible, well fed, well housed, and well clothed, with satisfactory outlets for their varied energies, was by definition a people capable of controlling not only its numbers but its quality; and it would exist on an upward spiral, sufficient goods creating energy and supporting intelligence that would result again in more goods which would become even more varied. This sequence opened out into a multitude of new services and an endless exfoliation of the arts. There were resources as great as atomic energy within men's own minds.

This was what the planner was useful for—to lay out the road which led forward and to warn against those which led into cul-de-sacs. Now his efforts must be respected and in the same way as were those of the natural scientists. As I thought of the failure to plan, the exaltation I felt from considering the unlocking of the new power faded away. What I—and others—had to deal with was a world already advanced in the technique of production but much retarded in humanity—meaning the willingness to share or to cooperate. To advance in humanity, planning would be necessary. It would not do to jump gaps or assume that we were farther along than we were.

It was sheer chance that I should be wandering on this day in the city where I had learned so much of my planning trade. From where I walked there were visible the scenes of numerous engagements in the various struggles through which, more than in any other way, I had learned it. There was an apartment house that had ruined a whole neighborhood by its theft of light, air, and space; along with thousands of others, it had bankrupted the city by adding to the costs of overloaded streets, congested transportation, shifts in school population, and so on through a long list of urban ills.

The interests involved had considered it an outrage that these social costs should be traced to their source; and my suggestions for their assessment had been denounced as subversive. There were streets, too, which I had helped to rearrange in some degree and about whose rearrangement, and what went below and above them, I had had to make calculations. Traffic was running in ways the Planning Commission, of which I had been the chairman, had considered again and again. A multitude of physical aspects in the city contributed to my sharpened wonder about the future.

We had not scrupled to think of the changes fifty years might bring. We had deliberately tried to create for ourselves a projected picture of fifty years hence as the only practical guide for planning. Hard as we had tried, however, we had not been visionary enough to be really practical. We had taken into consideration all we could learn of new methods and materials, new processes, and new ideas. Whenever we had had the least excuse, we had urged others to pay attention to what was significant in the future we must plan. But we had not imagined that atomic power would soon become available. We had not anticipated this Bomb. By extensive exploration we had decided that bombs did not then warrant the breaking-up and relocation of cities—perhaps wrongly, in view of what had since happened to so many metropolitan areas. But, at any rate, New York had survived, perhaps because we had crowded in on the Nazis six months or a year before their robot projectiles were perfected. If so, it was mostly luck. Yet here it was, our city—shabby and run-down, partly from war, partly from bankruptcy, but intact and alive.

In my experience of planning I had had opportunity to learn, if I had not known it before, how effective was the opposition of narrow local interests in a democracy in which legislative representation was not identified with the general interest. The difficulties with obstructions of this sort were no greater, however, than those which sprang from the resistance of departmental officials and of others who had interests in government to protect. It was not so strange, in a society whose production and distribution were intrusted to a profit system, that there should be objection to foresight, co-ordination, and control. But it was strange indeed that in the twentieth century there should be a government that had inherent in its very structure political resistance to planning as strong as any economic resistance. The gradual unfolding in my mind of the conviction that these things were so had become final in New York, and so I had more reason than other people to despair about the Bomb.

I was perhaps more depressed because this city was the scene of one of my own failures—a failure in analysis. I had concluded from my Washington experience that the cause of legislative bankruptcy in our country—that is, legislative unwillingness to defend or represent the general interest—was the geographic division of the electorate, so that those elected owed allegiance to a part of the whole and not the whole itself. From this defect in our Constitution came the system of blocs—cotton, silver, steel, aluminum, beef cattle, dairy, sugar, drugs, food products, and so on, all commodities which were localized. This, I thought, was the key to the situation.

Although other pressure groups with a wider spread, such as the American Legion, the National Association of Manufacturers, labor, bankers, insurance companies, realtors, public utilities, and the like, were able to win favors, I had thought it was done by uniting with the more sharply defined and directed commodity blocs that were utterly careless about what they let the public in for if they could carry their own point.

That this analysis was so defective as to be almost amateurish, I realized before leaving Washington; but I had not been willing to accept what was being forced on me until I came to New York. As a practical and practicing democracy we were farther from perfection than was evident in our theory. Democracy, I realized, could be found only in individual minds and hearts; it was so near the Christian ethic as in fact to be defined by the teachings of Jesus. Did they not center in selflessness, generosity, neighborliness, and co-operation and reject envy, hatred, recrimination, individualism, competition, and other manifestations of man's unkindness to man? Only decent and self-respecting but generous and actively co-operative individuals could make a democracy work. Ganging up to get the best of others was a fundamental denial that democracy was wanted. It was, indeed, the Fascist technique, which, if it comes naturally to a people, almost certainly makes them ineligible for immediate democracy.

Democrats were always at a grave disadvantage in dealing with absolutists. Their scrupulousness was easily taken advantage of; and men of violence know how to widen a breach in men's minds as well as in their economies. Since they were driven by motives which democrats had been purged of, or which had never been natural to them, they were underestimated. Their appeal was to the primitive, the uninstructed, the animal-like, the irresponsible, the warped, the envious. Even the wisest and most normal of men would have moments of distress and discouragement; and at such times their minds would be receptive to some element of the totalitarian offering. Such a man would come to himself and be ashamed presently because he would understand that his nature was being violated. But the less balanced and more envious would go on and on into extremes of viciousness from which there would eventually be no retreat and for which there could be only the justification of extermination—extermination of all men of good will. The war in the world was a war between these forces in the minds of men. The Fascists in the Europe of 1930–40 had got the upper hand; ours had tried and failed. But their failure had not changed their natures. They were always with us, with crucifixion in their books for all who clung to the dangerous doctrines of co-operation and tolerance.

We needed a machinery for democracy which would implement the kindliness in men rather than their hatred. The real weakness of our kind of legislative representation, I had come to see, was in its representation of the perverse and negative rather than the creative and positive. It was easy to get done a thing which injured many to favor a few. It was difficult to get done a thing which asked a sacrifice from a few for the sake of many. It was symbolic, somehow, that we had used atomic energy first for destruction and were still a long way from using it for production.

Here I was aware that I breached an old and unresolved argument. Do men take their natures from their institutions, or are these institutions so much the shadows of men that they have no creative effect? I had gone through many active years during which I had had no cause to question the assumption—if assumption it was—that a *few* men created institutions with the passive consent of others whose lives were largely determined by the institutions in which they moved. Progress in a democracy was fairly well measured by the number of those who were prepared to participate creatively in social arrangements. Men tended to become not only controlled but controlling actors in the drama of organized living. For a person like me this explanation had sufficed as an answer to the riddles of free will and determination.

The important question of social policy involved in the relation of men to their institutions was this: How far ahead of the majority who must live with them can institutions go? To put it another way, how far, how fast, may people be persuaded to accept new forms of industry, of government, or of educational, recreational, and other institutions? New ones were continuously being suggested, and old ones continuously reshaped. We knew that sometimes there was resistance and sometimes acceptance. We knew such crude facts as that acceptance was easier for changes in industry than in government, or in health and welfare than in religion and education. But knowledge of this kind was too gross and general to be of use.

We needed answers now to a whole series of questions that was of the utmost importance, for we were faced with an enormous cultural discrepancy. For a long time it had been obvious that there was a growing disparity between scientific advance, or, more specifically, the adaptation of science to industrial uses, and other contemporary institutions that ought to have contained, or at least have been related to, science in a controlling fashion. Now in one leap science had gone so fantastically far ahead of social thinking that even social scientists, and certainly political scientists, were paralyzed. The problem was so huge, so mystifying, so far beyond our grasp, and yet so cruelly deranging, that action and thought were immobilized. Certainly something had been created in atomic power for the majority of mankind, without their concurrence, that they would not have created for themselves. They were, furthermore, helpless to reject it. Just as the Scottish weavers had had to live with the close-following inventions that affected their trade in the eighteenth century, all the world now had to live with atomic fire.

If recent history might be taken as a guide, mankind had no very long interval to count on until the next war should grow out of the unresolved rancors of nationalism; and a much shorter time would see determining decisions made. Within the time allotted could the masses of men—perhaps half of whom could not yet read or write and nine-tenths of whom lived in the most unrelieved economic insecurity—accommodate themselves to institutions co-ordinate with this sudden scientific ultimatum? It seemed incredible that they might. Yet, if it could not be done, there stared us in the face the possibility of destruction, final, complete!

Imagine what was required. It was required not only that this terrible destructive weapon be handed over at once to an agency which represented all the world's people, not just any part of them, and represented them in so conclusive a way as to establish complete consent; it also was required that the institutions governing industry and commerce give way to others suited to almost unimaginably cheapened production. It seemed possible that the farthest Hottentot, Ubangi, Tibetan, Uruguayan, or Malayan might soon be rich as Croesus—if the world's goods were not monopolized. If they were monopolized and made scarce to a notable degree, so that whole peoples or whole classes were shut away from them, a resort to force would be inevitable. If they were not, if we overcame the enormous difficulty of disestablishing interests in scarcity, there was still the fact that illiterate savages were scarcely to be expected to become overnight as reasonable as Swiss or Scandinavians. And overnight was about all the time we had.

Christianity as a doctrine imbedded in people's hearts might have prepared the world to receive atomic power. Come to think of it, the wonder was that it had not. Certainly the Christian virtues were those needed to assure peace. The avoidance of vengeful violence, patience in co-operation, sympathetic mutual aid—these were at the heart of Christ's teachings. He had lived and worked at a time and in a part of the earth in which poverty, sickness, and tyrannical government were common and characteristic; his own people had been subjects of an alien power; the religion he had inherited was a monotheism infused with race consciousness and jealous exclusiveness that justified the exploitation of inferiors. To have persisted, as Christ did, to the point of getting crucified for preaching humility, mutual responsibility among men, and equality in a universal brotherhood was perhaps to have acted impractically for his time. But to have immortalized these virtues through hundreds of generations by the symbol of the resurrection and eternal reward was to have conferred a profoundly valuable gift on mankind.

There never had been a time when a majority of men had been practicing Christians. But there never had been a time when a majority (in the Western world) had repudiated the Christian doctrine. They had not dared. The Reformers, it is true, had created a Protestant ethic that had served for several centuries as apology for one of the great perversions, even reversals, of Christ's doctrine —capitalism. But always those who were acknowledged to be the best of men had lived Christian lives and denounced the sins of exploitation. And most of mankind felt the inner compulsions their outward lives seemed to reject.

I had grown up in what, as I heard it, was the gentlest of Protestant faiths—the Congregational. Its preachers in my boyhood had filled, not incongruously, their simple pulpits. But in those days, in rural America, the choices men had had to make had comported not too badly with Christian morality. There were no great perverters of the faith. Men worked for gain; but they helped one another, and exploitation was controlled by accepted concepts of what was fair—fair wages, fair prices, fair sharing all around—there was enough agreed on. And violators hesitated before the social opprobrium which is man's most useful insurer of conformity.

We had a different America now and a different world. It was one in which the transformations caused by technology had gone far enough to complete the paradoxical drawing-together of all parts of the earth and the simultaneous separating of its individuals. Neighborhoods were no longer the functioning entities they had immemorially been, and their moral disciplines were therefore no longer effective. It took only a short time to get from anywhere to anywhere else, and almost anyone could telephone to anyone else. But goods were produced for an impersonal market, and services were rendered only for cash. There was a tendency to guide one's conduct by a judgment of what could be got away with without the saving control of neighborly judgments. Christianity functioned less well in this modern atmosphere. It depended deeply on individual intimacy, on assistance for the erring—in fact, on a brotherly love and guidance that now had only a limited chance to develop or to express itself!

Those unusual individuals who rearrange physical things and thus create change were working in a new milieu and with more effective instruments. At the same time that morality was being weakened, the need for it—in the sense of guidance under new conditions—was becoming greater. Human sympathies were deprived of the material on which to work, and the compulsions of Christian teaching were lessened. It was an economy of surplus; the deficit days were past. But not for all—because the arts of withholding were well developed, brotherly feeling was wanting, and even "enlightened selfishness"—the classical economist's contribution to the Protestant ethic—failed to curb capitalistic possessiveness.

Why had not those who possessed that half of 1 per cent of unusual ability which characterizes human societies in all times and places seen what was happening and done something about it? I could think offhand of many possible reasons. First and most important was the ease with which, under our highly developed institutions, the young were conditioned to orthodoxy. Even those of unusual ability who found their careers in the social sciences seldom became genuinely creative or even critical. They worked within a system. It was a very elaborate and intellectually satisfying system. That it really had nothing to do with the dynamics of civilization many never discovered; or, if they did, after a long apprenticeship, they found it then extremely inexpedient to depart from accepted doctrine. Men have to live within the institutions that exist; and most of them, even the most intelligent, make an accommodation "which will do for their time." Only men of unusual courage, as well as ability, will risk what has to be risked in pressing for or even in suggesting fundamental social changes.

Science had had its struggle for freedom in the nineteenth century. But it never had been much of a struggle, because it had appeared at once that money could be made out of its results, and theologians and moralists have never yet won a short-run victory over money-makers. But scientists had presumed. They had thought, because they were not required to be orthodox, that they were superior people who needed to accept no direction and to work within no framework. It would be tedious to elaborate this: and with the fact of the Bomb there was no need. Whatever the evolution had been, the end result was equally grave. Science, working in relative freedom, had presented social science, working in a confined orthodoxy, with devastating evidence of futility.

How had we failed so dismally? I had become fifty-four years old the last month, and I had lived through and been part of the age which ought to have made the world ready for atomic power. I had a sense of responsibility combined with a conviction of failure. For I had possessed some knowledge, and yet I had been ineffectual in influencing my generation. My colleagues and I had been beaten by what the American language so aptly called "phonies"—those who buried reality under a scum of platitude, holding out to others the nostalgic dream of security in old ways while they exploited the new technology and undermined the old society.

In my generation there had been many merciless critics of our weakness for superficiality. Mencken in his way had been one; and Sinclair Lewis, of course, who had given a name to Babbittry. These were literary men who had had progenitors in W. D. Howells, Hamlin Garland, Sarah Orne Jewett, Upton Sinclair, and Theodore Dreiser. But a more serious critic had been Thorstein Veblen, whose dispassionate scalpel had exposed the corruption within the directive centers of our civilization; still another was my Patten, who had tried to open the way to a surplus economy and to insist on the beneficence of creativeness. There had been others. There had always been a few Socialists and a few others who devoted themselves to the co-operative movement. But the critics, and those with alternatives to offer, had caused no more than momentary sensations; and those who had other suggestions for replacing or modifying capitalism were like the small band of early Christian martyrs who were lost in the decaying splendors of Rome. No one of any importance could believe that they were more than fanatics. The apex of the capitalist structure glittered on a broad base of dirty factories, ravaged land, and miserable slums; but even the poorest faces were turned adoringly to its light.

How had I—and other dissenters—failed? That question very evidently required an explanation as complex as the phenomena visible even on the first day of the new age. It would, I suspected, require the most careful, sensitive, and persistent reconstruction if it was to be of the least use to the inquiring mind. But I was sure that I had to tackle it, sure with that instinctive feeling for the filling of an intellectual void which has probably been responsible for most serious efforts of sustained inquiry. Every scholar had now to stop and answer for himself the question which was so insistently asking itself of me. Not all would answer it in the same way. Some would even think they knew the answer without much inquiry. Those could be dismissed—for the fact of disparity here was so colossally evident that only a gigantic and destructive cancer eating at the mind could create a blind area large enough to hide it. Others would meet their conviction of sin without necessary response in outward action. They would be wholly honest and deeply serious, but they would feel no need to externalize or to share with others what truth they might find.

Face to face with so final a fact, the loneliness of the human spirit on this earth, so often remarked by poets and philosophers, was being rediscovered by even the most gregarious souls. Men had to explain to themselves because they were men. They did not have to explain to others, especially since it might very well be too late for such an explanation to be of any social use. To themselves in the new solitude of their universe they might say many things. But it was not a time for sharing such enormous conclusions as were shaping in their minds.

I knew, however, that I should never again have any peace until I had done my best to explain, not only to myself, but to those most dear to me and perhaps to others to whom as a teacher and leader I had an indisputable responsibility.

The inquiry I had in mind could obviously not be completed before the crisis arrived. That, I judged, would be sometime in the fifties. Such a dating could be arrived at—even if only very roughly—by judging what the technological acceleration was likely to be. It might be more or less, depending on the pressure exerted by the sense of urgency generated in the public mind. But that sense of urgency might be very great. A weapon capable of transforming war into genocide was now available. At the moment only the United States possessed it. But this monopoly would not last very long. And when the Russians also possessed the Bomb, the fear of destruction would rise to something like panic. This fear might be relieved in one of two ways: by the invention of a practical defense or by an international agreement to outlaw its use.

The first of these, we were told, was unlikely for some time to come; the second was entirely possible, but it would depend on a surrender of sovereignty more far-reaching than any ever achieved before. Such a surrender could only be carried out in an atmosphere charged with the absolute conviction that an atomic war would be futile—that neither side could win a real victory, because the decimation of both sides would amount to a holocaust. That conviction could be expected to influence American policy; but how the knowledge necessary to form this conviction could get through to the Russian public was not easy to see. The Politburo might very well be able to resist any surrender of sovereignty. By minimizing the threat and by assuming that the Americans and the British would not actually start a preventive atom war, Russian leaders might carry on into a period of terrible tensions when both sides would possess the Bomb.

This last development seemed the most likely. Such a prospect was a terrifying one. The years just ahead would be without parallel in history. There would always be the hope—until holocaust actually supervened—that the crisis might be got through somehow without war. If it was not, everything done in the meantime would be useless; if it was, some record of humanity's struggles under the whips of atomic compulsion would be useful. I thought I might undertake such a record on the chance that we might squeak through. Our fool's progress toward jeopardy, turning at last into progress toward peace and security, would certainly be the most dramatic incident since man's emergence from the slime. I resolved to undertake its recording.

A more revealing inquiry into causes could be undertaken when events had shown that it might be of some use.

CHAPTER II *1946*

HIROSHIMA had been in August of 1945; Bikini was in July of 1946.[1] Like many millions of others, I saw it through the eyes of radio commentators who spoke from the decks of the "Appalachian" and the "Panamint"; from the planes which were observing; from "Dave's Dream," the superfortress which carried it; and from Kwajalein, two hundred miles away. I heard Vice Admiral W. H. D. Blandy speak cautiously of the results. And, through several weeks following, I watched, with growing melancholy, the spread of belittlement and recovered confidence through at least the English-speaking countries. That melancholy gradually turned to a greater alarm than any I had felt before—an alarm which I evidently shared with the atomic scientists; only they did something about it. They abandoned their laboratories, wholesale, for legislative lobbies, a really excited reaction for people who had hitherto been wholly scornful of "politics." What might not happen to a world which so stupidly refused to acknowledge peril, they asked; and the answer seemed only too clearly indicated.

The spreading lethargy after the Pacific tests appeared to be a sudden change from the panic of 1945. In reality, as I came to realize, familiarity, together with the active efforts of powerful sub-verters, had already induced a contempt which Bikini no more than confirmed. Belief in disaster which does not arrive simply will not persist; or, perhaps more accurately, concern will not be sustained if any possible escape can be made plausible. And an active campaign of disparagement was now going on, which fell on too-willing ears. This reassurance came, as might be expected, from those who had either lived by the old kind of force or had sheltered behind it.

1. The air-exploded bomb was dropped on July 1; the surface bomb, on July 24.

It was unbearably obvious that, if the Bomb was really the apocalyptic weapon it had seemed to be immediately after Hiroshima, there would simply be no place at all for lesser weapons or for those who made and managed them. All the world's land armies, and especially its navies, might now be obsolete. Land armies could perhaps be thought of as having many police functions, but not navies. There might be no excuse at all for keeping the old military class on any considerable scale. The new weapon was the product of university learning; it had not been developed by, or even at the suggestion of, military men, a fact that seemed to leave them without any hold at all on public consideration.[2]

It is not often understood how widely the military shelter spreads and how many citizens of our society would feel nakedly exposed if it should cease to exist. For those with large commitments, those who depend in any degree upon national, as apart from municipal or state, strength for protection, the existence of military might is not only always a comfort but often a necessity. International or colonial ventures of all sorts especially require such support. The general and the admiral are the partners, seen or unseen, of all really intelligent top executives: They may grudge the taxes they pay for every other bureaucratic purpose but not those for the military.

The military, swollen from war, and the great interests, swollen from making munitions for war, were, in spite of their unprecedented size and strength, dazed and demoralized by Hiroshima. Like other citizens, they were at first merely frightened into irrationality. They were, for a time, not interests at all but were suddenly dissolved into individuals. Generals, admirals, chairmen, directors, presidents, and vice-presidents became mere scared human beings. Atomic explosions could extinguish luxurious headquarters, board rooms, offices, and clubs as easily as factories or workers' homes— more easily if they happened, as they often did, to be concentrated in urban areas.

Recovery from this first personal panic came rapidly. The powerful men began to find some comfort again in their solidly luxurious surroundings. They had not reached eminence without courage and

2. Actually, as Professor Harold C. Urey, who had had a central role in the proceedings at the Chicago laboratories, said, "No general ever invented a weapon." They had not less claim to this than any other. The real question was: Should they be intrusted with discretion as to its use?

ability, and they did not remain paralyzed for long. They met and talked to one another; and from this communion came the notion of capturing and containing even the knowledge of atomic fission—of intrusting it to military custody until it should be ripe for exploitation. There grew a kind of plot; if it could succeed, it would not only dissolve the lumps of fear in the bellies of the great men but might give them far more power than they had ever before hoped to command.

That this dream was unsubstantial simply seemed impossible to those who had it. It was so fortunate a thought. It was simple but, sadly it must be said, deceptively so. It would put the awful agency in a place which would make it safe for its controllers and an irresistible threat to all who should oppose them. But beyond this— just imagine!—if the military could preside over the development and production of atomic power and allocate its uses to carefully selected clients, as it had always done with war contracts, the powerful men might not only be made secure from danger but might also come into possession of a whole new technology which hitherto they had been eyeing apprehensively. In fact, they had gradually recognized that the tightness within them came not only from fear of dissolution but from fear of dispossession as well. Here was a way to end both threats at once. It simply must be possible.

The half-year after Hiroshima was largely characterized by the incidents of this conspiracy and by the various maneuvers of those who exposed and defeated it. On August 9 Nagasaki was bombed, and all mankind shuddered again. On August 12 Japan made the open offer of surrender, admitting that the force to which the Japanese people were exposed was intolerable even to a marvelously disciplined and amazingly submissive population. On August 16 the Smyth Report was released;[3] and this, together with Mr. W. L. Laurence's reporting,[4] opened to all who could read the amazing story of the Bomb's development and allowed the knowledge to filter everywhere into intellectual cracks and crannies, filling all of them until they ran over with the conviction that what had been reported and guessed at was inescapable fact.

3. H. D. Smyth, *Atomic Energy for Military Purposes* (Princeton: Princeton University Press, 1945).
4. Various issues of the *New York Times* in the days after Hiroshima.

Others in the community had duties and routines which could soothe nerves plucked by the harsh fingers of fate; intellectuals' nerves were still twanging with demoralizing insistence in October, when the President recommended to the Congress legislation for domestic control. Secretary Stettinius had already been authorized to say that the Security Council of the United Nations would be concerned.[5] On the day of the President's message, so that it seemed to be the approved administrative measure, a bill embodying the hopes of the conspirators was introduced into the House of Representatives.[6] It provided for military control of atomic energy. Among other incidental results, the publicity concerning the bill made Mr. Stettinius appear further out of his depth than many had already begun to suspect. But its most important result was that it awakened, not the social scientists, but the atomic scientists, who, being more familiar with what to expect, had been suffering less than others from shock; and its reverberations gradually reached and stirred the minds of other intellectuals and through them widening areas of threatened human beings.

Practitioners of the social sciences were completely unprepared for this crisis; nor were they ready for the re-evaluation of their disciplines which now faced them. They had ignored the swelling current of knowledge which had just produced atomic fission. They now had to tell themselves that this achievement was based on a formula already forty years old and so had been due as soon as any government had budgeted the large sums necessary to accumulate the critical amount of fissionable material. There could be no doubt that the failure to foresee this development was intellectual as well as one of limited imagination. There was no one in the literate world who had not heard of Einstein. True, the emphasis had been on relativity and its celestial measurement rather than on the transformation of mass into energy; but what social scientists thought physicists in a dozen familiar places were doing with the atom-smashing apparatuses, often pictured even in the Sunday supplements, it is hard to say. They certainly had not considered the goal

5. President Truman's message was sent on October 3; Mr. Stettinius had issued his statement on September 1 (cf. *New York Times* of relevant dates).

6. This came to be known as the May-Johnson Bill.

something which would affect profoundly the whole basis of the social disciplines—economics, political science, sociology.

By the time of Bikini, a year after Hiroshima, it was becoming more and more clear that social scientists should be indicted for irrelevance—for rationalizing and theorizing about social arrangements that would no longer serve mankind if civilization was to be preserved. How did they react to this exposure? Of course the less flexible considered themselves to have been betrayed! Events had not moved as they ought to have moved; something epigenetic had occurred—something which had come out of nowhere and which no one could have been expected to anticipate. This attitude was not universal, although it was distressingly common. There were others who could see at once that their most useful activity now would be the exploration of social consequences, and still others felt social, if not moral, pressure to adapt themselves to the new orientation. The economics, political science, and sociology texts would not be rewritten overnight; but the change would come—so I thought—now that the almost intolerable indictment of irrelevance was written in the skies.

Yet, even in this year, it began to appear that there was still life in the old concepts—free competition, nation-states, individualism— just as there was hope in the breasts of those who managed the vested interests. A strong impulse to thrust Alamogordo, Hiroshima, and Nagasaki far down into the unconscious where they would not disturb routine had its origin in the urgent need for defense, for security, for continuity, for protection of all the precious accumulations in the social scientists' treasure house. So powerful was the compulsion that Bikini, as I have suggested, seemed to have reinforced it rather than to have acted as a further and final exposure of futility.

Social scientists shared this retreat from reality with everyone who had an investment in the going arrangements of government, industry, and other social institutions. All alike wished with extreme intensity that atomic fission had not occurred and erupted into enormous social consequence; and the impulse was widely shared either to pretend that its significance was not really serious or to find ways of containing it which would relieve the intolerable psychic stresses of the August days when knowledge was a bludgeoning monster.

There was, furthermore, the added impulse to protect from depreciation all the accumulations of learned techniques, which the intellectuals guarded, used, and transmitted. There was not, for this
reason, the outcry there should have been against the great conspiracy embodied in the May-Johnson Bill. There were too many who
felt that it would be fine if the military would just put the genie back
into the jar and stand guard over it permanently.

The movement to bottle up the knowledge of atomic fission thus
prospered for some time and seemed quite likely to end in containing legislation. And it would have done so if there had not been
an unprecedented and undignified, because outraged, outburst from
the atomic scientists themselves. It is not too much to say that, if
civilization survives into further evolution of the contemporary culture, that survival will be owed in considerable part to this group.
When the social scientists stood aside, still paralyzed by their need
for reorientation, clutching their irrelevant concepts, and while
power-holding individuals conquered their fears and went to work
at making disaster pay, the atomic scientists swarmed out of their
laboratories and raised a row all over the nation until they got the
hearing they so loudly demanded. They discarded dignity, abandoned reticence, and adopted the gaudiest tactics they could conceive. They pleaded with women's clubs, luncheon groups, and congressional committees. From sedentary reasoners they changed into
peripatetic missionaries. They called attention to themselves in
every way they could devise. They demanded that they be heard.

They wanted to say that the impossible was being attempted and
that, because it was impossible, it could only result in a fatal impasse.
It was not so much a bomb which had been let loose, they
said, as the knowledge of atomic fire. The use of it for destructive
purposes was only a trick—a trick plus the immense expenditures
and the complex organization necessary to produce fissionable materials. It was the knowledge which was important, and the knowledge—up to the last engineering device and its manufacturing process—was common. It was, in fact, contained in the Smyth Report.
They estimated, from their own recent experience, and from what
they knew of the state of nuclear physics elsewhere in the world,
that other nations might easily begin to manufacture atomic weap-

ons within five years or even three. A policy of secrecy could only lead to a deceptive sense of security which would prevent us, but not others, from making further progress.

Senator Brien McMahon was among those who listened and was profoundly impressed.[7] On October 9 he proposed a Senate committee for atomic discussion. He was only a little ahead of those who would have pushed a measure there corresponding to the May-Johnson Bill in the House. But what he said, together with the growing public support for the atomic scientists, secured him the right of way; and for the first time it began to appear that adequate discussion of the public policy to be embodied in legislation might be had. The House Military Affairs Committee went ahead, however, and reported its bill, an occurrence which whipped the scientists into a renewed frenzy of opposition and showed that the issue could by no means be regarded as settled. It seemed quite possible that railroaded legislation might be on the books in a matter of weeks.

On November 1 the Federation of Atomic Scientists was organized. If no one else, no other group, was capable of understanding what was happening and what its consequences to civilization might be, the scientists, unaccustomed though they were to such work, were going to awaken the nation. That it would be a real effort was now guaranteed by organization and by the funds which they themselves, out of their meager resources, their university or foundation salaries, provided.

About this time it began to be plain that the Truman administration would not be able to maintain President Roosevelt's kind of relations with Soviet leaders. After the meeting in Potsdam,[8] Mr. Truman let it be known that there would be no more personal conferring among the chiefs of state. He had evidently been disappointed in his face-to-face contact with Stalin and had decided that it would be better to use American power at a distance, perhaps because he felt that power to be so overwhelming. The Potsdam meeting had been just before Hiroshima; in fact, the presidential announcement had been made from a ship on the way home. And

7. General Eisenhower, by now Chief of Staff, also listened. It was Professor Hogness who, hearing that the General was a sensible man, thought to call on him. The influence of this call was certainly considerable.

8. In July, 1945.

the consciousness of overwhelming strength, along with the belief that our equipment had enabled the Russians to do as well as they had, must have given him confidence that no more was necessary in the postwar world than to make known American wishes to have them treated respectfully by the only remaining formidable world power. Britain was now our second, but still a not inconsiderable, source of strength, with her widely scattered bases and her diplomatic finesse. The United States had, also, a navy which was overwhelmingly greater than all others in the world put together. And then, as he knew, we had the Bomb. What Stalin would think when he heard of its use a few days after the Potsdam exchange of confidences was apparently not considered. Pondering it afterward, Mr. Truman may well have felt that his reticence had had a flavor of underemphasis even though he had informed Stalin of its existence. And this may even have had something to do with his determination not to meet again with the other chiefs of state. Mr. James A. Byrnes became Secretary of State,[9] and there opened an era of degenerating relations with Russia which would, in no more than a matter of months, become the subject of open speculation throughout the world. By the time of Bikini, potential war between the Soviets and the United States would become an accepted notion with which people everywhere would have to try to live. How greatly this fact added to the tension already induced by the Bomb's existence, all who lived through it would always remember. I know I suddenly added a Russian war to my sons' possible futures, when, before, I had only thought generally of the dangers of the Bomb if some unfocused trouble should arise.

For the Soviet Union, instead of accepting the secondary role that our negotiations seemed to presuppose as the due of our might, acted rather as though she were the senior partner in the world's company of nations. She strutted, she growled, she exhibited bad manners, she talked to our emissaries openly in unprecedented language—and, on the whole, it might have been judged by an impartial observer that *she* had powerful partners, that *she* had the greatest fleet in history, and that *she* possessed the ultimate weapon. Before very long, America's ready hostile newspapers were openly suggesting that the war had better come now, before the fleet became ob-

9. July 3, 1945. He would resign in January, 1947.

solete and before Russians had been able to manufacture the Bomb. This was the atmosphere in which the agitation of the scientists had to go on. In this atmosphere, also, legislation for the administration of the atomic-energy potential had to be shaped, and discussions had to begin among the nations concerning possible arrangements for the same purpose. It was all difficult and unpropitious.

Mr. Vyacheslav Molotov, Soviet Foreign Minister, speaking to a party congress in Moscow on November 7, 1945, made pronouncements which underlined the growing hostility between the two greatest powers. He spoke of "atomic diplomacy" and in effect accused the United States and Britain of attempting to dominate the world. The evidence he cited was the unwillingness of the Western bloc to recognize the terms of the new balance of power. They insisted on questioning Russia's relations with the smaller nations of eastern Europe which she had every intention of maintaining as buffer puppets. The nationalist dogma was still strong in Western minds—more so in the American than in the British—and it seemed an injustice not to grant immediate local autonomy throughout the area east of the Oder. The difficulty with the American contention —or one difficulty—was that Russia's armies were in occupation, that no amount of talk could accomplish their removal, and that, so long as they were there, it would be Russia who would dominate eastern European policy. The Russians were no more than amused by American insistence on "democratic" elections. They argued that under the circumstances free choice would mean the return to power of the old capitalist-landlord classes and orientation toward the West. They had no intention of opening the Balkans to Western intrigue, and they said so.

Britain gradually fell into second place as asperity between East and West grew; and Mr. Byrnes and Mr. Molotov became spotlighted antagonists who played their roles in the full sight of all the world's peoples—except that news as reported was doctored one way in Russia and another in the United States. In fact, Britain's realism, which had for generations been her strongest resource in foreign affairs, led her to begin advising moderation. The old cliché of the Anglophobe American press, that American diplomacy was a tool of the British imperialists, could hardly survive this defection. For it soon became apparent that the Labour government was actually withdrawing from India and Egypt and was reassessing the whole conception of the Mediterranean lifeline.

While American generals and admirals were maneuvering for the preservation of their war organization and while the State Department was engaging the Soviets in perhaps the most acrimonious peacetime dispute in all history, the British somehow found the genius not only to reassess their own position in the new alignment of powers but also to produce a completely new conception of empire strategy. Its great virtue was that it was premised on the organization and the weapons which must be used in any future conflict rather than on those used in the last one. It was proposed to withdraw, militarily, from the Near East and to base on the vastnesses of Mid-Africa. In the crudest terms, Britain could be attacked there by guided missiles, having atomic war heads, with the minimum risk of damage; the destructiveness even of such terrible explosives might be absorbed in the endless forests and plains of the least-developed land area on earth without paralyzing effect. From there her own missiles could reach any likely enemy with sufficient accuracy.

This conception acknowledged, it will be seen, the essential unrealism of trying to press Russia with land forces or to threaten her from the sea. The air was now the military medium; and pilotless rockets were the inevitable weapons. American strategists might put up a show of bluster for old-fashioned institutions. Such bluster revealed them to be the Colonel Blimps of the new age. There were signs, however, that they saw the anachronisms in the present military establishment. They talked more and more, for instance, about limitation of weapons and rules for warfare. They also experimented on a grand scale with guided missiles in the empty deserts of the West. And they hinted that there was being prepared—that there already existed—a more dreadful resource than the Bomb. This was bacterial warfare, which supposedly could extinguish whole populations by loosing among them new strains of virus diseases to which no immunity had been established.

So far as atomic energy was concerned, matters took a turn for the better toward the end of 1945—domestically, if not internationally. The quarrel with Russia over other matters was still growing; but the conspiracy of the May-Johnson Bill had evidently failed. Military control of atomic power was not winning approval. Senator McMahon's committee had been organized, had held hearings, and had introduced legislation whose main feature was a provision for civilian control not only of fissionable materials but of enterprises growing out of the processes of fission. The most the military could expect to get was some participation of an advisory sort; their hope for a monopoly was lost. The scientists and their National Committee on Atomic Information had been too much for them. And at the end of the year the formation of a United Nations Atomic Energy Commission was announced.

It was just at this juncture of events, and coincident with the failure of efforts to hide atomic power in the Pentagon, that there began the active effort to promote the idea of limiting atomic weapons; and this was to be prepared for by a campaign of belittlement. It proved very difficult at first to suggest successfully that the Bomb was not really dangerous after all. It was not easy for most people to forget the dreadful shock of Hiroshima. The organs of mass communication had all recognized it as the "biggest news story of the century"[10] and had made quite as much of it as was warranted by this description for some time afterward. Reversal had to be gradual, but by the beginning of 1946 it was well under way. In fact, by the end of January the cautious progress toward a new attitude had gone far enough to enable the Navy to announce the Bikini tests.

This was a strategic time for the announcement; for in February President Truman backed the McMahon Bill, and, if this campaign of belittlement had not been in progress by then, the atomic scientists would have come off with a complete victory. As it was, Bikini, and the preparations for it, made their task far more difficult. By showing that the Bomb had its limitations as an instrument of destruction, the military hoped to prove that public control of atomic energy was unnecessary and that international agreement to limit

10. Lieutenant Colonel John F. Moynahan, *Atomic Diary* (New York: Barton Publishing Co., 1946), p. 38. Lieutenant Colonel Moynahan was the Army's public relations officer in charge of publicizing the event. *Atomic Diary* was his own account of what took place while the operations at Hiroshima and Nagasaki were prepared for and executed.

its war-time uses was a real possibility. In June a final attempt by the House committee to put military control back into the bill failed, but there were severe compromises in the measure as it emerged from conference. It finally passed on July 26 after both the first and second Bikini tests.

Meanwhile, the forces of reason had had the support of the so-called "Acheson-Lilienthal Report,"[11] which was so clear and matter of fact that much of the remaining mystery concerning atomic energy was dissipated and what had to be done appeared in terms which anyone who cared to could understand: Not just the national but the world public had to control the new source of energy. The report was published a few weeks after Mr. Bernard Baruch had been appointed to be representative of the United States on the United Nations Atomic Energy Commission and was obviously intended to serve as a directive for his work, although he was reported to have known nothing of it in advance and to have been annoyed because he had not been consulted.

I do not know whether others were as disconcerted as I was at Mr. Baruch's appointment. It seemed to me then, and has seemed since, to be part of the attempt at containment and monopoly of atomic power, now turning toward limitation of its uses. In fact, this movement now seemed to me to have become much more than a mere reaching for the benefits of atomic energy for one nation and one class within that nation. I thought I could see evidences that sinister interests might be taking general control of the government and managing foreign policy according to their own desires. Mr. Byrnes and Mr. Clayton, in the Department of State, could be thought of as serving such an interest.

As for domestic policy, by the summer of 1946, it had become a debacle. It seemed by then to have all the characteristics of the kind of reaction from the high tensions of war which had ruined Wilson's hopes for peace in 1919 and 1920 and had set the country off on the pursuit of normalcy under Harding, Coolidge, and Hoover— and, it may be added, had ended in catastrophe.

A strange situation in Washington reflected in some ways what was going on in the nation, but in other ways was merely a taking advantage of it. There was unrest enough. Everyone was sore: con-

11. This report was issued on March 28 by the Department of State.

sumers, because prices were rising; returning soldiers and sailors, because they could not find satisfactory readjustment after their service; workers, because of shifts from war to peace production; businessmen, because strikes interrupted the production of their enterprises and because labor was dictatorial. But most powerful of all was the discontent of business, large and small, over the controls which had been imposed during the war and which still, although shattered and wavering, remained. Businessmen were determined to shake loose from all the "bureaucratic meddling" which seemed to them so stupidly restrictive.

Mr. Truman was the more or less innocent victim of all these gathering discontents. Immediately after Hiroshima he had consented to the removal of certain controls at the instance of his new advisers. He had not then realized, apparently, the unbalance that shifting from war to peace production would cause and the turbulence among workers that would follow the reduction of their high take-home incomes; and no one had warned him that, once controls were loosed at any center of the highly articulated economy, readjustments would be made necessary everywhere else. When these readjustments occurred, as was inevitable, they were accompanied by civil disturbances of unprecedented violence. Almost at once the hardly attained morale of war production broke down in unhealable divisiveness. The administration was unready. Besides, the central organs of government themselves were losing strength and prestige. The Congress, increasingly irresponsible, was harrying them. They were being bled both of talent and of energy. The mediocrities with whom Mr. Truman persisted in manning the agencies of control were either unable to conceive their tasks or were actually determined to manage them in favor of private interests. The concept of a public interest, of the nation's wholeness, of the articulation of all initiatives in one purpose, which at the most intense moment of war had seemed at last to be grasped in the War Production Board, the War Manpower Commission, the Office of Price Administration, and, especially, in the overhead agencies, the Office of Economic Stabilization and the Office of War Mobilization, was now dissipated in vague confusion or in a raucous conflict. The nation was splintered. And it had no leadership.

At home people were unhappy and ashamed of themselves for

being so selfish; but they were unable to express through any existing institution any other than ungenerous impulses. Abroad our representatives were engaged in recrimination with Russia which could not possibly have a favorable outcome. To all this the nation had descended, the same nation which had displayed the superb capacities of the war years and the intelligence at their end to harness atomic fire!

Under the circumstances the possibility of limiting warfare to "civilized" weapons was certain to be explored. There could be no doubt that guided missiles with atomic war heads would, if actually used, be irresistible. It would be a relief from tension for others than the military to know that the next war, which, like the last two, had begun to seem inevitable, would not be worse than the others. Above all, it would be a relief not to face the incalculable labors, the degrading compromises, the uncongenial disciplines, the violations of tradition—all that would have to be undergone if a world state *had* to be brought into being as the only alternative to destruction. There were many who had begun to believe that it must be done; but there were very few who believed that it could be done. This terrible dilemma would naturally induce an almost frantic search for alternatives.

For the military, the idea of outlawing atomic weapons had an almost irresistible attraction. Consider how marvelous the old weapons had become! The battleship and the cruiser had evolved into things of technological beauty, indomitable on the sea. They were the darlings of the admirals, who considered that the airplane carrier rather supplemented than displaced the sister ships and that the submarine could be contained. The bombing plane, too, was mechanically marvelous; and electronic techniques were about to furnish it with the ability to see through mists and to strike at targets with "pinpoint" precision. On land the tank, repeating artillery, and motor transport had revolutionized battle tactics. To have all these new instruments, evolved with such a wealth of experience and mastered with such prolonged effort, simply thrown away was unbearable waste if there were any alternative at all.

The concept of limiting weapons was not new. Throughout history, indeed, until modern times, it had been accepted. Chivalry had been largely such a limitation. Codes of honor had been part of the military tradition right down to Clausewitz, though they showed a certain tendency to fail when there existed no possibility of reprisal. And, in the late war, both sides had prepared gases for use in battle—the gas attacks of World War I had been hardly more than experiments—but they had never been used, perhaps because each belligerent feared that the other would profit most. If gas, why not atomic bombs and bacterial warfare? It was a very natural question.

The answer was, unfortunately, only too clear. Not only had the victors already used the atomic bomb, but history seemed to run against limitation. Chivalrous war in the Middle Ages had been a kind of game, and even in the wars of ancient times there had been a large element of sport. Many of the tales on which children fed told of individual heroes who had represented their forces in personal combat with opposing champions. In modern times that custom had been reversed: The heroes lately had been represented by masses of soldiers; and, even more lately, national wars had brought into conflict whole populations on both sides. A new kind of war had accompanied this shift—the crusade, for a conviction of right is a powerful inducement for subordinating personal ends to those of national policy. Perhaps the first great war of conviction, if the Crusades are excepted, began when the Republican armies of France undertook to defend themselves against the Absolutists of the rest of Europe and, fed by success and betrayed into dictatorship, went on and on in enfeebling wars of conquest. Napoleon failed when the convictions of his people failed. This lesson was clear to the Prussians; and a succession of Prussian generals organized into a continuing staff succeeded in imbuing the German nation with fanatic faith and with devotion to force for its extension. The faith was very different from that of the Republicans of France; but it had the same utility to the staff of conquerors who created from it the mass armies that implemented the militarism of the years from Frederick the Great to Hitler. Like so many social phenomena which have begun in pursuit of admirable ends, crusading warfare seemed likely to annihilate the Westerners who had invented it. And certainly to talk of limiting the weapons to be used in a crusade was to be fatally unrealistic. In such a conflict the professional soldier, with his notions of fair play and his tradition of chivalry, is simply not in control. He is the servant of forces which are far more powerful than any restraints he can impose.

World War II demonstrated that, even when a soldier was not a crusader but an American draftee anxious to go back home, he could not escape participation in a campaign which, by way of bombing, particularly, punished civilians far more than it did soldiers. There had been something in the education and environment of the American which had brought him to accept the murder of innocents as necessary to national purpose. The Prussian generals lost World War II because of Hitler's unrestrained fanaticism; but the American generals won by violating—without a fanatic faith, even with reluctance—every canon of decency they and all their fellow-citizens professed. The shift from war as a game to war as a national struggle for survival had shattered the chivalric tradition upon which any agreements to limit weapons must be based.

Furthermore, the Asiatics had now acquired significant military powers. They had not the same chivalrous tradition and so would not recognize whatever restraint it might have imposed. It was no accident that both Port Arthur and Pearl Harbor were attacked without declarations of war or that Westerners should have been maddened almost beyond sanity by the treachery. The Japanese had understood the logic of the process they were in; but they had not understood the uses of hypocrisy. Nor, of course, would punishment teach them.

The situation was frighteningly easy to see: To a world without chivalrous restraints, in which ideological crusaders still dominated powerful masses, there had now been given a powerful weapon. It was no wonder that the American revulsion was so violent and the instinct to keep the weapon away from fanatics so ready. This instinct underlay the conflict between the Americans and the Russians. Give Russians the Bomb, Americans felt, and the subjection of the world to communism—communism operated as a world system from Moscow—would instantly begin. Without explaining to themselves how they happened to have used the Bomb, Americans still did not believe that the Russians could be classified among those who did not want to push other people around.

The nature of the weapon was such that he who used it first might well prevail even if others possessed it too. There was as yet no defense, and, theoretically, an adequate defense seemed unlikely to develop soon. True, a single attack with atomic weapons would not necessarily be final, and no nation could easily be annihilated in one strike; the power of attack had been greatly, but not infinitely, multiplied. Recognition of the finite nature of the Bomb was sensible and in accord with fact; but it may have encouraged the carelessness that was rapidly developing. Overlooked was the possibility that the technology of a nation might be destroyed or so impaired as to be useless; and, in these days of centralization and of dependence on the higher nerve centers of social organisms, this possibility was all-important. Not every citizen in any wide land could be killed by a few bombs; but all of them could be set back to pre-technological days and condemned to wandering about the countryside without direction. And, since defense could only consist in reprisal, this disaster might fall upon both opposing nations simultaneously.

Limitation set by agreement on the use of a small object with paralyzing power could only be effective under certain conditions. It was with despair that the first condition was recognized—no single nation could control the whole development of atomic energy. This was the real meaning of the Acheson-Lilienthal Report. No amount of disparagement or devious argument could change that fact; the report did not seek to do other than drive it home. The necessity of revolutionary modifications not only of attitudes toward national sovereignty but also of the American prejudices against public ownership and operation of industrial enterprises was quite apparent. There were two great questions quivering in the air after the report was issued: Would the Communist state consent to the necessary close communion with the capitalist West? And would the American capitalists renounce their hopes of exploiting this rich new source of profits? Bikini was intended to make both think the sacrifice unnecessary, as well as to preserve the Navy of the United States from scientific aggressors; such, at least, was the opinion I found myself entertaining.

Would the test succeed in hoodwinking its audience? There was, at least, a fine set of prejudices, predispositions, and vested interests to back it up if there should be the slightest encouragement.[12]

So we came to Bikini, that curious demonstration in the far Pacific. We had been reading about the project off and on since the spring. There had been differences about it, but finally the combined Chiefs of Staff had ordered it to be undertaken;[13] and, after postponement, preparations had gone ahead. It must have been a relief to such of the military propaganda officers as had not yet been demobilized to have the secrecies of war removed and to be able once more to surround an activity with the aura of excitement and glamour which they felt necessary to their work; anyway it was obvious that they had released a good deal of pent energy on "Operation Crossroads," as one of them had had the ironic wit to name it. They had had to overcome some stuffy objections from Major General Leslie R. Groves; but the Navy had been with them, and they had been able to organize splurge enough to suit the most exacting—correspondents' trains, specially fitted ships, and all the rest. Only the Bomb itself was hidden. But even about the Bomb it was allowed to be said that a small crane had hoisted it from a tent which had sheltered it on Kwajalein to a trench beneath the bomb bay of "Dave's Dream" and that it was at least large enough so that a twelve-inch picture of Miss Rita Hayworth could be pasted on its side.

There was good weather out there on the Pacific, the broadcasters said. At what was just before six, by their time, "Dave's Dream" lifted its load off the Kwajalein runway and went off toward the

12. Mr. B. H. Liddell Hart, in an article called "War, Limited," which appeared in March, 1946, *Harper's Magazine*, explored these matters at some length but with an obvious prejudice. That prejudice he stated as he began: "Today, there is a vast tide of sentiment, the world over, in favor of preventing war. But there is a very little awareness of the practical necessity, if that hope fails, of *limiting* war." He did not analyze the nature of the atomic bomb. If he had then known how clearly it is a mere by-product of developments in the producing of atomic energy sure to take place in many different nations, he might not have been so optimistic. The Acheson-Lilienthal Report was not optimistic. But it gave more real hope than any scheme for international agreements because what it proposed was *supranational*.

13. This made it a joint undertaking of Army and Navy, but the expedition was under the command of Vice Admiral W. H. D. Blandy.

small fleet of superannuated ships in the Bikini lagoon. For those who were most skeptical, this seemed to be a prejudiced demonstration which in no way simulated reality. What could be told from the fate of a few scattered ships on a lagoon, manless and inert? Others, even if they felt that what they were being shown was phony proof that navies were still useful, recognized that much would be learned. There were many hundreds of animals on the ships which would be exposed to the same shock and the same radioactive mists that had had such dreadful results at Hiroshima. Great pains had been taken to prepare them in all kinds of ways for the ordeal, and their experience would be revealing. It was the fourth dropping of the Bomb, and, for whatever purpose it was intended, everyone would wait in strained suspense until it was over. Hardly anyone yet felt quite certain that the scientists knew what precisely they were doing. In spite of belittlement, there was some remaining fear that all the earth's atoms might split in chain fashion and the world disappear in a flash of flame. They might not understand the meaning in any scientific sense, of $E = mc^2$, but instinct told them that its logic was not limited, but universal, and they wondered whether the fission experts knew how to stop the processes they had begun.

Up to the taking-off, the radio listener could follow matters. From then on he was subjected to a series of losses and recoveries of lucidity which made progress very hard to follow. Transmission from the "Appalachian" was so muddled that little more came through than an irregular series of ejaculations. Nevertheless, it was possible to know when all was ready and the bombing run had begun. There were repeated exhortations about listening to a metronome which apparently had been placed before an open microphone on the deck of the "Pennsylvania" within the lagoon. When the metronome stopped, the bomb would have been exploded. The metronome was only heard at the last moment, so its dramatic effect was lost. Not only the ticking of this instrument but most of the rest of the performance were drowned in a deluge of those weird, shivery sounds that convey so eerie a sense of illimitable distance and empty space. But out of this space there did come from the Fortress an excited voice crying, "Bomb's away!" Then silence—a kind of silence, filled with the screechings of those devils in the outer darknesses! There was nothing more.

After a while we were told that the drop was over. There had been a flash and the shock of compression. But the explosion had been so accurately gauged, so well prepared for, that neither the flash nor the shock was deeply experienced. The millions who were listening drew a long breath and said, as afterward the Russian observer was reported to have muttered, "Not so much, after all!" Bikini had been beautifully managed from the military point of view. The Navy's publicity men had caught the receding wave of terror and ridden it into a new period of assurance. For the ships that the admirals had so daringly and expensively exposed had not been sunk. They were, most of them, still indisputably there. The nearest were twisted and wrenched, but only two had been sunk outright. And, although nothing close to the explosion had lived through it, and probably no man would have survived out of the fleet's complement, the general impression was one of anticlimax.

That derogation, of course, was what was wanted. How eagerly the world's press embraced the finitude of the Bomb; how volubly it resolved in editorials that this was, after all, "just another weapon"! And how contentedly the military men rested on the "facts." Of course the pictures taken from the "Appalachian" and from the Bikini beach would show exactly the same phenomena as had been observed in the other three drops: the glaring flash, the swiftly spreading mist, the mushroom-shaped bulging, at incredible heights, of the column of disintegrated materials—but this would be later. On that Sunday, and all through the week following, all mankind was busy with self-congratulation. It need not face its doom quite yet. And, when the surface explosion occurred on July 24, no more attention was paid to it—perhaps not so much—than to the broadcast of the professional baseball games that were then warming up to the season's middle.

Between the two tests, being alone for a while, I had a chance to look back over the year since Hiroshima.

Our smaller immediate worries had little to do with the permanent problem we had been provided with by the scientists, except that they indicated how concerned all of us could be about taking care of matters which would be of no importance if the great issue were not settled. As I looked back over the year, I thought I had made some progress in discovering for myself the source of the great worry and how the unreadiness of the world for atomic power had arisen. As I gazed from a window at the Washington traffic, it faded out into a composite of several village streets and squares with a sharply nostalgic recall for me whose people had at least looked different, however much like these they may have been inside.

The United States was still—in spite of marvelous communications and transportation systems—full of village backwaters. (As I considered this fact, it seemed to me that there were many city backwaters too, if, by backwater, I meant intellectual pockets that the stream of culture had passed without affecting them greatly.) This, at once, became a complicated consideration of the sociologists' social lag; and the lag obviously had its opposite in lead. Of this, the presentation of atomic fire to a world like ours was ample evidence. Indeed, perhaps 80 per cent of the world's families were dwellers on primitive homestead farm places; perhaps 50 per cent were not directly influenced by mass communications—newspapers, the radio, and so on—because they were illiterate and could not read the one or because they lived out of hearing of the other. Even if they could read or possessed radios, their educations had not provided them with the background of knowledge indispensable to judgment. They were in process of obtaining self-government, all these masses, or what was called self-government; even in India, in Indonesia, in China, and in the Near East, and to a less degree in Africa, the responsibility for governing was devolving upon them. They were insisting upon independence, just at a time when independence was finally being made obsolete by new inventions. Asked about this problem, Jawaharlal Nehru, doubtless the most statesman-like of their leaders, had answered that only independent peoples could co-operate. But his answer begged the question rather than answered it. What was meant by independence? Was it freedom for the Hindu to govern the Moslem? And who or what were a "people"? Obviously, all those within the confines called India by geographers did not consider themselves to be one people. They might be made so by the effect of a constitution; but, within limits, so might the people within any area. Why not the world? Nehru had no answer to that question, nor had anyone else. There was no logical stopping place short of the world, because any "independent" people might use the Bomb on any or all of the rest.

But it was not only leaders like Nehru who had been arrested in midcareer, so to speak, being overtaken by a technology that had outrun their ideologies. Lesser folk, who had no cultivated resiliency, no surface of aplomb, to cover their bewilderment, had been overtaken too. They were also making question-begging answers to themselves, to their children, and to their neighbors. They were hiding their heads in the sand because there was nothing else to do, and their consternation was turning into the demand for relief that was being met by their leaders and by the organs of mass communication in hearty but thoroughly dishonest fashion. Belittlement was a soothing oil under the ministrations of which settling back into accustomed ways could go on without unendurable pains in the conscience.

I had not got so very far in explaining why atomic fire had been lit in a world still largely illiterate and still largely in the handcraft economy; or even why it had been lit in a Western world whose technology had not succeeded in feeding adequately more than half its population or in furnishing more than half its homes with electricity; or even why it had been lit in a nation which had had to reject half its young citizens because of physical disability for war service, and half of whose schools, houses, and hospitals were about to collapse from obsolescence. The contrast did not make much more sense than it had when I had first looked at it. I thought I knew now that the trouble lay in institutions rather than in people, but I was not yet certain; and anyway such a generalization had in it more than a slight hint of contradiction.

Social lag and technological lead, these had now become crucial problems: We had to get rid of backward peoples, it seemed, somehow—preferably by bringing them up to civilized standards. But actually I knew, as I thought about it, that backward peoples were much less a problem than the backward thinkers in our own midst. Many of those best furnished with polished chromium and glass surroundings, who had the finest motorcars and the most servants, because they had the most power were the most dangerous men in the world. They were on the make for themselves, not for society; and in our social order we had not succeeded in devising an institutional setup which would reward them for public service, utilize their initiative for the general good, control their dangerous, and unloose their useful, impulses. This was the real difficulty, the worst threat to our civilization. This was, in fact, what I felt the urge to explain.

Most young lives in my time had been to a tragic extent wasted. There must have been a way for some of the superior talent that had developed nuclear physics to have operated in the social sciences to create different institutions. It seemed, from what we know now of the richness and flexibility of human nature, that if school, home, economic system, municipality, and other institutions had been so shaped as to bring out socially directed initiative, drives toward co-operation, and appreciation of gentle virtues, the world—at least our Western world, or, at the very least, our nation—might have been ready to receive and use the energy of the universe with which we were now being presented.

Instead, I and my fellows in the village backwaters had been brought up to be David Harums. As I remembered the Harum philosophy, it was: "Do unto the other fellow as he would do unto you— only do it first." That exactly fitted the prevailing approach to life of small-town Americans. There were minorities, as there always are, but they seldom prevailed over those who believed in withholding, trading, going cautiously, exploiting others under the guise of "business" and "freedom," and generally getting to old age providently with money in the bank. That was what a boy was supposed to do in my day and place. And other boys, in city backwaters, were learning a worse approach. They were learning to be against the world in gangs, because the world was against them. They had to play in city streets full of peril and unamenable to the stretch of a boy's legs, or in vacant lots, cramped, filthy, and furtive.

Somewhere back at technological beginnings a wrong turn, on the path toward civilization, perhaps unnoticeable at the time and not located precisely now in any histories I knew of, must have been decided on by our ancestors. Men must have turned in time further away from the imperatives of civilization, and given heavier weighting to destruction rather than creation, so that now we had come to the end of that way and faced its consequence in catastrophe, unable to say how it had come about or where the tiny mistaken beginning had been made.

The first year of the atomic age had seen the start of an enterprise which, although it might have no practical outcome, was nevertheless of some satisfaction to me in the same way that the political activities of the atomic scientists must have been a satisfaction to them. A group called The Committee To Frame a World Constitution was set up. It had its first meeting at the University of Chicago in the fall of 1945. I was asked to join, and I accepted eagerly. The conception was that only genuine world government could unite the various peoples of the world in the operation of common institutions and that nothing short of a drastic modification of national sovereignty would keep nations from some time or other falling into quarrels and resorting to the use of atomic explosives. Mr. William Higinbotham, secretary of the Federation of Atomic Scientists, put the common feeling picturesquely when he said: "I don't know exactly what weapons will be used in the next war; but I know what ones will be used in the war after that. They will be sticks and stones."

This was the background of the committee. It had had its origin, probably, in the remarks of Chancellor R. M. Hutchins on the "University of Chicago Round Table" following Hiroshima.

Up to last Monday I must confess that I did not have much hope for a world state. I have believed that no moral basis for it existed and that we had no world conscience and no sense of world community sufficient to keep a world state together. But the alternatives now seem clear. One is world suicide; another is agreement among sovereign states to abstain from using the bomb. This will not be effective. The only hope, therefore, of abolishing war through the monopoly of atomic force is by a world organization.

Remember that Leon Bloy, the French philosopher, referred to the good news of damnation, doubtless on the theory that none of us would be Christians if we were not afraid of perpetual hell-fire. It may be that the atomic bomb is the good news of damnation, that it may frighten us into that Christian character and those righteous actions and those positive political steps necessary to the creation of a world society, not a thousand or five hundred years hence, but now.[14]

Our Committee To Frame a World Constitution was certainly not a "positive political step"; but, for us, at least, it was a "righteous action" and one utterly necessary to relieve the personal sense of guilt we all of us had. During the first year we worked conscientious-

14. Reuben Gustavson, Robert M. Hutchins, and William F. Ogburn, *Atomic Force: Its Meaning for Mankind* ("University of Chicago Round Table," No. 386, broadcast August 12, 1945), p. 12.

ly, trying by frequent and disciplined discussion to build up what
one of our number described as "a group memory"—that is, to explore each other's minds until we had no need for further controversy over elementals and could concentrate on the construction of
a document that should be adequate for our agreed purposes.

None of us had the illusion that what was being contemplated
was an actual constitution for any real government, although outsiders often supposed that we thought so. All of us were used to the
methods of abstraction and imaginary synthesis so necessary to the
discovery of possibilities, in which a concept is gradually unfolded
and becomes a plan for the unified institution which, if events happened as they were assumed to, would come into being. There is
nothing unusual about this procedure except that individuals do it
more often than groups. The utopists—Plato, Augustine, Harring-
ton, More, Bellamy, and many others—have done it individually.
Their utopias have not come into being; but they have had influence. True, the uninitiated are apt to ridicule such efforts because
they have never been adopted, and "utopian" is something of a
synonym for hopelessly futile wishing. But what such critics do not
appreciate is that prediction is not the purpose. The purpose is to
objectify possibilities.

That this purpose has often succeeded is shown by the kind of
criticism that the best of them have received: that they are not in
accord with "human nature." It is not often said that they are unde-
sirable, or, indeed, that they do not represent what ought to or could
happen; it is said that people are not good enough to accomplish
such things or to live with such institutions even if they were to
come into being. Such criticism is beside the point. People have
frequently rejected the good in favor of the bad—especially if the
bad harms mostly others.

As a planner, I was perfectly familiar with the method. It is the
planner's way to create a Development Plan first, so that subsequent proposed public actions can be measured by it. The Development Plan is a concept; it is something that should and can, with
the resources available, be brought into being. It is constructed by
a group made up of technicians, analysts, experts, each of whom
contribute something which is then made to articulate, to take on
wholeness, by the planner. For it is always *his* business to be con-

cerned with the nature of the organism, the operating whole—the city, if it is a city; the industry, if it is an industry.

Like More and others, the planner too is sometimes ridiculed as utopian; for, though better furnished than the utopians with engineers, architects, fiscal experts, and lawyers, he too, in making a Development Plan, is not making an organism which will ever be realized. What he gets up is the logical end of present possibilities. Its value is that, since it displays the end, it can keep present policies rational and consistent with the end in view rather than irrational and inconsistent with a number of mutually inharmonious ends. If the goal changes, then the road toward it will need to change too. The Development Plan, even if it is never achieved, can thus compromise differences, reduce friction, create order, and generally act as an institutional mind controlling a reflective organism. Through it society can cease to be an insane arena for the practitioners of laissez faire and become a more smoothly functioning instrument of disciplined impulses.

Our Development Plan, the putative constitution, would thus be a definition of what world government must and could be *as things were;* if things changed, and to the extent that they changed, the constitution would become irrelevant and would need to be amended.

Out of the first year of study and discussion there had come some progress toward agreement on framework. It was an amazingly difficult feat, however, for a group of people, even relatively detached people, to imagine the creation of a unified government for the world rather than for one nation-state in that world. A preliminary review of sovereignty was enough to show all of us how the concentration on international friction, or the fear of it, had shaped everyone's ideas about his relation to the state. Nations had existed since before the accumulation and transmission of cultural artifacts and records had become highly organized; and it was the nation on which thought had centered in the Western world since the possession of high and unusual ability in the race had been made almost universally available through accessible education and more equal opportunity. It was far from easy to conceive the disappearance of so highly symbolized an institution. The transfer of loyalty to a world government would lack for reinforcement many of the strongest ties the nations could count on between their governments and their citizens. Patriotism had been pounded into young minds everywhere as a first and deepest commitment. Dying for the country, if not a certain claim to eternal reward—and it was that in many lands—was at least a claim on the gratitude of fellow-citizens which would be perpetuated in deathless annals. The heroes of nationalism were honored and beloved above all others. What indeed could a world state have that would so stir and hold men's imaginations and compel their sacrificing services? Only the hope of forwarding the welfare of the race; so much was clear.

When the contemporary scene was surveyed, it could be concluded that, in spite of the millions lately dead in nationalistic warfare, the old ties were weakening and the new ones might answer to a deep need in men's souls. In the democracies the transference of sovereignty to their citizens had been almost completely accomplished in fact as well as in theory, and this transfer had liberated the people from the unquestioned obedience to authority that had earlier characterized their relation to the state. This liberation was a necessary preliminary to co-operative association, though it was accompanied by an almost fatal individualism and an imperfect understanding of the necessity for voluntary discipline. Only the free could co-operate; those who worked together involuntarily were no further along, morally speaking, than the individuals in a slave gang. (Equally unfree were those who were held together in groups for some reason other than the purpose for which the group existed. It was this servitude which fundamentally damned the American industrial system and made its continuance unchanged into a civilized future unthinkable.) And co-operative communities of free peoples might learn new loyalties to an even wider community.

Nations themselves, furthermore, were beginning to find that the old symbols were less effective because the old motives were weaker. National inferiority was an insupportable thesis. People everywhere began to see themselves as very like others—not all others yet, but certainly some others beyond their national borders. Citizens of the United States thought Canadians, Britishers, Scandinavians, and Germans their equals; and there was some uncertainty now in the old arrogance before Latins, Slavs, and Chinese, which might very quickly turn into genuine respect. To this extent national governments could count on less readiness to die in disputes brought about by diplomatic ineptitude. Western leaders had taken considerable pains to make the recent conflict seem inevitable; and Pearl Harbor had been indispensable as final proof of aggression for reluctant prospective soldiers.

Our group did not succeed in persuading itself that divorce from nationalism could be made complete. When it came to expressing sovereignty through institutions representative of it, we agreed that there must be assemblies representing not only world citizens directly but also nation-states themselves. The one was, however, conceived as primary, and the other as secondary, somewhat in the way the American House of Representatives, according to the original Constitution, represented the electorate directly and the Senate represented the states. It was not easy, of course, to define the difference between the interest of an individual citizen in Kansas or California and that of the nation of which he was a citizen in world government. Presumably he would be a citizen of the World State. If so, if his citizenship meant anything, it would carry civil rights, and he would be able to trade, travel, and communicate freely throughout the world—in other words, his relation to the World State would be the same as his relation to the government he now had.

Still, there had often been federations in which limited sovereignty had been granted to the federal government. The Swiss and the American were contemporary examples. Americans now had a dual citizenship. Examined in perspective, of course, it could be seen that the central government had grown stronger and the states weaker. It could even be seen that the states had been strong in the beginning only because they would not give up powers which logically they could not keep. If there should be established a Federal World State, the same development would undoubtedly take place. The constituent states would wither away; and this withering would be certain if they retained no armed forces or only ones which could not be used for successful aggression.

At the time of Bikini, and after prolonged discussion, we had decided on federation for our framework—but federation with a strong center. We had also agreed on the necessity of democracy for method, because nothing else could be permanent; and democracy, to us, meant equal voting rights, representation in lawmaking bodies, and election of an executive who, equally with the legislature, should represent all the people of the world. We had also agreed that there should be a judiciary to interpret law. The nature of these institutions was still vague; and there was still a great region of economic and social machinery largely unexplored. That there could not be immediate free trade and free movement was apparent. There must be a long effort to develop backward regions and their peoples before equality in these matters would be acceptable to peoples with advanced standards. This effort in itself would require novel institutions with sufficient central power to allocate resources. These new institutions, in turn, would necessitate a place in the constitution for economic and social planning such as had been consistently avoided in historic representative democracies.

I felt and said that the group lacked familiarity with economic life. Therefore, I made repeated recommendations for additions. Nothing came of them, however, and I began to feel that, for sheer lack of competence, we should not be able to produce a satisfactory document. I had begun to note in some of the others, too, a diminution of enthusiasm for the project. Yet I persisted, along with a few others, for the sheer need of doing something, however remote the chance that it might be useful in the deepening crisis.

That crisis seemed to be deepening, and I thought I saw a measure of it in one mind—a first-rate one which had found no way to be used in statesmanship—when Mr. Hutchins, the titular head of our Committee, suddenly took leave from the University of Chicago to devote himself to adult education, saying that there was no longer time to work with youth. If those already grown could not save civilization, it could not be saved; atomic fire would consume it. Mr. Hutchins did not say what his hopes were now, a year after Hiroshima and his declaration that a world state was possible; but I noted his irregularity at meetings of the Committee and drew my own conclusions.

CHAPTER III *1947*

THE second anniversary of Hiroshima approached. Professor Albert Einstein and others of the Emergency Committee of Atomic Scientists, meeting at Princeton, issued on June 29 another solemn warning to the world. It was necessary to make another statement, they said sadly, because their "appeal to reason" in May, 1946, had been wholly ineffective. The atomic scientists were not clear whether salvation required the creation of a world community, speaking in sociological terms; a new world government, federal or unitary, speaking in the technical language of political science; or merely an agreement among nations, such as the conferees of the United Nations Atomic Energy Commission had been sweating over at Lake Success all year. They referred to all three in the same public statement without being conscious, evidently, that controversy, intense, almost paralyzing, had arisen among the advocates of each. They only knew that catastrophe moved nearer.

The atomic scientists had made contributions of immense value in the great debate over policy. Since Hiroshima they had not ceased to demand action. They had been influential in the setting-up of the United Nations Atomic Energy Commission, in the passage during this last year of the Atomic Energy Act of the United States, and in the long Senate hearings over the confirmation of Mr. David Lilienthal as chairman of the commission authorized by the act.[1]

1. There was not much controversy over the confirmation of the other members, but action was delayed on all nominations by the attack on Mr. Lilienthal. The other nominees were: Robert F. Bacher, formerly associate director of the Los Alamos Laboratory and director of the Laboratory of Nuclear Studies at Cornell University; Sumner T. Pike, former member of the United States Securities Ex-

The atomic scientists were exactly as clear as—but no clearer than—others about what ought to be done in America and in fact elsewhere in the Western world. What they hesitated to acknowledge was what others also hesitated to acknowledge—that the United States was in process of deciding whether or not to accept responsibility for dominating the earth and all therein, not in the manner of the old imperialism, but by projecting the "American way of life" as universally suitable, and departures from it as unfriendly acts. If the latter-day cultural imperialists were to prevail, there was no hope whatever of avoiding the war that the scientists sincerely believed would be the end of everything.

If the scientists had been as learned in political as in atomic science, they might have discerned what had begun to some others to seem like a consistent impulse toward expansion since ancient times. The Romans had conquered their world, only to find that it was not a world; out of the forests beyond the distant Roman frontiers, hardier men than they had emerged. After medieval stasis, expansion had begun again; Spain, Portugal, Holland, Britain, France, and Germany each in succession had followed trade, religion, and national interest in outward-going thrusts until resistance had been met from another expanding power. In the resulting conflicts accommodation had sometimes been sought and sometimes temporarily found; but it had seldom sufficed to keep the peace for long. Since the world had become round—and so finite—there had been no ceasing from the struggle among imperiums to possess all of it.

Now at last it was known to everyone that an issue was joined which could end only in one of two ways: world domination by one

change Commission; Lewis L. Strauss, former admiral, United States Navy and member of the Interdepartmental Committee on Atomic Energy; and W. W. Waymack, editor of the *Des Moines Register and Tribune.* These appointments were announced in October, 1946, and the long hearings were begun which did not end until March 10, 1947. Confirmation was not voted until April 9, 1947. The law had been passed on August 1, 1946, after incredible proceedings that lasted some six months. Only at the beginning of May, 1947, almost two years after Hiroshima, and almost a year after Bikini, was the United States equipped to proceed with such atomic-energy development and control as could be contrived by one nation. The British had been both more expeditious and clearer. Their control act had been passed by the House of Commons on October 11, 1946. Its powers and responsibilities had been sensibly intrusted to the Minister of Supply under a broad authorization instead of to an awkward commission as in the American act.

people or an agreement, implied or explicit, for coexistence. If conquest was eschewed, an agreement to modify national sovereignty and to live in peace despite disagreement must be now established under firm auspices. People hoped that such a miracle would happen; but there were few historians or social scientists of any kind who were not skeptical. This pessimism may have accounted for their paralysis as the atomic scientists worked for peace. But by the summer of 1947 pessimism seemed justified and hope futile. The only hope left, really, was the uncertain one that the earth itself would not disintegrate in the last titanic grappling of the opposing powers. Conquest had not yet been given up.

The protagonists in the world struggle so plainly shaping up by 1947 were the Soviet Union and the United States. Each dominated a vast and productive area of the earth's surface which furnished the base from which to move outward. This common expansion was conscious, persistent, and ruthless. Because it was supported more by instinct than by reflection among people of the farms and the cities, it was the more easily managed by the policy-makers—the Communists and the capitalists—at the center of authority. Communism had both an advantage and a disadvantage in this struggle. Besides being based on the immense but undeveloped heartland of Eurasia, it commanded a religious devotion from its followers—it was one of those causes for which men gladly die. This devotion, furthermore, was not confined to Russians. Communists controlled by the Russian party formed a fifth column in almost every nation, for world revolution was a logical and acknowledged end of communism—an end never successfully disguised by Soviet diplomats. It was just this doctrinaire devotion, however, that weakened Soviet diplomacy. For two years now, Molotov and his colleagues had missed every opportunity to placate Western opinion. Their bad manners, their arrogance, and their sullen certainty of capitalism's inner weaknesses had resulted in unbelievably boorish performances at the meetings of the United Nations Assembly and its Atomic Energy Commission.

Capitalism in its turn had disadvantages. Its pretension to freedom no longer fooled the masses in the areas in which it prevailed. It was inherently exploitative and undemocratic, characteristics which had not been so obvious in its earlier stages as in the later ones now being reached. Devotion of a considerable percentage of its profits to proving that this was not so—the financing of elaborate propaganda—was no longer so effective as it once had been. It was most fortunate that the Russian alternative could be presented as utterly unattractive. However disillusioned American workers might be with their own capitalism, they were certain that Russian communism would be far worse. This certainly did not produce nearly so compelling an emotion as did the dream of world revolution; and it was altogether incapable of holding a core of devotees to a rigid and unquestioning discipline. This was the worst of its disadvantages.

Luckily, there were still those in America who did not believe that capitalism and democracy were identical. These consisted mostly of the traditional liberals, or—as they preferred to call themselves—progressives. But they were not many outside the labor organizations, and, to tell the truth, they were not too many there; they seemed, furthermore, to grow proportionately fewer or, at any rate, less effective. Capitalism, with its false front of freedom, possessed the wherewithal to assert a thousand times daily, and in a thousand different ways, that it *was* democracy. In 1947 it had better claim than ever before to this identity, for its ideas were dominant in one of the vital organs of the United States—the Congress.

Never in the history of the nation had the Congress seemed so submissive to self-seekers. A hundred battles won by great sacrifice through many decades for the suppression of exploiters and the protection of popular sovereignty were flagrantly reversed. The lobbies reveled in power. The lobbyists for the prosperous farmers, the real estate dealers, the big taxpayers, the National Manufacturers Association, and the United States Chamber of Commerce, as well as those for the oil, public utility, and railroad interests, found the national legislature eager to abase itself. Laws written by the representatives of predators often passed without record votes. In this way the Congress alienated great areas of the public domain, presented subsidies to industries, and furnished protection for all kinds of privileges. The word in Washington was "business." Whatever business wanted it could have; whatever it did not want commanded no attention.

One accompaniment of this grab for governmental favor was a

red hunt. Always a convenient cover for reaction, it was used in 1947 to expel from the public service virtually every employee, no matter how humble, whose conscience led him to put public concern before some private group wanting to use an agency of government for its own purposes. Thousands of respectable and earnest civil servants, presumably protected by the merit system, were driven out as "subversive," discharged without recourse. Nothing more damaging had happened in our democracy in all its long history. To liberals, it was an appalling exhibition of appeasement, reaction, and, as they believed, degeneration. But they could do nothing. Any protest induced a species of blackmail. Resistant voices were drowned in abuse.

The most prominent liberal or progressive of the year was Mr. Henry Agard Wallace, who had been cast out from President Truman's Cabinet because he disagreed with the expansionist diplomacy he saw developing as Secretary James A. Byrnes negotiated in Berlin with the Russians. Policy-makers had concluded in 1946 that nothing could be done with the Russians except by using the harshest methods. In the American vernacular it was called "getting tough." Since this policy tended to exacerbate differences, instead of conciliating them, Mr. Wallace and his fellow-liberals dissented. With the departure of Mr. Wallace, the last embarrassing objector appeared to be removed from the Administration. There then began an all but open subjection of foreign policy to military direction, a development contrary to every instinct of Americans and to a long tradition of civil control. Presently, however, the military made its inevitable mistake. It chose a line running from the Balkans east to Turkey and in effect said to Russia that she might come so far, but she must not come farther. It was exactly like a tough adolescent bully daring a weaker boy to cross a line and risk a thrashing. This uncovering of so stark and unyielding a policy for all the world— including the American people—to see was overprovocative. The reaction was adverse.

There had been one single consistent policy pursued by Russian diplomacy since that peoples' national existence had begun. This was the continued pressure, applied in all times and in every conceivable place, for outlets to the warm-water ports to the south. It seemed likely that, sometime in the future, air transportation would make this old struggle for seaports obsolescent, but that time, imminent though it might be, had not yet arrived. For the United States to draw a line far on the other side of the earth and forbid the Russians to cross it was incredible to most American ears, so different was it in every way from the characteristic American civilian approach. Even the militarists who proposed the scheme seemed dimly aware of incongruity, for they presented it as one intended to aid Greece and Turkey in reconstruction.

The line had originally been drawn by the British, but, because of their increasing burdens at home, they had confessed their inability to hold it further. Besides, maintaining it had been a Churchill policy, one which Labour, now in power, had found it hard to defend. For it happened that Greece and Turkey had governments which, by no stretch, could be called democratic. They were dictatorial and corrupt. Nevertheless, a Democratic administration in the United States had agreed to replace the British in holding the line. The intention was to prevent revolutions in which those who were protesting against flagrant abuses might prevail, in the fear that, if they did prevail, they might bring their governments within Russian influence.

This open challenge was resented by Russia as an affront; and so prevalent was favorable response to Mr. Wallace, when in a spectacular speaking tour abroad and at home he pointed out what way we were headed, that General George Catlett Marshall, wartime Chief of Staff and now successor to Mr. Byrnes as Secretary of State, presently entered a modification of what had been called the "Truman Doctrine." In the late spring of 1947 he proposed a "Marshall Plan." It was much more sensible than its predecessor policy for the purpose not only of aiding Europe but of opposing the totalitarians. The way in which the aid was offered, however, was significant. That a Secretary of State should promise, on his own responsibility, vast rehabilitation funds to foreign nations in furtherance of an anti-Communist policy, funds that committed Congress to expenditures of many billions a year, was unknown in our whole history. It could happen only because the plan was the product of a bipartisan junta—a junta that believed itself dominant in the Congress, the source of funds, as well as in the circles where administrative policy was determined. Yet, Mr. Wallace's was almost the only important voice heard to comment.[2]

Even Mr. Wallace, however, clearly as he saw the trend of events, could not object to European rehabilitation. Indeed, he had suggested something similar, and it was, in fact, what all liberals wanted—to see America's strength used in ways which would be helpful to the people of devastated countries. Nevertheless, this policy angered the Russians far more than the aggressive threat of punishment if a certain line should be crossed. The embarrassment of Mr. Molotov when confronted with a simple offer of helpfulness was revealing. He was certain that the gesture was not made in good faith; but his protestations weighed lightly in the scales against the promise of American food, clothing, and materials for reconstruction. World opinion went against him.

Mr. Wallace had the right to claim that he, singlehandedly, at least changed the Truman Doctrine into the Marshall Plan. He did not exercise that right; but everyone knew that it was so. For in his speaking trips he had drawn enormous crowds, who had listened to his alternative with the hunger of a people frightened to the bone by the approach of what now seemed certain war. They were, they could see, very nearly committed to conflict, and they wanted to try another way.

Americans had not ceased to be deeply concerned about the atomic bomb. They had heard much, moreover, this past year of another weapon almost equally frightful. This was bacterial warfare.[3] They sensed the expansionist movement which based itself

2. Actually, the Marshall Plan was a suggestion, made in an academic address, that the nations of western Europe get together on requests for aid—a suggestion which Messrs. Bidault and Bevin took up at once. Their requests would come to the United States late in September and be considered at a special session of the Congress in November, 1947.

3. It had begun to be intensively worked on in 1942 and had ultimately been brought to development on a scale suggesting that of atomic fission. In the *Bulletin of the Atomic Scientists*, October 1, 1946, there was published the very guarded report of Mr. George W. Merck, who had been in charge of these developments. Its closing paragraphs gave some hint of the extent to which research had gone and of the perils to peace in its results:

"While it is true that biological warfare is still in the realm of theory rather than fact, in the sense that it has not actually been used, the military findings of groups engaged in similar work in the United Kingdom and Canada have shown that this type of warfare cannot be discounted by those of this nation who are concerned with the national security. Our endeavors during the war provided means

on the immense productive power of which they were a part. But they had not the severe logic of the military mind, which gazed at the known facts and said that war had better come now before the enemy also gained possession of the weapons of which we presently had the monopoly.[4] So genuine was the revulsion against the expression of this view, which many organs of opinion had accepted from the military, that it was doubtful whether the war party would be able—even by progressing from provocation to provocation, even though aided at every step by Russian ineptness—to precipitate the open hostilities they apparently sought. If Russia had also possessed the weapons, the task, paradoxically enough, would have been easier. Fear would then have been added to irritation. But when the United States possessed not only two weapons of cataclysmic strength but a navy, besides, of many times the power of all the other navies in the world combined, it was difficult to contend that we had a cause for attacking another power, even the Soviet Union. There were those who wanted war; there was an indisputable agitation in that direction in certain higher levels of the Catholic hierarchy; and a certain xenophobic group which began to be identifiable was perhaps hottest of all to see it begin. But neither the political jingoes, the war-minded Catholics, nor the little group of self-conscious capitalists had facilities for persuading anyone but their usual allies. All of them still supposed that propaganda could effect their purpose; but a lesson had been widely learned in the Roosevelt years. Whatever the great newspaper publishers and

---

of defending the nation against biological warfare in terms of its presently known potentialities, and explored means of retaliation which might have been used, had such a course been necessary. Although remarkable achievements can be recorded, the metes and bounds of this type of warfare have by no means been completely measured. . . .

"It is important that, unlike the developments of the atomic bomb and other secret weapons during the war, the development of agents for biological warfare is possible in many countries, large and small, without vast expenditures or the construction of huge facilities. . . . It could proceed in many countries, perhaps under the guise of legitimate medical or bacteriological research. . . ."

4. Mr. Wallace had referred to this attitude and so brought it into public discussion in his letter to President Truman of July 23, 1946, attacking our policy with respect to atomic disarmament. The passage relevant here was the following: "There is a school of military thinking which recognizes that when several nations have atomic bombs, a war which will destroy modern civilization will result and that no nation or combination of nations can win such a war. This school of thought, therefore, advocates a 'preventive war,' an attack on Russia before Russia has atomic bombs."

magazine proprietors were willing to go all out for—that was against the people's interest.

On this automatic disbelief of many people in whatever they were put under pressure to believe, Mr. Wallace counted. They thought his credentials good because he had been ejected from a cabinet that no one any longer felt was Mr. Truman's. Much as they respected Mr. Roosevelt's successor, they had a profound suspicion that he was not his own man. He admired General Marshall too much; he was too often seen with Admiral Leahy looking over his shoulder; and there moved in the shadowy background the Joint Chiefs of Staff, the big businessmen, and the most vindictive among the prelates. These men wanted power; they represented a will to world dominion, or so many people thought. To dissenters from this movement Mr. Wallace made his appeal.

He was not a little aided by adventitious assistance from the great oil companies. Guided by big business's instinct for the malapropos, they chose this time to announce their own plans for vast capital expenditures in the Near East. These oil developments would lie just back of the line established in the Truman Doctrine and obviously would need protection. The American Navy, justified or not in its fear of oil shortage, supported these plans.[5] Many great publicity organs now united in a vast effort to prove to Americans how important Arabian oil was to their domestic interests. There would not be enough gasoline, it was said, for the growing number of automobiles if millions of tons could not be imported annually in the future from Arabia; and, to be convincing, importation was actually begun. No one took these protestations seriously. There were few who thought that anything more significant than oil-company profits was involved. This subject was one Mr. Wallace mentioned in his

5. See *Standard Oil Company (New Jersey) and Middle Eastern Oil Production: A Background Memorandum on Company Policies and Actions, March, 1947.* This pamphlet issued by the company has two parts: "Historical Background" and "Current Developments." The former relates to the between-wars period of the restrictive agreement which "specified and limited the activities of the signatories within a defined area." The signatories were the Compagnie Française de Petroles, the Royal Dutch Shell Company, the Anglo-Persian Oil Company, and the American companies. This old agreement was held to be made invalid by the occupation of France. A new one was announced in December, 1946, whereby Jersey would acquire a substantial interest in the Arabian American Oil Company. By this means it was expected to increase production greatly and to build another pipe line from the Persian Gulf to the Mediterranean.

educational campaign on the Truman Doctrine. It was one on which response was undoubtedly knowing.

There were not a few suggestions that Mr. Wallace was verging on disloyalty when he discussed the dangers of American foreign policy in Britain, Sweden, and France, suggesting about the same solution as was afterward to be known as the Marshall Plan. When he came home and started through the West from Chicago, his audiences ranged up to twenty thousand, and each individual paid for his seat, thus creating a fund for the use of the local and national offices of the PCA.[6] The policy-makers took notice. This was political strength, real and sizable. It could split both parties, but especially the Democrats; it could end almost anywhere. It might well have the power to defeat Mr. Truman in 1948, either in the convention or by offering a third ticket and so reducing the Democratic vote in the election. It would, moreover, undermine the effort, if there was one, to bring on an early war.[7]

Mr. Wallace had to be met. The Marshall Plan replaced the Truman Doctrine; the President, furthermore, in a series of startling reversals vetoed a Republican tax-reduction bill as well as the Taft-Hartley measure reducing the privileges of organized labor to something less than they had been before the Wagner Act. The second measure was passed over Mr. Truman's veto; but he sent a message to the Congress which embodied most of the arguments used by the Congress of Industrial Organizations in congressional hearings. The President thus did his best to appease labor and to steal Mr. Wallace's support. It might be too late. Secretaries Snyder of the Treasury, Anderson of Agriculture, and Krug of Interior—not to mention other and even worse appointments in lesser posts—had a policy, now in full course, of granting favors to bankers, to food and textile processors, to western exploiters of the great public

6. The Progressive Citizens of America was successor to Sidney Hillman's Political Action Committee, which had been so effective in 1942 and 1944. Its genius was Mr. C. B. Baldwin. It had always pushed Mr. Wallace, and he had always accepted its support. During this year there was a regrettable split in the forces of progressivism, weak as it was; Messrs. Wyatt, Ickes, Henderson, Franklin Roosevelt, *et al.* formed an alternate group called Americans for Democratic Action. It differed from the PCA in rejecting outright the Communist element its leaders claimed was undermining the older organization.

7. Polls in the early summer of 1947 indicated from 13 to 15 per cent adherence of voters, a much greater percentage than necessary to defeat a presidential candidate if it should be drawn from his supporters.

domain; and Marshall, Forrestal, and Lovett in the Cabinet seemed to be bringing the military-banker group into full control of diplomacy—it was too much! It seemed altogether unlikely that Mr. Truman could regain the confidence of progressives that he had to have.

Progressives generally regarded this situation as tragic. They liked Mr. Truman. He was nothing of a demagogue; he was, in most ways, a true liberal. But he was unable to associate happily with other liberals. Though he was now collecting honorary degrees voted by the trustees of great universities, he often made remarks indicating a feeling of inferiority because he had never earned one; on the other hand, the Roosevelt liberals all seemed to possess several. And perhaps the Roosevelt tradition in the White House and among the executive agencies, the reverence in which so many of the personnel held the brave, gay leader who had gone, had its irritating effect. For Mr. Truman, even though he still protested his desire to implement Roosevelt's policies, had obviously been ridding himself of all those who could carry them on.

He had, furthermore, a fatal disposition to appoint in their place mediocrities or outright illiberals. Mr. Snyder was one of these. During the year his influence had been instrumental in bringing the new International Bank well within the influence of New York's great banking houses, thus thoroughly justifying the Soviet refusal to associate itself with this auxiliary body of the United Nations. It was especially unfortunate that there should be suspicion about the bank, for *Pravda* and other inspired mouthpieces were thus enabled to label all the United Nations and auxiliary bodies as mere instruments of capitalism.

That the United Nations should fall into desuetude and disregard quite so rapidly as it had was an unexpected misfortune. In a desolate and almost hopeless world—one in which perhaps half the population was unable to command a sustaining diet or to protect itself from the hazards of exposure—there were no agencies, aside from those of the United Nations, by which the fortunate could assist the unfortunate. To have the only existing general world institution begin to die before it was completely born seemed a misfortune indeed.

Mr. Truman nevertheless spoke often and well of our duty to

others. We had made a loan to Britain and, finally, another to France; and our ocupation forces were supplying much food to Italy and to parts of Germany. But dollar balances in the European countries were running low. Inflation in the United States had reduced the buying power of other nations by almost half. American tariffs were still high; and immediately ahead there was a time when others could no longer buy from us for the old familiar reason— because we had an essentially isolationist economic policy.

The Marshall Plan had not come too soon. The question was whether it would suffice. For the militarists were more anxious to supply Russia's enemies with arms than with food. Even in South America, where the withdrawal of wartime spending had caused a rightist revolution in practically every country, the five-star diplomats thought only of standardized armaments for what they called "common defense." That such armaments meant orders for American munition-makers, jobs for professional soldiers, and eventual support in a war against Russia was painfully obvious; and American policy was coldly received by all but the dictators and military juntas in the unhappy lands to the south. The militarists went unchecked, and it remained to be seen whether the Marshall Plan meant anything more than an arousing of western Europe against Russia. Such aggression was its main objective, asserted Molotov, when in Paris in early July he met with Bevin and Bidault.

To the liberals in the United States, Mr. Truman seemed to have become the prisoner of dangerous persons and forces. They recalled now weaknesses that had not before seemed significant. There had been at first his insistence that he had not wanted to be President, with the inference that he felt himself incapable of carrying the duties of that great office. From this early modesty he had seemed to recover; but then he had shown a persistent tendency to lean on the military, grown so strong during the war. He made no secret of his admiration for General Marshall—he called him "the greatest American"—and finally made him Secretary of State. This appointment, together with the numerous appointments of generals and doubtful Democrats like Lewis W. Douglas to the most prominent diplomatic posts, convinced the country's liberals that the President's personal attitude must be regarded as a cover for the recapture by the business-military group of policy-making powers that President Roosevelt had more or less kept away from them since Mr. Hoover had left the White House.

The United States was a curious exhibit to an observer with any competence in economics or political science in 1946–47. One of those retreats from social responsibility, which had begun to seem an inevitable aftermath of crises, was in full development. Controls on prices were by now almost gone; those remaining on rents were fast going. The result was a jump of some 50 per cent in the cost of living, an inevitable raising of wages, with the usual wasteful phenomena of bargaining, and a reduction of the status of middle-class workers—teachers, clerks, supervisory personnel, pensioners, and so on. The social results of this irreponsible action were registered in widespread dissatisfaction. Many Americans who had resented controls, largely because of incitement to resistance by the press, found that their freedom was more costly than they had anticipated.

Many materials were still short, and so, of course, were all the goods made from them. The millions of housing units needed had not even been begun, partly because in the absence of priorities builders of commercial and amusement establishments could bid highest for the available supplies. People went on living in incredibly crowded and degraded conditions. They had race tracks, theaters, dancehalls, and amusement parks to go to in their leisure time; but there was a deficiency of homes in which to carry on a decent family existence amounting to seven or eight millions. And such homes as were built were not provided in public housing projects; they were not even provided in rental projects; they were those same incredibly jerry-built small houses from which speculators had long ago learned they could extract the largest profits. The real estate interests were operating on the American people in shameless fashion with the consent and collusion of their Congress. But real estate was only an example; organized trades of all kinds were doing the same thing. It was a sellers' market, and speculators were riding high.

There had been forecasts in great plenty in 1946 that 1947 would be a year of depression; the only disagreement had been as to how serious the depression would be. It had been expected that shortages would turn to surpluses, that the increases in productive capacity made during the war would, now that manpower was back and ready to contribute, turn out more goods than consumers could absorb. A rapid rise in prices, which would exhaust more rapidly not only consumers' savings but their credit, was expected to make this oversupply even more serious. The depression had not come, and the prognosticators were abashed; but clearly it had only been postponed. The anticipated surpluses of goods, instead of piling up at home, were going abroad. Hundreds of millions of bushels of grain and yards of cloth, not to mention vast quantities of steel, coal, farm machinery, automobiles, trucks, and so on, were still being shipped to the areas devastated by war. Part of this outflow was paid for by loans to other nations, Britain and France, for instance; part was distributed by occupying forces; and part was sent as gifts. The slowness with which the economies of Germany, Italy, and lesser European nations recovered their ability to produce anything for themselves could be laid largely to the stupidity of the victor nations that preferred, evidently, to supply the needs of those they had defeated rather than to let them work for themselves.

People in the United States had no rationing, but they had, instead, an unfair distribution of commodities. Goods went to those who had the highest incomes. Workers got raises by striking or threatening to strike; but, since prices rose faster than their wages, they were progressively worse off as the months passed, and many a pensioner who had thought his lifetime of work and thrift sufficiently rewarded by an old age or disability allowance found himself staring at imminent penury. It semed unfair, and there was much dissatisfaction, but no suggestion of renewed rationing or price controls was allowed space in the press; and in the Congress subservience to business simply produced one exploitative measure after another. Toward the middle of 1947 the signs of strain became unmistakable. The margin of purchasing power necessary to absorb the output of the mass-production industries was being supplied not only by loans or gifts abroad, which would never be repaid, but by a growing volume of internal credit.

In the absence of controls, ordinary business practices led to increasing margins of profit at each of the many steps in the passage of goods from producer to consumer. In the determination to make the most of the sellers' market, what had seemed fair profits a few years before were now regarded as foolishly moderate. President Truman, frightened at the rise in the cost of living and warned by his Council of Economic Advisers of approaching danger, early in the spring engaged himself in a contest of recrimination with Republican leaders in the Congress. He wanted to father responsibility on them. He had at last realized the political potentialities of the lag between consumers' income and consumers' prices. But the engagement was inconclusive. He had a poor case, for he had consented to the policy of disestablishing controls immediately after Hiroshima. On the other hand, it was the Congress that had killed the OPA and that was in process of surrendering control over rents.

The situation was this: In order to maintain the purchasing power which sustained the economy and provided employment, inflationary policies—expansion of domestic credit and loans abroad—were essential. It was a true dilemma. Either production could be slowed down, unemployment risked, and a deficit of buying power consequently incurred as the deflationary spiral turned in on itself; or inflation could be maintained with feverish production, expanding credit, dangerous speculation, and ever rising prices. Either course led inevitably to a situation in which prices would outrun buying power.

Already consumers were restive. They were paying more and getting less month by month. The Marshall Plan necessarily contributed to the inflationary spiral. True, it might sustain certain crucial agricultural markets—such as those for corn, wheat, meat, and cotton—and thus increase farmer buying power; but the American wheat, cotton, trucks, machinery, chemicals, glass, cement, and other goods going abroad were being paid for either by loans or by taxes. Loans which are not to be repaid are only gifts by another name, and gifts must be paid for by someone. The payment was being exacted currently not only in enormous peacetime taxes but, even more ruthlessly, in the hidden taxation of inflation, which came out of the consumption of every American.

These were stubborn facts. Every serious student of the economy felt that grave trouble lay ahead—that a time would come, as in 1929, when creditors would suddenly realize that the great volume of debts owing to them could never be collected, and each creditor would press his debtors for payment. Then there would be a crash.

There is only one way in which a so-called "capitalist" economy can function without periodic depressions during which debt is wiped out, prices are readjusted, and, after long deflation, an inflationary rise again begins. There must be established and maintained a mutual exchange among groups and organizations of the economy so that each can freely purchase the products of the other; and this exchange must take place without that exploitation which builds up, on the one hand, vast pools of sterile gains and, on the other, creates a deficit of purchasing power. This was the "balanced abundance," to use Mr. Wallace's phrase, or the "concert of interests," to use the locution President Roosevelt once had favored, toward which the New Deal had painfully worked its way through more than a decade of trial and error, but which business and its representatives now gaining control both in the executive and in the legislative had never accepted. The Republican congressional victory at the election in November, 1946, had brought into the national legislature new people to reinforce the old who had always opposed this New Deal program. Consequently, the trend begun by Mr. Truman's new associates was becoming a fixed policy. Governmental efforts to keep the balance became, in the press, practically identical with communism. Many of the agencies set up during President Roosevelt's time to maintain the balance were either already liquidated or were in process of being abandoned. Not all of them could be eradicated. Social Security, for instance, provided a national minimum; but its benefits were presently so undermined by inflated prices that its effect as an economic stabilizer was largely lost. The Taft-Hartley Labor Relations Act so weakened the power of labor in collective bargaining that it seemed probable that purchasing power would continue to be reduced—a consequence, in fact, that the supporters of the act had intended. When Mr. Truman disapproved the bill, he forced the Republicans to accept full responsibility by passing it over his veto; but it was not clear that the veto was more than a gesture of appeasement to the Wallace movement. His Cabinet and staff showed no signs of having learned how government must operate in a "free economy" if it was to be kept going at reasonable efficiency.

From what he said on various occasions, however, there was reason to believe that the President himself was learning. True, he still obviously trusted Secretary Snyder and others of the Cabinet beyond their competence, and especially beyond their loyalty to the liberal ideals he himself professed. But he was now discovering what every President has to discover—that, in all but the most exceptional cases, members of the Cabinet are a President's rivals rather than his servants. In the American system administrative authority runs very loosely up to the Chief Executive; Cabinet members are not so directly commanded by the President as in theory they are supposed to be. He has no effective means of supervision. They are not very amenable to the Director of the Budget in planning expenditures, and, when the director is subservient to a Cabinet officer rather than the President, his authority almost vanishes. As things were in 1947, the secretaries had practically independent relations with the appropriations committees of the House and Senate. Furthermore, the personnel of the federal departments had come to regard themselves as representatives or advocates of special interests—Commerce representing business, Labor representing the American Federation of Labor and the Congress of Industrial Organizations, Agriculture representing the more prosperous farmers, the Treasury representing the financial community, and so on. Cabinet members derived their independence and their strength as political figures from the backing they thus acquired. Their divergence in policy from the President, as a result of all these outside relationships, was often really considerable.

As this tendency among the President's subordinates had been combined with the various divisive local and special forces which played on the Congress—duty to represent a district, support from political machines, business interests, racial groups, and so on—the presidency as an institution, separate even from the Cabinet, had come increasingly to be the only federal organ which single-mindedly represented the public interest. The President was elected by all the people, and no other federal official, except the Vice-President, shared this relationship. Those who, like Mr. Truman, came into the presidency late in life, especially after long conditioning in the Congress, were apt to require some time for re-education to this view. President Roosevelt had not required such reorienta-

tion. He had belonged to the governmental executive by long experience. He had known how legislators or even Cabinet members tend
to develop their own policies and ambitions, and consequently he
had known how important it is for the President to be a leader. But,
while President Roosevelt had been trying to strengthen his office,
Mr. Truman had been in the Senate. It would not be fair to say that
he had opposed the Roosevelt intention; but senators naturally fall
into opposition to any enlargement of the executive power, and Mr.
Truman had been by no means immune. Consequently, it took him
some time to learn that the President is the President of all the
people and that no legislator, and only the most exceptional and
devoted Cabinet officer, is thus oriented.

By 1947, Mr. Truman had had many disagreeable experiences;
and in the course of them the powers of his office had leaked swiftly
through his fingers—it was possible that he had learned his lessons
too late. There never had been a Congress more given to the vice of
legislation through appropriation. The appropriations committees
of both houses were continuously interfering in executive matters—
negatively, of course, which made the interference worse and nearly
drove governmental administrators mad. In numerous instances
committees withheld funds for the payment of salaries either for a
specified individual or for a group, actions which amounted to
attainder; they even refused to act on appropriation bills until appointments satisfactory to committee chairmen had been made by
the President. Such humiliations showed Mr. Truman the fallacy in
his original belief that the legislative power belonged wholly to the
Congress. It was clearly essential to the American system that the
lead in legislation should come from the President, who should
formulate, suggest, and use his power as head of his political party
to establish a program and to see that it was implemented with personnel and funds.

Actually, part of this duty—the making of long-term and continuing economic and social plans—could better be done by a planning agency. The President has limitations as a long-run planner.
He is the head of a political party whose first instinct is to stay in
power; and he has a relatively short term within which to accomplish his designs. A planning agency, locked into the governmental
structure and integrated to its functioning, can borrow from legis-

lative, executive, and judiciary without interfering with the essential functions of any of them. Mr. Truman had no such agency to depend on, but he was at least discovering the utility of long-run planning by observing and experiencing its lack. Consequently, he paid some attention to his Council of Economic Advisers, and this body provided such realism and continuity as his program possessed by 1947.[8]

During the early part of his administration Mr. Truman had not only lost control of the legislative process in the Congress; he had put himself on record as wanting strong men in his Cabinet who would proceed on their own. This was the one kind of relationship it was fatal for a President to encourage in his subordinates. The presidential power is so great, and the prestige of sharing in it so attractive, that strong and ambitious men will always grasp for more if they are encouraged. And, even if they are not strong and grasping, the interests which they in effect represent will reach through them for the powers they need. Before Mr. Truman could begin to understand his position, he had lost more than he would ever regain unless he should vigorously assert himself over a long period of time. Secretaries Krug, Snyder, Forrestal, and Anderson had very large ideas, none of which was served by enhancing the prestige of the President himself.

Nowhere was this relinquishing of presidential leadership more serious than in foreign affairs. Here Mr. Truman had a double handicap: he had had no previous experience; and the military-financier junta—businessmen, international bankers, admirals, generals, and amenable foreign-service officers—was already half in power through its occupancy of high-level offices and its affiliations with the career service. Mr. Byrnes had given these men pretty much their own way; during his regime Mr. Truman had been hardly more than well informed as to the development of international relationships. When General Marshall had succeeded Mr. Byrnes, this group had moved confidently into control and had

8. This agency had been set up in the Employment Act of 1946. It was an acknowledged recognition of error by the Congress in having abolished the National Resources Planning Board in 1940. It had an improper relationship to other governmental agencies—that is to say, it was part of the President's office. It could give useful economic advice, but by its nature it could not carry on true planning functions (cf. *First Annual Report to the President, December, 1946* [Washington, D.C.: Government Printing Office, 1946]).

begun to make and practice the dangerously aggressive policy which had shown itself first in the Truman Doctrine. They had made a grave error—that is, they had gone too far—when they had written and had the President announce that doctrine. They recovered this lost ground in the Marshall Plan; but they were of the true Bourbon breed and were not really educable. They had never learned to support enlightened self-interest as a domestic policy; and, if they remained in control, they would continue an aggressive and perilous foreign policy until the war they had tentatively begun to talk of as inevitable was precipitated. Mr. Truman, as he contemplated what had happened, was frightened. He said so. But so inferior did he feel in his relations with General Marshall and other military men[9] that it seemed wholly unlikely that he could find the determination to recover the power and prestige he had so carelessly handed over.

There was much head-shaking over Mr. Truman's position throughout the country and especially among the Roosevelt progressives, who were used to a different kind of policy-making. It was not that General Marshall and General Eisenhower were not regarded as competent—even as great—generals. They had come out of the war with immense prestige. But the managing of an aggressive military campaign to defeat an enemy is not the same thing as managing a nation's relations with others. War may be in most instances the extension of diplomacy, as Clausewitz said it was, but in America it looked as though diplomacy was being used to extend a war, and to extend it not only in time but in space—against a former ally.

It was probable that the assumption by the military of control over foreign relations was only a forerunner of more of the same. As early as June, 1946, indeed, these events had been foreseen by Mr. Norman Cousins and Mr. T. K. Finletter, two citizens who had been more foresighted than most others in the atomic crisis and who had worked hard to avert the very developments now so inevitably in

9. This attitude apparently went back to his experience as a captain in World War I; it was openly acknowledged that during World War II while he was chairman of the Senate's War Investigating Committee; and it appeared in the many appointments he made of military men to civil posts and in the subservience he was glad, apparently, to show to them on every occasion when he could.

train.[10] In an attempt to warn their fellow-citizens of the dangers implicit in the foreign policy of the Truman Administration, they had sought to trace American errors back to their beginnings. They had found the roots in the use of the Bomb at Hiroshima. That act had placed us in a moral position from whose consequences we might never escape. How could we ever contend in the future what the use of atomic fire as an international weapon is indefensible? In the year which had passed since Hiroshima, our policy had developed nothing positive; it had been, on the contrary, one of "drift, default, and delay." It was doubtful, they thought, whether in all history there had been an "uglier or more ominous frittering away of critically valuable time." This judgment was hardly exact; as we looked back after still another year, we could see that a hidden struggle had been going on between the forces of the exploiters and those who exposed them, between moral and immoral men, between militarist-capitalist aggressors and those who would intrust the new forces of the universe to public, civilian, and profit-free control. It was not a time of drift and delay but of momentous conflict, which was now resulting in decision. Something was being gained—for instance, the passage of the McMahon Bill in place of the May-Johnson Bill. But something, also, was being lost—something of great importance. That loss was signalized and made definite when General Marshall became Secretary of State with Mr. Robert A. Lovett as his second.

Mr. Cousins and Mr. Finletter had had a clear view of the consequences if the loss should occur which now had occurred:

Do the American people know that an atomic armaments race means more than the manufacture of atomic bombs? Do they know it inevitably means the redistribution of population, the decentralization of our cities, the dispersal of our industries? Do they know that every American will be directly affected, that the required controls will of necessity be in the hands of the military, that it is a real question whether free institutions as we understand them can be maintained under the pressure of such vast and complicated changes? Do they know, finally, that America may be only a very few years away from such a readjustment and that the plans are even now being drawn up for that purpose?

This is not a matter of the military deliberately plotting to seize control

10. The discussion referred to here first appeared in the *Saturday Review of Literature* for June 15, 1946. It was reprinted in the *Bulletin of the Atomic Scientists* for July 1, 1946.

of the nation. What is happening is that our failure to create a sound policy for atomic energy and other weapons of mass destruction looking toward effective world control creates a vacuum which is automatically being filled by the military. No one would ever accuse General Eisenhower or General Marshall of plotting a military state; but a powerful momentum is being set up which will inevitably force the War Department to carry out the biggest and most complicated physical change-over of a nation in the world's history—with all that implies in the way of political and social readjustment and control.

Whether drift was responsible for these events or whether there had been more subterranean conspiracy, Mr. Cousins and Mr. Finletter must have felt themselves justified when some six months later the military had virtually taken over the diplomacy of the United States. By then many even of those who had theretofore been advocates of a policy of conciliation toward Russia had begun to wonder if the way out of the horrors they foresaw might not be to encourage early war. We might, just possibly, win expeditiously. Otherwise would we not have to become a military state, disperse our cities, go underground, become robots, in the interest of an always-coming struggle? Were the shapers of the new American policy in the summer of 1947 still counting on this reasoning? Did they expect it to make aggression seem justifiable in even the most strictly humanitarian sense?

There was no doubt that the Marshall Plan, without decreasing East-West tensions, rearranged the moral situation to the benefit of the United States. Unlike the Truman Doctrine, it de-emphasized aggression and threw the onus of initiative on the Soviets. Molotov was in an awkward position when he was called to Paris by Bevin and Bidault. He had no sounder objection to make when it was proposed that Europe should be rehabilitated with American aid than that the offer was a capitalist trick. This interference in the affairs of European states, he had to contend, was in the interest of the warmongers across the Atlantic. Since the proposal was that all European states should jointly propose their own terms, this argument had a hollow ring. When he left between dusk and dawn on a June night without the usual courtesies of farewell, and when Russia's satellites one after the other, including a reluctant Czechoslovakia, refused to confer, it was made just as clear as before that there were now two worlds; but it was Russian diplomats who were forced to underline the separation. President Truman had only to denounce the Russian choice. The antagonists had taken their stances. There would be no more searching for compromise.

Yet all was not well for those Americans who believed in ultimate resort to force. It was true that the Republican party belonged to business, that business was generally favorable to the military, and that the Congress was now controlled by the Republicans. But the Republicans, as they seemed so often to forget, had a rank and file; and they also had a theoretical commitment which had deepened all through their long opposition to the New Deal—a double commitment to isolation and to economizing. Many of those now in power, and linked with the military, had been opposed to war when the German conflict had been boiling up. They had belonged to America First—that is, they had been last-ditch isolationists—on the theory that Hitler was a bulwark of capitalism against communism and that naziism was the Wave of the Future, the apotheosis of big business. As economizers, they had been against the New Deal, against government interferences, against relief and compensatory spending; even more important, they had looked askance at the costly military expansion of the preparatory years because it was directed toward the suppression of naziism. Business willingness to support military expenditures had been tried too far and for the wrong purposes.

Now isolationism and economy-mindedness seemed to have an embarrassing persistence in the minds of their rank and file. Republicans even found in Mr. John Taber, chairman of their own Appropriations Committee in the House, a formidable opponent of Greek and Turkish aid, and, indeed, of the whole Marshall Plan intention. Mr. Taber was a simple man. He felt that if America was to have isolation, economy, and freedom from government supervision of business, the way to have these things was to withdraw from Europe, reduce spending, and drastically reduce the federal bureaucracy, including generals and admirals. He could not bring himself to approve the reverse of these policies after more than thirteen years of commitment. Many other prominent Republicans seemed to hold the same view.

Nevertheless, it appeared to be true that unless war was successfully precipitated and won within a short time—but no one could say just how short—we should indeed have to change our physical means of living and working so drastically that no businessman, except those few to whom it might somehow be made profitable, would voluntarily accede. There would have to be coercion. Consider, for instance, the situation of those real estate interests to whom the Congress of 1947 had been so subservient. If there were to be an intensified atomic armament race, American cities would logically have to be torn down and their facilities rebuilt in less exposed places.[11] Otherwise the United States would be in danger of having millions of workers and a large percentage of her productive capacity destroyed in the initial raid of the coming war. Not only real estate interests, but many other commercial interests as well, would oppose the adoption of such a policy with every means they could command; so would the political machines whose existence is coterminous with that of the cities they exploit.

Probably the opposition would be so formidable that it could only be overriden by the use of subsidy and force combined. To think of the billions of dollars necessary to compensate the owners of city equities all over the United States was to think in astronomical figures. To think of the public dissension which would be preliminary to the appropriation of such sums by the Congress was to think of a very deep split in opinion.

The summer of 1947 thus appeared to be a time of unhappy beginnings; and it was certainly one of uneasiness and deepened worry. There were, besides, unfriendly manifestations of nature: storms, floods, and droughts. Food production consequently was not so great as had been hoped; and the slight reduction was exploited by the food processors and the speculators. What with witch-hunts, inflation, apprehension over aggressive diplomacy, continued shortages of materials, and even worry about abnormal weather, Americans were harassed and beset. They were divided among themselves; they were refusing to put their best efforts into whatever it was they were doing because they found it not worth while; they looked forward to war and to the preparations for it with worry and, when they really stopped to consider, downright fear. No leadership appeared with any solution better than that offered by Mr. Wallace, and even he seemed to have been silenced by the Marshall Plan,

11. In August, 1947, the War Department announced the completion of a preliminary survey of underground building sites.

which was substantially what he had advocated. But the Marshall Plan had not served to placate Russia; it had seemed only to make the division sharper, to draw the issues more clearly. When Molotov left Paris and went home to Moscow in the middle of the night, the hopes of most American liberals went with him. Everything was now in the hands of distrusted policy-makers in Washington.

And the President traveled. He had a new DC-6, called "The Independence" after his Missouri home town, fitted up, the newspapers said, as a "flying White House." It let him escape from responsibility—or seem to. Meanwhile the two great powers of earth, Russia and the United States, intrusted their futures to little bands of men who worked in secret, protected by rigorous security measures—the Politburo, the heart of communism; the Joint Chiefs of Staff, the heart of capitalism. They plotted, as it was their business to do, against each other. The preparations they made were for the final war. At its end, if the plans of either were good enough, there would be only one power left. Would it be a Communist world or a capitalist world? There were many who hoped, without arguing to justify it, that the choice was not yet foregone, that accommodation was possible; but there was little faith mixed with the hope.

Just as the Congress was about to adjourn late in July of 1947—having insured inflation, insecurity, and a return to privileged exploitation, having abridged the liberties of all those who dissented from their doctrines, and having taken much vengeance on the dead Roosevelt—the United States Atomic Energy Commission made a kind of interim report to the home-going legislators. One of the commitments made in this report was to the further trial of atomic weapons after the manner of Bikini. It was, the commission said, necessary to insure American predominance until an international agreement had been reached which would insure world security from armed aggression.[12] This statement was significant because it reaffirmed a position taken from the very first by the policy-makers of the Department of State, one which had been consented to by the authors of the Acheson-Lilienthal Report, and which was the object of particular Russian attack. So strong was the Russian opposition that there seemed by now to be a permanent block which could be dissolved only by a retreat of one protagonist or the other; and such

12. This report was made on July 23, 1947.

94

a retreat would now require for either side a change in an already implemented policy. Russia had organized eastern Europe; the United States had adopted Greece and Turkey and had announced the Marshall Plan. There were those who still hoped that these were not the preliminaries of war; but they were not many, and their faith was fading as they watched General Marshall reverse himself on China in order to bring Far Eastern policy into concordance with that in Europe. When he had left China in 1946, he had said that nothing could save that unhappy land but compromise, efficiency, and democracy; yet he now seemed prepared to support the authoritarian, corrupt, and hopelessly inefficient regime of the Kuomintang and Chiang Kai-shek—either that or to withdraw in despair.

The warning of the United States Atomic Energy Commission that it was proceeding to insure American control of the world's most destructive weapon was an expected development. The year had been among the most discouraging in the whole history of mankind. During its course the United States had become the citadel of the active anti-Communists and had taken almost final decisions to implement aggression. There had followed the complete failure of the meetings of the United Nations Atomic Energy Commission at Lake Success.

This United Nations commission had its origin, not at San Francisco—for then "atomic energy as a deadly weapon had been unknown to the world"[13]—but rather as a result of the Conference of Foreign Ministers of the United Kingdom, the United States, and Russia in December, 1945, in Moscow. The foreign ministers, at that time more influenced by their awe of the fearsome weapon than by the priests of their respective religions, had agreed at this meeting to make a joint proposal—together with China, France, and Canada—to the General Assembly of the United Nations that there be established a commission which would "deal with the discovery of atomic energy and related matters." The Assembly, accordingly, had adopted the suggested resolution without change on January 24, 1946. On June 13, 1946, the commission had met for its first session and heard the American proposal, for the United States was

13. Opening speech by Trygve Lie at the first meeting of the United Nations Atomic Energy Commission, Lake Success, June 13, 1946.

appropriately taking the initiative in recognition of the responsibility of ownership. Meanwhile, perhaps appropriately also, Mr. Bernard Baruch had been made United States representative—certainly no one had a higher or more sacred status as a priest of the capitalist cult. It was he who had made the presentation.

"We are here," he had begun, "to make a choice between the quick and the dead." The succeeding eloquence had been an entirely satisfactory exposition of mankind's dilemma: A way had to be found to free the world "from the heart-stopping fears" which now beset it because its own institutions were predisposed to war. He had referred to the terms of reference of the commission:

> The Commission shall proceed with the utmost dispatch and inquire into all phases of the problem, and make such recommendations from time to time with respect to them as it finds possible. In particular the Commission shall make specific proposals:
>
> A. For extending between all nations the exchange of basic scientific information for peaceful ends;
> B. For control of atomic energy to the extent necessary to insure its use only for peaceful purposes;
> C. For the elimination from national armaments of atomic weapons and of all other major weapons adaptable to mass destruction;
> D. For effective safeguards by way of inspection and other means to protect complying states against the hazards of violation and evasions.

He had then gone on to propose on behalf of the United States the creation of an Atomic Development Authority

> to which should be entrusted all phases of the development and use of atomic energy, starting with the raw material and including:
>
> 1. Managerial control or ownership of all atomic energy activities potentially dangerous to world security;
> 2. Power to control, inspect and license all other atomic activities;
> 3. The duty of fostering the beneficial uses of atomic energy;
> 4. Research and development responsibilities of an affirmative character intended to put the Authority in the forefront of atomic knowledge and thus to enable it to comprehend, and therefore to detect misuse of atomic energy. . . .

In pursuit of these objectives, he had further proposed that with respect to this Authority the members of the Security Council should give up the veto power. He had then repeated what had been said in the Acheson-Lilienthal Report: that, if the United States were to relinquish the secret of the bomb, she would require assurances of safety—"a guarantee of safety, not only against offenders in the atomic area, but against illegal users of other weapons—bacteriological, biological, gas—perhaps, and why not?—against war itself."

Naturally the uncovering of the Russian attitude toward this proposal had been awaited with anxiety. It had come at the next session, on June 19, 1946. Mr. Gromyko had then proposed:

As one of the first measures to be carried out, in order to carry out the decision of the General Assembly of the 24th of January, . . . a study of the question of the conclusion of international agreements forbidding the production and use of weapons based upon the use of atomic energy for the purposes of mass destruction. The purpose of such an agreement should be to forbid the production and use of atomic weapons, the destruction of existing stocks of atomic weapons, and the punishment of all activities undertaken with a view to the violation of such agreements. . . .

At the end he had made harsh remarks concerning the proposal to give up the veto power. It was, he had said, an attempt to undermine the Security Council. It would be utterly incompatible with the interests of the United Nations, created as it was to preserve peace and security in the world.

There the position had stood. The proposals of the United States had been rejected by inference. The Soviets had proposed instead that, by the destruction of existing bombs and of the facilities for further manufacture, the United States should be put on an equal basis with all others. Then a committee of the Security Council could be set up to draft an international agreement to prevent any future use of atomic energy as a threat to peace. Obviously, since the agreement was to be international, it would be enforced by each nation on itself.

The deep discouragement of the summer of 1947 thus had been preparing for more than a year. The hopes built on the Acheson-Lilienthal Report, on the action of the foreign ministers at Moscow, and on the prompt response of the Assembly of the United Nations had turned to despair as the deadlock between Russia and the United States in the Atomic Energy Commission became known. In this atmosphere of depression, on July 23, 1946, Mr. Wallace had voiced the fears of American liberals in a letter to the President. If we want to understand Russia's attitude, he had said, we must try to see ourselves as they must see us. We have been mainly responsible for the victory over the Axis; but it has made us not only the most powerful nation in the world but prideful and vainglorious:

How do American actions since V-J Day appear to other nations? I mean by actions, the concrete things like thirteen billions for the War and Navy Departments, the Bikini tests of the Atomic bomb and continued production of bombs, the plan to arm Latin America with our weapons, the production of B-29s and the planned production of B-36s, and the effort to secure air bases spread over half the globe from which the other half can be bombed. I cannot but feel that these actions must make it look to the rest of the world as if we were only paying lip service to peace at the conference table.

These facts make it appear either (1) that we are preparing ourselves to win a war which we regard as inevitable or (2) that we are trying to build up a predominance of force to intimidate the rest of mankind. How would it look to us if Russia had the atomic bomb and we did not, if Russia had 10,000 mile bombers and air bases within 1,000 miles of our coasts and we did not?[14]

Mr. Wallace went on to show that the policy of the United States could only be understood as a military design of the old familiar sort: "The only way to preserve peace is for this country to be so well armed that no one will dare attack us. We know that we will never start a war." The trouble with this, he said, was simply that it would not succeed. "In a world of atomic bombs and other revolutionary weapons, such as radioactive poison gases and biological warfare, a peace maintained by a predominance of force is no longer possible." For (1) atomic warfare was cheap and so available to any nation; (2) having more or better bombs was no longer a deci-

14. This kind of thing was not being said for the first time by Mr. Wallace; perhaps it was not even original with him. It was being said everywhere by the kind of people who were able, in spite of their fears, to see themselves as others might see them. Mr. Rose, for instance, said something of the sort in responding to the Prime Minister in the Canadian House of Commons, December 17, 1945. This record was inserted in the *Hearings on S. 1717*, January 22, 1947, p. 25: "I am afraid that the damage which has been done will be hard to heal. . . . Scientists who know exactly what is involved have advised that we hand over the secret to an international committee right away." And he quoted, with approval, Mr. Leland Stowe, who had said: "If the Soviets had the bomb and had followed Washington's precise course since 6 August, how would the average American feel? I think the newspapers would be full of imperialistic, power-seeking Russians—and an awful lot of us would be plenty scared. . . . We would say: Why is Moscow treating us like second-class allies? Military men would be derelict in their duty if they didn't say: We've got to build a bomb of our own. . . . The very fact that they only talk about sharing after they've had time to make many more bombs themselves shows they can't be trusted."

All this was more than half a year before Mr. Wallace's letter. The spread of this feeling was very great. Mr. Wallace only gathered up a prevalent liberal opinion.

sive advantage, since a few bombs, well directed, might totally disrupt our productive facilities; and (3) "the very fact that several nations have atomic bombs will inevitably result in a neurotic, fear-ridden, itching trigger-finger psychology in all the peoples of the world, and because of our wealth and vulnerability we would be among the most seriously affected." This whole scheme, Mr. Wallace went on to say, was not only immoral and stupid; it was also contrary to all the basic instincts of the American people—so contrary that it could only be done under an American dictatorship. Fortunately, however, there was an alternative; and it was the very one on which Mr. Truman himself had settled. We must develop mutual trust and confidence, support atomic disarmament, and work out an effective system for enforcing that disarmament.

There had been a fatal defect, however, according to Mr. Wallace, in the Acheson-Lilienthal Report, in the Moscow statement, and in the American plan as presented to the United Nations Atomic Energy Commission by Mr. Baruch. This defect had consisted of trying to arrive at international agreement on this matter "by many stages." We would require other nations "to enter into binding commitments not to conduct research into military uses of atomic energy and to disclose their uranium and thorium resources while the United States retains the rights to withhold its technical knowledge until the international control and inspection system is working *to our satisfaction*." For this satisfaction there was no objective standard. We were to determine whether we thought the Russians had behaved in such a manner as to deserve our confidence. Is it any wonder, Mr. Wallace had asked, that the Russians refused? If we had been in the same position, we would have reacted as they had. "We would have put up counter proposals for the record, but our real effort would have gone into trying to make a bomb so that our bargaining position would be equalized."

Mr. Baruch had replied indignantly, but essentially ineffectually, to this letter. It had served its purpose. It had forced Americans to reconsider their position. Many of them had come to the conclusion that they had indeed been arrogant and that the nature of their proposals, as much as Russian suspicion, had been responsible for the existing deadlock. On this basis official reconsideration might have begun; but it had not. At the elections in November the Republicans won a congressional victory which established the business-military group in a much more powerful position than it had occupied when the McMahon Bill had been shaped during the previous year.

It was not a time for conciliatory gestures to foreign nations but rather for following to its tragic conclusion the very policy which Mr. Wallace had already called "not only immoral but stupid." There was even a tendency to undo the work of the McMahon Act. The military would try again and again for absolute control and would try to dominate the Atomic Energy Commission if it could not revise the act. The first attempt would be to secure amenable appointees. Mr. Lilienthal as chairman was a disappointment to them and to their allies, although there seemed to be no great objection to Messrs. Bacher, Strauss, Pike, and Waymack. One of the epic battles of the year between liberal and reactionary forces turned out to be that over Mr. Lilienthal's confirmation by the Senate.

The McMahon Bill became law on August 1, 1946.[15] The proceedings leading up to its passage have been referred to, but no short description can have characterized adequately the meanness of the debate. Yet, for all its bitterness, the discussion resulted in a bill unsatisfactory to the military because it provided for civilian control. For the moment the scientists and liberals generally seemed to have gained a victory, and they rejoiced. Nevertheless, this result, achieved only after the airing of the deepest disagreements and the exposure of the most serious divisions in American life, was unsatisfactory. The perils of these divisions and the narrow margin of consent had robbed the victory of most of its significance; and, if those who fought so long and well for the bill had foreseen that the midterm election in the succeeding November would result in Republican victory, their discouragement might well have caused them to withdraw and permit the militarists to have their way.

The scientists could not then know that the bitter fight over Mr. David Lilienthal's confirmation would be a re-enactment, in a more unfriendly atmosphere in 1947, of the battles of 1946. The Congress elected in November, 1946, would not have passed the Atomic Energy Act, whose passage preceded the election by no more than

15. Public Law 585 (Atomic Energy Act of 1946).

a few months. It would most likely have enacted a measure very much like the May-Johnson Bill giving the military complete control. Actually, the result might not have been very different in the long run, for, when General Marshall became Secretary of State, the military moved into a strategic position with respect to far more than the Atomic Energy Commission.

The act passed after so much controversy and with much obvious reluctance was subsequently described as almost revolutionary by the special counsel to the Senate committee, Mr. James R. Newman,[16] who had sat through all the hearings.[17] For, according to him, the three recurring questions in all the discussion had to be given solutions that the Congress basically mistrusted. The overriding consideration of long-run national safety forced the reluctant legislators to (1) decide in favor of civilian rather than military control, (2) provide that scientific inquiry should be free, and (3) forbid private enterprise to enter the field of atomic-energy development. Without these safeguards, the exploration of atomic energy might be so handicapped that the United States would lose the present lead. By the time the bill had been written and was being subjected to public examination, battles had been fought and won on each of these points. But the problem of what kind of government agency should administer atomic energy remained.

The legislative branch has always been jealous of the executive power; and when, in the past, public safety has required government regulation or control of business activities, the Congress has always

16. "America's Most Radical Law," *Harper's*, May, 1947. The documents of most interest will be found in *Hearings before the Special Committee on Atomic Energy, United States Senate, 79th Congress, Second Session, on S. 1717*, Part I, January 22 and 23, 1946; Part II, January 25, 28, 29, 30, 31 and February 1, 1946; Part III, February 7, 8, 11, 13, 14, 1946; Part IV, February 18, 19, 27, 1946; Part V, February 15 and April 4, 8, 1946. See also *Report To Accompany S. 1717: Conference Report*, July 25, 1946; and Public Law 585, 79th Congress (S. 1717), for the development and control of atomic energy, with Index to Public Law 585.

17. This series of hearings was preceded by a series on S. Res. 179, *A Resolution Creating a Special Committee To Investigate Problems Relating to the Development, Use, and Control of Atomic Energy*. This series began late in November, 1945, and ran through January, 1946. It may be found as follows: Part I, November 27, 28, 29, 30 and December 3, 1945; Part II, December 5, 6, 10, 12, 1945; Part III, December 13, 14, 19, 20, 1945, and January 24, 1946. Most of these hearings were devoted to the pleading of the atomic scientists for civilian control and for freedom of inquiry. The last, January 24, 1946, was an explanation from Vice Admiral Blandy of the results to be expected from the tests at Bikini.

refused to create a strong agency that could most effectively carry out this purpose. Instead it has created many-headed boards or commissions which so disperse responsibility and authority that each organization as a whole never finds the requisite unity and initiative. Usually the objective is partly lost, because private interests take advantage of weakness. But in such situations legislators find their influence strongest, and thus they are usually to be found pressing for an advantage which is on administrative grounds a serious liability. The commission form was originally developed for semilegislative, semijudicial functions such as the regulation of interstate commerce or the establishment of fair-trade practices; but, in coping with more recent government undertakings, the Congress has failed to distinguish between these duties and such administrative operations as the Tennessee Valley Authority, with a great construction job to do, or the Reconstruction Finance Corporation, with another kind of task requiring positive policy and executive competence. Both these have been forced to find new administrative forms within the commission structure—the TVA by setting up a general manager and relegating its board to policy matters, as is done in any corporation; and the Reconstruction Finance Corporation by making its chairman virtually its sole executive.[18] Both these organizations might have functioned far more effectively as regular departments of government, their executives subordinate to the President. But the Congress would not have it so with these or with most of the New Deal or wartime agencies.

Since the 1930's new functions for government have been forcing themselves on a reluctant Congress; and the Congress has seen in each of them a potential threat to its power. This threat has not been imaginary; more and more as the complexities of technology have increased and as organizations have been forced to enlarge in scale, the federal government has been found to be at the center of the vortex. Something has had to be done to conserve social processes. Reluctantly it has been done; but, because reluctantly, it has been done in half-measure. Thus these eternal commissions are responsible half to the Congress which creates them and half to the Executive which theoretically executes all laws!

18. Succeeding scandals would finally (in 1951) force the adoption of a single-headed administration for RFC.

Mr. Harold Smith, Director of the Budget, and Mr. Harold Ickes, Secretary of the Interior, both opposed the establishment of a commission for atomic energy in hearings before the Congress; but there was no chance that any other device would be considered for the control and management of this new force. The arguments mostly centered on the members of the commission. Mr. Smith recommended three, the smallest possible number; Secretary Forrestal and the other naval and military people advocated a large commission, a majority of them ex officio. Having lost their battle for control, they sought to keep what they regarded as a rival organization as weak as possible.

Finally, of course, a full-time commission of five was decided on. But there was also specified a general manager to be appointed, not by the commission, but by the President and to be confirmed by the Senate. Since the relation of the commissioners to the President was as hazy as their relation to the Congress, and since the relation of the commissioners to a general manager, who was not appointed by them, was at least equivocal, atomic energy had been thus launched upon the United States with an awkward, confused, and feeble administrative device to contain and develop its immense potentialities.

Why this tragedy did not engage more than casual attention is hard to say. Even the experienced industrial executives who had helped in one way or another to establish or operate the immense installations at Oak Ridge, Hanford, and elsewhere for the Manhattan District did not mention the grave handicap of administrative confusion. A curious blindness overcomes many persons who turn from private to public operations. They are unable to see that the elements of decent organization are just as important for public as for private concerns; and they are willing to see established in the very fabric of organization confused authority, inefficient operation, and conflicting relations with other organizations. It was so now. As the law emerged, the commission of five members was to be appointed by the President and confirmed by the Senate, but so was their presumed subordinate, the general manager. Furthermore, the internal divisions of the organization had been specified: research, production, engineering, and military application. Mr. Smith had emphasized that this was a peculiarly unknown, experimental field;

that changes were already within sight; and that, above all, flexibility was necessary to meet them. The senators had rejected with indignation all doubts of their omniscience.

There had been provided also a General Advisory Committee and a Military Liaison Committee. These were to represent, specifically, the scientists and the military, and both were vestigial recognitions of quarrels carried on both before and after Hiroshima. No one expected them to have an active part even in the formation of policy. Still they might well be a burden and a nuisance to harassed management; for, in order to placate the military, furious at not being intrusted with the whole development, a dubious invitation to interference had been included in the duties of the Military Liaison Committee: "If the Committee at any time concludes that any action, proposed action, or failure to act of the Commission . . . is adverse to the responsibilities of the Departments of War or Navy . . . the Committee may refer [it] to the Secretaries of War or Navy. If either concurs, he may refer the matter to the President, whose decision shall be final."

This provision would seem to have given the President authority over matters which might embarrass the commission. But, otherwise, the President's function, except as to appointment, had nowhere been defined. The commission seemed to be an "independent" body, subject to various interpretations of its duties and relations and to the harassment of those who resented its existence. Its relations with the President would not even be governed by the body of law and custom gradually formed through the decades since the establishment of the Interstate Commerce Commission in 1887. Everything about the Atomic Energy Act was special, and this relationship was no exception. The President, in submitting the names of proposed commissioners to the Senate for confirmation, was directed to "set forth the experience and qualifications of the nominee," as though he were the mere agent of the Senate in making the nominations; and he could remove a commissioner only for stated reasons: "Inefficiency, neglect of duty, or malfeasance in office." This protection no Cabinet officer had ever enjoyed, and no subordinate in a policy-making position can enjoy it with any propriety.

In order to understand these curious, perhaps crippling, certainly unwise, departures from normal approach to governmental activity, it has to be understood that the legislators did not regard energy development as proper government activity; but at the same time they had not been able to find any other agency than government to develop it with even a modicum of respect for national security. To trust it to private hands, in the light of what had been known about cartels by then, would have been a flagrant neglect of public safety. Yet every other instinct directed the legislators not to allow government a free hand either. All this pain and confusion was reflected in the "Finding and Declaration":

Research and experimentation in the field of nuclear chain reaction have attained the stage at which the release of atomic energy on a large scale is practical. The significance of the atomic bomb for military purposes is evident. The effect of the use of atomic energy for civilian purposes upon the social, economic, and political structures of today cannot now be determined. It is a field in which unknown factors are involved. Therefore, any legislation will necessarily be subject to revision from time to time. It is reasonable to anticipate, however, that tapping this new source of energy will cause profound changes in our present way of life. Accordingly, it is hereby declared to be the policy of the people of the United States that, subject at all times to the paramount objective of assuring the common defense and security, the development and use of atomic energy shall, so far as practicable, be directed toward improving the public welfare, increasing the standard of living, strengthening free competition in private enterprise, and promoting world peace.

Perhaps the most notable inconsistency here is the expressed desire to promote competitive enterprise and at the same time improve the public welfare. In very few pieces of legislation can there be found so open a declaration in favor of business or so open an espousal of the Smithian economics which identifies private purpose with public good. Yet Mr. Newman spoke of the legislation as being unique because it had established a "socialist enclave."[19] It remained to be seen whether "socialism" would develop. The commission, sensing the attitude of the Congress from under its thumb, would be apt to go far toward letting private enterprise in on the profits certain to come from the vast prospective developments. In

19. "It sets up in the midst of our privately controlled economy a socialistic enclave, with undefined and possibly expanding frontiers. Into a system happily being reclaimed for free enterprise in the postwar period, it deposits a large, alien and unassimilable lump. What the interaction between these opposing elements is likely to be Congress did not even discuss" (*op. cit.*).

fact, aside from the production of fissionable materials, it is evident that the commission was expected to proceed by licensing private enterprises. This is no more socialism than is an assertion of the public ownership of the air waves and the granting of permission, under certain conditions, for their use by profit-making concerns. From the discussions at the hearings it would appear that, aside from research and medical uses, the most likely civilian use of atomic energy was expected to be the production of energy; but of its distribution to consumers not one word was said. The socialist enclave seemed likely to be confined to the actual—and probably unprofitable—primary production of fissionable materials.

While the Atomic Energy Act of 1946 had been shaped, the Congress had been struggling with itself; the nation had been without a trusted and experienced leader; the military had been ascendant; and powerful forces at home had been conspiring with the Russians abroad to frighten everyone with the prospect of another war before the last one had been well over. The act reflected this fright and confusion. It put an emphasis, quite out of character for America, on control of information about what was called "restricted data"; and it included in restricted data anything having to do with "the manufacture or utilization of atomic weapons, the production of fissionable material, or the use of fissionable material in the production of power." The commission, however, might determine what data could be published without affecting "the common defense and security"—an obviously difficult and unwelcome judgment to make.

Take it all together, the commission would have a task almost impossible to discharge with general approval. Either it would permit the exploitation of its monopolized resource for private profit and be subject to criticism, or it would be accused of being hostile to business. It might define restricted data to the scientists' satisfaction so that their research could be carried on freely, but then it would risk continual jingo criticism for jeopardizing the national security; the choice was between the atomic scientists and, say, the Hearst press. The activities of the commission would have the gravest effect on foreign relations, yet it had no defined duty to accept guidance from the President or the Department of State respecting them; for all the guidance furnished by the act, it might pursue its own way, except for minimal and perhaps irrelevant standards and guides, regardless of its impact on either foreign or domestic policies of the government in which it formed, not a socialist enclave, but an alien nodule.

After protracted controversies had so long delayed the passage of legislation for domestic control of atomic development, it was hoped that the President would make his appointments to the commission promptly and that serious work could begin. Such hopes were disappointed. President Truman signed the bill on August 1, 1946, and he appointed the members of the commission three months later, after pressures and hidden negotiations which may be imagined; but the appointment of the members proved to be no more than a beginning. Many months of hearings on their confirmations were yet to be gone through, and before a committee with a new chairman—the Republican Senator Hickenlooper of Iowa. Furthermore, the new Congress was thinking second thoughts about the act itself; in view of the country's mood, should it put greater trust in businessmen and the military? Most of this soul-searching used Mr. David Lilienthal as a butt, for it was he whom the President finally chose to be chairman.

Mr. Lilienthal had many qualifications, among them long administrative experience in the public service and trial in fierce fires of controversy. He had been a member of the Wisconsin Public Service Commission when Mr. Philip La Follette had been governor and of the Tennessee Valley Authority in its formative period. More recently he had pleased many diverse people with his contribution to the Acheson-Lilienthal Report. No doubt this report led directly to his present appointment, and the warm support of the atomic scientists must have helped. Those who had known Mr. Lilienthal in public life or who had followed his career knew him for something of a liberal but one whose compromises were often hard to explain. To President Truman he was obviously the happiest of all possible choices. He had an enemy or two, it was true, but no one formidable until some of the more responsible Republicans— such as Senator Taft—decided that he was unsatisfactory to certain of those they preferred to protect. In the middle of the proceedings, though previously they had tacitly approved, they turned against him, but by then his confirmation had been made inevitable by the stupid, persistent, and ignorant opposition of Senator Kenneth Mc-Kellar of Tennessee, pursuing an old grudge about patronage in TVA into Mr. Lilienthal's new activity.

The hearings were abusive. To Mr. Lilienthal were plainly imputed communism, venality, lack of personal integrity, and other qualities of like absurdity; and he was questioned in the most brutal manner over and over on the same counts. For once, however, the press was on the candidate's side—which led to some suspicion that Mr. Lilienthal was tolerably at peace with those who hoped to exploit atomic fire for their own profit. It was Senators McKellar, Wherry, and others who suffered ridicule rather than their victim. Senator McKellar was speaking, it appeared, only for himself. He was not the agent for any sinister seekers after privilege; he was merely an old man with a grudge who was inexplicably allowed to use the majestic machinery of the United States Senate for its satisfaction.

The character of the proceedings was one more proof—if more proof were needed—that Senate confirmation of federal appointments constitutes interference with the executive without compensatory advantage. They were also, moreover, a waste of valuable time. A whole year of the five (or less) estimated by the scientists to be available before Russia produced the atomic bomb was thus allowed to be frittered away in utterly futile internal bickering, *after all the issues had been substantially settled*. The Russians some day might well erect a statue in Red Square inscribed: "To the Eightieth Congress of the United States, in gratitude for promoting controversy, contributing to the incapacity of democracy, and presenting the Soviet Union with a valuable gift of time." It would be appropriate.

Nothing of any importance was revealed in the hearings. They were mostly concerned with Mr. Lilienthal's character, such of them as were not questionings of what had been settled by the Seventy-ninth Congress in 1946. To be sure, the other members of the commission were interrogated, but no more than casually.[20]

20. Although somewhat more than casual attention was devoted to the question whether there was suspicion or resentment, as there should have been, at the provision for continued congressional interference represented by the Joint Committee on Atomic Energy. For instance:

"THE CHAIRMAN: May I ask you, Admiral [Strauss], whether you are fully in accord with the policy of constant and continuous liaison and mutual informa-

They were all of them extremely conciliatory. Perhaps they were following the policy of getting through the ordeal at any cost, knowing they could rely very little on the President's prestige. Or perhaps, knowingly or unknowingly, they were infected with the determination to protect the new resource from public development. Mr. Strauss, for instance, said to the chairman, without prompting and without rebuke: "I regard the task of the Atomic Energy Commission as a high public trust: that of being in custodianship of that charge until those problems are resolved to the point where the American pattern can be applied to this subject as well as to any other branch of science or industry." Significantly enough, no one spoke up to ask what he regarded as "the American pattern." Everyone knew. He may have been correct in assuming that this conception was now the accepted one. The elections of 1946 seemed to have disestablished the New Deal and what small challenge to the pattern its meliorativeness had brought. But there still existed, Mr. Strauss notwithstanding, many Americans to whom profit and competition were not an accepted way of life.[21] Unfortunately they were too concerned with sheer survival in a world possessed of atomic fire, but not of world organization, to busy themselves overmuch with the current aggressiveness of reaction. They did not appear to realize that both dangers were of one piece and that to fight the one was to fight the other. They worked ardently, as a matter of fact, for the confirmation of the members of this commission, all of whom, with the possible exception of Mr. Lilienthal, were at least conservatives.

tion between the Congressional Joint Committee on Atomic Energy and the Commission?

"MR. STRAUSS: I look forward to it. It seems to me that the success of the Commission depends upon it" (*Hearings*, p. 43). Which shows how little one member, at least, understood what lay before the commission.

21. The experience and qualifications of Mr. Strauss, as represented in the President's submission as required by the law, indicated the training and environment which produce this sublime faith in business. They may be found at pp. 38–39 of the *Hearings*. He had begun early as private secretary to President Hoover when Mr. Hoover had been Food Administrator. Afterward he had gone to work for Kuhn, Loeb and Company and had risen to be a partner. He had joined the naval reserve in 1925 and in 1941 had been placed on active duty as a lieutenant commander. His services in inspection, procurement, etc., had been such that he had risen to be an admiral. He had gone back, full of honors, to Kuhn, Loeb and Company in 1946, whence the President had plucked him to be a member of the Atomic Energy Commission.

Although the men of the right now so rapidly moving into the policy-making posts of government may have been confident, without good warrant, that they had popular approval, it must be said that the people of the United States were actually to be blamed. If, as most liberals believed, they had voted in a peevish moment in 1946 against the fancied source of their irritations and put in power those of whom they were fundamentally distrustful, there was nothing to show such a distrust. For the first time since 1929, the conservatives could claim a popular mandate. Others could only hope that, when the tide turned again and they no longer had a majority, they would not use their accumulated power to destroy the machinery of democracy. Such a pattern had been followed too many times in recent decades in other lands to be dismissed lightly. American institutions had been twisted toward dictatorship during the war. It had been a temporary distortion, administered by a convinced democrat; but the precedent was there, and the knowledge of its technique had not been lost. If the national crisis vis-à-vis Russia should deepen or be made to seem to deepen, democracy might well be in the greatest danger it had ever been.

On the anniversary of Hiroshima—and of Bikini—in 1947, some matters had begun to take recognizable shape in American minds. There was still a general attitude of puzzled confusion. The results of electing the kind of Congress that had been chosen in 1946 were being produced with terrifying rapidity but were not yet traced to their cause. The citizenry had voted against Washington's interferences and ineptitudes, real and fancied; they had not voted for higher living costs, privileges for big business, international ill will, and so on, which they were getting. Perhaps the fact that they were again disappointed in their political hopes was one cause of disillusion about other matters. Americans were angry at Russia in all possible ways. But their anger was beginning to have a core of reason. They saw the futility of recent expectation: that good will and economic assistance would lead, if not to friendship, then anyway to some kind of accommodation which would make it possible to get along. They saw now that Molotov, Vishinsky, and Gromyko, who were the Russians they heard about most often, were genuinely indifferent to American opinion. Ill will in the United States was an advantage to a Soviet diplomat who was operating as the rigid extension of a Politburo. Diplomats were tools used for Politburo purposes. Those purposes were to expand immediately the Russian borders and ultimately to create and control a Communist world. Americans, with their careless live-and-let-live attitude, half-indifferent and half-contemptuous, unless their sympathies were aroused, tended always to forget the persistent and implacable determination of the Politburo fanatics. They were becoming more realistic under Molotov's tutelage, more amenable, also, to the urgings of their own jingoes. But there was also a reaction from this—a drawing-back from the danger of a break.

They watched the proceedings at Lake Success. To be sure, these consisted of gloomy forebodings and futile lecturings by Mr. Frederick Osborn, who had by now succeeded Mr. Baruch as the representative of the United States on the United Nations Atomic Energy Commission; but they were profoundly disillusioning. They reviewed the complete futility of last winter's Moscow Conference of Foreign Ministers and the fiasco at Paris in early summer when Molotov had gone home between dusk and sunrise, thus shocking more millions of Westerners into a realization of Russian intransigence. They saw Britain shrinking in power and influence and weighed the necessity of going again to her aid in spite of her apostasy; she was, after all, they told themselves, only socialistic, not Communistic, and she was incorrigibly libertarian and democratic. It was, for the liberals of the world, a deeply felt misfortune that Britain's socialism did not have more of a chance to prove itself; her troubles were being used by business interests to demonstrate that their's was the only way, thus proving that capitalism and democracy really were the Siamese twins which capitalist apologists represented them to be. Mr. Winston Churchill, declined from his once-great stature, proclaimed that socialism was a failure and found more followers in America than in Britain.

Americans began, also, to have a more realistic understanding of the atomic fire which was burning under the crust of stiff international exchange. This understanding did not allay their anxiety; it rather added to their distress; but it may have been leading to the kind of general formulation of belief and attitude which might have formidable consequences. If time should be given, the weight of public opinion might prevail and be for good. The post-Bikini deprecation of the Bomb had disappeared. During the spring of 1947 Mr. Robert M. Hutchins was widely heard when he spoke of others, now perfected, of many times the destructiveness of that which had fallen on Hiroshima. This knowledge, together with the steady spread and deepening of the sense of guilt about Hiroshima itself, brought American opinion to a pitch of gravity concerning the Bomb on which, it did seem, a movement looking toward world government might be founded, provided the leadership could be found. But leadership seemed oriented in another direction.

It was a tragic accompaniment of this willingness in America to follow a way to unity if it could be found, even a sacrificial way, that the rest of the world should be suddenly indifferent. For indifferent it was. The Politburo kept Russians in ignorance; Asiatics were busy becoming nationalized just as nationalism was becoming obsolete; an amazing number of Africans were ignorant; and even western Europe seemed more interested in remaining merely alive today than in taking precautions about survival in any tomorrow. If the United States were to do anything about world government, it would have to be something more than a mere reluctant joining. Americans would have to create, support, and implement it, or it would never be created or live. This was to ask an amazing reversal for statesmen from Wisconsin, Texas, South Dakota, and other traditionally isolationist localities. Yet there was a movement going on which did have impressive power and unmistakable appeal to all sorts of folk. It rested solidly on the now-accepted proposition that there were only two choices: to unite or to perish. Knowledge of what atomic fire could do in careless, nihilistic, or hostile custody had brought even the most reluctant and suspicious patriots to this admission. They were among those who now sought the way.

Painted large on a sign outside a circus tent on the vacant lot nearest my dwelling place in Chicago, during the spring and summer of 1947, were the words: "World Survival Meetings: Daily at 8:00 P.M." A group of young university people thus did their bit for the continuation of our species. The arguments with which they sought to persuade their audiences were somewhat naïve and even sophistical. But they were given power by the fear in their hearers' hearts—a fear even greater than that which the old-time hell-fire-

and-damnation preachers had had to count on. Hell, after all, had been problematical; atomic fire was an immanent menace. It was even well and intimately known. Many people spoke frequently and intelligibly about neutrons, isotopes, and other phenomena which, not long before, had been part of a closely held means of communication among very specialized nuclear physicists.

It was by no means only journals of the intellectual quality of the *Atlantic Monthly* which maintained the current discussion of atomic fission and its consequences. But, as usual, the *Atlantic* did produce as telling an argument in short compass as was to be found anywhere. It was in the August number and in the department labeled "The Atlantic Report on the World Today":

The day of the Hiroshima bomb, 6 August 1945, was staggering both as revelation and as warning. It made known the results of a success achieved on 2 December 1942. That was the day when Enrico Fermi, Arthur Compton, and their associates in the Metallurgical Laboratory at the University of Chicago accomplished the first self-sustaining, or chain reaction in uranium.

The crux of the achievement is the fact that the uranium atom, when its nucleus is struck by an electrically neutral particle—a neutron—travelling at the right speed, and under the right conditions, splits into two atoms, one of barium, and one of krypton, releasing some two hundred million electron volts of energy and liberating several more free neutrons to produce the subsequent fission of more uranium atoms, the release of further enegy, the liberation of more free neutrons, and so on and on.

On this basis, in a succinct page or two, the *Atlantic* went on to summarize the significance of the discovery, showing that what appeared above the surface here was only about as relatively great as what might appear of a floating iceberg above the surface of the sea. It spoke of the politics as well as the physics of controlling so powerful a release of energy. In decades to come it would be a mighty source of industrial energy; for the moment its significance was military. And of the work of the United States Atomic Energy Commission it said: "Chairman Lilienthal has made it plain that the United States is determined to maintain and strengthen its preeminent position not only in atomic energy generally, but in atomic weapons specifically until such time as a sound system of international control has been established."

That was undoubtedly a correct summary. Mr. Lilienthal had already said that an area in the Pacific would be set aside for the testing of atomic weapons. There were to be more Bikinis. They would be better understood than had the first one. It could not be certain that their purpose would be altogether different; but their results might well be better. For now not only the bomb but Russia had come into focus. And, sharply, men asked themselves: was there to be war? Mr. Hutchins had met that question when the Atomic Energy Act was under hearing:

SENATOR MILLIKIN: Suppose we were to reach the conclusion that war is inevitable. Would you say that we would be warranted in using the bomb to destroy the nation that we figured would inevitably involve the world in war?

DR. HUTCHINS: I decline, Senator, to be brought into that hypothesis as a participant. If you say that, in your opinion, war is inevitable, then it seems to me—if you say that your first duty is to protect or defend your own country—you would be warranted in exerting all your efforts to getting war under way at once, because we are in a better position to win now than we may be in the future.

SENATOR MILLIKIN: Let us assume that you reached the conclusion that war is inevitable.

DR. HUTCHINS: You have my recommendation.

SENATOR MILLIKIN: I am delighted that you look that in the face and give that answer to it. It might come to that. As you look over the world, Doctor, what are the cheering prospects that will enable us to indulge in the assumption, so far as law-making is concerned, that we have seen the end of wars?

DR. HUTCHINS: Perhaps, Senator Millikin, we ought to make clear that we think there are two issues here: one is the issue of the foreign policy of the United States, which is not, as such, before this Committee; the other is the issue of what you are going to do with atomic energy.

Now, we have assumed that it is the foreign policy of the United States to maintain and promote peace in every possible way. We believe that atomic energy must be considered in the light of that policy, and that that is the only way really in which it is useful to consider it, because if that is not the policy of the United States, and if we are not going to find ways to implement that policy, then the thing to do is not merely to sit on the atomic bomb, because sitting on the atomic bomb will not protect us from the atomic bombs that other nations will shortly be able to produce.

The answer, if you assume it is not the policy of the United States to promote peace and that we cannot obtain peace, is to start a war.[22]

In August of 1947, a year and a half later, it was no longer a safe assumption that American policy, with respect to the atomic bomb was or could be based on the assumption of continuing peace. It was no longer even a safe assumption that our foreign policy was directed toward maintaining peace. Even the commission, set up un-

22. *Hearings*, Part II, January 25, 1946, p. 125.

der the legislation which had been the subject of this exchange between Chancellor Hutchins and Senator Millikin was, it said, devoting itself to preparations for war. War, indeed, seemed to have begun but to be in that stage it reaches before climactic outbursts of violence occur. The question was: Would some accommodation be found by which a partial armistice could be maintained? Even if it could, the instability of the world's political elements would be kept only from day to day and by devoted effort. The least relaxation, the smallest mistake, and the resort to force would be precipitated.

The meeting place in which these unstable elements met, seethed, glowered, charged one another with every conceivable delinquency, and failed, always, to agree on anything to be done (wherefore it could not be done, since there must be unanimity under the charter) was Lake Success on Long Island. It had got so that observers felt each day during which such exchanges took place without one or another of the protagonists marching out and refusing to meet further was a day of borrowed time. That time, they felt, furthermore, was borrowed from the essentially timeless infinities of the universe which would absorb the great shock of energy released into it as the mass of man, his works, and his planet were disintegrated in chain reactions of exploding atoms or dissolved in clouds of radioactive mists. The anxious years moved toward a climax; men watched its approach with dread.

By THE third anniversary of Hiroshima in 1948, the disruption of preatomic adjustments was well advanced, but the pattern of new arrangements to succeed the old was not yet manifest even to the most clairvoyant observer; or, if it was, that observer was silent and inconspicuous. Nations still clung stubbornly to sovereignty. There were even new independent political units, among them India and Pakistan, fifth and sixth most populous states in the world. There was war of sorts all along the borderland between the Soviet Russian and the West European–American areas of influence. Inflation was ruthlessly at work, everywhere destroying old and creating new classes, establishing insecurity, and breaking down, even in the United States, what stability remained. Revolution succeeded revolution in all the dependent areas as Russia and the United States concentrated on preparations for the active conflict which now seemed inevitable. The crisis in the world's affairs was still unresolved, still not even preparing for solution.

The most confusing situation existed in the United States. The country of the Bomb's origin, where there was wide publicity concerning atomic energy and its effects, the country most advanced technologically, appeared to be in the throes of a political reaction which came straight out of its pioneering past. It strove to move backward while it was relentlessly pushed forward. The American people seemed to have made up their minds what to do about Soviet Russia, their enemy; about atomic energy, their bête noir; and about communism, the frightening manifestation now enlarging itself in the ideological heavens. They would defeat Russia, ignore atomic energy, and suppress communism. The America of uncut forests and unplowed plains, of unregulated exploitations, of vigilantes and general primitivism, was thrusting through the crust of

116

an industrial civilization, a dream, a wish, a powerful urge to escape from crisis, from regulation, from constriction, and from anxiety.

Disaster was coming up over the horizon now, dark as a thunder cloud. Typical measures had been taken to dispel the black threat. Billions of dollars, to a number no one seemed able to count, had been cast into the face of the rising storm: billions to purchase surpluses, billions to prepare the nation for the approaching war by rebuilding the now obsolete military machine and by strengthening the Western allies along the enemy's border line. This double usefulness of funds borrowed from the treacherous treasury of inflation was regarded as most fortunate. The Republicans who had been weeping into their beards for fifteen years over Democratic spending—"boondoggling" had been their name for it—voluntarily joined a bipartisan coalition for the forwarding of the superspending now favored by business. And when the Eightieth Congress adjourned late in June of 1948, the military and the big businessmen were equipped with colossal funds to force the genie of failing purchasing power back into the vase from which it had been threatening to escape. The jar still stood, a looming shadow, in the sacred place of the capitalist economy. But a little time had been bought from its monstrous and insatiable inhabitant. Productivity was a Frankenstein.

The whooping politicos in Philadelphia in June sought to divert attention from its imperatives; and seemingly they succeeded. The same Mr. Dewey who had been defeated by sick old President Roosevelt in 1944 was the wonder-working medicine man of 1948. Mr. Dewey was an opportunist. He knew not only that the horse-and-buggy longings could not be realized but that those who had them wanted, really, to ride in the latest automobiles themselves. It was other people they hoped to see limited to horses and buggies. This problem is familiar to politicians. The electorate is always unreasonable in some such way. It wants government to do much but without a bureaucracy; it wants to intimidate foreigners but without the risk of war; it wants prosperity but without the regulation or controls which are the necessary conditions of prosperity. It had always been the task of political leaders to gain the necessary consent to unwanted controls, but the requisite courage seemed to have vanished.

In this dilemma lay the secret of Mr. Truman's decline in public favor, which now presented Mr. Dewey with his opportunity. Mr. Truman had been unlucky. Not only had he succeeded an extraordinary political strategist but he was faced with problems which not even a Roosevelt could have solved. To find a way to peace while preparing for war; to insure the continuance of the inflationary boom without permitting its rising prices to reduce levels of living; to maintain business freedom without incurring the penalties of un-co-ordinated activity—these were paradoxes it was not possible to resolve in action. Because he had not succeeded in showing how to do it, Mr. Truman and his party moved, in a kind of unwilling trance, toward what seemed certain defeat. Mr. Dewey, who progressed, on the contrary, with a certain majestic somnambulism toward victory, was not going to win because he advocated any positive policy, any more than Governor Roosevelt had in 1932. He had learned that lesson. He was sure to win anyway, he felt, and so the less he said the better. His contempt for the electorate was total.

The meager crops harvested in the fall of 1947 were being succeeded by bountiful ones in 1948. Here was good news for a hungry world, but it made the anticipation of coming surpluses keener among American farmers. In the welter of privileged legislation passed by the irresponsible Eightieth Congress, their lobby succeeded in extending the guaranty of prices. There was, of course, to be no limit on production. The elected President was assured, if war did not come soon, of still one more insoluble problem—how to dispose of some half-billion bushels of wheat, perhaps twice as much corn (largely in the form of pork), and several millions of bales of cotton in a world now prepared to raise its own wheat, corn, and cotton. For even Europe, where our potential surpluses had recently been going, was back almost to normal production.

We might continue to give away our produce. So long as Europeans were hungry, that policy had been approved by all Americans. Soon, however, European farmers would object to that kind of competition. What then? Would we give it to the Hottentots and other remote but hungry people? Or would our farmers accept the principle of restricted production? Either solution was politically dangerous. War with its limitless wastes and insatiable demands would seem more and more attractive as the time of reckoning ap-

proached. Farmers, like a good many shortsighted American workers, had concluded from recent history that they were best off when
war was either preparing or present. There might not be much real
opposition in spite of moralist talk.[1]

The program of containment was being more and more generously backed. A billion had been spent for bridgeheads in Greece,
Turkey, and Iran; and there were intimations that, if necessary, a
billion more might be spent to buy one in Spain behind the Pyren-
nes. Ideological differences with Franco and his Falangists seemed
no longer to bulk large in governmental calculations. Why should
they when the House of Representatives had already voted to include Spain in the benefits of the Marshall Plan? For liberals, this
was a shocking incident, but evidently it was accepted generally as
desirable if necessary; at any rate, few expressed any indignation.
This step was entirely consistent, in fact, with American affiliations
everywhere. In China, in the Near East, in South America, in
Europe, the United States gave preference to the right over the left.
In Italy a holy spectacle had been provided by American diplomats
running in harness with reactionaries to win an election with about
the same methods as were traditionally used by the less scrupulous
political machines in such large cities as Philadelphia, St. Louis,
and Jersey City.

Most American liberals, especially the unpolitical intellectuals
who had gathered in President Roosevelt's shadow and called
themselves "New Dealers," were *in extremis*. Mostly they drank
their bitter tea in silent retirement. But a few made futile and foolish gestures toward persuading some liberal candidate to succeed
Mr. Truman. Mr. Truman, however, refused to step aside; if his
refusal jeopardized the party, that was the party's lookout. The
spectacle of Mr. Leon Henderson, the Roosevelt boys, and even Mr.
Arvey of the Chicago machine pleading with General Eisenhower
to run, then trying to put him over on the party, then being repudiated by the General himself, was political tragicomedy in its highest

1. Cf. W. F. Ogburn and Jean L. Adams, "Are Our Wars Good Times?" *Scientific Monthly*, July, 1948, pp. 23–33: "The conclusion of this study . . . is that the
experiences at home in the United States of our social and economic institutions
and activities during the periods of our participation in the last two world wars
were much like those of the prosperity of the business cycle in peace years,
commonly called good times. . . ."

vein. For they might have supported the effort of Mr. Wallace to present a real alternative to prosperity by inflation and to a war of prevention toward which Mr. Truman now moved, and Mr. Dewey, if he should be elected, would move even more certainly. If Mr. Wallace had had the support, generally, of American Progressives, he might, more quickly and more firmly, have repudiated the support given him by the American Communists. His reluctance was easily made to seem partisanship on his part for Russia; and, since we appeared to move toward war with Russia, not many Americans were going to consort with a friend of the enemy.

A preventive war was now a fairly established activist objective. It was, in fact, the official bipartisan foreign policy. That aggression from the combined "free-world" forces was much feared in the Soviet Union was evident from the sinister consequences to be observed wherever the two power systems came into contact—along the borderlands, both in Europe and the Far East, and in such international meetings as continued to be held. The United Nations still functioned, though in very low gear and in a thick fog of uncertainty; but one by one its specialized agencies ceased—or almost ceased—to function. During the year the Atomic Energy Commission had given up; and late in July the Permanent Disarmament Commission agreed to disband until Russia and America should try for some compromise which would dispel the farcical atmosphere in which it now worked. So it went. The machinery of international conference dissolved; the groupings of East and West coalesced and hardened. And on Hiroshima Day in 1948 the crisis in Berlin was of such a nature that any short-tempered second lieutenant on either side might easily precipitate one of those incidents which turn uneasy peace into active war. No one thought that such a thing would happen—yet! But everyone thought that, when either side could see its way clear to a real victory, it would.

Why war should be less dreaded now than last year or the year before, it was difficult to understand. Yet so it was, as simple observation proved. One of the familiar polls of public opinion indicated that more than three-fourths of Americans felt that American policy toward Russia was not tough enough. The grounds for this opinion might be a guess that the Russians had not yet equipped themselves with the atomic bomb. Certainly such an attitude came close to approving the consequence of more toughness, and that would be a "preventive" war. Had the terrors of Hiroshima then been forgot? Were we willing to risk a bombing attack on America if it should turn out that the Russians possessed it? And were we willing to use it on Russians as we had used it on the Japanese? Above all, were we willing that the cataclysm of atomic fire should again be turned loose to destroy men and their works?

Recently the Bomb had been tried again. Bikini had been succeeded by Eniwetok. But the performance of 1948 was different from that of 1946. Bikini appeared to have been run by the Navy's highest-powered publicity men; Eniwetok was smothered in an almost complete mystery. Bikini had been widely advertised and numerously attended (even the Russians had had an observer present); Eniwetok was kept strictly within the family of the armed services and the United States Atomic Energy Commission. The publicity in the one test and the mystery in the other were both for the same purpose. The idea was to strengthen the confidence of Americans in their potential for aggression and at the same time perhaps to frighten the Russians. The approaches were different because the United States had passed from stealthy preparation for war by the armed services without authorization to the preliminary stages of a war which was authorized by an approving public opinion and backed by enormous congressional appropriations.[2]

There was no longer any need for such publicity concerning American terror-making power as had existed in 1946; the armed services could now retreat to their normal secretiveness. And the Atomic Energy Commission, under the circumstances, with the ad-

---

2. Following a cautious statement by the Atomic Energy Commission in its *Annual Report*, the President, on July 24, 1948, issued a statement which, besides saying casually that the bomb had been greatly improved, summarized, two years after its passage, the operations of the Atomic Energy Act. It stood, the President said, upon a foundation of four principles: (1) that a free society places the civil authority above the military; (2) that, until the technology of atomic energy is better understood, the role of private enterprise in its development must be restrained; (3) that, until international controls are established, the nation cannot afford to disclose the secrets which make it the most deadly of military weapons; and (4) that we must continue to probe the facts of nature both to supplement our defenses and to insure peacetime progress. He went on to say that, for two years at least, these objectives had been steadily pursued. Unfortunately, however, no progress had been made toward international agreement. This was because the Soviet Union had refused to co-operate.

mirals and generals always waiting to pounce on any lapse, were bound to be far more royal than the king. They avoided publicity and guarded their atomic secrets with fanatic care. By now, however, the imagination of people everywhere was quite equal to the task of picturing what must have happened to have enabled the President to say to the press that "the recent tests . . . in the Pacific have demonstrated beyond any question that our position in the field of atomic weapons has been substantially improved." What the mind's eye saw, as from so high a place above the world that it seemed really globelike—pictures of the sphere on which they lived, taken from rockets at a height of sixty or seventy miles, were now familiar to everyone—was a vast stretch of placid sea with miniscule islands from which missiles with atomic war heads had been projected upon other miniscule islands. The rockets were pictured as blazing through the stratosphere like comets. And, at contact, the sinister thunderhead of heavy mist boiling in incredible dimensions upward and outward over scores of miles of unoffending sea had as vivid a manifestation as could have been given it by the most skilful of press agents. Death, disaster, and devastation were still immanent, still waiting for some irresponsible fool or some ideologically crazed group to release them. And, seemingly, the mind of man which could ascend into the stratosphere and understand the consequences, upon a globe gone small, of released atomic fire, could not yet conceive of ways to contain it.

The two power systems continued to harden at their cores, to prepare new traps for each other, to shut off communications which might lead to conciliation—to bring, in a word, the hour nearer when that vast rolling mushroom which had spread over Hiroshima should rise over one another's cities and productive facilities. Nothing that men of good will, of foresight, or of imagination could do had any more the slightest effect.

The President said, and most Americans believed, that "the uncompromising refusal of the Soviet Union to participate in a workable control system has thus far obstructed progress." And in fact a vote taken on May 17, 1948, in the United Nations Atomic Energy Commission referred the whole question of international control to the Security Council, because, in the view of the majority, the Soviet

Union was determined never to agree to control.[3] Mr. Gromyko, for the Soviet Union, had objected to breaking off discussions; but the others had felt that he was merely playing for delay while Russia improved her position. Russian inscrutability made it difficult to be certain what lay behind the insistence that inspection must be carried out in such a way as not to infringe national sovereignty. Such an inspection—and Mr. Gromyko further limited it by entering an objection to aerial surveys—would be no more than a farce. And he must have known that it was futile to insist that the destruction of existing stocks of bombs must precede any control agreement.

The Russians felt either that those with whom they were dealing were acting in complete bad faith and were not to be trusted or that by delaying they could so improve their circumstances that they would be able to dictate. Perhaps they were operating on both assumptions. On the one hand, they may have expected to become powerful enough to conquer the West, or they may have expected the West to collapse from capitalist stresses. They could see that inflation built up from day to day and that American business refused to accede to any of the restraints necessary if an economic collapse in the near future was to be avoided. On the other hand, they may have felt that the business and military character of the Truman administration made it obviously untrustworthy. The American Secretary of State was a general; the American ambassador to Russia was a general; the American Secretary of Defense was a former president of Dillon, Read and Company and so might fairly be said to represent Wall Street. It was no different anywhere in the Truman administration. The Roosevelt influence had been completely liquidated. Big business and the military had taken over the government. Soviet statesmen may well have felt that the every move of such officials must be calculated to undermine and eventually to destroy such a collective state as theirs. Of course, the open alliance of these men with the Vatican, a most bitter enemy of the aggressively atheistic and anti-Catholic Communist complex, would confirm the certainty of bad faith in any proposal for joint action—especially of any action which had in it the power of life and death for the Soviet government.

There had been a time, about a year before, when some optimism

3. *Third Report of the United Nations Atomic Energy Commission.*

had been felt about Soviet intentions. It had been reflected in an editorial in the *Bulletin of the Atomic Scientists*[4] which suggested that the Soviet statesmen "might genuinely want, or at least realize the necessity for, international control" but that the means required to achieve such a control might be novel and abhorrent and might run contrary to their attitude toward capitalist nations in other respects. This interpretation would account, it was suggested, for the "slow dribble of concessions" which came from Mr. Gromyko, the Soviet representative. The latest of these had been the proposals of June 11, 1947, which had rejected aerial surveys and had favored reliance on national governments themselves for enforcement. True this proposal was "unrealistic," but might it not mark a step in a reluctant progress toward recognition of the inevitable? Even given such progress, however, the question still faced all those who hoped for peace: "How long will it take the U.S.S.R. to spell out the whole alphabet of an international control mechanism? Is there any hope that she can do it within the time which remains before the atomic armament race will destroy the last chances of reconciliation?"

This question furnished its own answer in the ensuing year; and the decision of the United Nations Atomic Energy Commission, on May 17, to abandon further discussion was the penultimate recognition of failure. Some kind of new beginning appeared necessary before more concessions could be wrung from the Russians. Either they were determined to engage in an atomic armaments race, or they feared that the other nations participating in the close relationships of joint supervision would use them to undermine the Communist state. The question then was: Would the Western nations give some reassurance, make some concession, which would move the reluctant Russians further toward consent? On Hiroshima Day in 1948 it seemed that they had decided to force the Soviets' hand. Hostility spread; disposition to tolerance declined. The Soviet Union became an enemy state.

This *Third Report* of the United Nations Atomic Energy Commission was uncompromising. The members of the Commission were thoroughly worn out from repeated attempts to influence the Russians. They were also thoroughly frightened by the prospect of failure. Their own thinking had progressed from reliance on inspection

4. III (August, 1947), 201–2.

of separately owned facilities for production to the conviction that nothing less than joint public ownership would be sufficient. As the editorial in the *Bulletin* had said:

How long will it take the Soviet Union to concede that . . . disagreeable provisions are inevitable in a control system based on inspection?

If and when the Soviet Union arrives at this stage it may begin to dawn on her why some scientists in America—without being in the service of vested coal or oil interests—have suggested the limitation of the production of atomic fuels to a level excluding large scale power production.

Perhaps she will realize that this limitation would greatly facilitate inspection and incidentally keep the margin between atomic disarmament and full atomic preparedness immensely wider than it can be if each nation is allowed to accumulate unlimited stocks of atomic fuels for power production.

Furthermore, will the Soviet Union at this state of spelling out the alphabet of atomic control, understand why Messrs. Lilienthal, Oppenheimer, Winne and Thomas have discarded the idea of control by inspection in favor of control by ownership and management?

Will the Soviet's next step be the reluctant concession that it is less distasteful to engage in common exploitation of atomic energy with the hated and suspected capitalist system, than to allow the agents of this system to fly over a large part of the Soviet territories and look at will into Soviet laboratories and plants.

Will she understand that managerial control has not been devised as an opening wedge for capitalist penetration into socialist economy, but as a provision for minimum interference by the atomic energy control agency with the diverse economies of individual countries?[5]

It was not likely that Soviet statesmen suspected the atomic scientists of any such Machiavellian plot; but that they suspected the representatives of Mr. Truman's administration, in concurrence with the Vatican, of just such intentions it seemed likely. Nor were they apt to be reassured by a change to an administration headed by Mr. Dewey. The prospect was for further separation. But the rift which already existed could hardly be widened. It already amounted to undeclared war.

By 1948 most of the ground gained in the legislative battle of 1946 had been lost. The atomic scientists had been defeated by an attack on an unprotected flank. In the Eightieth Congress Mr. Lilienthal had had to come up again for confirmation, this time for a "regular" term of five years.[6] But now the Republicans expected

5. *Ibid.*, p. 202.

6. One of the defects of the act had been the short initial term for appointees to the commission.

soon to come into power, and they wanted their own men in the Commission. After a good deal of trading they settled for a two-year concession; they could not be shamed into respecting their own act.

It was not easy to see what objection the congressmen could have to Mr. Lilienthal, aside, perhaps, from his former identification with the Tennessee Valley Authority. No policy sponsored by him could possibly be regarded as inimical to business. He and his colleagues had concentrated on furthering the destructive aspects of atomic energy; they had maintained a rigid secrecy; and Mr. Lilienthal himself had insisted that the Commission's results eventually should be handed to private industry for profitable exploitation. These policies were those favored by the majority of the Eightieth Congress, and, in fact, his opponents in the Congress could adduce no real objection. They fell back on unashamed politics. There was some criticism in the press for irresponsible playing with an engine of destruction such as atomic power was now recognized to be; but this criticism was faint by comparison with the quite general approval of the announced Republican policy not to confirm any more appointments at all—at least none for any federal jobs whose terms would run on into the probable Republican years after January 1, 1949. Such a policy the predominantly sympathetic press found too attractive to resist even if it did violate all the standards to which they had been disposed to hold the Democrats for the last sixteen years.

Thus the atomic scientists, who had fought a good fight in the public interest and who had won an initial battle, were now losing the campaign. The development of atomic energy was already dominated by the interests they had sought to exclude; and it was about to be bodily seized by them. How did the scientists feel, and how, now, did they conceive their role? Would they struggle against defeat? It was a sad fact that by now they had given up and that most of them were busily justifying their surrender. They, no more than other citizens, were able to resist the cumulative jingoism of the times. Propaganda had been too much for them. They still occasionally squeaked faintly, but the retreat to the laboratories was very nearly total. When they were heard from, it was not argument in favor of effective action to interrupt the progress toward war, or in favor of attitudes which would reassure the Russians; it was merely to the effect that war would be destructive. And that, by now, no one needed to be told.

Mr. Louis N. Ridenour expressed a view common to many.[7] He believed in working for a world-wide political organization and a social philosophy and political morality adequate to prevent wars. This problem, however, was "entirely unscientific." The scientist ought not to allow himself to get into the dangerous position of accepting a responsibility which was not scientific and which was, in fact, everyone's. He ought to do his part as a citizen, but not more.

Mr. John A. Simpson in the *Bulletin of the Atomic Scientists* for September, 1947, supported the same view.[8] He too was clearly in retreat from responsibility. He too felt that it was not reasonable to expect scientists alone to do what others should also be doing. He was more specific. We cannot continue, he said, to put all our time into this effort unless we are "to withdraw completely from the frontiers of scientific knowledge." He ended by saying: "We feel that this [effort] has been justified for the past two years, but cannot be justified any longer."

What were the real reasons for this retreat? It was not that the scientists did not believe themselves as omniscient as ever; it was not that they were now "too busy." At least neither of these reasons seemed at all adequate to the nature of the decision. Was it not that reaction in their ranks, as they had enlarged, had taken hold? And that those who were not conservatives yet anticipated a coming Republican regime? The bullying they had undergone and were still undergoing dismayed them, not so much for themselves as for their scientific work. Also, perhaps, they were tired of living in disfavor. The only people who took the menace of the Bomb and its fellow-weapons seriously enough to advocate a policy shaped strictly in accord with its menace were not respectable either in university or in government communities. They were, in fact, regarded as radicals; and, since scientists had always been notorious for their with-

7. Mr. Ridenour, who had been adviser on radar to General Carl Spaatz, was professor of physics at the University of Pennsylvania and one of the most widely recognized leaders among the newer scientists. The article discussed here appeared in the *Atlantic Monthly* for May, 1947.

8. Mr. Simpson was one of the most prominent of the younger scientists, a member now of the group at Chicago and formerly an important contributor to the first accomplishment of fission. He had taken a very active part in the battle for the McMahon Act in 1946.

drawing attitudes in social matters, they were repelled by such en-forced fellowship. In addition, there may have been a few who had some suspicion that natural scientists were likely, in the long run, to do more harm than good by blundering about with social institu-tions. But, if there were, they did not express themselves very clear-ly. In fact, Mr. Conant and Mr. Bush were reputed to be speaking for their scientific confreres when they opposed the inclusion of the social sciences in the bill for a scientific foundation which was being considered in Washington. It seemed more likely that the bullying, the ostracism, the charges of disloyalty, the constant investigation, together with the company they had to keep, induced the scientists to find important matters to be attended to in their laboratories.

Messrs. Einstein, Urey, Shapley, Szilard, Morrison, and a few others were exceptions. They continued to be tormented by the urgency of the situation and to join generously in the agitation for conciliation.[9] They were not bothered by loss of time expended for survival; and they had, they thought, earned a hearing concerning the future now so seriously in jeopardy. Also they were not modest about their political opinions. Received social science seemed in-effective in the crisis. Mr. Einstein addressed the Foreign Press Association of the United Nations on November 11, 1947, on the occasion of their presentation to him of an award "in recognition of his valiant effort to make the world's nations understand the need of outlawing atomic energy as means of war, and of developing it as an instrument of peace." What he said could be regarded as a rebuke to contemporary statesmen, and coming from his towering scientific eminence its implications hurt. There were, he said, in the opposing camps enough people of sound judgment to work out solu-tions for factual difficulties; the trouble was that they were not per-mitted to do anything. A forced separation now made even negotia-tion impossible. As for the statesmen who were intrusted with the awful duty of finding a way to peace: "As long as contact between the two camps is limited to the official negotiations, I can see little prospect of an intelligent agreement, since considerations of nation-

9. Mr. Szilard, for instance, addressed an open letter to Premier Stalin sug-gesting a means for *rapprochement* (*Bulletin of the Atomic Scientists*, December, 1947); Mr. Urey continued to work for conciliation; and Mr. Morrison joined Mr. Shapley and others of the Council of Arts, Sciences, and Professions in a public protest against aggressive American foreign policy in June, 1948.

al prestige as well as the attempt to talk out of the window for the benefit of the masses make reasonable progress almost impossible."

This speech drew a reply from four Soviet scientists of international repute.[10] They insisted that the world government for which Mr. Einstein was working was a device of the imperialist Western powers to divide the world and to ruin Soviet Russia, and they begged him to cease his naïve and harmful efforts. Mr. Einstein replied in his turn that the Soviet scientists seemed to have nothing to offer but rigorous isolationism. He agreed with them that a socialist economy was better than a capitalist one; but it would not by itself cure all the world's ills. To think so was to subscribe to a kind of mythology. He then entered a lively defense of world government based on the argument that failure to achieve it would mean mutual annihilation:

> If we hold fast to the practice and concept of unlimited sovereignty of nations it only means that each country reserves the right for itself of pursuing its objectives through war-like means. Under the circumstances, every nation must be prepared for the possibility; this means that it must try with all its might to be superior to anyone else. This objective will dominate more and more our entire public life and will poison our youth long before the catastrophe is itself actually upon us. . . . This alone is on my mind in supporting the idea of world government. . . .[11]

Workers for world peace, for conciliation, or for the establishment of an inclusive world government were a harassed and unhappy lot by 1948; and, of all these, the scientists who persisted in such activities were the most harassed and unhappy. It was no wonder that so many of them, like Mark Twain in the pilot-house of his Mississippi steamer when the bullets began to fly, recalled that they had urgent business elsewhere. The Un-American Activities Committee of the House of Representatives, which had found in Mr. J. Parnell Thomas a worthy successor to Mr. Martin Dies, continued its irresponsible campaign of innuendoes, unproved charges, and general character assassination. Under its mandate to investigate, it questioned witnesses without allowing them counsel, bullied and harassed them, and then issued statements concerning them which

10. November 26, 1947 (*New Times* [Moscow]). The scientists were Sergei Vavilov, A. N. Frumkin, A. F. Joffe, and N. N. Semyonov.

11. *Bulletin of the Atomic Scientists,* February, 1948, pp. 35 ff. The letter of the Soviet scientists is to be found in the same issue.

had no basis in known facts. Its bias was antiliberal and anti-intellectual. It served very well the purpose of the big-business–militarist group which was now dominant in Washington. And it emphasized how little representative the United States Congress had become.

This committee conducted a special campaign to discredit the director of the Bureau of Standards, Mr. Edward U. Condon, himself a well-known scientist. Without the presentation of any proof, he was called "one of the weakest links in our chain of security," with reference particularly to Soviet Russia and to the atomic bomb. This accusation implied treason. Mr. Condon was repeatedly investigated—had been, in fact, before the committee's statement had been made—and was cleared by the FBI and the Atomic Energy Commission. But many a scientist and many a lay citizen, seeing the ordeal to which a useful, high-minded, patriotic, and responsible person could be subjected because he was perhaps a little independent and perhaps slightly tinged with unorthodoxy, decided to think twice thereafter before risking such an unprincipled attack. In theory Americans might be free; they might think their country's welfare required some criticism of government or of the business system; they might believe it their duty to take part in public discussion, especially in subjects in which they were expert. Actually, any American who chose thus to do his duty, to exercise his right of criticism, was extremely likely to suffer severe penalties. He might be publicly castigated; he might be persecuted; he might lose his job. And all without any pretense at due process.

The Congress not only supported this Un-American Activities Committee; it also abused its powers of investigation in other ways. Any committee was likely to copy the methods of Mr. Thomas and his colleagues, and many did. Furthermore, there turned up a whole crop of bills based on the heretofore unknown principle in American life of guilt by association. None of them passed; but the principle was heavily relied on in the extensive loyalty investigations carried out by the FBI all during the year. In interviews with the FBI, in 1948, so familiar a characteristic of American life, the friends, acquaintances, or even enemies of all government employees were invited to remember the remotest contacts between the subject of investigation and "radicals" or even "liberals"; such contacts gave a person bad marks. This policy was in contradiction to the whole tradition of freedom. Americans are naturally curious and have always felt it their right, if not their duty, to find out what others think or feel and what makes them act as they do. A democratic consensus must be based, it had been supposed, upon examination of facts and ideas. Thus the expression of all kinds of isms, however fantastic, has been free. Nevertheless, there have always been those who have wanted to protect others by preventing the expression of unorthodoxy. Until now they had always been a minority, but undeniably they had the legislative upper hand. True, the Mundt-Nixon Bill did not actually become law; but it did pass the House by an overwhelming majority and only died in the Senate because of premature adjournment for the Republican convention. This bill would have enacted into federal law the principle of guilt by association. It would have outlawed and driven underground all political unorthodoxy. On Hiroshima Day in 1948 it still seemed not unlikely that when the Congress met again, safely Republican, this bill might pass.

Not only constitutional freedoms were in danger; American political sportsmanship had probably never fallen lower than it did in the treatment during this year of Mr. Henry A. Wallace. Fighting all kinds of chicanery and blackmail, Mr. C. B. Baldwin and his colleagues put together in 1948 a full-scale political party. This party in its convention late in July was given the traditional name "Progressive" and made Mr. Wallace and Senator Glen H. Taylor its respective nominees for President and Vice-President. The convention in Philadelphia had been preceded by months of work by local groups in nearly all the states. After the La Follette third-party campaign of 1924 some of the states—Illinois, for instance—had revised their election laws to make it all but impossible for a new party to be organized. Yet by July, in spite of this handicap, and in spite of a campaign of misrepresentation joined in by almost the whole daily and weekly press, the party was officially accredited in all but a few states. The public opinion polls indicated that its support was now confined to from 6 to 8 per cent of the electorate; but for technical reasons it was generally believed that this estimate was low.

When the Wallace progressive movement first got under way, the Democratic party, which seemed to be at a low ebb after the loss of President Roosevelt and the policy changes of Mr. Truman, had been expected to try to win back these progressive votes. Obviously their loss might very well be responsible for a Democratic defeat in the presidential election. There were, however, no concessions offered to Mr. Wallace. Apparently his comments concerning Messrs. Krug, Snyder, Forrestal, and Harriman and General Marshall and others in the presidential family had been too sharp. Mr. Truman tried to achieve the same result in another way. In the report of a presidentially appointed Civil Rights Committee and in leftward-leaning speeches he tried to recapture the appearance of Rooseveltian attitudes. He succeeded mostly in alienating the Bourbon southerners and the labor movement generally, the one because he was too liberal on the race issue, the other because he had made one or two mistakes in handling labor.[12] Big-city bosses—Mr. Arvey in Chicago and Mr. Hague in Jersey City as well as Mr. James Roosevelt (now Democratic chairman in California) and Mayor O'Dwyer of New York City—joined in a futile and foolish movement to draft General Eisenhower. They were humiliatingly forced to go back to Mr. Truman when the General turned them down. And so the Democratic party began its campaign in so rickety and ramshackle a condition and with so weak a candidate that victory seemed improbable even though there were now, after the Roosevelt years, more Democrats than Republicans.

By July, Democratic defeat seemed to the professionals quite certain, for several million votes estimated for Wallace and Taylor could not now be bought back even at the expense of Democratic disruption. They might have been, say, in January or thereabouts, if Mr. Truman had been willing to turn to progressives instead of militarists and businessmen for advice and help. It was judged to be too late now. Lacking a political miracle, said the professionals, Mr. Truman was going to be defeated. This defeat would not bring about much change in a foreign policy which had been bipartisan and reactionary anyway; but anticipation of its defeat made other nations reluctant to deal with the Truman administration unless they could be assured of Mr. Dewey's consent. This impasse had occurred before in American history—it had occurred when President Hoover

---

12. He had, for instance, proposed drafting railway workers into the Army when a strike had seemed imminent in 1945.

132

was going out and President Roosevelt was coming in—but it had never happened before in the midst of so serious a crisis.

The convention which made the Progressive party a legal entity was held after those of the other parties. The atmosphere was thick with the hostility of the press. The Union League, across Walnut Street from the Progressive headquarters in the Bellevue-Stratford, seemed to have its very cornices drawn up in an outraged stare. It was said that the Communists had organized the party and that they ran the convention—wrote the platform, determined the rules, and so on. Mr. Wallace said frankly that he would not repudiate any support for his campaign, Communist or other. He was intent on peace, freedom, and abundance for Americans; and anyone could come along who wanted to. Many liberals who had refused to join the Progressives, even though they were alienated from Mr. Truman's administration, regarded the reports from Philadelphia as confirmation of their wisdom in staying out. Their position was buttressed by a formidably determined and unanimous attempt of press and pundits to make out that Mr. Wallace and his followers were subversive. The platform rejected the Truman Doctrine, called for abandonment of the draft just now going into effect, and asked that aid to needy people abroad be intrusted to the United Nations. This was the Communist program, too; and it was said to be all but disloyal, considering the state of American-Russian relations.

So the Progressive party of 1948 came into official being with even less approval among the conservatives than had those of other years, 1924, 1912, and earlier. The enlargement of its numbers would obviously be difficult with the faint aura of disloyalty about it. Mr. Wallace might well have prayed to be delivered from some of his supporters who were in fact known to be Communists and some others who were their sympathizers. He felt unable to repudiate Communist support without himself being antiliberal; but Progressives who were repelled by this association felt that Communists need not have been allowed to dominate the party machinery. Consequently, Mr. Wallace failed to attract the support he should have had; and, after the widely publicized convention, his strength steadily leaked away.

What was not much noticed by the press, for obvious reasons, was the seriousness with which the Progressive's platform treated the idea of world government. Theirs was not mere lip service to the United Nations and some smooth words about its enlargement; they made a full-scale acknowledgment that peace was only possible in the framework of government and that government was only possible if all peoples were included. They evidently meant world government as it had been defined by the framers of the World Constitution.

This constitution had been published in the spring.[13] It was obviously the result of much thought and prolonged discussion; it showed many compromises; it was deficient in the economic machinery needed in a complicated global society; but, for all that, it did approach the outline of a world organization. It achieved its defined intention: to show what it was that those who advocated world government must be talking about and so make its discussion more realistic.

The published document did at least dispel the foggy penumbra that surrounded the idea of one law for everyone. The mechanism outlined in this constitution *would be world government* until some new draft should be offered or until this one should be amended. For the drafters had met most of the issues any constitution-makers would have to meet and had outlined a possible settlement of each of them. They might not have settled problems satisfactorily; but they had visualized them.

One of the most difficult questions they attempted to answer was: Is there an institutional device which can keep the peace without performing any of the other functions of government?[14] After two years of debate and research the committee decided that any such approach would be embarrassingly like treating the symptoms of a disease without understanding and reaching its causes. The disease would not be reduced in incidence, and there would always be a good chance of its escaping from control—with fatal results, since the disease itself was now so deadly.

13. "Preliminary Draft of a World Constitution," published in *Common Cause*, March, 1948. The preliminary draft was signed by R. M. Hutchins, G. A. Borgese, M. J. Adler, Stringfellow Barr, Albert Guérard, H. A. Innis, Erich Kahler, W. G. Katz, C. H. McIlwain, Robert Redfield, and R. G. Tugwell.

14. Elisabeth Mann Borgese, "Why a Maximalist Constitution?" *Common Cause*, July, 1948, pp. 199 ff.

Having determined that there could be no security without justice and freedom as well, the committee was free to ask itself: What are the fundamentals of any government? They answered: In any effective government there must be ways to make laws, ways to execute them, and ways to interpret them; and there must be means by which the society can anticipate and shape its future. All such institutions must be of global scope; the unity in the physical and social structure of the world, in so far as we understand it, must be recognized and given expression in the instrument of government. If it is not, the potentialities of mankind will never be realized in full. Properly conceived, laws are an expression of man's relations to his whole environment, including other men; they define the ways in which he must act in order at worst to survive and at best to prosper. They are thus not only ways of settling disputes among litigants or of avoiding them by establishing rules; they are the embodiment of natural law in society.

The constitution presented by the committee was recognized to be only a poor and relatively ineffectual approximation of a document which expressed the need of man for guidance on his journey toward harmony with nature. There would be others later on far better suited to this purpose. But it was at least a beginning. It provided a way of selecting a world legislature to make laws; it provided an executive to carry them out; and it provided a judiciary for interpretation. Furthermore, it specified several bodies, not adequately fleshed out, but still suggested, for visualizing the social future and for keeping society knit together and harmonious as it advanced. It was bothered, naturally, by many transitional problems —problems so apparently insoluble that after a look at them so ingenious a social engineer as Mr. Beardsley Ruml had dropped out of the discussions altogether. The committee's work had seemed to him premature. Perhaps it had been. But the alternative to a fairly quick *modus vivendi* now might well be destruction. After a look at the difficulties and at the alternative, the rest, except Mr. Reinhold Niebuhr, who said world community must precede world organization, had gone on with their task.[15] Perhaps Mr. Niebuhr, too, may

15. Mr. J. M. Landis dropped out later for other reasons.

have been right. The rest of the committee felt, however, that he was putting the cart before the horse.[16]

The first thought of most of those who looked at the tentative document was that it was a brave effort. The second thought of many was that there ought to be further attempts and that these ought to make more use of social engineers and of fundamental physicists, both those who were investigating the universe-like microbodies within the tiniest atoms and those who were becoming familiar with the vast spheres in what we call "space." In these realms lay the fundamental materials of which societies as well as visible physical phenomena were only the obvious manifestation. There the secrets of life, of nature, of society were to be found, and there, in fact, they were now being searched for.[17] It already appeared that the universe was a universe and not a pluriverse and that the universe opened out into the subatomic spaces as well as those far ones toward which the new telescopes were now reaching for observation.

Man's earth, and man, occupied a place somewhere between the small and the great. He was not the center about which the universe was organized; he was rather integral with it, a part of its arrangement, unique only in being able to think about it more connectedly than could any other form of life. As he accumulated knowledge with the new instruments at his disposal—cyclotrons, betatrons, enlarged photographic telescopes—and disposed his knowledge in more meaningful ways, he would be able to apply it. He might manage not only materials, forces, plants, and animals but himself, so that, as Emerson had long ago suggested, he might at last come

16. Mr. Hutchins' answer to Mr. Niebuhr ran as follows: "The Swiss, by living under the Swiss constitution, have formed the Swiss community. . . . We, by living under the American Constitution, have formed the American community and the American state. It is possible that the peoples of the earth, by living under a world constitution, might form a world community and a world state. If a world community were a prerequisite to a world state, we should never need a world state. If men were angels, we should not need law and government. Law and custom are among the greatest of all educational forces. . . . Enough has been said to suggest that because a world community does not exist now, we need not suppose that a world state cannot arise" (address at the opening of the University of Wyoming's Institute of International Affairs, June 15, 1948 [*Common Cause*, August, 1948, pp. 1 ff.]).

17. Cf. R. G. Tugwell, "Notes on Some Implications of Oneness in the World," *Common Cause*, November, 1947, pp. 165 ff.

into tune with the universe. Only then would he be able to shape a really useful government. For the present he was under pressure. Before he knew nearly enough, he had to take emergency social measures simply to avoid annihilation. What it seemed possible for him to do, at least, was to go in the direction which he understood already was required of him for survival. This he could do under the constitution suggested by the committee. Under it he could take those precautions necessary to prevent the frictions in society from overcoming its productive power. Under it, also, he could center the control of destructive force in world-public instruments and take them away from those individuals, corporations, or nations that would, if they were allowed to, risk using force for their own advantage, even now that force had been so horribly implemented.

It was true that this constitution could not claim more than the roughest adjustment to modern science, and it was able to suggest solutions for no more than part of the pressing issues which were only now being visualized. Take, for instance, this basic question: What contribution are the different peoples of the present to be allowed to make to the future population? There was a dilemma to be faced here. The peoples least well adapted to civilized living would, if allowed, maintain the highest birth rates. And if, in a unified world, health measures and general sharing of food brought death rates into equalization, or came near doing so, the future would obviously belong to the Asiatics. In a few generations the contribution of Anglo-Saxons would have almost disappeared and that of the Latins would have diminished greatly. What kind of men were to inherit the earth? What prejudices there were to combat, what prides to conciliate, what difficulties to overcome in gaining acceptance for any decision on such a question! And how rough an approach to it was represented by the electoral regions proposed in the committee's constitution! And how ironic that it should be the Anglo-Saxons, perhaps about to disappear into an interracial mélange, who should be almost alone in having any interest at all in world government!

There were other questions, a multitude of them, of almost equal difficulty. For instance, were those nations or peoples who had attained high productivity, and so a high level of living, to be allowed to keep this level? Or would they be required to find a laissez faire accommodation with others who had not progressed in this way? Was there, in other words, to be free trade, free immigration, and free access to resources and to capital? Or would the have-nots consent to a very gradual equalization which would have the effect of bringing up their standards rather than of reducing all peoples to the level of the lowest? In spite of the increase in productivity in recent decades, both agricultural and industrial, man had been so incredibly thoughtless and wasteful as he multiplied from a few hundred thousand a millennium ago to well over two billions in 1948 that his increased numbers depended on nearly exhausted mineral and plant materials. The magic of invention, of taking thought, might substitute itself for many of these materials. Energies might be conjured out of air or sea, and it could be seen how man could get along without wood when his forests were gone and oil when his wells were pumped dry. But what would he substitute for the minerals in the top soil, which supplied the necessary trace elements for human life, when the top soil had mostly run down into the rivers? And what would he use for food? There was hunger among three-fourths, perhaps more, of the world's people now. How would it be when erosion had gone on for a few more decades and the population had risen to three billions and more?

The constitution had provisions under which these problems could be approached. But they were weak and very tentative. Not nearly enough had been done to estimate needs of the future or to shape it in accordance with the requirements for continued survival. It was strong in matters of freedom, but it did not visualize at all the problems of discipline within a collectivism; and these were at least as important for the coming decades as the securing of men's rights. True, it emphasized duties along with privileges, but it did not appear to make duties as compelling as the respect for rights.

The constitution was, in these and in many other features, a tentative, even an obviously defective document. Yet, faulty though it was, the justification for devising and publishing it was ample.

It may be profitable to examine the provisions of this constitution more concretely. One of the first problems was: What should be the composition of the lawmaking body? Whom should the legislature represent? Trying to find a solution which would conform to reasonable requirements that an advanced and restrained peoples be given weight and that the canons of democracy be respected, the committee experimented with a number of devices. A unicameral legislature with equal representation for existing nations it immediately discarded. This imitation of the United States Senate would give Nicaragua and Norway the same representation as India and France. The directly opposite solution would apportion representatives according to numbers in the population. This arrangement would please the populous nations, but it would anger the small ones; and, besides, it would make technical difficulties of some importance. If the smallest nation was given one representative and the others multiples of this number, the legislature would have several thousand members—a nice opportunity for demagogues but not for serious lawmakers. Besides, India and China between them would have a majority. It seemed so unrealistic to suggest this solution that it was abandoned.

There followed an attempt to modify popular representation by weightings of economic position, fertility rates, literacy levels, and so on. There was an uneasy feeling, however, that these represented wealth rather than anything else, and opposition to them grew. But there was no better solution so long as extant states were taken as the basis of representation. In the end the committee divided the world into regions for electoral purposes only. Local government of existing states was not to be interfered with. This solution achieved a reasonably small legislative body. But it did not satisfy those who felt strongly about the administrative inefficiency of small states or who saw remaining possibilities of troublemaking. It was, in fact, a compromise.

The committee hoped to create a strong but not dictatorial executive. It felt that the executive should be responsible to the legislature rather than independent. Independence leads to checks and balances, a system more suited to the calmer, less dynamic eighteenth-century than to the present. A modern government carries large responsibilities for economic life, social welfare, and technological progress. Its institutions need to be mobile, elastic, energetic, capable of originality. Necessarily much of this kind of responsibility should fall on the executive under broad policy authorization of the legislature. Contemporary governments have been moving in this direction, some eagerly, some reluctantly.

The committee finally hit upon a plural executive, whose economic and welfare powers were broad. It also provided for the creation of such special agencies as might be required to carry out the granted powers. The President was to have a subordinate, the Chancellor, who would carry the more onerous administrative operations and who would deal with the legislature.

To a Chamber of Guardians was intrusted the whole system of force. The President was made a member, of course, of the Guardians; but the provision of colleagues for this duty was a really important division of his office. The Guardians represented the response of the committee to anxiety about irresponsible use of atomic fire or of a chemical or bacteriological weapon. To them was assigned exclusively "the control and use of the armed forces of the Federal Republic of the World." The membership was fixed at seven, to be elected by the Council; their number was to be enlarged by the addition of one former President; and their chairman was to be the President "acting in his capacity as Protector of the Peace."

The Guardians represented a deliberate blurring of the classic distinction among legislature, executive, and judiciary. They not only supplemented and divided the executive, but they were also given power, in time of emergency, to "demand and appropriate such . . . funds as the emergency demands. . . ." True, the state of emergency was not lightly to be entered on; it was to be "proposed by the Chamber of Guardians and proclaimed currently by a two-thirds majority of the Council and a two-thirds majority of the Grand Tribunal for a period not in excess of six months. . . ." But during such an emergency the Guardians would have not only control of all lethal weapons but unlimited power over the funds necessary to multiply and use them. They would be, then, the whole of government.

The judiciary, as set up in the committee draft, also blended somewhat with other branches of government. The President was to act as Chief Justice and as chairman of the Grand Tribunal. Both the executive and the legislative were thus brought into the judiciary. Otherwise, the Grand Tribunal was to consist of sixty justices, to be divided into five Benches. Each Bench was to have special duties, one to deal with constitutional issues between the primary organs and powers of the World Government, another to deal with conflicts between the World Government and any of its constituent units, and so on through to the adjudication of conflicts among individuals when they affected the interpretation of federal law. The Supreme Court, for review and for decision as to competence among the Benches, would be composed of representatives from each Bench with the Chief Justice-President as their chairman.

Supplementing this judicial system was a Tribune of the People. He was to be a "spokesman for the minorities." In this capacity he would "defend the natural and civil rights of individuals and groups against violation or neglect" by the government.

Finally, a Planning Agency was provided to estimate future needs and bring society into accord with its possibilities. It would have twenty-one members, appointed by the President for terms of twelve years. Their duties, however, were no more than sketched. They were to envisage income, prepare budgets for expenditure, and pass on all "plans for the improvement of the World's physical facilities"; and plans for the productive exploitation of resources and inventions were to be submitted to such agencies for this purpose as it might establish.

This was the alternative to chaos proposed by one group of scholars. It was widely discussed.[18] But whether it made its way into the main stream of thought among the world's people, it was hard to say. It seemed doubtful. The Russians were inclined to reject it summarily as a cover for the aggressive plans of the "monopolists and ideologists of the bourgeoisie."[19] The scholars who produced it had hoped that the Soviets would recognize as sincere this attempt to furnish a neutral mechanism; and they went on hoping that such recognition would yet prevail. But the climate was undeniably hostile. War had been imminent for so long that efforts to avert it were regarded as necessarily insincere. It had not been possible to secure the collaboration of Russian scholars in the enterprise; and it was probably too much to hope that any such scheme produced exclusively in the West would ever be acceptable to the prideful and suspicious Russians.

This last seemed to have been one reason for the breakdown of

18. It was reprinted whole and commented on in the *Saturday Review of Literature.*

19. *Common Cause*, August, 1948, p. 34, quoting Radio Moscow for May 3, 1948.

the atomic-energy discussions and, indeed, for the state of desuetude into which the United Nations had by now fallen. For the United Nations was all but moribund. Its bureaucracy functioned at Lake Success; its subsidiary agencies held conferences and passed resolutions; its Assembly met on stated occasions; and its Security Council had not yet broken up. But it was being bypassed more and more frequently by the great powers; and the most serious issue—the mutual aggressions of the Soviet Union and the United States—it was completely helpless to settle. Everyone was by now aware that the labors at San Francisco in 1944 had not resulted in a world government. The only hope in the United Nations lay in its amending provisions, which, by a tour de force similar to that effected in Philadelphia in 1787, could be the means through which a government might be established. The United Nations as an institution was, in fact, obscured from view by the mists of conflict. Not much was heard of it during the year—except for its action on Palestine, and, in that, it was shamefully abused. The United States was by now so used to taking unilateral action that it did not hesitate to act unilaterally through the United Nations, thus completing the degradation of the supposedly international institution.[20]

The disillusionment of all those who had hoped that the United Nations was something which it was not was now nearly complete. Some felt that this disillusion was the prelude to a healthier realism. In an age in which there was time for such impulses to spread and have their effect this might be so. But time was now incredibly truncated. In so far as communication was not cut off by iron curtains,

20. Cf. Summer Welles's *We Need Not Fail*, a résumé of policy in the Palestine case and an exposé of cynical attitudes toward the Jewish people which can seldom have been equaled in American history. The case of Palestine happened to engage American interests in several ways. For instance, American oil interests wanted to exploit the immense oil reserves of Arabia; and this created an impulse to support Arabs against the Jews. But also Jews were important in American politics in strategic states like New York, and 1948 was a presidential election year; this impelled Mr. Truman to conciliate the Jews. At one time Mr. Forrestal, as a Wall Streeter and Defense Secretary, was almost openly opposing Mr. Truman's reelection. Then too there was the complication that Palestine was in that borderland between East and West where local conflicts might at any time turn into general war. The Palestine issue was therefore a continuously delicate matter, too delicate to be left to the United Nations, in the opinion of American policy-makers. But these policy-makers, being in conflict and sometimes being confused, made of Palestine during the year a horrible example not only of how not to treat an international agency but also of how not to advance the best interests of their own nation.

as in Russia, or corrupted by widespread misrepresentation, as in the United States, it was swifter; but many times swifter was the tempo of destruction which might be let loose by the Bomb, by bacterial warfare, or by chemical destruction. Mr. Trygve Lie in his annual report pointed to a full-scale race in the preparation of these apocalyptic weapons. It seemed unlikely that reason and realism would work more rapidly than the forces for destruction. Yet reason was working. In any other time its advances would have been notable.

The people of the globe had had lessons in geopolitics during the war which immeasurably advanced their education as world citizens. It would not be true to say that there were no provincial thinkers still remaining, any more than it would be true to say that nationalism as a psychological phenomenon had been eliminated. But that striking advances had been made in both these matters, there could be no doubt. American boys had flown across the top of Africa to the Persian Gulf and on to Burma and China. Journeys across the Arctic to Russia were to them commonplace. Nowadays—since the war—hundreds of flights a week were undertaken on regular schedules across oceans which had recently been regarded as barriers to intercourse. These would be completed in hours which would correspond with days or weeks a few decades ago. Many a family got its son or daughter back from jungle, desert, or island which had been literally unknown before. The earth was not only round; it was small. It was all visible and comprehensible at once. Its divisions and conflicts were bound soon to become absurd. But would they seem so soon enough to prevent its quarrels from ending in destruction?

The old geopolitics was as dead as the old physics and the old economics. It had been based for two centuries on a sea-power–land-mass formula which air transportation and radio communication, in their latest phases, were making wholly obsolete. During this year a military plane had repeatedly flown at speeds considerably faster than the speed of sound. This was a piloted plane. But experiments were known to be going forward on unpiloted and much faster missiles. A rocket, steered by radio, proceeding at several thousand miles an hour and equipped with an atomic war head was now the prospect for the next open conflict. The consensus of scientists was that there was no defense.

There was still a difference among the experts as to whether the Soviet Union was equipped with these weapons, but none as to whether presently she would be. The United States was not yet satisfactorily stocked—that is, so equipped as to be able to destroy Russian war potential in one massive attack. The American military apparently felt that neither side wanted open conflict for some years and that the sparring all along the European–Near East border line would not be allowed to result in so provocative an incident as to make it unavoidable. Nevertheless, the tension there was serious, and apprehension concerning it was extreme throughout the world.

It was surprising how quickly people had abandoned the old geopolitical concepts. The United States Navy tried to maintain the fiction of sea power. It began the construction of a vast supercarrier and worked at the improvement of the submarine. But it was obvious that sea power was now supplementary. So with the Army: The talk was that after all it was the Army which had to do the real fighting; it would provide and defend the necessary air bases; it would follow and consolidate air attack; it would occupy. But it was obvious that these too were supplementary functions. They belonged to the age of railroads and steamships, of artillery and tanks. People generally were well into the psychology of the push-button war, even ahead, for once, of the technicians. They thought in terms of vast and rapid airlifts, of continents as islands, of resources as less important than know-how. It was an age of miracles, and they expected the miracles to be produced.

This was the West. What of the East? Was it true, as Mr. Hutchins suggested, that the East was interested not in security but in hope of improvement? And was it true, as Mr. Toynbee suggested, that the religious heart of civilization lay in the West? Mr. Toynbee also suggested that it was Western technology which had created the crisis which could only find a religious resolution.[21] The East's teem-

---

21. Mr. Toynbee's *Study of History* in its abridgment by D. C. Somerville and more especially his *Civilization on Trial* (London: Oxford University Press, 1948) were being read by great numbers of Americans in 1948. He was, in fact, a kind of phenomenon. He seemed to bring people a larger view, to establish a more commodious framework within which to judge the seriousness of contemporary problems. Atomic fire was easier to look at with the perspective of al-Gabartī and

ing millions lived in a misery which had been little mitigated by Western technology. So far, perhaps, technology had had the opposite effect. It had reduced the death rate, but not the birth rate, and had not communicated the improved techniques of production which alone could have caused a higher level of life as population increased. Could the East—India, Indonesia, China—acquire these techniques, or would the uncontrolled reproduction rate there drive living standards even lower? The most careful students of these matters were the most doubtful whether standards could be raised. Yet the making of two worlds into one depended wholly on such an equalizing of living conditions as would bring both to the same concern for the future, to the same sense of brotherhood.

There was much surviving religious rivalry. The Roman center and the orthodox center in Moscow were militantly set against each other. But these were churches, not religions; the antagonists were hierarchies, not peoples. It might still be true, as Mr. Toynbee said, that religion was likely to be "the plane on which the coming centripetal counter movement" would declare itself.[22] A social scientist, however, found it easier to think that the evolution of technology would settle East-West differences. If, as Mr. Toynbee suggested, the center of civilization might be expected to locate itself somewhere between the western pole of the world's population in Europe and North America and its eastern pole in China and India, air transport, instantaneous communication, and divorce from orthodox resources seemed more important to the shift than did religion. But it was interesting that Mr. Toynbee would plant the future capital of the world hypothetically in the neighborhood of Baber's Farghana "in the familiar Transoxianian meeting-place and debating ground of the religions and philosophies of India, China, Iran, Syria, and Greece."

In that day the West and the East would be one. It was interesting to speculate whether world government would assist in bringing one-

---

the emperor Baber. The easy and familiar mention of men long gone, and of their civilizations, lessened the tension, somehow, by making it seem less important what happened now. Then too Mr. Toynbee was somewhat comforting about the Russians; and he was deeply religious. All this gave him a vogue which few intellectuals attain in their lifetimes.

22. *Civilization on Trial*, p. 94.

ness about or whether world government would be a product of the world community thus established. This is a question we have met before. Mr. Hutchins disposed of it summarily. But deeper examination made no substantial change in his conclusion. The civilizations of the past which had lasted longest and made the greatest contribution to succeeding ones had been those which had grown up in, and been fostered by, a containing framework of law. Laws can only be made by governments; the making of a law is a process of government. Where individuals, groups, and peoples came into a system of this sort, there was mutual tolerance, a process for the hearing and acceptance of ideas, and peace in which continuous work could be carried on by scholars as well as farmers and craftsmen. Such conditions prevailed in the Roman imperium, for instance, to which the modern world owes so enormous a debt. Such were the conditions in the great days of Islam, to which we owe most of what we do not owe to Roman-Greek thought. When these imperiums went to pieces, there ensued what were quite correctly called the Dark Ages. The distinguishing characteristic of this long period was lack of government. Lack of sufficiently general government allowed incessant wasting conflict during which accomplishments were registered only in isolated undisturbed communities—monasteries, small mountainous principalities, or islands.

However one looked at the problem, the containing structure seemed necessary to the development of high culture, and the time had come when no containing structure could be less than worldwide. It could not otherwise rid itself of the same incessant conflict, or the prospect of it, which had tormented medieval states. In the year 1948, even in the United States, most powerful of modern nations, science had been driven underground. Great areas of it had to be carried on in closets without that fructifying interchange and open discussion which are the life of scholarship. It would not be different, apparently, until the world had been unified politically as well as technologically.

CHAPTER V *1949*

AUGUST to August, 1948–49, was "a year of jitters and yammers." It was hard to recall a time when those in charge of political affairs for the human race had seemed so incapable of reaching the arrangements common folk demanded. Though it appears paradoxical to say so, Western capitalism and Eastern communism were both enormously stronger on August 6, 1949, than they had been on August 6, 1948—a dangerous growth of power that further demonstrated the universal refusal to learn the lesson of Hiroshima. Violence seemed all the time more likely to break out when either of the protagonists possessed sufficient confidence in its own strength. The only hope was recognition by each that the overwhelming predominance present strategy called for was unattainable.

I had no reason to change my estimate that the year 1952 would be about the end of the required technological term; from then, jeopardy might well be total unless a standoff came to be mutually recognized. And even now the United States appeared to be losing faith in the persuasive potency of capitalist doctrines. Free-enterprise theorists still believed that their system could produce more than any alternate system, but there were signs of diminishing confidence as something like depression threatened to stifle the Western economy. James V. Forrestal, Secretary of Defense, destroyed himself in an access of despair about his nation's ability to survive the coming crisis. The Congress floundered among innumerable futile investigations, determined to find a Red Devil to blame for American moral inadequacy. At the same time, communism, though it moved toward a defeat in western Europe, made incredible gains in China, thus demonstrating what theorists had been afraid to con-

147

clude from the single instance of Russia: that totalitarian political organization (whether Communist or any other) was very well suited to the governing of the earth's backward places.

Whether Russia was to be solidly backed by China in the coming crisis remained to be seen; even if she were, she would not necessarily strengthen her position thereby in any specific conflict. For China, of all places on earth, was backward, amorphous, and diffused; and she would, it was thought, be generations in finding her own direction and organization. By that time the conflict now impending would be over. But the acquisition of a powerful—if only potential—ally was now a fact.

On the other hand, American misgivings not withstanding, the West had become immensely stronger during the year, although the business-military influence in Washington had suffered a noticeable decline. There had been some disappearances—Messrs. Clayton and Draper, for instance, had gone, and General Marshall had been displaced as Secretary of State by Mr. Dean Acheson. No one of these changes necessarily had any significance by itself; but the fact that Mr. Forrestal, General Marshall, Mr. Harriman (as Secretary of Commerce), and Admiral Leahy had departed diminished by a good deal the visual cohesiveness of the group which Americans had identified with the preventive war that was their immediate danger.

If capitalists no longer had sufficient faith in the persuasiveness of their doctrines, neither, it seemed, had the Communists. They too were in a mood for violence, and 1948–49 was a year in which they took such enormous risks that only the inability of their opponents to believe what they saw and heard, together with their unreadiness for war, enabled the Soviets to get through successive provocations without being attacked.

The focus of provocation throughout the year was Berlin. The Berlin of these years was the product of Yalta and Potsdam; but back of Yalta and Potsdam lay those differences which had been so imperfectly reconciled as the late war had drawn to its end. Russia had been an inscrutable and mysterious presence in the councils of Europe from earliest days. Her mighty masses of men and vast stretches of undeveloped land had lent her an influence far greater than was ever warranted by her ability to bring it to bear on any given occasion. But in the last war she had unexpectedly found new resources of technological competence and practical leadership. Those strengths and riches, which had never before been more than potential, had suddenly emerged as real and present. Stalin had brought them with him proudly to Teheran (where he had asked the famous question about the Pope's divisions); and it was he and the new Russian competence, rather than American argument, which had determined the decision, against Mr. Churchill's resistance, for a second front in Europe even after the Allies' successes in Africa.[1] Undoubtedly there were now statesmen who regretted that Operation Overlord had not taken place in 1942 rather than in 1944, before the Russian avalanche had buried all eastern Europe in its advance. The Communists were now in possession there; and how or whether they would ever be displaced was a question to which no one could see any answer.

Here, the immovable object (Russia) and the irresistible force (the United States) were meeting. Here they theoretically shared the governing of one of the world's great capital cities. Actually they maneuvered for advantage. What particular incidents were from time to time used as excuses was immaterial. It was clear that both sides, in spite of verbal violence, wanted neither a settlement nor a final break which might result in hostilities. Such a state of tension without an outbreak of actual war might seem almost impossible to maintain by mutual (tacit) agreement; but they managed it. And on August 6, 1949, matters looked no better and no worse than they had on August 6, 1948. But meanwhile the home folk of both sides had lived in deathly fear of that final provocative incident which would commit them to destruction. Thus, although matters looked neither better nor worse in Berlin, they looked far worse in Washington and in Moscow.

The Berlin blockade and the answering airlift—Operation Vittles —was one of the strangest interludes in modern history. It began with a breakdown in the four-power governing body of the city, a

1. Churchill's amazing concentration on the integrity of the old empire, which younger statesmen knew had already disappeared, appears in every account of the high-level negotiations—except Churchill's own. The Churchill who had planned Gallipoli would have planned another in 1941–43 if he had been permitted, in order to shut Russia out of Europe and protect the Mediterranean lifeline to the East.

cumulative failure to agree which finally resulted in abandoning sessions. The city, in so far as is possible for a social organism, ceased to function. Diets, already at a level of malnutrition, fell ever further; unemployment increased; reconstruction, except for listless clearing away of rubble, almost ceased. Yet, in spite of the folly of such an arrangement, it could not be discarded by either side without loss of face; a point in the maintenance of prestige became more important than the business of getting on with the repairing of the ravages of war. The blockade itself was begun as one of those curious Russian *démarches* to which withdrawn bodies like the Politburo are apt to resort in their ignorance of the outside world and in forgetfulness that others than Russians may not be forced to accept a palpable falsehood. They closed the railroads and then the highways and canals into Allied Berlin "for repair." The thought was, apparently, that, when the Berliners in the Allied sectors had suffered enough, they would force the Allied officials to accept Russian conditions for municipal management (including the Russian currency). Either that or the Allies would withdraw altogether from such a hopeless situation and leave all eastern Germany to be incorporated into the Soviet system. The airlift was the amazing response to this pressure.

It soon became obvious that the Berlin episode was likely to turn into a glorification of American airpower. Such a result could be prevented in Russia, where the press was official; but the rest of the world drew its own conclusions—including the Germans themselves. For now the Berlin incident, besides being the contact point of antagonistic imperial systems, was turning also into an incident in a contest for the favors of the former mutual enemy. By spring Western Allies and Russians alike were engaged in an unseemly effort to persuade the German nation that its best interests lay in affiliation with East or West. Each was posturing and beckoning as though no unpleasantness had to be remembered. Hitlerism was far from dead; but no one outside Germany seemed now to recall its dangers.

The strange fact that, with a war against naziism hardly over, the wooing of numerous little Nazis should begin before the trials of the big ones had ended was remarked by a few carping observers; but mostly attention centered on the regard of the Germans for one or the other of the occupation forces. Yet the competition was obviously silly and futile. That Germans (or any other people) should love or even admire their conquerors was against nature, especially German nature. And that they had not recovered from their recent delusions of grandeur was painfully obvious to the most casual newspaper reader. Unless the occupation ended promptly, its most significant effect would be a mere political overturn; the Hitler crowd would be superseded by another no more humble, no more realistic, no less devoted to authoritarianism.

It had been part of the Yalta-Potsdam policy to divide Germany not only in order to satisfy the occupying nations but to weaken the Reich. During the war there had been put forward a plan, which had seemed to emerge from the vengeful rage of the Jews who had suffered so from Hitlerism, for reducing Germany to an agricultural, perhaps even a pastoral, level. At one stage President Roosevelt had consented to this scheme, a consent which he regretted and from which he withdrew—but never frankly and wholly; and remnants of this kind of thinking had gone into the final plan for division. The Yalta-Potsdam policy was intended to break up the German organization, to humble the German people, to encourage such elements of divisiveness as the South German jealousy of Prussian discipline and efficiency. It completely overlooked the major contribution of Germany to the European economy. This oversight became painfully apparent as time passed and as American billions were annually needed to feed, clothe, and reconstruct an artificially paralyzed western Europe.

Out of this obvious situation, to which the new school of German politicians called attention over and over, the contest for authentic sponsorship of unity arose. Both Russians and Americans began to pose as workers for reintegration, and, before the dismantling of heavy industry had been completed, big business in America and Britain was attempting to prevent decartelization. One of the worst internal quarrels of the year centered in this issue. It was feared that American and British capitalists were at work to control German industrial power and use it to dominate the economy of all Europe. Some such process was certainly in progress, reinforced by the absurdity of division, by a reviving German nationalism, and by a growing reluctance among American taxpayers to support their former enemies in idleness. To add to the confusion, the Allies were far from agreed on the meaning of the democracy they offered in competition with Russian communism. To the Americans it might be identified with capitalism; but there was after all a Socialist government in Britain, though it sometimes seemed that neither the Foreign Office nor the Colonial Office had discovered it; and France, though mixed in economic opinion, to a man wanted Germans and Germany kept in such a condition that France would be safe from another attack.

In the climate of confusion and recrimination, among the Allies and between them and the Russians, the essential problem of European recovery had little chance for solution even with the generous Marshall Plan subsidies. There had been formed a European Recovery Administration to administer American funds, and under American prodding some semblance of European organization had come into being—but only a semblance, only enough to conciliate American opinion. That Europeans ought to help themselves was an entirely reasonable idea to Americans; but that they should be expected to do it at the expense of nationalism seemed utterly unreasonable to most European politicians. On this difference, as well as on conflict over the German contribution, the recovery efforts seemed in the summer of 1949 to be breaking down. The Marshall Plan conception that American aid need continue only until 1952 was obviously insufficient. American aid would have to continue indefinitely unless (1) Germany were allowed to become unified and productive and (2) unless something like a European federation should come into being, so that economic co-operation might replace the nationalistic competition which Marshall Plan funds were undoubtedly being used to bolster.

Unity was something Europe probably would rather sacrifice American aid than accept. For the old Great Powers were the European headquarters of empires whose richest regions lay elsewhere in the world. A United States of Europe was an attractive conception to Americans, who saw it as a bulwark against Soviet power; but French, Dutch, and especially British statesmen thought, not in European, but in imperial terms. Americans could never quite understand this preoccupation. Their imperialistic moments had been fleeting; rather, their businessmen had earlier learned how to exploit backward peoples without the extension of sovereignty, so that their imperialism was of a different species. When the flag was said to follow the dollar, what was meant was that, if necessary, the marines would collect bankers' debts from recalcitrant nations. It was cheaper and less troublesome not to have the responsibilities of governmental affiliation.

This procedure the old nations of Europe, with their centuries of imperial tradition, simply could not bring themselves to adopt. To them it was an abandonment of responsibility, a cynical disregard of obligations long since undertaken; and, when confronted with the demand for independence now sweeping the remotest reaches of hitherto loyal colonial areas, they cited the undoubted fact that the peoples there were not competent to carry on civilized governmental operations. Behind this reasoning lay not only tradition but the long adjustment European nations had made to their roots in colonial lands. Without this support their large populations, their industries, their enormous service organizations, would wither away. For colonialism, European federation was simply no substitute. Americans might answer that colonialism was an anachronistic system which could no longer be maintained anyway and that desperate new measures were urgently needed; but Europeans were bound to cling desperately, as long as they could manage it, to their empires.

That the United States should attempt to force economic union as the price of Marshall Plan aid thus made sense to American, but not to European, statesmen. The issues involved a reversal of many historic arrangements and traditions. Americans were not ignorant of this fact and were not unsympathetic. But, being removed from the problem, they were undoubtedly inclined to overlook difficulties and complications and to dwell exasperatingly on essentials. If the old colonialism had to give way to a new pattern of voluntary co-operation in which no nation, merely because of tradition, would be able to maintain a favorable place, it seemed to Americans that this necessity might better be recognized sooner than later—especially since the expense of maintaining the empty pretense fell largely on them. If the empires could forget their vanishing glories, much could be done to make Europe self-sufficient. But even Socialist Britain and the Communist parties in Holland, Belgium, and France had strange theoretical lapses on the colonial issue.

It was partly to the resolution of this dilemma (as well as to a strengthening of the "free" world against communism) that American policy was now being directed. It consisted now not only in the Truman Doctrine, the Marshall Plan, and the Atlantic Pact, but also in a general offer of aid which was becoming known everywhere as the "Fourth Point."[2]

When he had made his proposal, the President had had no program for the implementation of this "Fourth Point." It was variously interpreted as meaning the extension of American private investment, of governmental aid to backward areas (both where the governments were independent and where they were part of some Empire system), and of technical assistance, in contrast with financial aid.[3] The interpretations were obviously in accordance with the interest of those who made them. This indefiniteness aroused a good deal of criticism, and undoubtedly it would have been better if the elaborate studies of the ensuing six months, made by many agencies, constituting an interdepartmental committee, had been made before rather than after the announcement. As it was, there were determined attempts to capture the program. Since the Department of State was in formal charge, however, the outcome could fairly be

2. It had been put forward in President Truman's inaugural address to the Congress in January, 1949, and had happened to be the fourth in his enumeration of issues.

3. What President Truman actually said in this inaugural address, January 20, 1949, with respect to the Fourth Point was this:

"We must embark on a bold new program for making the benefits of our scientific advances and industrial progress available for the improvement and growth of underdeveloped areas.

". . . We should make available to peace-loving peoples the benefit of our store of technical knowledge in order to help them realize their aspirations for a better life. And, in co-operation with other nations, we should foster capital investment in areas needing development.

"Our aim should be to help the free peoples of the world, through their own efforts to produce more food, more clothing, more materials for housing and more mechanical power to lighten their burdens. . . .

"Such new economic developments must be devised and controlled to benefit the peoples of the areas in which they are established. Guaranties to the investor must be balanced by guaranties in the interest of the people whose resources and whose labor go into these developments.

"The old imperialism—exploitation for foreign profit—has no place in our plans. What we envisage is . . . democratic fair dealing. . . .

"Democracy alone can supply the vitalizing force to stir the peoples of the world into triumphant action, not only against their human oppressors, but also against their ancient enemies—hunger, misery, and despair. Events have brought our American democracy to new influence and responsibilities."

forecast in advance: That Department had never been known to waver in its identification of democracy with capitalism; and its most earnest efforts had always been given to the extension and protection of American financial interests. Under the President's urging, there might be a considerable extension of technical assistance to backward peoples, such as both the United States and the United Nations were already undertaking. But there would be no great extension of direct governmental financial aid. For one thing, by the summer of 1949, America no longer felt so rich as she had during the first days of victory; and the Congress became more economy-minded than ever when the subject of possible foreign aid was mentioned. The President might plan; but it was clear that what would happen would be late, reluctant, and miserly.

Yet this conclusion overlooked the long-run certainties. For the technological oneness of the world was surely, even if intermittently, forcing the equality which is the inevitable concomitant of oneness. Through tax and welfare legislation, such a redistribution of wealth had already been going on within the Western nations, though more slowly in the United States than in Europe. There had been a time when various parts of the United States, for instance, had shown enormous contrasts in well-being; there had been Fifth, Delaware, and Euclid Avenues, Rittenhouse Squares and Nob Hills; and there had been East Sides, Hell's Kitchens, and Barbary Coasts. Even when the automobile had outmoded the city estate and left it to become that most degraded of all slums, the decayed mansion, the trend had not yet been recognized in America. The income tax, together with the equalizing welfare legislation it paid for, had come earlier to Europe than to America. But it was only a delay, not a difference in development. The Tories in England, as elsewhere in Europe, still regretted the past; but only Mr. Churchill and his little group seemed seriously hopeful of bringing it back. The Tories of the United States were more successful in their delaying action. But it required nothing less than blindness to miss the inevitable drift. For rising taxation and welfare legislation, stubbornly resisted though they were, embodied themselves bit by bit in law and administration. Fair shares were on the way.

It was true that these developments were delayed in America and that it was a serious matter for the nation to be out of concordance with the cosmos. The power and place of the United States in the world required leadership in such matters which it was a constant struggle for those of her statesmen who felt the responsibility to gain. And they had not yet nearly secured it.

The change was symbolized by the new housing for the "poor" in New York—Red Hook, Vladek, Stuyvesant, Abraham Lincoln—which was at least as desirable from the point of view of sheer amenity as Park Avenue. There were cleanliness and order, comfort and convenience, health and dignity, in the new housing. Whatever could be said about its crowding—its most disappointed proponents called such projects potential slums—and its high rents, it represented a trend toward shared well-being which ran all through modern life.

The minimum wage and the various social security programs were other equalizers. They made sure—to an extent—that the distinction between the "two worlds" of rich and poor should at least be blurred. If equality did not go so far yet as in England, for instance, it could be seen that presently it would. It would probably come faster because it involved a sharing of riches, really, rather than, as in England, a sharing of hardships—though the "austerity" there was cleverly exaggerated by Mr. Churchill's gift of language. Between the half-sharing of 1949 and the genuine equality of, say, 1969, there would be many opportunities for people's champions; but they would win.

The same influence was now being felt throughout the world. As water seeks a level, so, in a world technologically one, do nature's riches. Perhaps the analogy is even more striking than at first appears, because there is no gathering of human wills and abilities to force the leveling of water. It merely seeks its natural state with persistent passivity. But behind the current demand of men for well-being and justice there was an unresting human purpose. To overlook this aspiration was to neglect the most formidable force at work on the planet men inhabit. It had been interrupted often or diverted to selfish uses, but it had always swung back to its original direction. Its manifestations could be seen in a thousand places, but perhaps its most spectacular embodiment in all history was to be in the program subsumed under the Fourth Point in the President's inaugural; that is, if it meant what it seemed to mean.

Everyone knew that the Administration had sponsored the Fourth Point to gain allies in the struggle with Russia; and it was possible that the program might so strengthen the West that it would be emboldened to challenge the Communist colossus. Point Four might, in other words, lead to a holocaust which would destroy all civilization. But this dilemma had been latent in technology all along. Wise men had seen that sometime the power of man to control his own inventions—with the penalty of destruction if he could not—would be tested. That time was rapidly approaching and was to be precipitated, apparently, by the ideological struggle between the Americans and the Russians. This struggle was expediting rather than hampering the drift toward equality—witness the Marshall Plan and the Fourth Point. We were now to make a virtue of necessity and tune ourselves to the cosmic drift; if not this year or next, then soon, as history goes.

Thus, although the Marshall Plan, and its accompanying programs, was part of the march toward war, it was also part of the march toward a higher civilization. It ought not to be forgotten that, when that plan was first suggested, Russia had been in all sincerity invited to join. She had chosen not to, for reasons which suggest themselves. She had wanted to preserve the purity of her ideology rather than allow herself to become mixed up with the doubtful peoples of the West. There had been no plebiscite on the question, of course; the Politburo had decided it, as it decided everything, as yet, for the people of Russia. It was idle now to speculate about what might have happened. What *had* happened was the first rift, followed by the development in the West of the will to aggression which was moving now toward obvious crisis.

Everywhere in 1949 there were evidences of movement toward equality. Not only was the United States sharing with Europe—and other parts of the world besides—Europe also was sharing with Africa and the East (such part as would accept anything). Great Britain got large sums from America, but she paid out more than she got, and other Europeans did what they could. There was the work, furthermore, of the Rockefeller corporations in Venezuela and Brazil,[4]

4. Descriptions of these ventures in practical philanthropy were available only in private material to be had from the American International Association at Rockefeller Center, New York. But see also R. G. Tugwell, "To Succor the Weak," *Common Cause*, March, 1950.

and of Mr. Edward Stettinius and his associates in Liberia. Of even more importance was the steady though unspectacular increase in American technological assistance to almost every less-developed area of the world. Men from the departments of Agriculture and Interior could be found working, sometimes in teams with Europeans, in Africa on the tsetse fly; on the central railroad needed to market the products of Tanganyika and Ugandi; or in China, imparting technical knowledge of poultry husbandry or drawing plans for dams. They were literally all over the world—even Britain was utilizing teams of efficiency experts in industry. *Expertize* was spilling over from where it existed in surplus to where it was in obvious deficit; and it could be seen that the process would go on and on until the whole globe had achieved substantial equality.

The United Nations was playing its only vital role in just this process, not supposed to be its main business. For it was often the conveyor of surplus to deficit areas in ways which appeared merely to be co-operation—and all member nations were alike entitled to co-operation; such gifts involved no loss of dignity. The auxiliaries of the United Nations, the Social and Economic Council, the Food and Agriculture Organization, the World Health Organization, and others, had for some time been as actively at work everywhere as their budgets (always objected to by Russia, who was not a member of any auxiliary, fearing "invasions of her sovereignty") would allow. Mr. Truman's Fourth Point, his official advocacy of such assistance, inevitably meant a vast enlargement of their work. Almost at once, indeed, in response to criticism for having proceeded unilaterally, the United States through the American members of the Social and Economic Council asked Mr. Trygve Lie, the Secretary-General, for new and enlarged proposals.

These were published in June.[5] They suggested no more than a beginning, really, but, added to the informal assistance of the United States and what the United Nations had alread begun to do, it was a real beginning. Eighty-five millions of dollars, spent over two years, would not transform the world; but even such a sum would make a start at its transformation. Mr. Lie, in making his proposal, had to maintain the appearance of practicality—there were economy-minded legislatures to consider, especially in the United States. The

5. *New York Times*, June 3, 1949.

truth was that such services, in their early stages, had to find firm administrative foundations somewhat slowly and had to avoid overwhelming the recipients of aid and raising the hackles of demagogues who are always ready to pillory progress as an invasion of men's rights to suffer and die in hunger and filth.

One rather disquieting comment in Mr. Lie's introduction was that the main purpose of the United Nations' plan was to "prime the pump" in the underdeveloped areas so that at some later date it would be practicable and profitable to pour private investment funds into the same regions. This idea seemed to suggest that the funds were to be loaned by those who expected them to produce a profit; and what that policy led to—or always had led to in the past—was "imperialistic capitalism," as the Russian propagandists were not slow to point out. President Truman had said that such exploitation would not and must not occur; but President Truman would long since have ceased to have any influence when loaning operations really got under way. He might not even have much influence on the immediate program, since the State Department bureaucracy was in charge of it. What might be in the making, in spite of the President's good will, was a vast push into all the backward countries of American capitalist ventures for profit, guaranteed against risk by their own government.

As Hiroshima Day arrived in 1949, men of good will were hoping that this was not the interpretation of American intentions which must be accepted. But they had not much to base their hopes on except President Truman's initial words and perhaps the belief that imperialism on this pattern was so anachronistic as to be somehow impossible. In truth, everything, even the bill finally introduced to implement the program, which was produced by the Interdepartmental Committee and sent to the Congress by the President in July, was disconcerting. It looked more like help for American business than relief for backward peoples.

The man who had started this boom in one-worldism, however it might develop, was himself a man of good will. He meant well. And the people of his nation demonstrated in November, 1948, how well they knew it. In spite of the great contrast everyone felt between the majestic Roosevelt and the unimpressive Truman, given a choice between a man who meant well and the arrogant, insincere, and un-human Dewey, the electorate had chosen the lesser of the evils. Mr. Wallace, who had seemed for a while to be an acceptable alternative, and who was obviously in intellect and in moral power much more nearly in the dead Roosevelt's class, had come out simply nowhere. His vote was something over one million in some sixty millions of votes cast.

The final result left a bewildered and chagrined press. This lesson was even worse than those provided by Roosevelt's victories. The journals had been almost unanimous for Dewey and had considered that, because Mr. Wallace would attract the whole liberal wing of the Democratic coalition, President Truman's chances were nil. They figured this vote at one point, as late as May in 1948, at some seven or eight millions; so, of course, did Mr. Wallace's supporters. There had been at least two courses open to the Progressives. One was to bargain with the Democrats for a more liberal policy in ex-change for support; the other was to proceed with their organization as a separate party and, with Mr. Wallace as a candidate, offer a determined bid for the presidency. Admittedly this last course was practically certain to elect Mr. Dewey, and they would have to bear the responsibility; on the other hand, the Truman administration was so dominated by big businessmen and generals that it was honestly hard to believe that the Republicans could be worse. And, finally, as the crisis deepened, liberals were finding it harder and harder to support Mr. Truman's foreign policy.

The Progressives were harried by the press from the very first. In spite of Americans' demonstrated distrust of the newspapers, the campaign of villification and lies was so massive and determined that only a hundredth part of what was alleged had to be believed; and about that percentage perhaps was believed. No one thought that Mr. Wallace was a traitor to his country, ready to hand it over to Russian Reds; but there were many who felt that the crisis had developed too far for appeasement and that appeasement was what Mr. Wallace intended. It is, of course, hard at best to distinguish between determined friendship and truckling, and Mr. Wallace stub-bornly refused to make the distinction with the required sharpness—because, said many even of his liberal colleagues, he was too closely influenced by the group of Communists and fellow-travelers who seemed to be in charge of his campaign.

While Mr. Wallace was losing out to fright of Russia and to misrepresentation of his real intentions, Mr. Truman, after the Democratic convention in June, suddenly appeared with an entirely new public character. He himself seemed to turn progressive, almost radical; and he began a vigorous campaign which was as much as was possible at variance with the policies of his administration. At first the people to whom he appealed were obviously skeptical, and the press, having written him off anyway, was loftily indifferent. His stand was sheer demagoguery, the newspapers said, and turned approvingly to the Dewey promises to end the drift toward socialism. They made no issue of foreign policy. There was a bipartisan agreement between Republicans and Democrats all through the campaign on these issues—as Mr. Wallace pointed out. One was as firmly committed to "resistance to Russian aggression" as the other; in fact, toward the end of the campaign, Mr. Dulles, who had been Dewey's "adviser" on foreign policy and had been taken into State Department counsels, carried more weight in these matters than did Mr. Truman's own Secretary of State—not that there was anything to choose between them!

President Truman's own Cabinet—Messrs. Krug, Forrestal, Harriman, and Royal and General Marshall—seemed to listen in shocked silence as their chief, who had appeared so tractable, now espoused one after another of the Progressive doctrines and forced Mr. Wallace to outbid him constantly in order to make an issue of any domestic matter; indeed, in the end Mr. Wallace had to conduct his campaign almost entirely on the issue of Russian relations. This was clever strategy; and it worked. For Americans were by now almost universally belligerent; they were reconciled to war, relying upon the assurance that their nation alone possessed the atomic bomb and upon the atomic bomb to make the war one in which armies would not be really engaged.

On foreign policy Mr. Wallace's voice cried loudly but went unheeded; on domestic policy the electorate could choose between what President Truman said he intended to do and what, under his superintendency, had been going on in Washington. He did not try to excuse his administration; he laid it all to the Republicans. They, he said, together with a few reactionary Democrats, had consistently opposed his liberal policies. What liberal policies Mr. Forrestal, Mr. Harriman, or Mr. Krug might be expected to carry out, even if they had been voted, he did not say. What he did say was that the Eightieth Congress had been "the worst in American history" the most amenable to "influence," the most unrepresentative, the most opposed to any development of the general interest. And he made his indictment stick, largely, because what he said about the Congress was beyond question true. Representative legislatures had seldom sunk to the depths of the Congress of the year just past.

That Eightieth Congress, aside from having heavy debts to pay for easing the way to election, had believed in the system of localism and of business enterprise—although the contradiction between local interests and nation-wide business empires had been often enough pointed out. Republicans and Democrats had joined together to repeal and reverse all the New Deal legislation. They had passed the Taft-Hartley Act to please the National Association of Manufacturers; they had allowed the real estate lobby to delay and emasculate housing legislation; they had revised neither the minimum-wage nor the social security laws to take account of an inflation which, since all price control had been summarily repealed, had doubled the cost of living. Business profits were now swollen, consumers were being squeezed, the worker's right to protest was sharply curtailed, and the economy was rapidly approaching a crisis comparable with that in foreign affairs. Savings were being exhausted, buyers were refusing temptation, the signs of recession were too plain to miss.

The President campaigned for renewed controls on prices, for the right to allocate scarce materials to necessary occupations, for enlargement of security benefits, for a higher minimum wage, and for repeal of the obnoxious Taft-Hartley Act. He hammered in speech after speech on the subservience of the Congress to special interests, with plenty of documentation and, on occasion, with picturesque language. The country was first slightly surprised at the seeming transformation, then grudgingly admiring, although skeptical because it was hard to forget the kind of associates the President had chosen. People ended by believing that he meant what he said; and, since they distrusted Mr. Wallace's affiliates and were inclined to credit somewhat the newspapers' claim that he was an appeaser of Russia, they elected Mr. Truman.

The American people, like others, concentrate on their own interests. They resist making up their minds on complex issues. They knew that the President had been right to oppose, and the Congress wrong to insist on, abandoning economic controls at the end of the war, although they had favored the Congress' stand then. They expected their leaders to be wiser than they and to persuade them toward policies, not necessarily popular, but effective. There is an old lesson about representation to be seen here. People must learn the arts of delegation; they must consent to be represented in reality rather than literally. For uninformed and self-interested individual reactions, when translated into national policy, have often had disastrous results. Yet it is an axiom in the Congress that ideally legislation should give expression to literal public wish and that, as a matter of practical politics, public wish and the private ends of lobbyists should be made to coincide. When the policy thus enacted has world-wide consequences, legislative behavior takes on a sinister significance.

Thanks in part to a powerful and equally irresponsible press, the public has often backed policies which favor special groups rather then its own real interest. And if it has happened to be irritated by a public personality, irked by control or regulation, or perhaps convinced that taxes were too high, it has rebuked its own best representative, usually the President. For many years, in every half-term election (except that of 1934) the President has lost out to the combination of special interests and public irritation; and he usually has had to face, during the second half of his term, a hostile and completely irresponsible Congress. This fate had fallen upon Mr. Truman; but fortunately the penalties of irresponsibility had this time been quick and obvious in the doubling of the cost of living. Two years later, even though people still looked back to Roosevelt's day as halcyon, forgetting how they had failed him so often, they decided to back the man who had so obviously been right when they had been wrong.

Presidents, however, are not infallible, and Mr. Truman's fallibility lay in his foreign policy, which had little attention in the campaign of 1948. In foreign policy, in fact, he followed the Congress;

and the policy was thus founded in local rather than world-wide interests and fostered the welfare of a special group, the American businessmen, rather than of peoples everywhere. It was on this issue that progressives had most difficulty in abandoning Mr. Wallace. They had to gulp hard, forget for the moment their fears of atomic forces let loose, and decide that domestic issues were even more important. It was a terrible choice for many of them; and the certainty that Mr. Wallace could not be elected played a great part in their decision. He offered the only alternative to the business-military policy of aggression which was official in Washington; Mr. Truman stood for no change in foreign policy. But there might be great progressive reforms at home. On domestic issues, therefore, and because the Wallace cause was hopeless, liberals plumped for what seemed like a transformed President.

For him it was a wonderful, a satisfying victory; and he as well as those who had elected him could legitimately expect to see his program translated promptly into law. There was, of course, that collection of disbelievers in the Cabinet; but they had been all but outrightly disloyal to the President during the campaign, and they were soon cleared out. Now that there was a Congress with a clear mandate to support the Truman program, there was such a pervasive optimism, such self-satisfaction for having done the right thing, as seldom spreads over the American democracy. But the elation did not last. By midwinter it had melted like the snows of spring.

Only by comparison with the odious Eightieth could the Eighty-first Congress be said to be better. The lobbies seemed to have just as much power as ever to prevent the passage of legislation for carrying into effect the President's campaign projects; and one after another these were compromised, diluted, or altogether abandoned. Nothing the President could say or do had much effect. The coalition of Republicans and southern Democrats was as effective as ever. Moreover, it was consolidated by an error in Administration strategy. The battle for civil rights was fought out first. It required weeks of maneuvering and ended in the old familiar way—nothing was done. Thereafter the coalition held together on all the other issues. Only another referendum and a new mandate could possibly change matters. But there had been a mandate given in every one of the last five presidential elections, and the Congress—even the new members—had refused to recognize the obligation. They had taken their chances instead with their own affiliates. The lobbyists still offered more than the electorate.

So serious was this congressional misrepresentation becoming that political scientists were quite generally at work suggesting devices for improvement, some old, some novel, but all calculated to modernize the legislative process. There had been, over a period of years, many changes and reforms in the executive department but practically none in the legislative branch.[6] In 1938 a formidable effort to reorganize the executive had gradually resulted in some reform under the constant prodding of President Roosevelt.[7] It had, in fact, been indispensable in the enormous expansion of executive agencies as the war situation had developed. And at this very moment the "Hoover Commission" was about to suggest new changes. But the Congress' only concession to modernization had been to enlarge its own prerogatives. It had not changed its attitude of persistent hostility to the executive; it had not confined itself to the work it was prepared to do. It persisted in interferences, in negative resistance, in stealthy service to private and local interests, and in neglect of the national interest.

The Congress not only made the development of any consistent policy impossible but hampered every effort to apply the conciliatory tactics which alone could ease the nation across the dangerous months. There were times, many times, during the winter and spring, when war seemed about to emerge from the latent into the active stage. And it was clear that, if war came, it would, at least immediately, be the result of the formidable handicaps imposed on American diplomats. They were following a delicate and dangerous

6. The La Follette-Monroney Act, notwithstanding. That act, before it had become law, in 1946, had been so amended as to be ineffective for its purpose and, in the one respect in which it might have made an improvement—in budget matters—had been completely ignored. The act provided for a long-delayed change in procedure which would at least have curtailed the worst log-rolling abuses and had set up a joint committee to decide on an over-all amount. It was hoped that there would develop a genuine executive budget, approved or disapproved by large items, instead of one written in detail in months of hearings and bargainings by the committees of both houses. But the hope was in vain. No one seemed to know what to do when the Congress refused to obey its own laws.

7. The Committee on Executive Reorganization, whose members had been Mr. Charles E. Merriam, Mr. Louis Brownlow, and Mr. Luther Gulik, had made the report on which the President's recommendations were based.

line. It was provocative and aggressive; but they obviously did not want it to result in hostilities at any time soon. The military were not ready. Yet the Congress pulled and hauled at them constantly. It was not that any different policy was desired. The Congress wanted to register an active aggressive hostility, to be outrageous and insulting to Russia on every occasion, and yet not to be held to account. It could not be guided in its forays of this sort—speeches denouncing Russia, investigations of Communist "infiltration" into government, even denunciations of the United Nations for "harboring" Communists—by any sense of timing or any judgment of probable consequence. It was an irresponsible and constantly perilous performance. How the nation got through the year to another Hiroshima anniversary, no one, looking back, could explain. It must have been because Russia also had not wanted war. In spite of her belligerence and her denunciations of capitalism, the Soviet Union also was not yet ready.

Meanwhile a kind of test went forward of the Communist theory that capitalism would destroy itself. Indeed, the Russian forbearance in the face of so much insulting provocation may have been the limited patience of a disciplined group of men—the Politburo—whose theory it was that they would never have to fight the capitalists if they could merely stave off a showdown for a certain time; for sooner or later the breakdown would come, and the nations now opposing them would become easy prey in the chaos of capitalist dissolution. The Russian armies, it was conceived, would never have to invade. Fifth columns would simply hold out the constant alternative of a constructive communism to gradually growing groups of sympathizers. First a Communist Europe, then a Communist America, would permit the organization of the world on the Communist pattern. The Far East might already be considered to have been won, for Chiang Kai-shek was by now in exile.

This attitude must have been encouraged by the development during the year of an unmistakable recession with all the familiar concomitants, modified by such New Deal dams against the floods as had been allowed to remain in being—for instance, price support for agriculture and the social security system. Unemployment, that old bugbear of capitalism, was back. The experts differed about its amount; but it was enough at least to call up disquieting recollections of the 1930's. During the early months of 1949 the President was forced to shift from advocacy of a program for combating inflation—price controls and all the rest—to one of preparation for recession. It looked as though the familiar New Deal devices would need to be dusted off and put to use again. All of a sudden it was found that there had been no planning for public works. For some reason this discovery seemed to be a surprise, although all such plans had been a forbidden subject on Capitol Hill for more than a decade; and certainly no authorizations for planning had been made.

It was a peculiar recession, not to be understood by orthodox reference. Although there was constant talk of buyers' markets and of a new sales resistance, and although some raw materials were reduced in price and some staple industries—cotton textiles, steel, and so on—had had to reduce operations by a quarter, the cost-of-living index showed no decrease. To the enlightened the occurrence of a serious business crisis without price reductions in consumers' goods indicated that there had developed such rigidities and resistances in the economic structure that it no longer responded to price impulses as, in theory, it was supposed to do. Indeed, it was no longer expected to do so. Now factories—at least those in the "administered-price group"—shut down during a recession, and their workers were discharged. Prices were not much lowered; they might even be increased, since, when manufacturers sold fewer units of their goods, they had to make more profit on each unit to maintain their net return. The net incomes of many of the slowed-down industries were actually as favorable as they had been in the feverish postwar years.

In a supposedly free-enterprise economy—that is, one in which there are no public controls—such courses, if they are persisted in, must necessarily lead to a crash. Those who are thrown out of work have only the incomes from unemployment insurance with which to make purchases. As they stop buying, there is even more need for contraction of production schedules. The malaise spreads. Presently the idle factories and hungry people present the free-enterprise dilemma all over again—as it was presented in 1893, 1907, 1921, and 1929, not to mention innumerable other occasions reaching far back into Western history. For, when there is industrial paralysis, financial paralysis soon follows. Debts cannot be paid; yet everyone wants what is owing to him at once. Something approaching panic then occurs. The last crash had taken place in 1929; and on President Roosevelt's first inauguration day in 1933 all the banks in the nation had been closed. How to get them open again and credit flowing, no one had seemed quite to know, then; and no one knew now. The economy had revived in the months and years which followed, blunderingly and unhappily; and when many debts had been written off and the dollar had been devalued by a third so that some obligations could be met, it was certainly arguable that the losses might better have been taken earlier as price reductions. If they had, infinite suffering might have been prevented, and the nation might have been enormously richer for having had the goods which the idle factories had not made.

The lesson had never been drawn; and, indeed, there was no way of administering such an adjustment. No compulsions to force decency in the interest of continuous exchange and the maintenance of activity had been accepted; there was really no way of accepting them. The war, furthermore, had furnished a devouring customer, one who never asked questions about prices and who settled accounts by inflation. The war was over; but a new war seemed imminent. There were vast expenditures for armament and for stockpiles of materials; there was an army to absorb the unemployed. In addition, aid for foreign countries still amounted to four or five billions a year. How, then, economists asked, could there be any real cessation of buying? Yet so enormous had American productivity become that all these voracious customers could not absorb the output. The American consumer must still take the greater part of it, and it was now being priced out of his reach. The profits demanded by business stopped the circuit flow of funds, channeled them away from consumption. By Hiroshima Day in 1949 the signs of depression were too numerous to be explained away even by the organs most devoted to the capitalist ideology. In fact, nearly everyone was worrying more about the recession than about the impending war, with its fatal recourse to atomic fire.

It was immensely important to the West—and, indeed, to all the world not attached to the Communist center—that the economy of the United States should stay stable. Everything, literally everything, depended on this stability. The slight recession of the spring, which had frightened Americans, more than frightened others. The British, for example, were progressively less able to sell their goods in the American market (or any other in the dollar area) and so were less able to buy goods from America. Some of those goods were very badly needed—food, for instance, and the means for carrying out the determined drive for higher efficiency in industry. What was true of Britain was true in other European countries, but, because the British economy was of greater consequence in the world, it made more difference what happened there. The inability of British manufacturers to sell in the American market created a dollar shortage, as they called it, for which the only ready remedy, aside from devaluation of the pound, was the desperate one of reduced buying. The reduction annoyed American exporters and their congressional friends, who had fancied that all the billions appropriated for foreign aid would be spent to maintain the market in which home consumers were now reluctant to buy.[8] When, in the late spring, the congressional appropriations for foreign aid (ECA) had to be renewed, there was notably less enthusiasm than there had been a year before. The whole program seemed endangered. It finally passed, but only after its appropriations had been considerably reduced; and everyone understood that notice had been given of early termination.

The Congress had always been annoyed that aid was going to Socialist Britain to maintain "a welfare state," a phrase intended to denote a certain coddling of the workers. It was true, of course, that British labor was in control and favorable to itself. Several centuries of middle-class predominance were giving way to the "century of the common man." What there was to criticize in labor rule, an impartial observer could see, was not free health services, subsidies for food and housing, controlled allocations of goods, nationalization of certain industries, and so on, but the failure of industry to make return in greater productivity. One reason for Britain's failure to sell her goods in the American market were her costs, and her consequently high prices—both as much the fault of management as of

8. The farm-bloc lobbyists as usual tried to earmark a percentage of the funds for buying American cotton, corn, and wheat.

labor. The only industries nationalized so far had been losing ones—railways, coal mines, electricity, and the like. Up to now, aside from their intention to nationalize steel production, the Socialists had gone no further than many a progressive in the United States had wanted to go.

As the 1949 anniversary of Hiroshima approached, Britain was in crisis. She had "lost dollars" at an alarming rate over the last quarter. Her attempted cure so far had been to restrict buying in the dollar area, a program which her politicians ought to have known would have fatal repercussions in the United States when the question of further aid came up. The truth was that little else was available as a remedy. Becoming more efficient, either by better management, by new infusions of capital for modernization, or by working harder, was not a program to be put into operation at a moment's notice. That she was not pushing this program hard enough was certainly true; that her politicians were deceiving their constituents was also true. But all she could do at the moment constituted a tragic act which would make more tragic acts inevitable in the year to come. She could devalue; but devaluations usually involve reprisals, and their gains are therefore short-run gains.

Would economic pressure break up the Atlantic community? This question was in a great many minds, disconcerted already by the undoubted fact that Marshall Aid (ECA) funds had frequently been used to strengthen nationalistic economies rather than to free European trade. Strangely enough, Britain was the worst offender, but France ran a close second. True, there were some elementary attempts at political *rapprochement*—the Council of Europe was due to have its first meeting at Strasbourg on August 16—but these seemed very feeble gestures when put beside fanatical political and economic nationalism. There was a recrudescence of this nationalism in West Germany, too, where the first electoral campaign under the Bonn constitution, so diligently worked for by the occupation administration, was under way.

It was at least an open question whether the nationalism which had issued in two world wars would be stifled even under the threat of a new one—a clear and present danger. Americans were puzzled by this defeat as by almost nothing else in contemporary life. Did Europe, they wondered, really not fear the Soviet threat as it professed to do? They always tended to forget what no European ever forgot, that Europe had not for centuries been able to live by and within itself. Adding France, Italy, Benelux, and even Germany to Britain would not create a viable economy in modern terms. If Britain was "a few islands in the cold North Sea," the others were worse off (except for France, which was able, at a low level of life, to be almost self-sufficient). By modern standards western Europe needed eastern Europe to live; and eastern Europe now belonged to Russia.[9] The real choice for western Europe was between two great power systems. If Americans did not recognize the nature of this choice, and soon, the Soviets would absorb what they rejected. If Europe was left at the mercy of a grudging Congress, lurching in the aftermath of an American depression, it would not long survive to receive niggardly aid from across the sea.

As we have seen, not only nationalism but imperialism had survived the war in Europe. Western Europe had not the resources to be self-sufficient, nor had it the tradition. Its people still cherished the imperial dream, though the war had shattered the reality. All the national entities except those in Scandinavia had overseas colonies, managed from headquarters in London, Paris, Amsterdam, Brussels, Rome, Madrid, or Lisbon. Even the Germans, coming late to the dividing of the backward areas of earth, had made a bid for the privilege of exploiting less-advanced peoples; and, as they crawled about in the rubble of their bombed cities, many of them probably believed that the war had been primarily a maneuver to exclude them from the benefits of imperialism.

Nearly every nation in western Europe received necessary economic support from overseas colonies. The Spanish and Portuguese empires were miniscule now; but Spain and Portugal were starving. The African Congo was so important a source of profits to Belgium that hardly any Belgian could be got to contemplate its independence. The stubborn reluctance of the Dutch to recognize nationalism in Indonesia was founded in a knowledge that the homeland could hardly continue to exist alone; perhaps a quarter of the national income came from the East. The French were similarly reluctant to regard Indochina as a national entity. Even Italy still had unlikely

9. Cf. Arnold Toynbee, "An Historian's View of American Foreign Policy," *Common Cause*, July, 1949, p. 472.

imperial aspirations. Without colonies she did not know how she could live. Only Britain—having given up India because she could not have held it longer against the forces of nationalism there— seemed prepared to give way in other areas; and, if she were to give up exploiting the rest of her subject peoples, she would have to find some alternative way of life for the homeland. Already, the British Commonwealth was no longer British but only a commonwealth. Britain hoped still to stand at the center of this free association of peoples and to live by exporting those services she had been so well paid for in the past. Her relations with the new India were a crucial experiment in this role—an experiment for which ground-work had been laid by the consummate tact of a great proconsul. Lord Mountbatten would always represent to Indians a symbol of Britain at her gracious best; and the memory of his services would go a long way to erase memories of a long line of dreary viceroys living in the empty splendor of a dying imperialism.

For the moment, Britain was hanging on elsewhere, notably in Africa, whose peoples would be the last in the world to catch the fever of nationalism. Even a Socialist government could not seem to devise an alternate to the exploitation of new resources and subject populations. Yet the British economy was collapsing anyway. By the summer of 1949 the latest resort to restriction of dollar imports had told the people of the United Kingdom that they were in for a bitter experience. But their politicians, if they had any notion of the funda-mental difficulty, were not telling any unpleasant truths. Sir Stafford Cripps was the one hard, clear, and honest intelligence in the murk of London's self-deception. As he consistently pointed out, what lay behind the "dollar shortage" was the failure of Britain to convert herself from the rather slothful capital of an imperium—living on interest, profits, and payment for services—to an industrial nation of fifty millions resorting to industrial efficiency, clever inventive-ness, and hard work.

When in July the crisis became inescapable, Britain's first con-vulsive act was to ask for a greater share in Marshall Aid funds. But the council which made recommendations was made up of the re-ceiving nations and was cold to this proposal. Each nation had an economy to be kept going, and when Britain said frankly that unless she were given a larger share, she might collapse and carry all

Europe with her, the others pointed out that they might do the same. With less to divide, the need was not smaller but greater, because what had been spent had not been sufficiently effective. What could be done? The question had not been answered by the summer of 1949. By then Sir Stafford Cripps was in a Swiss hospital; he might come back rejuvenated; but his effort to meet the challenge now presented to the British was failing before the querulous timidities of his political colleagues. Some even hoped to lose the impending election and thus escape the odium of economic collapse.

As the Council of Europe—a kind of regional United Nations without any but "consultative" powers—prepared to meet in Strasbourg, Europe seemed less than ever to have unity. Each nation was concentrating far more on regaining colonial possessions, lost or alienated during the war, than on co-operating with her neighbors. Mr. Averell Harriman, America's "roving ambassador," and Mr. Paul Hoffman, head of the European Co-operation Administration, talked about "freeing trade," "mutual interchange," and the like; but the nations, Britain in the lead, refused all such suggestions when they went beyond the harmless consultation of the Strasbourg meeting. Even the occupation officials in West Germany were trying to establish a national balance of payments and to shape the German economy in the direction of nationalistic self-sufficiency.

This renewed nationalism was inherent in Europe's decision, made tentatively and a little reluctantly in 1946, to side with one of the then-polarizing power systems—the United States—and thus give a feebly renewed life to "the Atlantic Community" which had been drawn together for the defeat of Germany. The United States had demanded this support as the price of assistance in rehabilitation; but a large and vocal minority of Europeans would have had Europe instead become a Socialist commonwealth, opposed both to Communist totalitarianism as represented by Russia and to "monopoly capitalism" as represented by the United States—a Third Force. It had been the Labour government in Britain that had weighted the balance in favor of the United States, a choice probably determined by the inability of the British to make up their minds to abandon colonialism and become the major unit in a United Europe. For the offer of assistance from the United States had not precluded help in rejuvenating colonial ties, and, in fact, American aid to the colonies —through Britain—had been very generous.

When American administrators talked peevishly about the refusal of European nations to co-operate economically, they were therefore being thoroughly inconsistent. The United States had perpetuated colonialism—it had saved Indochina for the French, Indonesia for the Dutch (although the Dutch had afterward lost it through stubbornness), and Malaya, Hong Kong, and other Eastern possessions for the British. True, it was American policy to ask for some modification of the old colonialism. Thus the Dutch were not allowed to impose the same old regime in Indonesia, but they made changes reluctantly and resentfully. The French in Indochina, in the face of a revolt certain never to end short of independence, persisted in the attempt to reimpose French sovereignty there. As the year ended, Hong Kong, which President Roosevelt had vainly tried to persuade Churchill to abandon, was a tiny outpost of empire, perched on the periphery of Communist China, preparing to defend its collection of expatriates against armies which had conquered the whole nation. If necessary, the British intended to involve the whole West in the defense.

If the United States had been basically responsible for perpetuating colonialism as a bribe to the Europeans and so had naïvely prevented the European union so ardently desired for a united front against Russia, she was busy in 1949 trying to repair the damage. She was forming a military alliance. She was even prepared, in spite of still formidable dissent, to depart from the tradition of noninvolvement on her own initiative and to guarantee the integrity of all the nations of western Europe through the Atlantic Pact, the rearmament of western Europe, and the setting-up of a joint military command to administer the armaments.[10]

10. There was continued dissent to these adventures in all the nations involved. It was led, in the United States, by Mr. H. A. Wallace. He however, had lost much of his authority in the electoral defeat of 1948—although he was defeated for other reasons than this dissent. In Britain Mr. Konni Zilliacus and Mr. Lester Hutchinson became such intolerable nuisances to the front bench in Parliament that they were expelled from the Labour party (cf. Mr. Zilliacus' pamphlet *Why I Was Expelled*). It was not that any of these, or any of their colleagues, favored Russian nationalist ambitions, which, indeed, they deplored. It was that they could not consent to a united aggressiveness such as was represented by the Pact and the military preparations now going forward so openly. So, in the congressional hearings on the bill for arming Europe, Mr. Acheson and the Chiefs of Staff no longer hesitated to name Russia as the enemy and to outline the strategy needed to defeat her.

The North Atlantic Treaty was signed in Washington during the first week of April, 1949, and was subsequently ratified by all the signatories. Its military implementation followed at once. There was some difficulty with the Senate—not that the senators wanted any change of policy but that they were fearful of their prerogatives, one of which was the power to declare war. Under modern conditions this power was a mere formalism; wars were the outcome of long-prepared diplomatic arrangements, such as were now being made; and they began, also, in ways which left legislatures no choice, the bombing of Pearl Harbor, for instance. Nevertheless, the Senate haggled over any commitment in advance to use force in supporting allies. Consequently, instead of an outright guaranty to come to the aid of an ally, the treaty merely provided that "the Parties will consult together whenever, in the opinion of any of them, the territorial integrity, political independence or security of any of the Parties is threatened."[11]

The European nations, unwilling though they were to modify in the least the economic nationalism which rested on colonial exploitation, nevertheless established during the year a joint military command at Fontainebleau of which Lord Montgomery was head. Just as the atomic year ended, the American Chiefs of Staff, Generals Bradley and Vandenberg and Admiral Denfield, made what amounted to a visit of inspection to the European outposts of their military domain. They were received with obviously mixed feelings. The visit was generally thought to be part of the campaign of the armed forces to secure passage of the Military Assistance Program, then having some difficulty in the Senate, but it was rather widely resented in Europe as simply an inspection of the expendables in the coming struggle. General Bradley was, in fact, strangely frank in

11. Article 4. Article 5, also, had to be modified, and finally read as follows:
"The Parties agree that an armed attack against one or more of them in Europe or North America shall be considered an attack against them all and consequently they agree that, if such an armed attack occurs, each of them, in exercise of the right of individual or collective self-defense recognized by Article 51 of the Charter of the United Nations, will assist the Party or Parties so attacked by taking forthwith, individually and in concert with the other Parties, such action as it deems necessary, including the use of armed force, to restore and maintain the security of the North Atlantic area."
But the treaty, in Article 9, established a council with the power to set up subsidiary bodies and a defense committee which was in effect already in operation before ratification.

an outline of strategy before the House Foreign Affairs Committee.[12] It would be the job of the United States, he said, to deliver the atomic bomb, a statement that recalled one congressman's remark sometime earlier that Europeans were going to be the cannon fodder of the coming war, whereas American boys would be kept at home. The strategy had become all too plain to Europeans, whose politicians had made their choice for them in 1946. Europe was to fight a holding action while America attempted to destroy the Russian centers of power with atom bombs. And would those centers of Russian power not be European as well as Russian cities? For how were the few divisions with antiquated equipment available in France (there were no more than perhaps two others) going to hold back the armored Russian hordes so generally reputed to be available no farther away than eastern Germany? Would not the Russians be in Paris, Amsterdam, Brussels, and all the channel ports in a matter of days or weeks after the beginning of hostilities and would not the Americans have to bomb them out of those cities?

For Americans, however, the real questions were the efficacy of the atomic bomb and the reality of the American monopoly. It was a minor matter whether the engagements were fought in western or eastern Europe, provided that they were won and provided that none of them took place in America.

Doubt had arisen during the year concerning the Russian atomic program. Had that nation developed a bomb and so destroyed the American monopoly, or even the American lead in production? There was, of course, no way of knowing. The confidence of President Truman, Secretary Acheson, and Mr. Lilienthal seemed monumental; and, unless it was assumed for the purpose of maintaining general morale, it indicated that they still believed in the American monopoly. They had access to intelligence sources closed to ordinary citizens. But the scientists, who had only their guesses and estimates of possible Russian progress to go on, were not so sure. It would be more accurate to say that they were divided, with the majority favoring an assumption that the Russians were now near success. Some said, as scientists had said from the time of publication of the Smyth Report, that there was no secret and that any na-

12. Released on the day the Joint Chiefs reached Frankfurt, July 29, 1949.

tion willing to devote a few billions to the development of a bomb, together with the appropriate engineering talent, could design and manufacture a satisfactory weapon. Russia had certainly allocated the funds; she was known to be digging frantically at all the sites under her control where there were uranium and thorium ores, including those in the part of Germany she held. She was, indeed, working forced labor, under frightful conditions, around the clock, indicating an urgent use for these ores. Besides, she had a defense budget by far the largest in her history—larger than that of the United States; and a good deal of it was known to be for strategic bombers.

This emphasis upon bombs, of course, seemed like a counter to the American emphasis upon a fleet of long-range planes, as invulnerable to attack as they could be made, which would be capable of delivering at Russian targets the bombs manufactured since Hiroshima and held in stock. No secret was made of the American strategy. It was so openly discussed—for instance, by Generals Bradley and Vandenberg before congressional committees in July—that there was obviously method in the openness. Presumably the military were confident of their monopoly and were counting on the deterrent effect of knowledge among the Russian chieftains of American readiness to use the most awful weapon of all time. Outsiders— which meant the whole American people—could only speculate and hope that such open warnings were no bluff, for one thing, and, for another, that terroristic talk would really be a deterrent. Illustrations of hesitation from such a cause were difficult to find in recorded history; on the other hand, there had never been so fearsome a weapon at the disposal of military strategists. Perhaps they were justified in depending on its threat.

There had been more tests at Bikini; assurance had been given both by Mr. Lilienthal and by the President that the weapon had been greatly improved since Hiroshima; and on April 19, the Atomic Energy Commission announced the testing of still another "atomic weapon" at Eniwetok. The sixth Bomb had been used. Absolutely nothing further was disclosed. This very secrecy, necessary as it might be to a nation preparing for war, was a corrosive. However horrible reality may be, the tortured imagination can enlarge it and, what is worse, can intensify its immediacy. The people were often told that the use of the Bomb in its improved form would result in such destruction that civilization itself would be jeopardized, but, because of the need for security, they had not the information necessary to judge whether these statements were true or to determine under what conditions and for what purposes the Bomb should be used for offense or defense. That democracy completely broke down in these circumstances they did not need to be told. Their fate was not in their hands. The generals would deliver the Bomb when *they* determined, not when the people judged it necessary.

There was some audible protest, as there was bound to be, in circumstances of such importance for the democratic will; but there were few suggestions for any remedy. Senator McMahon asked whether the size of the Bomb stockpile ought not to be made public. But senators, generally nosy enough about other people's business, shuddered at the thought of such a disclosure, and nothing came of this or of other demands for more knowledge in the interest of public control.

It would be helpful, it seemed to me, before coming to a statement of the strategic situation as it appeared in the summer of 1949, to review the chronology of atomic-energy development. The publication of hitherto unknown facts and the memoirs of those who had played important parts in the chain of events since 1939 made such a project feasible. Any complete review, of course, would go far back into the history of science, perhaps to the Greeks, certainly to the Renaissance, but, for the purpose of understanding the structure of strategy being built by contemporary statesmen in 1949, it was impractical to go further back than the earlier work on atomic fission.

An extraordinary decade can be said to have begun on January 26, 1939, when Niels Bohr reported to a meeting at the Carnegie Institution in Washington (later to become the headquarters of the Office of Scientific Research and Development) that Hahn and Strassmann in Germany had produced barium by bombarding uranium with neutrons and that Lise Meitner and Otto Frisch (Jewish exiles in Denmark) had guessed that "the absorption of a neutron by a uranium nucleus had caused that nucleus to split into two approximately equal parts."[13] By the summer of 1940 all well-

13. James Phinney Baxter, *Scientists against Time* (Boston: Little, Brown & Co., 1946), p. 240.

informed physicists knew that it was the isotope of U235 in which fission had taken place and that both slow and fast neutrons could produce this result.[14] Even by March, 1939, Mr. Enrico Fermi, then at Columbia University, had informed a representative of the Navy Department of the possibility of achieving a controllable reaction with slow neutrons or an explosive reaction with fast ones. The following summer Leo Szilard, Eugene Wigner, and Albert Einstein had interested Mr. Alexander Sachs in the problem because they thought he might have access to President Roosevelt; and, in fact, he did induce the President to appoint an advisory committee.

This advisory committee met in October, 1939, and again in April, 1940. Its resources consisted of $6,000 granted by the War Department for supplies, an amount later enlarged to somewhat over $100,000 to be used for isotope research. By this time Mr. Vannevar Bush of the Carnegie Institution, already chairman of the National Defense Research Committee, was active in pushing the work, and the Carnegie Institution allotted $20,000 of its own resources for further research. A merger resulted: the advisory committee was placed under the National Defense Research Committee (NDRC) on June 15, 1940. Immediately $140,000 was requested for further measurement of fundamental constants and for experiments with uranium and carbon, but in smaller amounts than the "critical amount" estimated to be necessary if a chain reaction was to maintain itself. For this work a contract was signed with Columbia University on November 8, 1940, and others followed with the universities of Chicago, Harvard, Minnesota, Iowa, Princeton, and California.

By April, 1941, the combined developments were ready for appraisal, and, for this purpose, Mr. Bush requested President Frank Jewett of the National Academy of Sciences to appoint a committee of scientists. This committee, of which Mr. Karl Compton was chairman, met on April 30 and May 5, 1941. It recommended a strongly intensified effort. When the National Defense Research Committee met on June 12, therefore, it had before it this recommendation proposing that special emphasis be placed during the next six months on intermediate experiments with uranium and carbon and on methods for quantity production of heavy water for use as a slowing-down agent in a pile.

14. *Ibid.*, p. 422.

Events followed rapidly. A month later the Uranium Committee (of which Dean George Pegram of Columbia was chairman) recommended that operations be stepped up and a central laboratory established; and in the same month the committee voted approval for fourteen research contracts. These contracts were for studies of chain reaction and for work looking to the separating of uranium isotopes in quantity, since by now it appeared that these were the only ones in which chain reaction could be brought about in a mass small enough to be carried as a bomb.

British scientists had independently reached the conclusion that a bomb could be constructed from U235 produced by a diffusion plant. But not until after a long conference with Vice-President Wallace and President Roosevelt was Mr. Bush free to work out an interchange with the British, and then only within a small group. Only Secretary Stimson and General Marshall, together with Mr. Bush and Mr. Conant were authorized to discuss policy. Mr. Bush could not even transmit British findings to the whole Academy committee. In November this committee came out for an expanded program focused on the development of a bomb. Its report said that "a fission bomb of superlatively destructive power will result from bringing quickly together a sufficient mass of element U235." Before Pearl Harbor, on November 27, 1941, Mr. Bush transmitted this Academy report to President Roosevelt and pointed out that it was somewhat more conservative than the British reports, perhaps because of the inclusion on the committee of some hardheaded engineers; it predicted less effective bombs and visualized the time and expense of production as considerably greater. Nevertheless, the President pressed for advance, and almost at once the administration of the program was reorganized. Mr. Conant, Mr. Compton, and Professor Ernest O. Lawrence of the University of California were added to the committee which would henceforth report direct to Mr. Bush. The physicists engaged on the bomb problem were grouped under three program chiefs, Mr. Compton, Mr. Lawrence, and Mr. Urey.

After Pearl Harbor the policy group agreed to press the work as fast as possible to the stage of constructing pilot plants. They also agreed that, when large-scale construction became imminent, the Army should take over. Success came into clear view during that fateful year; one problem after another yielded to a series of brilliant intellectual efforts. Mr. Lawrence and his group in California perfected the electromagnetic method of separating isotopes; others determined what amount of fissionable material would be "critical"; and Mr. Fermi and Mr. Szilard at Chicago devised the first atomic pile—lumps of uranium imbedded in a matrix or lattice of pure graphite—which on December 2, 1942, induced the first chain reaction. It was now certain that a bomb could be made.

There were events other than scientific to be recorded as having significance in the perfection and use of atomic fire. One of these was certainly the personal interest taken by Vice-President Wallace and, less directly, by President Roosevelt. Another, not so clear then, was the appointment of Mr. James F. Byrnes to be Director of Economic Stabilization (a title changed after about six months, on May 2, 1943, to Director of War Mobilization); for Mr. Byrnes immediately became known as the "Assistant President" and very soon in fact occupied a much more strategic position than that of Vice-President Wallace. On him President Roosevelt relied to suppress any embarrassing questions in the Congress about the mysterious expenditures, now reaching huge proportions, for atomic development. He became perhaps the most important member of the decision-making group. His appointment had been made necessary not only by the President's desire for administrative relief but also by the growing disaffection of the southern conservatives, who, even in the midst of the nation's greatest crisis, were driving hard political bargains. As the price of consent to war expenditures, they were insisting in particular upon the liquidation of the few remaining vestiges of the New Deal. Over this extinguishment Mr. Byrnes presided; he secured the political price for which the New Deal was being bartered.

How necessary this appeasement had been the election of 1942 demonstrated; for it went strongly, almost disastrously, against President Roosevelt in spite of all his concessions. The Republicans became almost coequal with the Democrats in the Congress, thus placing the conservative democratic group precisely where it wanted to be—in a position to dictate because it controlled the balance of power. Not the least of the necessities for which the New Deal was sacrificed in the ensuing bargaining was immunity from exposure for the atomic-energy program.

It can now be seen that at this time the pressure on the President was almost beyond human endurance. Quite apart from the vast administrative burden of preparing for war in the midst of war, there was the worry that Germany might well be, probably was, ahead of the Allies in work on an atomic weapon.[15] It is pleasant to think that there was some relief for a harried President in the great success at Chicago. It had come within a year after the administrative reorganization which had assembled, under the now unused stands at Stagg Field, and in some hastily contrived temporary structures, the mysterious "metallurgical project"[16] about which other Chicagoans wondered in such silence as they could manage. And this was only the more spectacular of many successes that Mr. Bush must have done his best to convey to President Roosevelt. Although even Mr. Bush could not be certain that the enemy was not considerably ahead in the race to produce a weapon, progress was sufficient for a statesman not unused to great risks to build upon.

From December, 1942, when certainty of success—though not of victory in the race with German science—seemed assured, to July, 1945, when the final assembly of the Bomb began in an old ranch house on the desert at Alamogordo, New Mexico, the pressures were never relaxed. Intensive engineering exploration went on; vast expenditures were authorized, and extensive building projects were undertaken to produce materials for fission by alternative methods. On July 16, 1945, there occurred one of the most dramatic moments in all history, as the assembled scientists crouched behind a barrier,

15. Secretary Stimson referred to this possibility in his much-discussed article, "The Decision To Use the Atomic Bomb," *Harper's Magazine*, February, 1947, p. 87. In fact, the Germans thought they were ahead. As late as July, 1943, the chief of German civilian research wrote to Göring that, although the work would not result soon in the production of useful engines or explosives, "there is certainty that in this field the enemy cannot have any surprise in store for us." This was stated by S. A. Goudsmit in the *Bulletin of the Atomic Scientists*, November, 1947, p. 343. There was confirmation in the remarkable interview of Waldemar Kaempffert with Dr. Werner Heisenberg (Nobel laureate of the Max Planck Institute for Physics at Göttingen University) after the war (reported in the *New York Times*, December 28, 1948). This interview was a confession in avoidance. In it Dr. Heisenberg sought to excuse the German scientists for not having produced the Bomb. They knew enough, but they were not supported.

16. To this division the Columbia group under Mr. Fermi, most of the Princeton group, and some others had been brought.

not entirely certain that the reaction would occur and, if it did occur, that it would prove to be as limited as theoretically it ought. They were not even certain that the entire material universe might not break apart in one final explosion. When it was over, relief and exaltation were almost equally present.

But Alamogordo had a setting. Not only had intensive effort been poured into the development of the Bomb but also the vast war had come to a virtual end. V-E Day was past; and Japan had for months been seeking a way to surrender. The effort was relaxing. But it had not been relaxed for long. The Germans had fought back in the Battle of the Bulge; and, in the same month of that battle, Professor Gerlach had written to Bormann, the German minister: "We . . . are still considerably ahead of America." If the Germans still thought themselves ahead, the Americans agreed. In spite of the scientists' unremitting toils, one problem after another presented itself as an obstacle.

Although success had seemed certain at some point, the time had been unpredictable until very late in the process—perhaps a few months before Alamogordo, perhaps not until after President Roosevelt's death. In 1944 the President was far from being out of the woods. Expenditures on atomic energy were at their height, concealment was becoming more and more difficult, and appeasement of a nasty, hostile Congress was more and more impossible. The election of 1940 had brought down his majority, and the off-year reverse in 1942 had brought painful losses. The election of 1944 had only to follow a normal curve to result in victory for the Republicans, and his opponent, Mr. Thomas E. Dewey, was confident that this would be the result. Mr. Dewey was wrong, but not by enough to give the winner a very free hand. The southerners again controlled the balance of power, and Mr. Roosevelt faced another period of appeasement, compromise, and bargaining for his more precious policies.

One of the incidents of compromise was the ditching of Vice-President Wallace as running mate for the campaign of 1944 and the acceptance of Senator Harry S. Truman. Another, equally serious, was the trading at Yalta of concessions in the Far East at China's expense in return for the Russian promise to enter the Japanese war. For even by February, 1945, it was not certain how the war would end. Germany was not yet finished; perhaps she might produce the first atomic bomb as she had produced the V rockets which were then falling with appalling effect on helpless British cities. And from the Philippines to the home islands of Japan was a long way.

In March, 1945, Secretary Stimson has recorded,[17] he talked with President Roosevelt for the last time about the great adventure of the physicists. Someone not named had sent the President a memorandum questioning the whole project, and he had sent it on to Mr. Stimson. They agreed to ignore it.

In April, Japanese representatives approached Mr. Leland Harrison, American consul in Berne, to inquire whether peace feelers would be received by the United States. Simultaneously, or almost so, tentative proposals began to come through the Vatican to Allied representatives and continued to come throughout May.[18] But April was a tragic month. On the twelfth President Roosevelt died, and the consequences to the world were of unimaginable dimensions, for he had known how to get the most possible for his liberal aims out of the coalition he had shaped. His compromises may have been heartbreaking, but the bargain he made was always a shrewd one. His death—coming just at the end of the war, when the militarist-capitalist strength in America, swollen by war profits, occupied strategic places in the American power complex—made it possible for them to move swiftly toward those objectives they would never otherwise have been able to reach.

The Roosevelt successor was not a man of ill-will; he was not even a weak man. But he had not been in the President's confidence, and he was not accustomed to executive responsibility. He began badly, weakly, and advantage was taken of him. It may even be, as Professor Blackett charges outright,[19] that the decision to use the Bomb on

17. In the *Harper's* article previously cited, and again in his memoir *On Active Service in Peace and War* (with McGeorge Bundy) (New York. Harper & Bros., 1947), chap. xxiii.

18. The authority for this statement is Admiral Ellis M. Zacharias' *Secret Missions* (New York: Putnam's, 1946). *Secret Missions* will be referred to again. The feelers referred to here came through the Archbishop of Tokyo, who was a brother of Matsuoka.

19. P. M. S. Blackett, *The Military and Political Consequences of Atomic Energy* (London, 1948).

Japan was one of those tours de force of the militarists which Mr. Truman's innocence and his naïve trust in generals deceived him into permitting. The evidence is not clear. But, then, Professor Blackett may simply have been innocent about American politics and may not have realized how important it must have seemed to those in the White House after the President's death that the expenditure of two billions of dollars should be vindicated by the use of the instrument which had cost so much.

Any recital of the events that led up to Hiroshima must take account of Professor Blackett's charges. His most serious allegations are two. (1) The decision to use the Bomb was clearly a political and not a military consideration. The war was won, the Japanese were suing for peace, and a memorandum was before the White House statesmen with a protest from the atomic scientists. Secretary Stimson speaks of need for haste when there was no need, unless it was to forestall the now imminent Russian attack on Manchuria. (2) The American atomic-energy proposals (the Acheson-Lilienthal Report and the Baruch proposal to the UNAEC) were not made in good faith: They were intended to make Russia helpless if she accepted them and to put her in the wrong if she did not; either decision could be exploited by American capitalism. Even supposing they were made in good faith, they would have to be judged incredibly naïve; they did not recognize how much more basic than the American was the Russian need for the power which lies at the basis of a rise in living levels. The UNAEC, dominated by America, could easily have so allocated plants or limited operations as to prevent Russian development and to favor private capitalist utilities in the name of security and have invoked sanctions amounting to war for no more than attempts to carry out the socialist development Russia had determined on.

This argument would not have so serious a claim to attention if it did not represent beyond any doubt the position both of the Russians during the years since Hiroshima and of many Europeans whose doubts of American good faith were very deep indeed. Even American liberals, though they had no desire to view decisions taken by their own statesmen in this unpleasant light, felt that much in the series of allegations needed to be cleared up. Mr. Wallace, for instance, had become more and more convinced that a militarist-capitalist conspiracy was afoot to cripple or destroy Russia, and it was his saying so that led to his ostracism by Washington.

How deep Mr. Stimson may have been in any conspiracy—if it was anything more than a shared attitude such as had led the British and the Americans into the White Russian adventure of 1918—no one can tell. His writings do not show that he had any motive other than the legitimate desire to save the American lives which would have been sacrificed in an invasion of the Japanese home islands. Professor Blackett asserts that there would have been no invasion. And, if there had, it would not have come until the next spring. Why, then, did the Bomb have to be used on August 6, 1945? Clearly because the Russian invasion of Manchuria was due to start on August 9, and the United States must not be forced to share with Russia the occupation of Japan.

Let us look at the events upon which Mr. Blackett bases his charges. On April 25, 1945, Mr. Stimson and General Groves explained the nature of the problem to the new President, "a man whose only previous knowledge of our activities was that of a Senator who had loyally accepted our assurance that the matter must be kept secret from him." It is not easy to imagine Mr. Truman's sensations as he heard the disclosure. He must have been overwhelmed. Had he already been told that the Japanese were seeking peace? We do not know. We do know that these feelers were not taken seriously either by the generals or by the State Department, and this attitude may have been conveyed to the new President without much detail or documentation. Mr. Truman had already displayed that bad habit, from which he was slow to recover, of making snap decisions on important matters without sufficient thought. Permission to use the Bomb may have been one of them. The memorandum on which this conversation was based was persuasive; doubtless many War Department civilians, perhaps some scientists, certainly the military, had all collaborated on it. At any rate, it resulted in the formation of an Interim Committee on which Mr. Byrnes[20] was the President's representative; and, until after Hiroshima, he was the White House policy-maker with respect to atomic energy.[21]

20. It was already generally known that Mr. Byrnes would become Secretary of State in July, 1945.

21. The other members of this committee were Undersecretary Bard, Assistant Secretary Clayton, and Messrs. Bush, Compton, Conant, and (acting for Secretary

At this point many scientists, particularly those at the University of Chicago, began to feel deeply disturbed. True, those on the scientific panel of the Interim Committee were still of the opinion even after V-E Day that the Bomb should be used on a military objective. But Professor Szilard, representing many others, had prepared a protesting memorandum even after V-E Day in March, which he had tried desperately to present to President Roosevelt without success. After the President's death he had been referred by the White House secretaries to Mr. Byrnes. On May 28, in the backwash of victory in Europe, and only six weeks before Alamogordo, he had a conversation with Mr. Byrnes which profoundly depressed the scientist and his colleagues. They then knew that there was not much chance of preventing the use of the Bomb. On June 1 this impression was confirmed by a report of the Interim Committee, which said that, "after discussions with the scientific panel," it "unanimously adopted the recommendation that the Bomb should be used against Japan as soon as possible."[22] The unhappy Chicago group then persuaded the director of the Metallurgical Institute to appoint a committee on social and political implications.[23] On June 16 the scientific panel of the Interim Committee reported that "we can propose no technical demonstration likely to bring an end to the war; we see no acceptable alternative to direct military use."[24] So great a disturbance within the Chicago group followed that Mr. Compton requested the director of the Metallurgical Institute to take a poll. It presented five alternatives, ranging from all-out use of the Bomb to no use at all. One hundred and fifty scientists were polled, and more than half voted for "preliminary demonstration on a military objective."

Stimson) Mr. George L. Harrison. The scientific panel was composed of Messrs. Compton, Fermi, Lawrence, and Oppenheimer.

22. Secretary Stimson in *Harper's*, Feburary, 1947, p. 100. Mr. Byrnes, in *Speaking Frankly* (New York: Harper & Bros., 1947), sets this date at July 1, 1945, one month later.

23. It consisted of three physicists, three chemists, and one biologist; and the chairman was James Franck. Secretary Stimson, it must be noted, nowhere mentions this group or its activities, although he was well aware of both.

24. Secretary Stimson relied heavily on this report for justification of the decision to bomb Hiroshima, as he frankly says in his *Harper's* article. He evidently felt that the weight of this group was far more impressive than that of the Franck committee.

It was on the strength of this judgment, as well as of his own, that Secretary Stimson, together, probably, with Mr. Byrnes, and with President Truman consenting, decided to attack Hiroshima. On July 2 Mr. Stimson presented to the President the memorandum (quoted in his *Harper's* article) outlining the determination first to warn Japan and then to attack her with intent to compel complete surrender. The Bomb was not mentioned, since Alamogordo was still two weeks in the future, but the intention was clear to the scientists. Either this decisive memorandum, with all its background of scientific support, was not known to Professor Blackett when he made his charges in 1948 or he ignored it. If he had studied the material available, and if he had been at all aware of the political pressures felt by an executive that had spent two billions of dollars on a weapon wrapped in complete secrecy, he might not so easily have convinced himself that a capitalist conspiracy against Russia had been responsible for the dreadful event of August 6, 1945—especially since he had nothing more to go on than a suspicious concurrence of dates.

It is true that the Japanese had been putting out feelers of a sort toward some kind of peace. But it is true, also, that the new President, even in the aftermath of European victory, confronted very serious political obstacles—for instance, a rebellious Congress; and what the Congress could have done with the discovery that two billions of dollars had been spent on a fantastic weapon never brought into actual use is all too clear. It is not nice to picture the holocaust at Hiroshima as an incident in American political controversy; it is, however, at least as realistic to picture it that way as to regard it as a deliberate and specific conspiracy to rob Russia of the fruits of victory. It may be that some of those who had a hand in the decision had in mind the facts regarding time cited by Professor Blackett; but there is no evidence to support such a supposition. There is evidence, on the other hand, not only for the obvious political motive but for others: The scientists had declared impractical a nonmilitary demonstration of the bomb, and Mr. Stimson has stated that the motive for a military demonstration was the saving of American lives. The statesmen may have had other motives than those they have been willing to record, but not the panel of scientists.

The Japanese approaches, furthermore, had been less than forthright. Even Stalin at Potsdam[25] did not take them seriously enough to refuse to join in the ultimatum sent thence to the Emperor.[26] It is quite possible indeed to conclude that Hiroshima and the whole complex of events associated with it were a colossal error in which all the statesmen, including Stalin, and all the scientists, except Professors Szilard, Franck, and the rest of the Chicago minority, were alike implicated. Morally, politically, militarily, in all ways, it seemed by 1949 to have been a dreadful mistake. But the mistake could not be attributed to anyone, or to any one group, alone. In a sense all mankind was involved in it. Certainly as a result of it mankind was brought face to face with the consequences of the careless and disjointed development of human civilization. The shock was perhaps needed and in the end might prove salutary; but surely there must have been other roads to the decisions which must now be made.

Whatever the truth of Professor Blackett's aspersions, the fateful event was now decided on. Sixty-four of the scientists associated with the metallurgical project sent a memorandum of protest to President Truman one day after Alamogordo, but in the high excitement and the moral depression of that success it seems not to have affected matters in the least. There is nothing to show that anyone actually read it; and certainly it was not allowed to affect the development of events between July 16 and August 6. For the military was now in charge; and the delivery of the Bomb had been transformed from a moral issue into a technical problem. It is interesting to speculate on what kind of Japanese action might have stopped the delivery. The likelihood of any such interruption was finally seen to be ended on July 28, when the Japanese premier, in an access of blind obstinacy, issued a statement saying that the Potsdam Declaration was "beneath notice." How much louder than statesmen's words was the scientists' Bomb!

On the sixth and on the ninth the Bomb was used; and on the

25. On July 24, President Truman, at the close of a meeting, told Premier Stalin about the Bomb. He seemed not to be much impressed (cf. Byrnes, *op. cit.*, p. 263).

26. This ultimatum followed closely the Stimson memorandum of July 2. Since Stalin had been told of the Bomb two days before, he was apprised of the "capitalist" intent. And there is no record that he made any protest or indicated in any way that he thought Russia was being circumvented.

tenth the Japanese offered to surrender, with certain reservations protecting the Emperor which they had reason to believe were acceptable. They had, in fact, been listening to the Zacharias broadcasts for many months, and these had always held out hope of reasonable terms, including continuation of the imperial system. Admiral Zacharias naturally felt that the various approaches—through Russia, through the Vatican, through Berne—were the result of the psychological attack he had directed; and it seemed to him that they had not been diligently followed up. A passage in *Secret Missions* indicates as much:

> It is left to the judgment of history to explain why it was necessary for the Soviet to take its course of action and why the allies, assuming they knew of Japan's approaches to the Soviet, refused to exploit the opening provided by Japan herself. If the detailed interpretations of the unconditional surrender formula had been forthcoming in June rather than the end of July, *the war would have ended without Soviet participation* and before the dropping of the atomic bombs—It is an undeniable fact that the diplomatic situation provided an opportunity for peace many weeks before mid-August, at which time it was generally thought that Japan had bowed to the supernatural force of the atom bomb.[27]

This passage is one which the scientific panel—Messrs. Compton, Fermi, Lawrence, and Oppenheimer—must have read with shuddering regret. Secretary Stimson seems to have remained unshakably convinced that he made the right choice, an attitude that lends some plausibility to Professor Blackett's charge that urgency about using the Bomb was not military but diplomatic. Is there an echo of such diplomatic maneuver in the casual clause italicized above, which does read as though it were common knowledge among naval intelligence officers, at least, that circumventing the Soviets was a consideration of some importance? Will there be other revelations? It semed not unlikely in 1949, for there were many of those who must have had personal knowledge of that whole decision-making process in June and July, 1945, who had not spoken at all.[28]

These melancholy recollections have their importance as commentaries on the moral condition of the world's statesmen when one

27. Pp. 367–68. (My italics.)

28. There was, for instance, Undersecretary Bard, who was the only member of the Interim Committee to vote against the use of the Bomb, even after the scientific panel had approved it; and there must have been other participants—secretaries and so on—who will someday speak.

war was ending and another—as many of them seemed to believe—was beginning. If it had not been necessary to drop the Bomb, it had not been necessary, either, for Russia to invade Manchuria. The Bomb seems more horrible now than the kind of blitz the Soviets staged in the last days of the war. But was there actually any moral difference? Was not the damage inflicted and Manchuria occupied in order to circumvent Western control of northern China and give the Politburo an advantage in the peace negotiations? Professor Blackett makes no reference to this whole range of subject matter. The moral degradation seems to him to be wholly on the Allied side. It is doubtful, however, that long-run study of events by historians will sustain him.

Of much more importance—and validity—than these charges is Mr. Blackett's well-reasoned argument that the Bomb is of far less military importance than the Westerners seem to imagine, or, at least, that it has less diplomatic value, because the Soviets do not regard it as a final weapon in terms of their strategy. It is elementary, Mr. Blackett seems to believe, that a continental power should think of defense in depth; and it is true that, since the Napoleonic campaigns, Kutuzov's strategy has dominated Russian military action. The belief that the Russians will continue to rely upon this strategy, however, depends upon the grand assumption that they visualize purely defensive campaigns. This assumption does not seem consistent with the obvious Communist intention to conquer the world, unless we accept another assumption: that the Russian strategy rested solely on the internal conflicts of capitalism. To the neutral—say a Swiss or a Swede—this dependence must have appeared either fatuous or strictly temporary. To the western Europeans the whole assumption seemed unlikely. The distance from Berlin to Amsterdam or Bordeaux looked very short, and they had only a handful of troops to oppose the reputed one hundred and seventy-five divisions of Russia.

One of the Russian attitudes most mysterious to Westerners all during the postwar diplomatic melee had been an apparent lack of fear. It was amazing, first of all, that Russian intransigence should have been stiffened rather than softened by Hiroshima—an attitude explicable only on the double hypothesis, first, that the Soviets regarded the Bomb as having been intended more for them than for the Japanese and, second, that they were not in the least impressed by it. If the first was true—as Mr. Blackett alleged—it was a secret to all but a handful of Americans; the rest, at least, were not even now convinced that it was true. The second might follow from the first thus: The capitalists had made a demonstration of willingness to use terrorism against their enemies and had, in fact, destroyed a Japanese paper city or two; should the tough Russians, who had just withstood the high-style German blitz, now succumb to capitalist bluff? Or, even if it were not bluff, should they not still have faith in Kutuzov? And, being the smartest people alive, might they not stave off attack by confusing maneuvers while their scientists worked at the production of a bomb which would equalize matters?

These days no one in the West suggested that communism was not intended for export. On the contrary everyone by now believed that Russia visualized Moscow as the future capital of a Communist world, just as they had finally believed that the Nazis had intended the world to center in Berlin. The question was: How did the Politburo intend to bring about its victory? Westerners were willing to risk competition, short of war, between democracy and totalitarianism. They had a profound instinct that, given present knowledge and social organization, a totalitarianism bureaucracy would stumble into some fatal conflict with nature. The general impulse in all society, it might be admitted, was toward rationalization and integration. There were planning endeavors even in capitalist America and certainly in Socialist Britain. But Westerners did not believe that complete centralization of all social activity was yet safe from the crazy, self-destroying possessiveness of a Hitler or a Mussolini; and the whole Russian state, together with the economy and all social organization, was centralized in the Politburo. Its few members had power to commit the entire organization to any adventure. They would, it was true, have expert advice, but the deciding power would nevertheless be theirs. Already they had shown an intolerance of any expert who opposed what they had determined from prejudice or theory. For all practical purposes, a tiny body of ill-informed, narrow, doctrinaire, and ruthless men had the absolute power to decide the policies, internal and external, of a great continental nation, and the Western liberals were almost certain that these leaders would, out of ignorance or prejudice, make a fatal error—sometime or somewhere. The Russian people could then resume a normal evolution toward the democracy, freedom, and self-discipline which Westerners believed to be the only safe foundations for a viable society.

Thus each side believed the other would fall by its own hand. The advantage in this contest of beliefs was, however, with the Russians. They believed that the fated capitalist crashes were immediate, or nearly so, and that inexorable forces determined their approach. In contrast, Westerners did not have any sense of immediacy about the Politburo's fatal mistake. It had been demonstrated that a conditioned and disciplined Russia could be managed internally so long as it could be persuaded that it had dangerous external enemies. The Politburo's mistake might bring conflict not only with nature but with Western civilization, as had Hitler's mistake; and war was something which most Westerners—in spite of military preparations —profoundly did not want.

Furthermore, the belief, so sustaining to Victorian generations, that progress toward freedom and plenty was a natural principle had been expelled from the Western mind by several hard lessons. Twice the Germans had been almost successful in bringing the "degenerate" democracies to heel. Equally disturbing were the technologies science had created—technologies that humans doubted their competence to control. Logically the totalitarians were right to force social integration. Unless humanity moved very rapidly in the direction of establishing the control of the group mind over social action, technology was likely to prove an irresponsible and destructive monster and was certainly open to capture by adventurers. Because men had not moved rapidly enough toward the enthronement of social reason, adventurers had been able to seize the controlling ganglia which reason ought to direct. The ousting of these gangsters once they had gained a central citadel had been possible only because a more powerful force had been mobilized. There could not be many more such conflicts, so closely integrated had the world become, and so nearly was it polarized now into two power systems. There could very likely be only one more; and its outcome was far from safely predictable.

Not only were Westerners less certain than the Soviets that inexorable social forces guaranteed their victory; they suffered another handicap. They were divided. For many of them capitalism was an unsupportable evil. This division, which was wholly unresolved, was a serious weakness, since there was little hope of substantial healing in the time left before the West must confront a monolithic Soviet bloc armed with weapons as powerful as those the West now possessed.

Furthermore, supposing that war rather than nature was to settle East-West differences, the centralized state had the advantage when it came to military preparations. The capitalists possessed the wherewithal to manipulate Western power up to a certain point only; beyond it they must reckon with recalcitrant public opinion. And, when they maneuvered their governments toward war, they had always to do so in the name of defense. During 1949, it is true, there was no trouble about appropriations for the military, for Russia had been very generally visualized as a danger. But any relaxation in tension would affect these preparations.

What, then, were the relations between the West and Russia by Hiroshima Day in 1949? The tension had, in fact, diminished. In the spring, at the height of the Berlin crisis, the foreign ministers of the Four Powers had met in Paris. They had accomplished little of importance. The Russians had proposed going back to the four-power government, based on the rule of unanimity, that had been in effect before the blockade had begun. The other powers had refused, especially since one of the conditions of settlement had been the abandoning of Allied plans for a separate West German government. Yet, in spite of this seeming impasse, the blockade had been lifted, and the airlift had been abandoned. When General Lucius Clay and the American commander in Berlin had been removed, the principal Western personalities identified with aggression were gone. Though the Bonn government, once in being, would make East and West Germany a fact, it might not in the long run delay German unification, and in the meantime it gave the Allies more moral standing with the Germans themselves.

Even though the immediate crisis was safely past, the fact remained that the Atomic Energy Commission of the United Nations was in adjournment, no longer even attempting to reconcile the differences between Russia and the United States. The contenders for world hegemony might for the moment be operating at a slightly safer distance from each other; but each was preparing for "eventualities"—and this preparation meant an armament race. Such competitions are costly and dangerous, but neither contestant saw any alternative, because there existed no hope of reconciling their deep differences. They could not seem to shape an agreement to live and let live—an agreement which reasonable folk saw now as the only hope—and so, although war appeared to everyone a pyrrhic solution, each moved toward it almost automatically.

Professor Blackett stated what had become almost a last hope: that, although areas of tension would develop, Russia most certainly did not want war and would avoid it. He saw the main danger arising in America from a double fear, first, of the depression that seemed to be creeping upon the economy and, second, of the now imminent loss of the atom-bomb monopoly—for Russia must by now be coming close to success in the effort to produce such a weapon, and Americans feared that she would not fail to make immediate use of it. Since the United States herself had used it on a civilian population, Russia, devoted to Communist ruthlessness, could hardly be expected to be more reluctant in its use.

These arguments reinforce the view that Soviet Russia will be careful to avoid precipitating a military show-down, while at the same time will do her best to increase her defensive strength. The more she succeeds in this twin policy, the more acute does the problem facing the Western Powers become; it becomes especially acute for America, just because of the widespread acceptance of the view, however false the view may be, that Russia will drop atomic bombs on American cities just as soon as she had any to drop, and irrespective of any possibility of a subsequent invasion and occupation. The "horrors of Hiroshima" propaganda, and the thesis that "weapons of mass destruction are the essence of modern war," have come full circle, and have faced Americans with the dilemma of having to choose between waging preventative war and, according to their own way of thinking, of waiting to be annihilated.[29]

But the United States could not undertake a "preventative war" without a pretext strong enough to carry American opinion. This pretext, Professor Blackett thought, Russia would go to any length not to provide. If war of this sort could not conveniently be begun by America within a few years, Russia would inevitably come to have a matching equipment of atomic bombs. By then, "if each were equally vulnerable, each might be deterred from using them on the other." The prospect of continuous tension of this sort might not

29. *Op. cit.*, p. 182.

be pleasant, but it seemed to be what the people of the world might have to face. If it did not turn into open conflict, furthermore, new personalities, changes in outlook, or other modifying circumstances might eventually make possible a *modus vivendi.*

Admittedly, Professor Blackett was not far from right in his assessment of the American fear of Russia. But in 1949 the jingo press was having more difficulty than before in maintaining its stereotyped picture of Russians in the public mind. The bearded, bearlike monster with smoking bomb in hand refused to come out as clear as in the past. Nor had the militarists so free a hand in Washington. The Americans were getting used to insecurity, to living with fear. The danger of an American-inspired preventive war seemed substantially diminished.

Professor Blackett's strictures perhaps reflected a tendency fashionable in British intellectual circles in 1949 to dislike Americans for their comparative prosperity and power. It was fortunate that these sentiments were not allowed to shape government policies. Of course, the fact that governments were officially friendly and agreeable to the acceptance of aid allowed the intellectuals to despise their own governments as well as Americans. But it prevented a cultural collaboration which was now the only possible salvation for nations whose political power had diminished. For several hundred years Europeans had in one way or another managed the world. They could not manage it any longer; they could, indeed, hardly live. No American, however selfish or isolationist, wanted them to die. What Americans could do, however, was dependent on Europeans overcoming their envy of American riches and refraining from the disparagement of all things transatlantic. Only then could imagination and initiative be mobilized with American aid for the salvation of Europe.

As Hiroshima Day approached and the Berlin impasse receded, not only was tension relaxing but new beginnings seemed possible. In the calmer mood of resignation which was replacing the frantic postwar search for absolute security, there were indications that new approaches to a *modus vivendi* might be found. A story which appeared first in the *United Nations World* was worth repeating in front-page prominence in the *New York Times* of August 5. It asserted that recently there had been an off-the-record talk between

Mr. Andrei A. Gromyko and "a top-ranking American business-man." According to the article, Gromyko told the American that Premier Stalin had gradually reversed a pro-American attitude to one of suspicion and distrust that could be corrected only by a series of tangible deeds on the part of the United States. There followed a list of such deeds:

Elimination of all discriminatory trade practices and resumption of normal trade relations, stimulated by a $2,000,000,000 loan; cessation of what was termed United States and British "support of subversive Fascist and Hitler-ite elements" inside the Soviet-bloc nations; four-power unanimity on all questions concerning Germany; and Western "generosity" on reparations for the Soviet Union as provided in the Potsdam agreement.

None of these was so unreasonable as to seem an unlikely basis for negotiation. And, even though this was not an official approach, its authenticity seemed possible. It was known that, before Mr. Gromy-ko had returned to Moscow to become Deputy Foreign Minister, he had had talks with several prominent men of affairs; and it seemed likely that this may have been the theme running through all of them. At any rate, the publication of the story had its effect, along with other occurrences, in dampening the ardor of the Washington adventurers and lowering the temperature of the jingo press.

More hopeful still was the publication of a report delivered to Secretary Acheson by the American Friends Service Committee. A committee of fourteen prominent Quaker leaders had studied the possible ways of resolving the Russo-American crisis. Being Quakers, they had faith in the healing power of good will and a certain trust in men's faith and intelligence. They had talked with Americans and Russians, including Mr. Gromyko, and had come to the conclusion that the United States must now give evidence of good intentions. This evidence, they thought, might well consist in (1) promoting East-West trade and ending "economic warfare"; (2) working for a unified "neutral" Germany; and (3) proposing an agreement to place all atomic stockpiles under United Nations seal.

The Quakers understood the nature of totalitarian theory, but they believed quite simply that good will could overcome its most brutal intentions. They knew well enough that Communist doctrine holds inevitable a final conflict between communism and interna-tional capitalism, but it seemed to them that there were flexible elements in the Russian ideology, and even certain precedents, which made a fundamental change of attitude not impossible.

These were small indications. They might not, for all that, be unimportant, for they did indicate that men of sense and faith were beginning again to assert themselves against the purveyors of fear and hatred who had for some time been in power. Were there similar men in Russia? No one in the Western world knew. The warmaking machinery was still moving ponderously forward. The opposition to it was pitifully weak; but it existed, and it might grow.

CHAPTER VI *1950*

ON AUGUST 6, 1950, the American Congress was engaged, not in reducing taxes as it had fondly planned to do, but in devising more of them. It was appropriating billions for the Army, the Navy, and the Air Force; it was "imposing new security measures"; and it was lifting the statutory limits on the armed forces. The Congress was, in other words, stepping up the enlargement of the military apparatus.

The British Parliament had adjourned until October, but it was expected to reconvene before then to pass new legislation required by the emergency; and there had been an acrimonious last-day debate on military matters, climaxed by Mr. Churchill's denunciation of the government for its unreadiness. "They bear," he said, "a fearful accountability."[1]

The occasion of this attack, as of the Congress' sudden, almost hysterical, reversal, was, of course, the outbreak of hostilities in Korea. Berlin was now quiescent, no longer the center of anxious interest; and the airlift had been liquidated. General Clay had been succeeded by Mr. John J. McCloy, a civilian; and West Germany had become a Federal Republic, even if a clumsy-footed one. There were still monthly (or thereabouts) incidents in Berlin which made disturbance chronic, but for some time none of them had seemed likely to touch off immediate hostilities. Korea, however, was war. True, it was not literally the war with Russia which was now universally anticipated; but the difference seemed to split a very thin hair. The arms and the instructors and advisers of the North Korean armies were Russian, the planners and officers were Koreans from Siberia, probably Russian citizens, and the choice of time for the attack was clearly Russian.

1. *Hansard*, July 29, 1950.

Officially the Soviet Union was not engaged. The United States, however, was. Her armed forces found themselves overnight up to their necks in a disastrous and humiliating engagement, for they were obviously and almost pathetically unprepared for the task they were required to assume. In the first stages, the troops thrown into the path of the highly mechanized and well-trained North Korean armies were ridden down and slaughtered almost as though they had been savages opposed to civilized power. The British and French in Kenya, Malaya, and Indochina also had "brush-fire" wars to contend with. When they spoke of their opponents, they still talked about "terrorists" and "bandits"; but the bandit armies they had been fighting for several years had been successful enough to engage practically the whole of their regular armies. The only one of the really great powers of the world not engaged in war was Russia, a circumstance which disconcerted the West perhaps more than any other. For the maneuvering by which the Russians had succeeded in involving first France then Britain and finally the United States in costly and embarrassing struggles with her satellites, without herself appearing at all in the open, showed a finesse which made the Western diplomacy by comparison seem clumsy and loutish.

It had looked for a long time as though the Western Powers would refuse the gambit so temptingly offered in the Far East. If the United States intended to oppose the spread of communism in the East, why she should have allowed China to fall was a completely unanswerable question unless there was postulated a sudden reversal of long-pursued policy. A well-known group of Republicans had for years been pushing for such a change. During the year just past they had been responsible for continual persecution of Secretary Acheson in the now-familiar congressional blackmail pattern and for embarrassing, repeated attacks on the Department of State.[2]

These congressional pushers for a Pacific-first policy were actually the backers of a grand strategy whose chief author was General

2. It was only an extension of the lead furnished by the Knowland-Bridges-Judd-Hurley-Taft group which Senator McCarthy exploited in the Huey P. Long tradition. Senator McCarthy became an actively embarrassing appendage of the party. His Republican colleagues tried to look innocent and detached as his antics became more and more irresponsible; but actually he belonged to them and they to him.

Douglas MacArthur. General MacArthur was still in Japan in command of the forces of occupation, acting more and more like a lama, pompous, remote, and dictatorial. He had not been back in the United States since Japan had been conquered; but he had been a contender for the Republican presidential nomination in 1948, and his connections with the congressional group were well known. General Chennault and General Wedemeyer were among those in the military high command who also favored an aggressive policy in the Pacific. But General Marshall and General Omar Bradley (the former Chief of Staff and the present chairman of the Joint Chiefs of Staff) were known to believe that American power ought not to be risked in Japan, in Formosa, or in the Philippines—fringes of the vast continent of Asia, more than five thousand miles from the west coast of America. To take such a risk, they had felt, was, in General Marshall's phrase, to "overdeploy." And what he had meant could now be understood from the Korean disaster. For the choice was at once presented of sending all available forces and equipment there or of risking defeat.

Either was an intolerable choice. For Russia, with a vastly superior army, which could operate on interior lines of communication if she herself should be engaged, formed a core of continental power which was fringed on every side by fanatically dedicated satellites only asking the word of their master to be released. Korea, where American arms had been so humiliated, was almost the smallest and least significant of these surrounding allies. Suppose, while America was busy there, and the British and French were engaged in Malaya and Indochina, the armies of Poland, Romania, Hungary, and Czechoslovakia should be let loose on Yugoslavia and Greece, and the fully armed East Germans on unarmed West Germany? What could be done? And, if the Russian divisions were added, how much less could be done! They *could* be in Calais and Boulogne in a few weeks—as the more realistic of French leaders were insisting.

Debates in the House of Commons[3] had brought up facts well known even to casual newspaper readers. Indeed, on July 28 Mr. Emanuel Shinwell, Minister of Defense, had been quite frank in presenting the figures on which the government relied. The Russians, he had said, had 175 active divisions. Mr. Churchill was well

3. *Hansard,* July 29, 1950.

within probability in assuming that this figure meant some 80 ready to be launched without delay and possibly 300 ready in half a year. He also referred to the recent statement by Mr. Vinson (chairman of the Armed Services Committee of the House) that the tank strength of Russia stood at about 40,000, seven times that of the United States and more than seven times that possessed by the powers of western Europe. To reinforce his point, Mr. Churchill went on to consider what known strength there was to oppose the Russian juggernaut:

> Let us see what the Western Union can put against all this. M. Reynaud last week said that we and our European allies have in Western Germany two British divisions, two American and three French. For the rest, he said, the French have four divisions in Europe and I think the Belgians one—a total of 12. I should think that M. Reynaud is tolerably well informed upon these matters. On this assumption, Western Union would have 12 divisions, against more than 80; and of which less than two are armoured, against anything from 25 to 30.

That Mr. Churchill was substantially correct no one questioned. It was perhaps not strange that Europeans, already concerned, had begun to lie awake nights with worry.[4]

It was not so much war in Korea which was causing worry as the total reorientation of American policy. For this, Europe was unprepared. When President Truman had decided to meet aggression with resistance in Korea, there had been universal approval. But he had linked Korea with intervention in Formosa, with a new Philippine policy, and with enlarged assistance for the French against Ho Chi-minh. This action was more than a meeting of aggression with resistance; it was very nearly an adoption of MacArthurism. And MacArthurism, Europeans knew, was incompatible with Western defense.

For three years the United States had refused aid to Chiang Kai-shek, saying repeatedly that his was a corrupt and unrepresentative regime to which no further help would be given. By now the Nationalists held no continental territory; only Formosa remained in

4. Captain B. H. Liddell Hart, making an estimate on his own, a few weeks later put the proportions a little differently. Speaking at the Liberal Summer School at Cambridge University, he said (according to the *Times*, August 8, 1950) that "if war in Europe were to come tomorrow Russia would have 70 divisions and the Western Powers about seven. Even with the atomic bomb seven divisions could not resist 70, and one had to reckon with a quick Russian surge to the Channel in two to three weeks."

their hands, and, as the Korean War broke out, the Communist forces were gathering for an attack on that island which no one thought could be successfully resisted. At this late stage President Truman had suddenly announced that the Seventh Fleet would be interposed between the Communist hordes, already publicly committed to "liberation," and Chiang Kai-shek's last remaining island.

This action not only saved Formosa for the moment; it permitted the United States to maintain that Nationalist China should continue to be represented on the United Nations Security Council.

Although Secretary Acheson had repeatedly disclaimed responsibility, the United States had so far prevented action to seat the representatives of the new Chinese government. As long ago as January, indeed, the Russians, after objecting for some time to sitting with the unrepresentative Nationalists, had begun to boycott all meetings of United Nations agencies at which the Nationalists appeared. But the American attitude offended others than the Russians. India, for instance, though tormented by Communist agitation and Communist-inspired insurrection, sympathized with the Chinese struggle for freedom from domination by the West and for the establishment of economic reforms that would raise the standard of living. She had recognized the Communist government there, and Premier Jawaharlal Nehru was known to object strongly to the policy of excluding it from the Security Council. He might approve the opposition to aggression in Korea; but he could not be got to support an American alliance with the reactionary Kuomintang. The United States might well be embarked upon a costly policy that would alienate Europe without gaining Asia.

The absence of Russia from the Security Council proved useful to President Truman. When the North Koreans attacked South Korea, and Washington policy-makers decided to make an about-face, the convenience of acting for the United Nations occurred to someone. There followed a hectic night of telephoning and consultation. The Security Council met next day, and in the absence of Russia it declared the invasion of South Korea to be an act of aggression and invited the South Korean president and the Secretary-General of the United Nations to organize resistance. General MacArthur was designated commander-in-chief of the United Nations forces and was asked to fly its flag.

Shortly afterward, Mr. Trygve Lie, the Secretary-General, invited all the members (some fifty) who had signified their approval to send co-operating forces. Not until the last of July did the United Kingdom indicate that it would send ground forces. Until then, although some Australian air units and British and Canadian ships were in operation alongside those of the United States, the attack was mainly absorbed by American units flown in from occupation duties in Japan or ferried hastily across the narrow sea. There were never enough. They were always outnumbered in the early weeks by ten or twenty to one; they had at first to face tanks with not much more than hand weapons whose missiles bounced harmlessly off the steel armor. As might have been expected, furthermore, the Koreans proved to be masters of guerrilla tactics. The Americans fought a slugging, stubborn, retreating campaign, the most difficult kind for green troops, without ever winning a battle, or hardly an engagement, driven from one position after another. In a matter of four weeks, when the first few fresh troops from America began to land, the two divisions which had absorbed the punishment of the long battle in tropic heat and in the rainy season were utterly exhausted.

Time, a little time, had been gained. But the North Korean armies had proved to be tough and capable, aggressively led and well equipped. It was a question whether the United Nations forces could hold even a bridgehead around Pusan. General MacArthur, in his first report to the Security Council on July 29, had said they could —"there would be no Dunkirk"—but there were the gravest doubts in every mind.

The British were slow to act in Korea, primarily because of the decision to defend Formosa. The British had recognized the Communist government of China; and Formosa—as Secretary Acheson had repeatedly admitted and as had been agreed at Teheran and Yalta—was part of China. How could they oppose the attempt to consolidate Formosa into the Republic? And, if they did, the reaction not only in India but throughout the East might be severe; for the peoples of the East seemed determined to be quit of Western interference.

Even worse, the protection of Formosa might entail engaging American armed forces directly with Communist China. A greater disaster for the West could hardly be summoned to the mind. Yet it had always been inherent in MacArthurism, and MacArthur would certainly not trouble to avoid the clash.[5]

The whole swing to MacArthurism, indeed, was an embarrassment to the British. They may have reminded Mr. Truman of Premier Nehru's repeated warnings to the West that Asian nationalistic movements must be respected. In January, at a Commonwealth conference in Ceylon, Nehru had refused to consent to any proposal to assist the French in fighting Ho Chi-minh in Indochina and had spoken plainly of the unwelcome activities of colonial powers in the East. Yet Secretary Acheson had since announced that aid was to be given—and given not only to the government of Indochina, Bao Dai's puppet regime, but to the French as well. How Nehru must have regarded this violation of the national principle the American policy-makers may not have realized to the full; but the British knew well enough, and they were aghast.

When the President qualified his first announcement of the defense of Formosa with the remark that it "would be without prejudice to any future political settlement," Mr. Attlee publicly accepted the statement as satisfactory; but it can hardly have satisfied neutralist Asiatic statesmen.

Mr. Attlee finally came up to scratch—not with enough enthusiasm to suit Mr. Churchill, but with enough to be approved by the *Times*—and, when Parliament had adjourned, he spoke to the British people over the radio. The British probably had no considerable illusions about America—indeed, there was widespread distrust of American motives, especially among the workers who were Socialists. But they shared with the American capitalists a belief in what Mr. Attlee decided to call the "moral law":

The attack by the armed forces of North Korea on South Korea has been denounced as an act of aggression by the United Nations. No excuses, no propaganda by the Communists, no introduction of other questions can get over this: Here is a case of aggression. If the aggressor gets away with it, aggressors all over the world will be encouraged. . . .

I would ask you all to keep ever in mind the value of the things for which we stand—freedom, democracy, justice, and the supremacy of the moral law. All over the world we are face to face with fanatics who believe in another

5. On August 6 Mr. Averell Harriman, who was President Truman's newly appointed adviser on foreign policy, was in Tokyo conferring with General MacArthur. It was hoped by all those who sensed the gravity of the issues at stake that the President was about to check the haughty general.

creed. I think it is an evil creed, but there is no doubt that there are those who find in it an inspiration just as did the Nazis and Facists in their creed. All of them deny the whole moral basis on which civilization has been built.

Our fight is not only against physical but against spiritual forces. In Britain and the Commonwealth and in the democracies there are diverse creeds, but their adherents all believe in the supremacy of a moral law.

Let us, then, arm ourselves against evil with an equal enthusiasm to preserve and protect the higher creeds in which we believe.

It is doubtful whether Britishers—or Americans, for that matter—sincerely believed themselves so very superior morally to the Russians. What they did believe was something simpler: that fanatics on the loose had to be stopped. And they were willing, if need be, to go to war to stop them. It was tragic, as Mr. Attlee acknowledged, to have to turn aside from the reconstruction of British life which was going so well; but, if it had to be done, the hardships could be borne. It would not be easy. The aggressor could always pick his time and would always have an initial advantage over his victim, just as the armed burglar has over the peaceful householder; but a community determined to have law and order would eventually have it.

It was with difficulty that Pandit Nehru followed the British lead. President Truman's conversion to MacArthurism was too sudden, for in the East it was firmly believed that MacArthurism was deeply set in the old colonial tradition. He and his American supporters were regarded as classic reactionaries who believed in exploitation and the subjection of "lesser peoples." If there was one thing certain about the East, however, it was that national independence was now going to sweep everything before it. Indochina and Malaya were in rebellion—a rebellion with which India, nurturing still fresh memories of her own struggle for freedom, deeply sympathized. India was having her own troubles with Communists, and she had no love for a Russia that fomented those troubles. But, if she was to join in repelling aggression, such action would have to be clear of any interference with national self-determination. This policy was not only a matter of Pandit Nehru's preference; it was a political necessity. In July, however, India announced that she would send an ambulance unit to Korea.

Since the United States policy placed Pandit Nehru in difficulty, both politically and personally, he did a very characteristic thing. He suggested to both sides a way to prevent the conflict from spreading. The Americans had made difficulties for him; he now made difficulties for them. He simultaneously wrote letters to Secretary Acheson and to Premier Stalin. He suggested that the new Chinese government be seated on the Security Council and that Russia use her influence to stop hostilities in Korea.[6] Secretary Acheson, tardily followed by Prime Minister Attlee, rejected the proposal. The North Koreans would have to stop their attack and withdraw behind the thirty-eighth parallel whence the attack had been launched. Then other questions could be discussed. Premier Stalin, however, anticipated the American refusal. He not only agreed cordially to Nehru's proposal but published his response in Moscow. It was a considerable propaganda victory, or so it seemed at the moment. There was, nevertheless, a hardening determination in America, in Britain, and, it seemed, even in France and Italy to stop aggression and to stop it at once.

The British and Americans have never been inclined to discuss peace while war has been going on. This attitude might seem strange, since any settlement would presumably be only a definition of what the fighting had been about; but over and over again it has proved to be a democratic weakness. To the North Koreans nothing was said but that they must withdraw—that is, aggression must be stopped. But what was to happen to a Korea in which the northerners had withdrawn? What then?

Probably the specific aim of forcing Communist withdrawal to the line fixed at Potsdam, following the Yalta Agreement, was already obsolete. President Syngman Rhee had said that it was in several interviews, and President Truman had seemed to agree. The Potsdam settlement, of course, had never been a reasonable one. It had done about what the Treaty of Versailles had done in Austria after the 1914–18 war—divided the country so that substantially all the agriculture was in one new nation and all the industry in another. Nothing would do, now that the issue was in jeopardy, but some kind of reconstitution of the nation as a whole.[7] There appeared to be no

---

6. *Times* (London), July 15, 1950.

7. This had been the objective of a United Nations commission which had been in Seoul since 1948. But the northerners—no doubt preparing for the 1950 attack—had not consented to free elections. They had refused, in fact, to have anything to do with the commission.

chance now that the Communists would withdraw; they would have to be beaten back. They would then be convicted aggressors and so outlaws. No doubt there would be an interim administration and then elections under United Nations auspices. The Communists would be defeated and disgraced; most of them might even be in exile, so that an election would mean the loss of Korea to communism, at the very least. Meanwhile, presumably, the Syngman Rhee regime would be in control.

The prospect that Rhee might be put back in power over all Korea would be one which the East generally would resent, for his government had been corrupt and inefficient to a degree apparently matched only by that of the Kuomintang in China. Insiders had been exploiting the peasants and the nationalized industries, manipulating the political machinery, and generally making themselves rich and powerful at the public expense. These had been the characteristics of Kuomintang rule in China which had lost it the confidence of the nation and determined the American policy of nonsupport. General Marshall, particularly, had been unable to persuade himself that such a crowd ought to be supported. If such a government was too corrupt in China for American approval, it was also too corrupt in Korea—until MacArthurism made its conquest of Washington. Now the United States was getting into bed with any discredited regime —Chiang Kai-shek's, Syngman Rhee's, Bao Dai's—which would oppose the Communists. It was a fair inference, and probably the people of the East were making it, that the settlement, if America prevailed, would put the dictatorial regimes back into power. In consequence the American armies would have the task of suppressing the revolution which was sweeping the East—so dangerous a position that it seemed imperative to escape from it. Yet it was what MacArthurism implied.

A general idea of American intentions was outlined in a speech by Mr. John Foster Dulles on August 1. Mr. Dulles had been taken into the State Department in the spring of 1950 in an effort to reconstitute the bipartisan foreign policy that American refusal to give further support to the Chiang regime had destroyed. That he was an extreme conservative he had proved when he had run unsuccessfully for the Senate in 1949; he had offered the electorate an outright repudiation of President Truman's domestic policies. As the official representative of Republican thought in foreign affairs, the part he had played in the recent reversal of Eastern policy can be imagined.

Mr. Dulles' most recent appearance in the press had been his address to the Korean legislature, under the auspices of President Rhee, only about a week before the Communist attack. He had assured that assembly of American good will and support, and President Truman had done his best to make good Mr. Dulles' promises. Thus when he spoke again in San Francisco on August 1, 1950, what he said deserved to be regarded with respect. It was more important to know what Mr. Dulles thought than what Secretary Acheson might think. The Secretary was by now a convicted waverer; he and Dr. Jessup had had to eat a good many words when they embraced MacArthurism.

Mr. Dulles dealt with Russian intentions as the Republicans in the United States viewed them and with the policy America must develop as a counter. He thought, he said, that the attack in Korea opened a new chapter of history. It was the moment chosen by the Russians to risk armed attack.[8] Indirect Russian aggression was now being checked both in Europe and in Asia. Communism was either on the wane, as in France and Italy, or being repulsed, as in Indochina. In Europe the Russians wanted the Ruhr, in Asia they wanted Japan, because the possession of these two industrial areas would greatly alter the world's balance of power in their favor.

The American war aim was to contain communism, supremely difficult though that task might be with Russia at the world's strategic center. To this end Japan must be re-established in the East and Germany in the West as part of the "free world." Mr. Dulles did not go further and say that, beyond this aim, there lay the task of eradicating communism from China, from the East European countries, and ultimately from Russia. But what other conclusion was possible from the continual diatribes which now issued from every source of publicity in the West, including the speeches of statesmen, even of heads of governments?

It had been a year of spectacular success for the Politburo strategists. The entire capitalist and colonial world was in the turmoil inevitable when an offense has turned suddenly into a defense. Three

8. Comments on Mr. Dulles' San Francisco speech are based on the report of it in the *Times* (London), August 1, 1950.

years before, Russia had been regarded more as a nuisance than as an enemy. The Western planners had clearly determined that the Communist center should be destroyed in good time; but they had supposed that delay was an advantage. The atomic weapon in American possession made it possible to drive a hard bargain—so hard that perhaps war might not be necessary. Now communism was a threat far worse than the German-Japanese-Italian axis had ever been, more powerful, more fanatic, more united, more subversive! Russia, the hard core of the Communist area, was now completely surrounded by shock-absorbing satellites. These were even capable of making thrusts at the capitalist world on their own—serious thrusts, already engaging and holding down all available forces of the West. Germany and Japan would have to be rearmed; but half of Germany was Communist, and Japan had no supporting empire. Unless each was turned loose to conquer its own hinterland, neither could develop any great power. On second thought they might not be much more than outposts. Would they be willing ones?

The power vacuum created by the final defeat of the Axis powers in 1946 had been filled partly by Russian expansion and partly by Western support of weak border states—Greece, Turkey, and Iran, for instance, and, until recently, Korea. Russia, however, had the overpowering advantage of expanding from a continental center toward continental borders. America was the encircling power, and it was General Marshall's judgment that the task was requiring a dangerous "overdeployment." It was a poor bluff, because the enemy was in a position to assess the weakness. The position of the West had become progressively worse; in Europe there now were eighty Russian divisions to the Western twelve, and in the East a despised little people could attack and humiliate the United States.

Perhaps, when, in 1946, Molotov had withdrawn from the Marshall Plan discussions, his move had been smarter than had appeared at the time. For Russia, without burdening herself to supply the kind of aid the United States had since given to such European countries as would co-operate with her, had succeeded in gaining allies. How faithful they were there was no way of knowing. Czechoslovaks, Hungarians, and Romanians lived under a typical police-state regime, so that, if there was any opposition, it could not be expressed. In Asia, however, the co-operation appeared genuinely fanatical, because Russia appeared to be on the side of liberation from centuries of Western hegemony. This domination all those nations were determined to end once and for all.

It was this push for national self-determination with which Pandit Nehru sympathized so strongly; and in allowing itself to be put in the position of opposing it—as MacArthurism required—the West risked alienating its one strong ally in the East. The first evidence that India's feelings had been deeply exacerbated appeared in the early August meeting of the Security Council. The Russians had boycotted this body for seven months, refusing to sit with representatives of Nationalist China; but on July 30, Mr. Malik, the Russian representative, notified the other members that he would assume the chairmanship for August in his regular turn. There was much flurried consultation as to what this sudden change of view implied. When Mr. Malik proposed that the first order of business should be the admission of Communist China rather than the Korean situation, it appeared that the Russians had come back to follow up their advantage in accepting Pandit Nehru's mediation proposal, which the United States and Britain had rejected. He was voted down; but India voted with him. It appeared that for the moment, at least, the Russians had succeeded in splitting India off from the West—another victory without resort to force.

Up to Hiroshima Day the conflict in Korea had not spread to China, but the behavior of the Russians at the meeting of the Security Council raised the suspicion that they intended that it should. Obviously, if the Western nations could be embroiled with China, an endless sink would be opened up for all their wealth and manpower. It must be said that American stubbornness suited this design very well. By continuing to refuse what Easterners regarded as the real government of China a Security Council seat, the United States lost all the friends she had or might have gained in the East—unless, indeed, defeated and occupied Japan could now be said to be a friend.

Even the conservative London *Times* was appalled by the gulf which was being opened up between East and West by the combination of Russian astuteness and Anglo-American mistakes:

If they—the Western members of the United Nations—are to win more of the sympathy of the Asian peoples in the Korean war it is not too soon for them to prepare and put before the United Nations their own proposals for the future of Korea. It may be argued that the future will be determined by the course of the fighting, but Soviet propaganda in favor of peace and Korean unity (however hollow to Western ears) has a disturbing effect on peoples with no near knowledge of Russian methods. To offset the propaganda it would be wise to reaffirm in the clearest manner that the future of Korea lies with the United Nations and that the United Nations will still strive to establish a united and independent Korea, led by a Government based on the peoples' choice. . . .[9]

By Hiroshima Day, this had not been done. Clearly the propaganda battle was being lost in the East, as was shown by India's stand. The West, by linking Korea with Formosa and Indochina, had allowed itself to be pictured there as attempting by force to re-establish the old discredited imperialism. This could never be done except by a military effort which would take years and might well wreck the Western economies. What way out would be found, short of another reversal—which would now abandon the East to communism—was not apparent.[10]

There may have been something in what Europeans had been saying about Americans for some years—that they were thoroughly undone by the prospect of atomic warfare because they had so much to lose! Certainly the Americans had been amazed at the temerity of the Russians in the face of atomic threat; the Baruch proposals had met a stony resistance which seemed completely unreasonable. It could only be explained by supposing that Russians had an attitude toward the possibility of atomic destruction entirely different from

9. Editorial, August 3, 1950.

10. In a temperate dispatch from Tokyo to the *Observer* (August 6, 1950) Mr. Michael Davidson had this to say:

"This war has brought political lessons, too. It has brought again into prominence that lamentable weakness in the Western political armament in Asia—the sort of 'leaders' whom choice or opportunity have set up as the figureheads of Western-sponsored democracy: Syngman Rhee, Chiang Kai-shek, Bao Dai, and certain politicians nearer Tokyo. These are men despised by the people they are supposed to inspire; it is not pleasant to think that British lives might be lost in support of such people.

"There is some disquiet here over General MacArthur's visit to Formosa. It is felt that nothing could be more impolitic in Asia than parleys, apparently as allies, between the American Commander-in-Chief and the discredited Kuomintang boss. Indeed, the feeling here goes further: there is regret, among the Americans and others, that President Truman's declaration on Formosa was not accompanied by the condition that Chiang Kai-shek should leave the island—voluntarily or under duress. Only then could opinion in South-East Asia be convinced that the American action is solely anti-Communist; to any Asian, parleying with Chiang means treating with a corrupt, detested and reactionary clique. . . ."

that of Americans. They could not be ignorant; indeed, there was reason to suppose that they were approaching the successful manufacture of atomic bombs themselves, though only the scientists thought that the problem could be mastered before 1952 or 1953. Meanwhile, if the Russians believed half what they said about the "warmongering" of the capitalists, they had been living in imminent danger. Yet they had been acting as though it was they, and not the Americans, who had the Bomb. They had been aggressively defiant. They had successfully developed a ring of buffer states, taken by Russian-fomented Communist revolution in defiance of specific treaty provisions designed to insure free elections. The West had been bluffed successfully. The time had passed when preventive war of the costless sort could be considered. Now, in 1950, the West believed that Russians had the preponderance; and it was presumed that they were beginning to risk something more than "indirect aggression."

Such a program seemed, on analysis, to be beyond Russian strength. They did not, for all their territory and numbers, produce more than twenty million tons of steel a year. Britain alone produced almost that much. Yet they had in being armored divisions of such magnitude and proved efficiency that no one doubted their power to overrun all Europe, to seize the Middle East, and so to possess themselves of the whole of the Eurasian continent. They might not be able to keep it. American preponderance of atomic bombs might destroy their cities and administrative centers if they could be located; and certainly a mighty effort would be made to reconquer the territory they would have taken. But their land forces were undoubtedly greatly superior to those of the West. How could they have built the vast air fleets, the multitude of tanks, and the hundreds of submarines they were reported to possess? For they had had also to rebuild cities devastated by the Germans just as the Europeans had, and with far less productive capacity for the task.

No one knew the answer to this riddle. It could only be assumed that, if Russians had used their steel for tanks and submarines, it could not have gone into transport, buildings, and machinery. Recovery must have been postponed. Europe, on the other hand, had hoped for no more war and had chosen recovery; and there was no doubt that it was well along. Europe, thanks to the Marshall Plan,

began to have almost as much to lose as America and began, therefore, to take a much more frightened view of a prospective war.

Recovery was well along in Europe; but America was experiencing a real boom. The year had begun with a recession in prospect,
but it had ended differently. In the weeks before Hiroshima Day the
steel industry produced at more than 100 per cent capacity—more
than a hundred million tons a year! The anticipated depression had
had a good start: Unemployment had risen to six, then to seven millions; prices had shown some weakness before consumer resistance;
but government measures to expand credit and induce buying had
halted the decline. The federal budget had been unbalanced, and inflationary policies resumed. These measures had been good for business, even if bad for pensioners and others with inelastic incomes—
such groups had, in fact, been the sufferers from the policies pursued ever since 1933 and by now, through the loss of purchasing
power, had had their incomes reduced by more than half. The tax
policies of the Congress and the credit policies of the federal agencies, it was demonstrated, had the power to check deflation. It remained to lift the burden from those least able to bear the losses
from inflation; but there seemed to be no intention of attempting
such a task.

The hundred million tons of steel produced annually had gone
into new automobiles, railway equipment, buildings, and machinery.
It was almost true to say that during the war and postwar years industry had been wholly re-equipped. New plant and new machinery
had replaced the old; and with every such change efficiency had increased. Transportation, communications, and record-keeping had
improved immensely. There had been, in fact, something like a new
industrial revolution. It had been very uneven. There were still backward industries—building was the most notable—but they were on
the defensive. On the whole, American industry was now coming
into that phase of efficiency which had been anticipated since the
invention of scientific management some seventy years before.

There was not yet the social organization necessary to the continued steady functioning of this economy; it depended on inflation,
and overoptimistic allocation by profit-seekers of capital for expansion caused enormous waste. The government, however, filled in

some of the gaps left by private capital through the continued functioning of its credit agencies, by now familiar, if not accepted, institutions. They had been established in the depression of the 1930's and had grown to meet the needs for expansion in World War II. There were recurrent drives to curtail or abolish all such functions. They emanated from conservatives in the Congress, acting at the instigation of local bankers; but the truth was that the functions were so necessary that they could not be dropped.

There was, then, in the United States, a machine whose productivity was without precedent—a machine capable of what to the uninitiated must seem miracles of performance. It had swamped Germany with guns and armor, ships, motor transport, communication equipment—all the apparatus of mechanized warfare—in 1944–45. Yet it was essentially inefficient. From now on—until America had accepted the principle of socialization—the advance would be appreciably hampered by insistent adherence to freedom of enterprise. In the years to come the superior linking-up of industries, the establishment of planned relationships, and the calculated allocation of resources in the Socialist systems would undoubtedly prove their superiority. But they had first to catch up with American industry's enormous capacity to produce. And that day would be some time ahead.

If the Russians did not know how far ahead, it must be because they could not read or because their ideology distorted their view of facts as much as the capitalists' view was distorted by the irrelevant Russian elements in the planned industrial system of the Soviets. The Russians had an enormous continent, what had been called by the geopoliticians the "heartland" of the world. Its resources, in what counted in this generation, were immense, even if sometimes exaggerated. There was every likelihood that inherent superiorities of system might in fifty years enable Russia to equal or even surpass the productive power of America. But until then a challenge to a trial of strength would be foolhardy. True, the Russians could overrun western Europe, the East, and the Middle East by sheer weight and numbers, and the United States probably could not prevent them. But American productive power could exploit any beachhead, and meanwhile atomic bombs would be falling on the centers of control so necessary to a planned system. Russia would be very foolish to risk a trial of strength now. The only question was whether the shut-in Politburo members were aware of it.

The Iron Curtain had been amazingly efficient in shutting off travel and communications. It was the theory of the West, of course, that the curtain would stifle progress of all sorts in the confined countries. When Russians were not allowed to travel abroad, read Western literature, or even talk to Westerners, they must lack everything they could learn from such contacts. Such enforced isolation was typical of a police state which feared competition. It was not so often realized that the Iron Curtain might be a specific preparation either for an imminent war or for an imminent collapse of capitalism; it could not represent a permanent policy unless the directors of the police state believed their own propaganda—that the capitalist nations were so decadent and far gone in rottenness that nothing whatever could be learned from them. And this belief, in turn, was hardly consistent with the facts turned up during the year in the Fuchs case in Britain and the Gold case in the United States. The Russians had risked a good deal to steal atomic secrets.

The Russians might believe that conflict was being forced upon them. They often said so. They talked about encirclement exactly as Hitler had once talked. Western statesmen were inclined to the notion that this talk was only propaganda for internal consumption—to keep low-standard workers from questioning their condition. The West certainly had no concerted plan for attack, whatever might be in the minds of some inner circle of official or unofficial strategists. The Russians may have believed, nevertheless, that so powerful a nation as the United States, with strong allies and with a deadly enemy, *must* be intending conquest.

The weakening of communism in France, Italy, Belgium, and Holland, its disappearance from Britain (practically speaking), and its diminution even in western Germany was a measure of the reestablishment of prosperity. All the indexes of production were on the rise. It is true that the Atlantic nations were basically capitalist (even Britain) and so linked with the United States as to be dependent for their prosperity on hers; but the establishment of an Atlantic community provided a wider and more secure basis for every part of it. Russia might have the heart of the continent; but Europe had always possessed its brains and its culture and for some time to come would continue to possess these. Europe, furthermore, might still gain strength from its colonies, past and present: the British Commonwealth, the French Union, and the Belgian and Dutch colonies and connections. The transformation of empires into federations might turn out to be successful. India, Pakistan, and Ceylon were already loyal members of the Commonwealth, even though they had independent notions about international relations. The Western nations might find ways of tying Africa, the Middle East, and the Far East to the West.

They were, anyway, making a good try. During this year the United Nations had been busy setting up its administrative machinery for aid to underdeveloped areas; the old empires had been turning into commonwealths; and President Truman's now famous Fourth Point had, after a severe struggle with the Congress, been implemented, even if only feebly, by an authorization of twenty-five million dollars. There was a strong current toward independence running in people's minds everywhere, and it was the American intention to take advantage of it. By raising the standards of backward peoples, the viability of their economies might be more assured. Their independence, when they got it, would not then disappoint them. They would be less envious neighbors in the contracting world, and they might get used to looking for leadership in its old accustomed places rather than in the new Mecca, Moscow.

Britain had lost a child and gained a friend in India. She had the same chance elsewhere; and probably she would take advantage of it. The French Union was a valiant attempt to bring all the French colonies into equal relationship with the homeland. Many of them did not appear to appreciate the privilege of becoming French; but the effort to persuade them was genuine. Indonesia gained independence through Dutch stubbornness and bitter refusal to recognize realities until it was too late to save anything. Whether these efforts would suffice to counter the attractions of communism—which assumed the false face of independence everywhere—it was too soon to say.

It was not certain that the West yet knew how to develop the backward areas or that it would persist in their support. It was only within the past few years that national budgets had begun to allocate substantial funds for development abroad. There had, of course, been foreign investment for profit-making purposes, most of it involving loss from the point of view of good will, since it required exploitation of the grossest sort; but this use of tax funds for expenditure in other lands without expectation of return except in friendship was something new. There were many Western taxpayers who doubted the necessity or utility of these expenditures, and their skepticism was reflected in legislative reluctance to vote the funds. Even less auspicious was the evident tendency of the American Fourth Point program to degenerate into a new attempt at exploiting backward regions for the benefit of American investors. The United Nations would presently enlarge its efforts to develop these areas. Whether the empires would step aside for United Nations efforts was something not yet decided.

Of these programs, the British Colonial Development and Welfare Fund was least subject to homeland opposition and to pressures toward exploitation. It had originated in depression days, when an epidemic of riots had spread everywhere in the colonies, beginning in the West Indies. The disturbances had been attributed to the prevalent depression; but a royal commission, of which Lord Moyne had been chairman, had dissipated that notion. The colonies were so backward, and had begun to have such vivid ideas of the contrast between their own condition and that of other peoples, that they found it intolerable not to take some action. Parliament had responded at first in a small way but later, as the idea became a familiar one, more generously. There was, nevertheless, always a question whether the resources of Britain would stretch far enough to do any real good. Cleverness can sometimes be substituted for capital. But in the British colonies cleverness had to operate through an almost impermeable bureaucracy. In order not to disturb the upper classes, the British civil servants shaped the fund as a welfare enterprise. They approved a modest supply of schools, hospitals, and sewage disposal works, but any economic development which threatened monopolies or interfered with the supply of labor or the rate of wages they regarded as a threat.

Like the British program, the American Fourth Point program was hampered by lack of funds. The Congress evidently planned, not to lend needed capital without expectation of return, but to prepare the way for American private investment for profit. The scare furnished by the Korean incident might make the Congress more generous with taxpayers' money. But it took a long time for developmental enterprises to make much change in the economies they operated in—decades, in most instances, rather than years— and there did not seem to be decades left now in the terrible struggle for men's minds and souls into which the skeptical Americans had been drawn. Twenty-five million dollars was a dangerously low bid for new allies in 1950. It was probably far from enough to compete with communism. America could have afforded far more, but of course the Congress genuinely did not believe that more would be of any use.

Nothing seemed to count now but military might. The Congress appropriated twenty-five million dollars for aid to backward folk, but five billions (or more—the amount was not specified) to the Western powers for rearmament and some twenty-five (at least) billions for the armed forces at home. That contrast was the measure of the Congress' feeling about the utility of good will in 1950.

One must consider, of course, what the contemporary climate was like in the United States. The automotive industry was breaking records week by week, and the roads and streets were crowded with shiny new cars; electric household machines of all sorts were being absorbed into family life with undiminished enthusiasm; cities were throwing out satellite circles of prosperous suburbs (thus ruining themselves); the railways were offering air-conditioned travel in silver-seeming trains; and the airlines were expanding their services with huge new planes. A catalogue of goods and services available to consumers would be long and varied, suitable to a maturing electric age and a people avid for its products. This material prosperity was the background for profound changes in living which were now coming to a kind of climax, just as the scientific management, which made them possible, had come to a kind of apotheosis.

No one—or so few as not to count—any longer resisted the momentum of change and talked about the good old days and ways. There were people who "would not have a television set in the house"; but most of them gave way gradually under the pressure of juniors in the home. Old people discovered the superior comfort of journeys in planes; and nice old ladies smoked and sunned themselves on endless miles of beaches. The mobility of people led to impermanence of home places. Middle-class families learned to be at home anywhere; fewer of them possessed houses and, when they did, seldom had them paid for—credit was made so easy by federal guaranty of mortgages—before they were ready to dispose of them and move on. Circles of friends were not old and accustomed. There were fewer and weaker roots going down into local and regional soil. One place was, to Americans, much like another; and, indeed, it would often be hard to tell, from looking at a street, or even at a city, where, geographically, it was. These signs and symptoms of modernity were sometimes deplored, sometimes praised; but they had undoubtedly come to stay. For, once they were accepted, they seemed agreeable to those who consumed the goods and lived in the ever growing and changing cities and towns. It was a maxim that everything an American now possessed would be changed for the better within a short time. Television would have color; automobiles would have superhighways to travel on; houses would have earth pumps for heating and cooling; cities would be better planned. It was not to the half-satisfactions of the present that Americans consented but to a vision of their perfection.

Everyone, generally speaking, was won over to the economics that supported this way of living. Factories had to be rebuilt, perhaps relocated, certainly retooled, with great frequency, necessitating high profits and high allocations out of profits for depreciation and expansion. There were enormous wastes, but there were also some spectacular successes. There was no sentiment for nationalizing industries and planning their future with a view to making the best use of national resources; it was felt, instead, that those who were engaged in the current investment spree ought to let more people in on it. The boom was not quite like that of the 1920's. It did not operate on such thin margins; its excesses could be checked by government action; but the essentials were the same. There was a whooping prosperity which need have no end.

The American boom was catching. It enabled the more staid British to follow in the wash and allowed most of them to think their welfare state safely established, though members of the government knew better. It did not, however, lead to any feverish emulation in spite of the transfusions of efficiency so enthusiastically carried out by the Economic Co-operation Administration. The British budget showed a characteristic surplus; the British workmen, if they struck less, did not work harder; and the British people had not torn themselves loose from old roots to the same extent as had Americans. The recovery of Britain, furthermore, was not a safe and stable one, although the "dollar gap" had been closed sooner than anyone had expected, and the standard of living (except for some remaining shortages—meat, sugar, fats, and so on) was undoubtedly higher for the workers than it had been before the war. There existed what the *New Statesman* called "an Indian Summer." Winter would come when the climate in America changed. Then Marshall and other aid would dry up, exports to the dollar area would diminish, and fifty million people would again become conscious of living in a confined island with very limited resources. For the moment, however, all was well.

All was well in France, too, in a comparative sense. It was her spiritual and social troubles that were not cured. Her defeat by the Germans was not easy to live with; and years of occupation had enforced the humiliation and made it semipermanent. France was, if possible, feeling even sorrier for herself than was Britain, and in French hearts, far more than in British, the canker of defeatism enlarged. In reality France was prosperous. Her countryside was fruitful again, even though this year's crop did not promise well. Devastation had been mostly repaired with extremely generous American assistance; her cities teemed with busy workers; her factories were operating. But she had not learned some essential lessons. Her farmers were still grasping and unco-operative; her well-to-do still found ways to evade their taxes. Her cost of living was rising so rapidly that the workers, even with continual strikes and threats of strikes, were falling behind in real wages. In consequence of this fall and of deficient social devices, her slums grew worse, and living standards declined; and, again in consequence, the industrial and white-collar workers were disaffected and unco-operative, and the bureaucracy slowed down and became more obstructive.

This catalogue of social diseases could with even greater truth be applied to Italy and, to a less degree, to Belgium and Holland. Europe was a sick society, in spite of prosperity of a sort. Her leaders were the center, perhaps to some extent the cause, of the sickness. There were notable exceptions, but most of those in power were rightists, allied with clerical, military, and business groups. What the Russians said of the United States was far more actually true of western Europe. In the United States there was an openness, a freedom, a progress, which dissolved neo-Fascist conspiracies before they came to anything. But on the continent of Europe the faction which could not win in America had a fast grip on political power. Strangely enough, it was a grip which was tightened by American action, for those who administered the fiscal aid represented by the Marshall Plan and defense assistance belonged to the very sort who had been repudiated in one American election after another for twenty years. They were the natural allies of Fascist-inclined Europeans. They meant to keep their friends in power; and they so far had.

Evidence that this policy led to the maintenance of large Communist, and therefore disloyal, minorities in every European country seemed to make no impression. In spite of the statesmen, as recovery came, the liberal fringes of communism were trimmed. Natural socialists returned to their old faith. The alliances made by the ECA representatives and the diplomats thus appeared justifiable; but actually they were a nearly fatal drawback. For the death wish in every European nation, fostered in the people by the conviction that nothing was to be gained by fighting for their ruling classes, was likely to precipitate the very disaster America sought to avert— the overrunning of all western Europe by Communist armies. In 1950 there would hardly have been more than token opposition to a Russian march to the Channel, and Americans who thought otherwise were living in a dream of their own conjuring. Indeed, the inroads of MacArthurism induced a deeper wave of pessimism in Europe, for Americans were now embarking on absolutely fatal policies in the East which would eat up all the resources they could get together. Europe, so long as the Eastern sink was swallowing up American men and material, was on her own and was thus defenseless. If this abandoning of Europe seemed inconsistent with President Truman's expressed convictions—and those of Secretary Acheson—it was still fact, not fancy, and had to be reckoned with.

The American legend was still strong in Europe, but the Korean debacle was damaging it. On Hiroshima Day the bridgehead around

Pusan had narrowed to a hundred-mile circle, and, although the Marines had landed, the North Koreans still had the initiative, and the narrowing was continuing day by day. Dispatches from the front—especially the frank ones to British papers, but also those from Mr. Homer Bigart of the *New York Herald Tribune,* for instance—pictured the Americans as having mediocre equipment, inferior training, and a good deal less ability to stand up to the terrible requirements of warfare in the oriental tropics than had the Koreans. Mao Tse-tung had said that the American army was "a paper dragon," a cruel quip which had flown speedily all over the East. The East was eager to believe that the American legend was fiction; Europe was not eager—at least that part of it which was not communist—but faith was shaken. So long as there was a choice between a Communist police state and a kind of American hegemony, the choice would be easy. But Europeans were beginning reluctantly to doubt whether the choice could really be made.

Europeans were far less impressed with supposedly high American standards of life than they had been. While young Americans were fighting with old, reconditioned equipment[11] and stumbling into action without proper preparation or leadership, the whole of America, evidently, had gone on a hoarding spree, determined not to be without luxuries and comforts even if the fighting men suffered. She was heading into certain inflation too; even Mr. Baruch had said so.[12] Although prices had jumped, the President had stubbornly refused to consider controls or even taxes which might check the competition for goods. European workers wondered whether their security might not after all be greater than that of American workers. There were other signs which were not reassuring. There never had been such profit-making from national emergency as was being recorded now.[13] Yet month after month the concerns receiving these profits raised their prices. The resulting pressure on the standard of living was enormous. The conditions were being established

11. According to Mr. Bigart, *News-Chronicle* (London), August 9, 1950.

12. *Time,* August 7, 1950.

13. Seventeen United States steel companies reported combined profits for the first half of 1950 of $327,000,000, which was 18 per cent more than for the previous six months. General Motors' six-month profits were $485,000,000, which was 59 per cent greater than for the previous six months—which had itself been a record period. So it went through the whole list of industries.

for the kind of inflationary spiral all economic planners most dread. The government was about to spend many billions for war materials; and this expenditure would intensify the competition for goods, would drive prices higher, and would make life more difficult for those with fixed incomes. It seemed likely that the President would be forced to accept some sort of responsibility for stabilizing the economy. But it obviously seemed to him unnecessary.

Europeans could not understand such shortsightedness. They wondered whether the Americans believed that what they had got into in Korea, and were possibly about to get into in China, could be taken in their stride without extraordinary measures. It was true that the national income was up to 267 billion dollars, that 61 million people were at work, and that 15–25 billion dollars' worth of war materials could probably be made by cutting down the automotive and radio industries by not more than 20 or 25 per cent—which would do no harm. But 15 billion dollars would not be the total. If MacArthurism prevailed, it would hardly be a start.

They were, in short, skeptical of American intentions toward themselves and shaken in their belief that America was wisely led or normally cautious about commitments. The wisdom of an Atlantic pact seemed more questionable now than ever before; yet the United States was urgently pressing Europeans to say what they could do, with and without American assistance, to increase and speed up their military preparations. They were told bluntly that they were proposing too little and that it would be too late. Europe produced new proposals, but attached prominently was the proviso that these should be paid for with American funds.

America was willing to pay. This was one of those times of panic when the Congress loses all its native caution. Matters about which it had been niggardly for years were suddenly financed with ridiculous lavishness. The President was now being asked to accept enough funds to choke all the administrative services. But politics was not adjourned; and Europe was more impressed by the strange, muddy compromises of Washington—especially the compromise with MacArthurism—than by the sudden spendthrift atmosphere.

Mr. Churchill had said in his speech on defense in the House of Commons that the sole protections of Europe were the bomber squadrons in East Anglia and the stock of atomic bombs possessed by America. Everyone recognized the truth of what he said. There was no infantry, no armor, to match the Russians'; and there was now displayed a deplorable, even a demoralizing, weakness in arms of the traditional sort. No war with Russia could be won now unless atomic weapons counted. But what the comparative strengths for this kind of warfare were probably no one knew. Secrecy in the United States had been carried to such lengths that, according to the practicing atomic scientists, it interfered seriously with further progress in research. Since the Fuchs case[14] the restrictions had been redoubled; and in June the President, in what must have been a purely political gesture, urged the Federal Bureau of Investigation to further efforts. The United States was just next to a police state now. But it was known, because the Atomic Energy Commission said so, that new types of bombs were being made and were being stockpiled in such numbers as to assure a safe lead in competition with Russia.

It *was* competition with Russia, now, not open competition, but a horrible kind of race, run in the dark, down obscure ways toward destruction. On September 23, 1949, the President had announced to a stunned Western world that there had undoubtedly been an atomic explosion in Russia. He did not say when the event had occurred or how it had become known. He was as reassuring as he dared to be in the circumstances; but the official consternation was perceptible in immediate protestations that the event was not unexpected and that it changed no plans. That such reassurances were nonsense no one needed to be told. The Russians were at least two, perhaps five, years ahead of the schedule set for them in strategic calculations. They might soon forge ahead in the race.[15]

In this crisis it was again the physical rather than the social scientists or the statesmen who came up with constructive suggestions.

14. Dr. Klaus Fuchs was head of the department of theoretical physics at Harwell, the most important British atomic-energy research center. He had been an important member of the working team which had produced the first bomb in the United States. He was accused of passing secret information to Russian agents at various periods from 1943 to 1947 and was convicted and sentenced to fourteen years' imprisonment on March 1, 1950. Others who had been part of the spy ring were later apprehended.

15. See statements to this effect by prominent American scientists in *Bulletin of the Atomic Scientists*, October, 1949.

The scientists had had by now several years not only of rough-and-tumble political fighting but of time to think. Some of them had withdrawn altogether from work on the atomic problems connected in any way with warfare.[16] Some had even given notice of complete objection to war work and had organized the Society for Social Responsibility in Science, of which Dr. Victor Paschkis, director of an engineering research laboratory at Columbia University, was president.[17] Other scientists might perhaps try, by giving or withholding their knowledge, to control public policy. They felt, at least, that events had justified a new demand that their superior qualifications as policy-makers be recognized.

The *Bulletin of the Atomic Scientists* for October, 1949, carried a suggestion from Professor Leo Szilard that seemed to offer a practicable alternative to present American policy, and its possibilities were to be further developed by Professor Hans Morgenthau, who would bring to it the knowledge and skill of the political scientists.

Professor Szilard's idea was to abandon the Atlantic Pact and neutralize Europe. The pact had seemed sufficient security to some people once; it could seem sufficient to no one any more. He wrote:

> Clearly, the time is not far off, when in case of war Russia will be in a position to deliver bombs anywhere in Western Europe and to deliver them in significant quantity.
> If the time thus comes when Paris, Brussels and Amsterdam face destruction within twenty-four hours after the outbreak of war . . . will it be much consolation for them to know that, some ten or fifteen years after their destruction, the United States may be victorious and might then help them to rebuild . . . ?[18]

Western European countries ought to be allowed to withdraw from the Atlantic Pact. Not that we should abandon them to their fate; we should in fact promise (1) to go to war if Russia should attack or occupy any of them; (2) to respect their neutrality as long as it was respected by Russia; and (3) to refrain from using atomic bombs or strategic bombing of any kind so long as no atomic bombs were being produced on their territory. Having made such a promise, we ought to go on assisting these nations and even encourage them to build up modest armaments of their own. They would then be

16. For instance, Professor Harold Urey.
17. *Bulletin of the Atomic Scientists,* November, 1949, p. 312.
18. "Shall We Face the Facts," *Bulletin of the Atomic Scientists,* October, 1949.

strong enough to be genuinely neutral, even toward us. Presumably Russia would prefer a neutral Europe to a Europe that she would have to occupy in case of war with the United States in order to prevent American use of it. This neutralization of all areas caught between the power systems of America and Russia would remove the most important area of conflict. What would the United States and Russia have to fight about if all the rest of the Western world were neutral?

This ingenious suggestion of Dr. Szilard was made in the fall of 1949 just after the announcement of the atomic explosion in Russia. Evidently no one paid any attention to it. In fact, after an interlude in Washington of what could only be described as panic, our statesmen resorted to intensifying the same policies which had presumably caused Russia to turn all her resources into the perfection of the Bomb. The considered American riposte to the Russian explosion came in January. It was announced that H-bombs would be made.

The events which, taken together, informed the lay world of what the scientists had always known—that it was possible to build weapons a thousand times more powerful than the atomic bomb used in the Bikini tests—were so fantastic as to seem like occurrences in a nightmare. To tell a person whose intelligence has made the supreme effort of comprehending the Hiroshima occurrence, and whose nervous system has tried to accommodate itself to its possession by an enemy with whom his own country is rushing into war, that the threat is now to be multiplied a thousand times is to ask for demoralization. The moral and psychological condition of most Americans could be fairly described as demoralized already; and this new demand on the human system was altogether too much. There followed a series of occurrences such as might be expected only in a horrible fantasia of some sort, the kind of thing from which there ought to be an awakening and a recovery of sanity. The sleeper ought to be able to chase away such a dream, the observer to walk out of the theater into the cooling air of night. The most dreadful feature of the January disclosures was the waking, the going-out into the air, and the knowing that there was to be no relenting, no end of the fantasy. The worst, the worse than worst, was true. Somehow it had to be lived with. It could not be, yet it had to be.

One of the finest minds and most morally sensitive persons in America was F. O. Matthiesen, professor of English and American literature at Harvard. As James Forrestal, as fine a mind but with a different view of the world, had done a year before, he destroyed himself. Accommodation was simply impossible. The horror could not be lived with. Matthiesen left a note explaining that this was so. He had believed, especially, that it was man's duty not only to develop his intelligence but to have the moral courage to do what his intelligence directed. He had been a stalwart in every movement for freedom and unity in his generation. He had suffered for it the displeasure of those who found conformity to convention easier; and he had often been warned to behave. But he had never compromised. He had always faced reality and followed his conviction about what it required of him. But this reality had implications beyond his ability to accept. His mind brought him face to face with the probability of human destruction. And there was nothing he could do which would, to the least degree, affect the inevitable progress of events to the climax in destruction.

There were many more ordinary men who suffered, in only less degree, these same spiritual agonies. They saw that the end might well be the reduction of the planet to a cinder; they saw too that there was little if anything they could do to influence events. But somehow they found the reserves of courage to live with terror until the end, if end it was to be, came on. Perhaps it was not courage they possessed. Perhaps they were able to go on because they were neither so intelligent nor so sensitive to their responsibilities. At any rate, most of them still went on. But there was turmoil in many a soul whose body did its daily routine tasks, read about the war in the East, the maneuvers of Malik at Lake Success, or the rearmament of western Europe, and shuddered—but still went on. Newspapers were published, families went to the seaside as summer came, students read their books of law, politics, geography, philosophy; physicists went on making bombs too. But it was only rather careless young men or women who could feel any confidence in the future, as they went to work, read the papers, swam in the sea, or did their reading. Their elders seemed to retreat into a stupor. Many, perhaps most, carefully avoided any discussion of the only thing in the world which really mattered now. They did not think of it if they could help it; and in this way they managed to carry on.

The source, the heart of the malevolent emanations, was what the newspapers, reducing the incredible to print, called the "H-bomb"— "H" standing for hydrogen. It seemed now not only that the unstable isotope of uranium, U238, was to be available for destruction as fission took place but that the lighter materials at the other end of the atomic scale could be detonated in the thermal conditions established by the fission of uranium. Such temperatures had never been available before, since they were such as had only existed in the sun; but they were approximated when the now conventional A-bomb went off.

Physicists had long understood the principles of the H-bomb; but it was not they who precipitated the discussion. For example, when in March, 1950, the *Bulletin of the Atomic Scientists* published an article called "The Super Bomb," by Professor Hans Thirring of Vienna, the editors pointed out that they had held it in abeyance for four years, hesitating to publish it because of the fear that "any discussion of this subject might foster the belief that America was actively engaged in developing thermonuclear weapons, and that this might stimulate the atomic arms race." True, the article had already been published in Austria as one chapter of a book[19] but its information had not been conveyed to the general public anywhere —an interesting illustration of scientific separation from ordinary cultural media. Professor Hans Thirring had not had any monopoly of the knowledge, of course. Every physicist in the world had possessed it.[20]

It was not the scientists but one of their anti-intellectual enemies who began the fantastic disclosure; and he began it as part of the campaign, ironically enough, against the scientists. The editors of the *Bulletin*, with accumulated rage looking out from every line, said:

19. *Die Geschichte der Atombombe* (Vienna, 1946).

20. There was an immediate spate of pent-up discussion, "within security limits," after the President announced the policy of going on to manufacture the thermonuclear bomb. Cf., for instance, the article of Professor Louis Ridenour in the *Scientific Monthly*, March, 1950. Professor Hans Bethe in the *Bulletin of the Atomic Scientists* for April, 1950, discussed at some length "some of the scientific, moral and political aspects of the hydrogen bomb."

It was left to the monumental indiscretion of Senator Johnson, and to obvious leaks of official information to journalists such as the Alsop brothers, to precipitate a public discussion of what has since become known as the "hydrogen bomb" in the American press. Apparently the only people who take secrecy in atomic matters seriously in this country are the much-abused scientists who, according to Senator Johnson, cannot resist the "yen" to tell everybody all they know about the atom. As soon as a subject gets out of the hands of the scientists (and of the equally maligned Atomic Energy Commission) on to the desks of high military or civilian authorities, or Congressional Committees, "top secrets" begin, not to leak, but to pour out in torrents.

The Alsop brothers[21] mentioned by the editors of the *Bulletin*, preparing to commit their own "monumental indiscretion," were loftily caustic about that of Senator Johnson. The difference seemed to be that they knew what they were doing and that the Senator had not:

There was altogether too much comedy in the recent incident of Senator Edwin C. Johnson and the 1000-power atomic bomb. Here is a pompous law-maker pleading with the television audience for more secrecy in American atomic development. And in the midst of his bumbling discourse, the Senator commits the worst violation of security rules that has occurred to date.

He discloses, in fact, that the Atomic Energy Commission is working hard to devise an atomic weapon 1000 times more powerful than the bomb that fell on Hiroshima. With the Senatorial foot thus securely placed in the capacious Senatorial mouth, the curtain quickly descends, and the audience dissolves into roars of happy laughter.

The Alsops, having ridiculed the Senator, then went on to confirm and enlarge on the disclosure. Everyone should understand, they said, that there was no comedy about this. All that the Senator had let out so carelessly was true: "A 1000-power atomic bomb is more than a simple possibility. In the long run such a bomb is a probability, if not a certainty," and "the job is actually farther along than was the making of the Hiroshima bomb when the Manhattan District was established." They went on to disclose something very few people could have known at that time. The Navy's ram-jet project had evolved an interim guided missile for use against high-speed planes. "By marrying a beam-rider guidance system to a solid-propellent rocket, the navy scientists have already produced a prototype." With all-out effort "unprecedented security against air-delivered atomic bombs could thus be attained in a relatively short

21. Widely published newspaper columnists. The column quoted here appeared in the Paris edition of the *New York Herald Tribune*, December 8, 1949.

time." But it was such people as Senator Johnson, with their witch-hunting and their economy-mindedness, who were preventing it.

The witch-hunt referred to by the Alsops was becoming a real menace. It was not new for members of the Congress to abuse, in the grossest fashion, their powers of investigation; and it was not new for elected officials to browbeat and humiliate their intellectual betters, a process which seemed to give them a certain cheap but mordant satisfaction. But the intensification of these phenomena until they reached incredible proportions took place in this year. The first hero of the political assassins who were intent on discrediting anyone of more than ordinary intelligence in public life was Senator Bourke Hickenlooper; but he had a worthy successor, once he had subsided, in Senator McCarthy.

Senator Hickenlooper made headlines with a vicious, yet ludicrous, attack on the Atomic Energy Commission and, in particular, upon David Lilienthal, the chairman. His attack centered on administrative management—something the commission could hardly be held responsible for under the statute, since the general manager was at that time appointed by the President—and for the happenings he objected to he proposed to hold only Mr. Lilienthal responsible. These confusions of mind only got worse as delving into the cost of garbage cans, the operational minutiae of the reserved communities, and other like matters went on. Because none of the evidence seemed very damaging or very important, the Senator kept changing his tack, bringing up one triviality after another, and trying to force Mr. Lilienthal to accept responsibility. An ordinary mortal would have thought Mr. Hickenlooper was making himself so ridiculous that he had better drop the whole matter as quickly as possible. But American politics had arrived at a stage below such ordinary considerations. An assortment of patrioteers had been awaiting the opportunity to attack Mr. Lilienthal ever since the military had failed to get control of atomic-energy development. They could not afford to have him triumph. His character and abilities simply had to be blackened. There was, furthermore, a lingering conception that he was somehow radical, a notion fostered by all those who had lined up against the public power program of the TVA. The whole affair turned into the familiar witch-hunt.

Nevertheless, it died. Mr. Lilienthal came out of this renewed ordeal, as he had come out of his others, quite untouched. But he would have to be confirmed again presently, because under Republican pressure the terms of appointments had been reduced. He decided that he had had enough. His endurance may have been pushed beyond bearable limits; if so, no one had a right to be surprised or to deny him relief. He may also have felt, as others before him have felt, that the work which had come to mean more to him than his personal fortunes or comfort was suffering rather than gaining from his connection with it. Such a feeling is natural after personal persecution has gone on for a long time and has become a kind of cause among a public servant's enemies. It is mistaken. Persecution is not personal. The object of it has only been stereotyped and, for a purpose, made into an object of abhorrence. If he goes on being himself, the stereotype will crack, the persecution will die down, and he can be useful again. But he may not have been able to withstand the demoralizing nervous strain of the unremitting ordeal. The victim of one of these lynchings can be forgiven for escaping into the peace of private life. Mr. Lilienthal had not only been persecuted; he had lived with such enormous responsibilities as almost no man before him had had to shoulder. And he must have felt an irresistible longing, after a while, to escape from them as well as from his persecutors. Whatever his reasons, he decided to depart from his chairmanship and went with the applause of all decent people in his ears.

So was lost a long fight of the scientists to secure a firm and fair administration of the commission. In an obvious effort to appease the anti-intellectual, pro-business element of the Senate, a law partner of Senator McMahon, chairman of the Senate Committee on Atomic Energy, was appointed. This event was followed very logically by the resignation of the general manager, Mr. Carroll L. Wilson. Americans, by Hiroshima Day in 1950, had cause for the gravest doubts about the conduct of their organization for the manufacture and control of atomic energy. If the Russians had the intention of going all out to win the atomic armaments race, this was their opportunity.

Senator Hickenlooper's performance was followed by Senator Joseph McCarthy's, for which it provided a model. Mr. McCarthy, however, did not center his attack on the Atomic Energy Commission, since Mr. Lilienthal had now resigned, and there was no longer a clear target; he moved on to the State Department and its head, Secretary Dean Acheson.

Groundwork for the attack had been laid by the Chiang Kai-shek bloc in a long campaign. Among the more prominent members of this bloc were Senators William F. Knowland and Kenneth S. Wherry and Representative Walter H. Judd, all animated by one evident purpose—to establish Chiang Kai-shek in power. They had never admitted any of the charges of corruption and inefficiency made against his regime. It is part of the strength of determined congressional blocs that they do not have to admit anything. They cannot be effectively combated, because they have made no open commitments. They make known their demands by indirection and enforce them by alliances which gather strength in ramified affiliations. The campaign of the China bloc, furthermore, was abetted by very strong sections of the press, notably the "impartial" Luce magazines. Nevertheless, the bloc had not been able to influence General Marshall, who as ambassador to China and then Secretary of State had clearly recognized the weaknesses of the Chiang regime and had modified American policy so that it had no longer appeared to support the Kuomintang.

This policy was one to which Secretary Acheson was also persuaded, and for which he was to suffer. Secretary Marshall, almost sacrosanct though he had been at the war's end as a simple and dedicated patriot, had himself been attacked by the Chiang bloc. If he had not had to resign, the attack would have become formidable. The signs of an embryonic plot for political assassination of the familiar sort were all present. Secretary Acheson inherited the opprobrium; and the momentum of the attack quickly shifted to him when he assumed office. His defenses should have been adequate. He had made a formidable attempt to reach a broad understanding with the public and had apparently succeeded. Dr. Philip Jessup had been sent out to the East for study, and there had been prepared a careful and compendious White Paper analyzing the whole Eastern position and showing in convincing bulk why the policy now being followed was necessary. Chiang and his regime had helped by becoming more and more inefficient and corrupt until, in 1949, Communist successes had forced him to withdraw to the border island of Formosa.

Still the Chiang bloc in Congress and in the American press did not quit. Financed indirectly by appropriations which had not quite run out—the Congress in every Marshall Aid bill had forced either an earmarking of funds for Chiang or an informal understanding of assistance—Chiang's regime settled down in Formosa. The congressional bloc now set out to replace Mr. Acheson with a more compliant Secretary. He had, of course, to be discredited first, and every ingenious method, however indecent, was resorted to. The Secretary, when he attended meetings of the foreign ministers of the Atlantic Pact nations, was accompanied by a din from Washington intended to intimidate his opposite numbers and to give notice that his credit at home had run out. It was in these difficult circumstances that the foreign policy of the United States was conducted in 1949–50. And it was in these circumstances that Senator McCarthy started out to force the growth of his bid for power.

He began by charging that the Department of State was infested with Communists. In his first speech there were a large number; but in subsequent speeches the number and the exact description were progressively watered down. A Senate committee under the chairmanship of Senator Millard Tydings set out to investigate. Mr. McCarthy was asked to substantiate his charges. Many witnesses appeared, but no evidence whatever turned up that would support anything he said. Not one single Communist was discovered. It was interesting, however, that neither Senator McCarthy nor the press supporting him were in the least embarrassed. They went on making charges. The less there was to say, the louder the Senator said it, and the more voluminously it was repeated. Finally the whole country was in an uproar—over nothing! And it was reported from many parts of the country that Mr. McCarthy had made a deep impression!

Throughout the investigation the press connected the State Department not only with Russian but with Chinese communism. The personal attacks on Mr. Acheson, as Secretary of State, appeared to be directly connected with his refusal to be bullied by the Chiang bloc in Congress. I do not venture to suggest how this connection was managed, but it was sufficiently plain. Mr. Acheson had to go if Chiang were to be supported in reconquering China for the Kuomintang.

Thoughtful democrats everywhere, watching the growing irre-

234

sponsibility of their representative bodies, wondered where the remedy lay. There was an incorrigible tendency to respond to special pressures and to local demands. The national interest, except in the emergencies brought about by the systematic neglect that preceded them, was simply smothered in these other, special interests. Old Senator McKellar's long persecution of Mr. Lilienthal because of his refusal to accede to patronage demands; Senator Hickenlooper's sudden decision that it would be politically useful to persecute the already persecuted—these had been no more than obvious developments of methods used in other years on other people and other causes. Senator McCarthy simply carried the method forward as it was open to any gifted demagogue to do. Yet there was no sign of any limitation by the Congress itself on these gross abuses of democratic privilege.

That there was a close connection between these abuses and the sudden success of MacArthurism when the Korean crisis broke, there were many observers to testify. The United States would go to war rather than sponsor another international appeasement; for she believed that appeasement knew no end, that, if aggression was condoned in Korea, there would be new aggressions in Iran, in Turkey, in Yugoslavia, in western Germany. Yet, in order to re-establish a nonpartisan foreign policy, the President was willing to adopt at home the very methods he so bitterly condemned abroad. When he appeased the China bloc about Formosa, he opened the door to a blackmail which would not end until he had repudiated the policy and reversed himself.

It was evident that the thermonuclear bomb would create an utterly unprecedented situation. There had been those who had been unimpressed, or had said they were unimpressed, by the Hiroshima Bomb.[22] Its use, they considered, would not have effects very dif-

22. Among these were certain officers of the American Navy. When in 1949 Secretary Johnson abruptly vetoed the naval proposal to build a giant carrier, insubordination broke out. Naval officers carried their fight to the public and precipitated a congressional investigation. They attacked the whole theory of intercontinental warfare as an untried fantasy. They claimed, in the first place, that the B-36 plane was not capable of delivering the Bomb. It would be intercepted and driven out of the skies. The only safe course was to develop giant carriers from which bombers could be flown. But they also argued that the Bomb itself—this was before the H-bomb—was far from an ultimate weapon. The whole affair was a disgraceful instance of insubordination, for which Admiral Denfield was relieved as Chief of Staff and Admiral Sherman substituted.

ferent from those of the mass bombings of the last war. The strategic air force carrying jellied gasoline bombs had done as much damage to Tokyo as had the atomic bomb to Hiroshima. But what would they say now that the atomic weapon promised, through thermonuclear action, a thousand times as much explosive power?

Americans as yet had almost no information about the new bomb —a dangerous state of affairs if democracy was to function. On February 26, 1950, however, Professors Bethe, Brown, Seitz, and Szilard discussed the hydrogen bomb on the program of "The University of Chicago Round Table." If anyone was entitled to speak about this matter, certainly these four were. Their remarks were factual and realistic. They pointed out that the blast destruction of the H-bomb would be a hundred-fold that of the A-bomb—a city the size of Metropolitan New York could be destroyed by a single bomb. Its flash would severely burn people twenty miles from the center of the explosion. Defense against such a weapon would necessitate the dispersal of the population of coastal cities and thus colossal government expenditures. Indeed, radioactivity from such a blast could destroy life on earth, especially since it would be difficult to control the spread of radiation.[23]

To these remarks Mr. Lilienthal, now no longer chairman of the Atomic Energy Commission, took violent exception. Perhaps he had been a bureaucrat so long that realistic treatment of a dangerous subject appalled him. In the course of a Town Hall address on March 1, 1950, he deplored the "cult of doom" encouraged by the "Round Table" discussion, characterized as nonsense talk of evacuating cities, and criticized the scientists for speculating in public on possible uses for the Bomb that the Russians might not have thought of.[24]

To this, Professor Szilard, when he had recovered from his surprise, replied that "Mr. Lilienthal criticized statements which we made over the air, not on the ground that they were not true, but rather on the ground that the truth was frightening, and that scaring people served no useful purpose." Americans need to know, he said, what the H-bomb will do, to both the nature of war and the cost of

23. This discussion is printed in the *Bulletin of the Atomic Scientists*, April, 1950, pp. 106–9.

24. *New York Herald Tribune*, March 2, 1950. This account is reprinted in the *Bulletin of the Atomic Scientists*, April, 1950, p. 109.

defense, yet neither the President nor the Atomic Energy Commission has told them. There is no more reason to suppress speculation as to the effects of the Bomb, he pointed out, than to suppress Mr. Walter Lippmann's speculation about foreign policy. The American people might agree with Mr. Lilienthal that the relocation of their coastal cities was impractical, and Congress might refuse to vote funds for it. "But if that happens, and if the atomic arms race continues and if the cold war goes on and on, there may be a price to pay. It is the people who will pay the price, and it must be their decision to pay it, and they will have to discuss it before they will be able to decide."[25]

There naturally followed a good many other discussions of the proposed thermonuclear weapon, both in the United States and abroad. The matter of radioactive poisons, indeed, began to take on a baneful importance of its own, not necessarily in connection with bombs. For instance, Professor E. S. Shire spoke, at the Liberal Summer School at Cambridge University on the day following Hiroshima Day in 1950, of the possibility that radioactive substances might be laid in an invisible film on the ground.[26] Professor Shire thought that the poisons from a million-kilowatt pile could cover an area the size of Greater London and that the United States had atomic piles totaling much more than that. The circulation of such poisons in the air as dust, furthermore, could even be more dangerous—perhaps as much as a hundred times more effective than laying a poison carpet on the ground. Professor R. F. Bacher referred to such possibilities in a discussion in the *Bulletin* for May, 1950; and, two issues later, Professor Louis N. Ridenour reviewed what was known about radioactive substances in warfare.[27] They had been referred to in the Smyth Report in 1945; but for five years not much had been heard of them, a silence which suggested either neglect or very secret exploration of their possibilities. The general conclusion from these examinations was much more realistic than anything previously published. It was undoubtedly not fantastic any longer to talk

25. Letter to the *New York Herald Tribune*, March 4, 1950, reprinted in the *Bulletin of the Atomic Scientists*, April, 1950, pp. 125–27.

26. *Times* (London), August 8, 1950.

27. His article was largely a review of Hans Thirring, "Ueber das moegliche Ausmass einer radio-aktiven Verseuchung durch die Spaltprodukte des U235," *Acta physica Austriaca*, II (1948), 379–400.

of a "death-sand"; and the previous silence was judged to be an indication of secrecy rather than neglect.

Professor Ridenour referred to the results of radioactivity at Hiroshima and Bikini. It seemed that the Hiroshima and Nagasaki bombs were deliberately exploded in the air so that the radiation particles should blow away and the United States not be accused of using an inhuman weapon (an accusation which was made anyway); but, after the underwater explosion at Bikini, "the contamination caused by spray carrying radioactive elements resulting from the explosion was so severe that it caused the eventual scrapping of the whole target fleet." Yet, when "radiological warfare" was spoken of, what was meant was, not just the by-products of a bomb, but the delivery of a mist or dust of poisonous radioactive substances. This can, said Professor Ridenour, "be regarded as a horrid and insidious weapon, since the person in the poisoned area has no way of knowing he is in danger. . . . He may receive a lethal dose of radiation two weeks before he knows he is endangered, and yet a few days later he may be dead."

Whether atomic fire was to be loosed as a bomb or as radioactive dust on the ground or in the air, there was no doubt of its mortal fearsomeness. Mr. Lilienthal had his hands full if he intended to enter on a crusade for keeping men's minds off the possibilities they faced. Too many irresponsible agencies might decide, for their own reasons, to use such a weapon. Especially dangerous, the scientists thought, was its escape from democratic controls in the West.[28] A decision to use atomic weapons could be made in the United States by a few people without any kind of real reference to the electorate. Such a decision, in fact, had resulted in Hiroshima. The London *Times* (January 27, 1950), in an article on the President's decision to go ahead with the manufacture of the H-bomb, ended somberly: "There seems little doubt that within a few decades, if not a few years, it will be possible for any Power with modern industrial resources to destroy the world as we know it." It appeared, furthermore, that the Power could be rather small if it possessed industrial apparatus. There seemed, literally and absolutely, no way out for mankind, when the H-bomb should be perfected, but a rigorously implemented agreement not to use it.

28. Cf., e.g., R. F. Bacher, *Bulletin of the Atomic Scientists*, May, 1950.

It was clear at once to those who had all the elements of the situation in mind that, when President Truman so hurriedly reversed himself on Korea, he also shifted the whole basis of the American strategy vis-à-vis Russia. The Americans had relied entirely on intercontinental warfare, its chief instrument being the great new planes carrying atomic bombs, at least until radio-guided long-range missiles were ready. Whether the devisers of this policy ever seriously believed it might be put to use, no one can say; it looked at least like a logically conceived deterrent threat. But by accepting the Korean challenge, which meant warfare with all the Soviet satellites on their own terms, the United States, in effect, renounced the Bomb as a weapon—at least for the kind of war which was now to be carried on.

The idea had to be entertained that, if Russia could maintain the fiction that she was not a party to the wars of her satellites, she might conquer all of Asia, and all of Europe, too, by proxy. If the United States were to oppose the aggressions of satellites, she would have to fight the old-fashioned kind of war all around the borders of the Eurasian continent. For Asia had no central ganglia to be destroyed by bombs, and it seemed unlikely—a contingency to be contemplated with horror—that the United States would destroy the old capitals—Paris, Brussels, Rome—to dislodge the Russians. If this Soviet strategy were not somehow countered, the Russians could get possession of the whole land mass from the English Channel to the China Sea, leaving the Middle East, India, and Africa in such a ferment as to be completely unreliable.

It was the sudden recognition of the implications in the decision to make a stand in Korea, rather than the actual demands of the campaign, that caused the convulsive effort to rearm in the summer of 1950. The campaign was not a major one—yet. But the decision to oppose Russia on all the fringes of her domain without making use of the atomic weapon was a major decision. Like all democratic choices, of course, it was not necessarily a final one. Much would depend on the nature of the H-bomb, including what certainty there was that it could be made. One thing was clear, however: The H-bomb could only be used against the real enemy, Russia. Fringe warfare was completely inconsistent with H-bomb strategy. The old ships had now to be taken out of mothballs, infantry had to be recruited and trained, tanks and fighter planes had to be manufactured, in short, all the paraphernalia of the last war had to be resurrected.

If the Russians had contrived this shift in strategy, they had been diabolically clever, for old-fashioned war was ruinously expensive. A few years of it would move the whole West toward bankruptcy, and at the end Russia would still be as secure as ever, like a spider in the center of a very large, self-sustaining web. If Russia had not planned but had only stumbled upon this debacle, the United States seemed incredibly innocent. A serious admission faced her—that it was to her interest to keep out of the entire Eurasian continent, because any part of it to which her pretensions stretched would have to be fought for, and fought for with infantry and tanks.

Would this be to abandon Europe to Russian conquest? No more, it might be said by others, than Russian impotence on the American continent abandons Mexico, say, or Brazil to conquest by the United States. Europe would have thenceforth to live in the shadow of a power overwhelmingly greater than any she could muster. But she was having to anyway. Perhaps the Russians would not tolerate the clerical-military reaction dominant in Europe anywhere within their reach; but it seemed unlikely that they would resort to anything more than the familiar propaganda—always the cheapest method of penetration—to gain their ends. And the phenomenon of Tito in Yugoslavia might dampen the enthusiasm of the Politburo for even this form of conquest. It could not have escaped the Politburo entirely, furthermore, that Communist strength in all western Europe had begun its spectacular recession at the time in 1948 when all good party members were forced to declare that they would not fight Russia, even to defend their own nations. Frenchmen, Italians, Belgians—few were so far gone in disillusion or so wedded to Russian Marxism as to espouse that doctrine. It had been a colossal error; and the error had never been repaired. Together with the Marshall Aid, which had helped in economic recovery, it had lost western Europe to communism, at least for the time being. The West had begun to believe that communism as a social and political reform was merely a propaganda device for forwarding Russian imperialism—that Russia wanted the whole continent and wanted it Russian. France and Italy as outlying provinces of a Russian imperium might seem fantastic in nineteenth-century terms; but the colossus of the earth's heartland had always been there, huge and rich, even though for a long time lethargic and supine, and so far behind the West in technology as not to count as a contender among the great powers for world hegemony. At the moment of greatest opportunity, Lenin had had the insight to make technology a cornerstone and to discover that it fitted communism with a hand-in-glove niceness. During the nineteenth century free enterprise had created economic strength; but it was becoming clear that, in the twentieth century, collectivism would create even more strength. Russia had already taken her rightful place as a world power.

The truth was that capitalism could only go a certain way with technology. Unless free enterprise passed over into oligarchy and made of society an organism in that way, it constantly created inefficient units under the pressure of competition and conflict; and oligarchy was morally intolerable to Western man. Technology led logically to a wholly integrated, an organic society; capitalism—except as oligarchy—led to divisiveness, and so to fundamental weakness. Westerners, looking at their own history and at the Russian police state, tended to think that capitalism was essential to the representative institutions they valued at least as much as they did economic efficiency; but, in fact, the inefficiency and instability of free enterprise was a far greater danger to democracy than the disciplined co-operation of a collective economy. In a world subject to inevitable technological progress, organicism in this sense was as important to the growth of democracy as to the efficient utilization of resources.

It was immensely significant that the marriage of technology and communism should have as the place for its physical embodiment the world's heartland in Eurasia. If the planning and administrative problems could be mastered, the potentialities of this marriage in the early nineteenth-century terms of coal, oil, steel, and so on were enormous. The only rival—and that, in the long run, not an overwhelmingly preponderant one—was America.

But, for Russia to reach her apotheosis, an evolution was required which could be forced, it is true, but not syncopated into a few decades. America was ahead in that race. A challenge to both capitalism and communism, furthermore, had been thrown out by the Axis powers, and time had been taken out to crush this pretension in the irresistible nutcracker of the two representative powers. Then, suddenly, the whole of the strategy, both of conquest and of re-source development, was thrown into confusion overnight by the scientists' discovery of the uses for atomic fire. The imperium which made the most rapid use of this new tool and the most rapid adjustment to its imperatives would be destined to rule the world, or, at the least, to share that rule.

What to do? If nothing was done, the power vacuums in western Europe and the Far East were certain to be filled by inrushing currents from America and Russia. Each would be sustained by the firm belief that the other intended, not merely conquest of the disputed area, but of itself. Each, clashing in Europe and on the borders of the Pacific, would be fighting a defensive war. The propaganda build-ups for these campaigns could be imagined in advance. Not only patriotism would be invoked but the preservation of civilization as well, for each would picture the other as unspeakably brutal. Such propaganda, indeed, had begun in 1950. "The Voice of America," for instance, did not confine itself to praising Western institutions. It had made a determined start at damning those of Russia.

In March, 1950, Professor Hans Morgenthau reviewed in the *Bulletin of the Atomic Scientists* the situation into which Russia and the United States were being so relentlessly carried:

The two fundamental facts which determined the policies of the two nations during that period were the temporary American monopoly of the atomic bomb and the military preponderance of the Soviet Union on the continents of Europe and Asia. The paramount interest of the Soviet Union was to make the period of American supremacy in atomic weapons as short as possible, while perpetuating this preponderance. The United States was vitally interested in maintaining her monopoly of atomic weapons as long as possible and in reducing the Russian superiority on the two continents. The policies of both countries regarding disarmament were the true reflection of those facts and interests.

The conflict between the United States and the Soviet Union, like that between France and Germany of the early thirties, then, was fought on two levels: on the superficial level of disarmament and on the fundamental level of the struggle for power. On the level of disarmament the conflict resolved itself into a controversy between two theoretical conceptions: security first, equality later *vs.* equality first, security later. On the level of the struggle for power, the conflict is posed in terms of two antagonistic policies: defense of the status quo *vs.* overthrow of the status quo. The American insistence upon security is the equivalent in terms of atomic disarmament, of the

1950

American policy of the status quo, as the Russian emphasis upon equality is the expression, in terms of atomic weapons, of the Russian policy of expanding and making unassailable the ascendancy of the Soviet Union in Europe and Asia.

Such is the nature of the power conflict between the United States and the Soviet Union. Of this conflict the controversy on atomic disarmament is but an outward expression, following the contours of the conflict as the cast of clay follows the shape of the form into which it is molded. As the cast can only be changed by changing the mold, so the problem of atomic disarmament can only be solved through a settlement of the power conflict from which it has arisen.

The political factors which have hindered attempts at atomic disarmament will inevitably militate against disarmament with regard to the H-bomb. As long as the struggle for power between the United States and the Soviet Union rages unabated and unsettled, the impasse with regard to disarmament will continue, whatever type of weapon may be chosen as an object and however ingenious a legal formula and institutional device may be contrived to make disarmament effective could it be agreed upon. Shall we then persist in an error which led the United Nations Atomic Energy Commission into an impasse, which condemned the world Disarmament Conference of the thirties to futility, and which for more than a century and a half has strewn the road of humanity with disappointed hopes and ever more frequent and destructive wars? Are we to continue trying to doctor the symptoms and let the disease, unattended, take its deadly course?

The question asked by Professor Morgenthau was one which was being asked, here and there, by thoughtful people in all countries. The statesmen continued to believe—or to act as if they believed—that the only position from which they could negotiate was one of "strength." But if both sides insisted on this position, there could never be any negotiation because there never would be a situation in which both sides would be satisfied that they possessed an advantage. Rearmament would be allowed to reach—if it had not already reached—that stage at which the use of what had been produced so expensively was practically inevitable. There was good reason to think that the expense of the atomic bomb had necessitated its use at Hiroshima. The same consideration would be likely to precipitate the using of the H-bomb if ordinary statesmanship prevailed. Only if mankind could be awakened to the fact that the H-bomb was a method of genocide, not just another weapon, only if its use could be denied to the statesman, could the holocaust it portended be averted.

In 1950 there seemed little chance of such an awakening, if only because the two powers were more securely locked away from each other with each passing month. Americans could not deny the Bomb to their military if the Russians did not to theirs. And the two peoples were kept utterly isolated from each other and were being charged to overflowing with fear and hate. Presently each would come to believe that the only way to salvation lay in destruction of the other.

Nevertheless, men like Professor Morgenthau continued to believe in negotiations. He believed in them because he could believe in nothing else. Disarmament was an illusion. Like competitive arming, it was a symptom of the underlying political relations—either of a raging political conflict or of a conflict peacefully settled:

> As long as the United States and the Soviet Union advance contradictory claims for the domination of Europe, of which the focus at present is Germany, it is idle for them to talk about disarmament; for they are forced by the very logic of this power contest to compete for armaments. . . . If we cannot settle the political conflicts which threaten to involve us in war with the Soviet Union regardless of the prevailing technological conditions, we must face, as we must threaten, destruction with the latest technological means of destruction available to men. If the United States and the Soviet Union can settle these conflicts peacefully by safeguarding their vital interests and compromising on secondary issues, the technological progress of mankind will, by that very fact, have lost its threat. They can then afford to agree upon limitation of their armaments. Disarmament, in turn, will contribute to the general pacification. For the degree of the disarmament agreed upon will be the measure of the political understanding achieved. . . .
>
> There are only three ways by which international crises can be settled: Overwhelming power, war, negotiations. Since overwhelming power is no longer at our disposal and beyond our grasp for the foreseeable future, the choice is between war and negotiations.[29]

Toward negotiation Mr. Trygve Lie, during the month of May, made what seemed to be at the time a hopeful contribution. He journeyed to Washington, London, Paris, and Moscow, was received by the chiefs of state, and returned with "a firm conviction that the United Nations remains a primary factor in the foreign policy of each of these governments and that the reopening of genuine negotiations on certain of the outstanding issues may be possible." On June 6, 1950, he made public a letter to each delegation saying that the memorandum he inclosed might be brought before the Security Council or the General Assembly at any subsequent meeting: that was a Secretary-General's privilege. The

29. *Bulletin of the Atomic Scientists,* March, 1950, p. 99.

memorandum's first two points were of most interest. The first was a proposal that there be periodic meetings of the Security Council at which foreign ministers or chiefs of state would represent their governments. There had not been such a meeting in all the four years of the Council's existence. It seemed useless to Mr. Lie—and most people shared his feeling—to go on having meetings of low-ranking officials who could not negotiate but instead jockeyed for propaganda advantage. Such meetings certainly could not result in negotiation and would eventually result instead in the withdrawal of one or another nation that had been insulted once too often in a particularly sensitive spot.

The second point called for a new attempt at atomic-energy control. He reminded the governments that at the autumn meeting in 1949 the Assembly had adopted a directive requiring the exploring of "all possible avenues" and "all concrete suggestions." There had, he said, been various suggestions for a fresh approach; and he mentioned two. The Security Council might instruct the Secretary-General to call a conference of scientists whose discussions "might provide a reservoir of new ideas on the control of weapons of mass destruction and the promotion of peaceful uses of atomic energy." These ideas could thereafter be explored in the United Nations Atomic Energy Commission. Or it might be that "an interim agreement could be worked out that would at least be some improvement on the present situation of unlimited atomic arms race, even though it did not afford full security."

But by the time Mr. Lie had returned to Lake Success and written his letter to the member nations, the Korean War was in full course, and suggestions for negotiation, even if they had been acceptable to either antagonist, would have had to do with stopping open hostilities, not with settling the atomic arms competition. Yet the only alternative to war was still negotiation. The third possibility mentioned by Professor Morgenthau, overwhelming strength, had now disappeared. Of course, these notions of mutually exclusive possibilities might be part of outmoded classical thought. Perhaps the half-war being waged around the Russian border, or the half-negotiations being carried on at Lake Success, represented the relationships of the future.

Professor Morgenthau was persuasive, even if he did speak in

the downright language of sincerity, which was seldom heard emanating from Lake Success or, for that matter, from any official
source. In the world of insincerity, verbal twilight had confused all
communication. It was a phenomenon as frightening as any in our
queer times. To Professor Morgenthau, who was not only learned
in the phenomena of power politics but was, because he was learned,
a realist, it seemed to be a law of international politics that only
those international agreements have a chance to be effective which
in fact express "the identical or complementary interests of the contracting parties." He thought also that agreements last only as long
as interests continue to coincide. It was, therefore, useless to hark
back to Yalta and Potsdam. The Russians were guilty of breaking
agreements they had made. What of it? A list a mile long could be
made of agreements broken by those who now professed to be horrified at Russian perfidy. We must search for areas of agreement
and negotiate their legal embodiment. As Lord Salisbury had said:
"The only bond that endures is the absence of all clashing interests."
American foreign policy in 1950 was wrong, Professor Morgenthau
concluded, because no attempt was being made to find coinciding
interests and to eliminate nonessential controversies. There was continual harping, enlarged by propaganda, on unrealistic legal commitments. Such behavior could never end in anything but war.

Perhaps the real aim was to wait for the precise time when negotiations would have the best chance; Secretary Acheson had made
it clear that in his view we had to talk to Russia from a position of
strength. But America had had a position of strength from 1945 to
1949 and had made no progress. Her present rearmament could not
possibly make her position as strong as it had been; time was, in
fact, running against rather than for her. What, then, was she trying to do? It was impossible to say. Logically she ought to bring on
a war with Russia at the first possible moment. Only in terms of
such an intention did her policy either at Lake Success or in Washington make any sense. But no one believed war to be her intention.
Ordinary folk in the West were naturally confused. They hesitated
to believe that Washington was divided, unled, and utterly irrational; but they were being forced to such a conclusion.

What the United States ought to be doing, Professor Morgenthau was certain, was to find a division of the world to which Rus-

sia would agree and which matched American interests. Such a division ought then to be made the basis of negotiation between the two powers. To go on "accumulating strength" at the points of conflict was to risk war constantly. The result could be favorable only if all the risks proved empty and if time was on the American side, so that in due course Russia would make the approach and a favorable settlement could be reached. But the risks were real; and Russia had already made approaches which had been arbitrarily rejected. Though these proposals had never been officially acknowledged, there could be no doubt that they had been made.[30] Professor Morgenthau's comment on the American summary rejection was caustic: Was it not better, as Mr. Churchill had remarked in 1946, "to have a world divided than a world destroyed?"[31]

The whole of this quotation from Mr. Churchill had been as follows: "It is better to have a world united than a world divided; but it is also better to have a world divided than a world destroyed." Was it now quite impossible to have a world united? The answer seemed obvious to Professor Morgenthau and to many others. Yet the movement for unification did not die. It was, it could be said, a kind of technological imperative. Professor Morgenthau would say that hope for unification was naïve, impractical, and perhaps pernicious, since it prevented realism from determining events. But there were those who said that such realism was only a seeming realism; that division, being unnatural, would not last; and that the only settlement which would bring peace would be one which unified the world and gave it a government. Masters of *Realpolitik* had been

30. Professor Morgenthau referred specifically to a dispatch from Mr. James C. Reston to the *New York Times*, March 13, 1950, which was titled "Soviet Move Seen for Deal with U.S. To Divide the World." Mr. Reston had quite obviously explored official attitudes all around Washington and had found that there was "no evidence that officials here are even slightly interested in such a deal." There were four reasons given for this lack of interest: (1) such an agreement would force Yugoslavia and China into satellite status and so strengthen the Communists; (2) it was believed that Russia would not be able to integrate China and European satellites; (3) it was not believed that the problem of transferring power after Stalin's death would be easy; and (4) it was said that spheres of influence were somehow immoral and violated a principle of American policy.

31. The discussion by Professor Morgenthau referred to here is contained in an article, one of a series of three, examining the present crisis, called "On Negotiating with the Russians" which appeared in the *Bulletin of the Atomic Scientists*, May, 1950.

incensed a few years before at the stand taken by the University of Chicago's Committee To Frame a World Constitution: "World Government is necessary, therefore it is possible." Yet if the *necessary* and the *possible* were examined and given content, they might turn out to be as realistic as that balance-of-power arrangement which seemed so realistic because it was a recognition of existent fact.

Existent fact was rapidly changing. The new industrial revolution might not yet be so very apparent in everyday life, but its phenomena could be foreseen by those who were not blind. The bases for such changes in living standards as had never happened before were being laid in laboratories, in the planning rooms of factories, in machine-tool shops. These changes would extend also to the facilitating mechanisms—transport, communications, paper work, vocational training—and would not only offer to tie the world into one whole but impose penalties for keeping it divided. World government was, day by day, becoming necessary not only to human survival but to technological progress. It was also possible, if by "possible" was meant the means for governing; these existed—political forms, representative devices, and bureaucratic competencies were all adequate.

Devotees of *Realpolitik* did not give "possible" this meaning; they identified it with expedient—expedient to those who possessed power. They did not, in other words, regard world government as an alternative to wars of conquest or to negotiation for spheres of interest. Russia, they said, regarded all proposals for integrating arrangements, even functional ones, as Western devices for advantage in the struggle for world control. And it was true that advocates of world government often weakened their case by their answer to the objection that Russia would never join: "Go ahead without her," they said. But Russia now controlled China, Poland, Romania, Hungary, and Czechoslovakia—half the world, if India was regarded as neutral. Thus any mention of world government without her was absurd. Until there could be resumption of progress toward functional arrangements in which "the peoples' democracies" joined, it was futile and even dangerous, said the critics, to talk of world government as a possibility.

Yet the talk of world government remained necessary. Russia had refused to join, or had withdrawn from, most of the subsidiary organizations of the United Nations—the World Food Council, the World Health Organization, the International Monetary Fund—and all of them met in a perpetual haze of ineffectuality because their coming to life depended on their being organs of a whole and living world, not a quarter or a half of it. They were nevertheless rudimentary organs of a whole which would have to assume its being. Perhaps one half would have to conquer the other half first (and there might be very little left to go on with then); but such a war was not yet the only means by which this whole could discover its identity. If atomic-energy development, both as a weapon and as a source of power, ceased to create division, the members of the United Nations might still join in mutually necessary functions. Such co-operation would be the check to division and conflict which ordinary men had hoped for so ardently in the postwar years. The hope had about given way now to resignation; but how easily it could be revived! And, if it did revive, then the climate in which the "necessary" world government might grow would at last be established.

Negotiation in the minds of *Realpolitiker* was defined as negotiation about spheres of influence; but negotiation could also be about the control of atomic energy. Atomic-energy development was far more important in creating strength than was territory held or populations ruled. If so, why was it not more realistic to negotiate about atomic-energy control than about territorial acquisitions? Such negotiations might seem by Hiroshima Day in 1950 a forlorn hope; but there seemed to be no other.

THE year that stretched between the Hiroshima days of 1950 and 1951 was readily typed by historians as one "of passion and confusion beyond anything else the United States has known in our time."[1] Anger, fear, and division had persisted throughout the year. These emotions had, however, been at their worst in two seasons— the first in December, just after the Chinese intervention in Korea, which resulted in the terrible battles of winter and still another United Nations retreat; the second in April and May, during the angry reaction to General MacArthur's dismissal. By Hiroshima Day in 1951 there was the relief of cease-fire negotiations at Kaesong—a kind of last pause for consideration in the rising climax of world conflict. But anger and division still persisted.

The Korean incident[2] seemed about to be liquidated by general consent; but there were troubles of only less acuteness all around the Communist periphery. The war in Indochina still continued; so

1. Mr. Bernard DeVoto, speaking from *Harper's* "Easy Chair" (*Harper's Magazine*, July, 1951, p. 48). He was commenting on "the MacArthur episode" of spring, also discussed by Messrs. R. H. Rovere and A. M. Schlesinger, Jr., in the same issue, a discussion afterward enlarged to book length in *The General and the President* (New York: Harper & Bros., 1951). After General MacArthur was removed by President Truman from his several commands in the Far East, he at once flew back to testify before a joint congressional committee about his removal and to engage in a campaign for the support of the policies he represented. Millions of words of testimony were taken; at the end no agreed report could be made. But the episode had at least served to bring into the open the activities of the China lobby, to force a taking of sides on the issue of coexistence versus preventive war, and to inform the American people at large about the wider issues involved in their struggle with communism.

2. If a conflict which had cost an estimated one and a half million lives and incredible suffering among the civilian Koreans can be called an "incident." The term was very generally used; but the belittling could only be accepted by contrast with the world conflict of which it was part.

did the insurrection in Malaya; in Iran the nationalists were in process of ousting the foreign interest in the oil fields, thus establishing a precedent for other uprisings in other Middle East nations; and in Africa the nationalist ferment continued to rise. Furthermore, a Japanese peace treaty wholly unacceptable to Russia was prepared for signing; and the West was ending its state of war with West Germany, preparatory to drawing it closer to the Atlantic nations. It seemed not unlikely that this last event might prove to be the most troublesome in the immediate future. It was on the German question and on the building-up of Atlantic Pact strength that the five-month-long meetings of the deputy foreign ministers in Paris during the spring had broken down. The prospect of a cease-fire in Korea offered a tiny hope of arrangement for peace; but no one could see how the difficult questions ahead could be compromised.

The quarrel between East and West was not eased by the approaching ratification of the Schuman Plan in Europe. In other times and circumstances this long step toward European union would have been regarded as a triumph of reason. It seemed to promise the liquidation of century-long quarrels between France and Germany which had resulted three times in invasion. As things were, however, its most important immediate effect was to increase the already dangerous tension. To Russia it seemed a new threat added to those she already regarded as just short of intolerable.[3]

The road to Kaesong had lain through Paris. The road to all future negotiations lay through that seemingly most futile of all international meetings. Kaesong, in fact, might be the first of many demonstrations that the efforts at Paris had not, after all, been wasted. The conference had broken up without achieving its avowed purpose of making arrangements for a higher-level conference. Yet perhaps its exposure of what matters were within, and what without, the area of negotiation had served to bring both sides nearer

3. Because, in spite of Britain's nonadherence, it added new strength to the Atlantic Pact nations. The plan amounted to the socialization of two basic industries, coal and steel, by a governmental organization created for that purpose. It was not at all clear how it would be possible for the organization to operate except as a government of Europe. That, at least, seemed implicit in the plan. And that it was implied was soon confirmed by a move to integrate the industrial plan with a similar authority for defense—parliament, court, and all (*New York Times*, July 25, 1951).

reason. Kaesong seemed to indicate as much. For Kaesong began in Moscow, not in Korea; and it was repeatedly saved from failure by Moscow. Evidently the Russians were about to explore the hard limits within which coexistence would be agreed to by the West. So matters stood, on Hiroshima Day, as the first preliminary moves were being made in the vast, dim ambient of diplomacy.

The decision of June, 1950, to resist aggression in Korea had been taken so suddenly that adjustments to its implications had all to come after the event. The decision itself was logical, considering all that had gone before, but Americans had not until that moment faced the probable consequences of the policies to which they had given assent. Thus, when the necessity for action presented itself, they squirmed uneasily and looked around, too late, for alternatives. They looked also for an author of their ills—a scapegoat—and found him in the person of Secretary Acheson. There was a widespread feeling that somehow the diplomats ought to have prevented outright conflict; and on the basis of this feeling there ensued one of those utterly confused debates which democracies periodically find necessary while minds are being cleared. Gradually it was accepted that the engagement in the Far East was a strictly expected one if Russian expansion was to be resisted and that probably there would be others of a similar sort. Attention gradually centered where it should have centered from the first—on an estimate of the possibilities for conflict and of the relative strengths of the antagonists.

Since, without noticeable dissent, the United States had set out in 1945–46 to contain Russian imperialism, containment had been the one firm tenet of her foreign policy. Such a policy has certain disadvantages: the instruments of containment—such as diplomacy or war—are not necessarily those of the container's choice; they must be determined by the force behind the expansion to be repressed and by the means used by the challenging power, as well as by the resources immediately at hand. The challenger, moreover, chooses the time and place for conflict. Korea had been thought a less likely spot for such incidents than Yugoslavia, for instance, or Iran. But, in Korea, Russia proved to have found a weak spot; the United States suffered there two of the most humiliating military defeats in all her history, first in the retreat to the Pusan beachhead and then in the withdrawal from the Yalu. The incident took place, furthermore, at a suitable remove from the Russian heartland so that the fiction of noninvolvement could be maintained quite without penalty.

Americans were taken by surprise, it can now be seen, because they had not fully understood what the Soviet answer to containment would be. The hopelessly innocent may have believed that Russian intentions did not encompass world hegemony, proceeding outward from her borders. But there were others, not innocent at all, who had trusted too much in what they had believed to be Russia's own self-interest. This, they had thought, would require consolidation of the enormous gains of recent years before she risked more than propaganda upon further expansion. Their views turned out to be miscalculated; they had underestimated the expendability of satellites. The official American view, as could be seen in 1951, was sufficiently realistic, but it required actions for which a suitable preparation had not been made either in military strength or in public opinion. For this reason, many months after the Korean decision, after the commitment of ground, air, and naval forces, there was still a dangerous doubt concerning its necessity. Even in realistic minds there was a question whether the Korean incident had furthered or had hindered the policy of containment. It was still being asked whether the first defense of the principle ought not to have been made elsewhere.

Even while the debate concerning the Korean involvement was at its height, the Administration was forced to undertake the task of preparing for other incidents. The consequence of accepting battle in one situation was that thereafter there could be no compromise in any similar situation. There were intense efforts to rearm, but they had to be undertaken in confusion and with haste; for it was not clear at first what kind of rearmament was necessary for such situations. The lessons had to be learned before there could be any profit from them, and the felt urgency was unable to emerge into effective action for some time. Since appropriation had to precede procurement, and retooling had to precede production, new arms were frighteningly slow to come as the Korean struggle developed.

One fact was instantly clear: A power vacuum existed all along the borders of the Russian imperium; and it was a vacuum which threatened the existence of Western civilization. Russian power had already been allowed to overflow unopposed into the heart of Asia and to advance in Europe to the Elbe; and there were other threatened areas, notably in the Middle East. It had evidently been conceived in the West that Communist regimes in East Europe and China were the agents, not of Russian imperialism, but only of Communist organization; and recovery from that illusion was slow. This *must* have been the prevalent illusion. Else why had so complete a demobilization of the once-vast American force been carried out? When Russian intentions were finally assessed, American strength-in-being was utterly unable to support the policy necessary to successful opposition; and this military weakness had presented the Russians with a prestige out of all proportion to basic national strength. They could not be talked as to equals. They were the superior power, and they behaved as such.

Westerners discovered their weakness only gradually; for there had been a prevalent theory, which died hard, that the old kind of war had disappeared into limbo. They had thought themselves strong for a new kind of warfare. That was the result of the last incident of World War II—Hiroshima. The application of force in settling human disputes seemed there to have reached its absolute. The possession of atomic fire and the ability to direct it at will, they had thought, superseded all other kinds of military agents. This weapon belonged to the United States; and it had seemed unthinkable that there could be a challenge which would risk its use. It had therefore been counted on to temper and hold in check Russian ambitions, even though they might be as aggressive as the worst pessimist feared and might be supported by vast ground armies. With such a weapon at hand, what use could there be for a large military establishment of the conventional sort? From this point of view demobilization had seemed reasonable, and recovery from the illusion was reluctant and slow.

It was impossible, furthermore, for Americans to realize that anyone could question their good intentions. They were so fundamentally centered in self-development and, beyond that, in willingness to extend a practical neighborliness to all who were less fortunate that they had listened with incredulity to the first measures of a Russian hymn of hate. As the cacophony had continued into one climactic movement after another, they had been moved first to an annoyed

amusement, then to indignation, and only finally and late to any calculation of its possible significance. There had been two successive
incidents which had shaken even the most complacent Westerners.
Russia had refused to accept atomic disarmament, offered, as Americans felt, in all good faith; and she had rejected for herself and for
her satellites all participation in the Marshall Plan. These were evidences that America was undoubtedly regarded in the Communist
realm as a kind of monster seeking to devour the world. But, since
most Americans could find in themselves or their neighbors none of
the characteristics or motives attributed to them in those incredible
speeches of Molotov or Vishinsky, they had been thrown back on an
incredulity that had manifested itself chiefly in isolationism. It took
the Russian development of the Bomb and the outbreak of old-style
war in Korea to demonstrate to Americans that they could not withdraw behind a curtain of atomic fire.

During most of the postwar period before Korea there had been
no real negotiations between the power groups centered in Moscow
and Washington. Both sides had tended to become immobilized by
their conception of themselves and of their opponents. Both had been
governed by illusions. Americans had come to believe that the Russians intended to reduce the capitalist strongholds by propaganda
and infiltration, neither of which they greatly feared; and the Russians had believed that the West intended presently to invade their
territory and destroy the centers of communism. The struggle had
ceased to be one for the bordering areas between the two power
centers and had come dangerously close to an accepted war for survival in which the only tolerable end would be the destruction of
one or the other. Any geographical definition of spheres had seemed
to be disappearing in the conflict of ideologies which accepted no
territorial limits.

If any negotiation had been possible, the West, even after the Russians had developed the Bomb, would undoubtedly have been quite
willing to settle for coexistence with some guaranties against further
aggression. There had been indications that Russia held the same
general terms in reserve. But it had not been just the inability of
diplomats to implement this mutual unwillingness which had paralyzed negotiations or even the mutual illusions they had harbored.
It had been, and continued to be, the existence of the genocidal

agent which each knew the other to possess. With its use there was the possibility of imposing the "way of life" of one on the other—a possibility quite unthinkable with conventional armaments. How could negotiations take place in the presence of the atomic bomb? Obviously only if each could be convinced that the other would somehow be restrained from its use and that conventional conflict, if resorted to, would result in stalemate. Neither side could see any way to such a mutual arrangement, for the mere possession of fissionable material, together with engineering ability and an industrial system, constituted all but the final step toward possession of lethal weapons; and fissionable material was evidently basic to new industrial advances to which both were committed. Neither was willing to forego a possible atomic industrialism, if indeed it was possible to sterilize the science which made it inevitable.

The meaning of the Bomb can best be understood by imagining for the moment that no such weapon existed. If there were no Bomb (and the United States had demobilized in 1945–46), Russia would now be potentially the master of all Europe, probably all Asia, and of the Middle East. The West would have lost the struggle against Russian imperialism. Western rearmament would not be allowed on penalty of Russian occupation clear across Europe to the English Channel. But the atomic weapon did exist, and it was, until 1950, an evidently effective substitute for the Western armament sacrificed in demobilization. Russian possession of the weapon, however, had changed the terms of the struggle, official pronouncements to the contrary notwithstanding. And the Korean War was demonstrating that the West must match Russia in conventional armament, backed with industrial strength. To use an atom bomb in Korea would be to chance Russian retaliation on Western industrial centers, an almost unthinkable risk for the highly integrated economies of the West. Luckily, although the Russian economy was not so highly integrated, it was still sufficiently so to be itself vulnerable to mass atomic attack.[4]

The risks of war were roughly equal so long as the West possessed a stockpile of bombs larger than Russia's and so long as the Russian stockpile was not large enough to paralyze Western production

4. Something like 70 per cent of Russian industry was located in European Russia; and the policy of decentralization to trans-Ural sites was reported to have been abandoned as impractical.

in one initial blow. The Russians were preponderant in land force; but this advantage was offset by American possession of the A-bomb. It was judged by most rational calculators that power of both kinds could not be equalized for several years—possibly two, more probably three. At that time Russia would still be behind in stockpiling bombs; but she would have reached the point at which comparisons of strength would be useless, since either side could deliver an initial devastating attack. But by then the West would be able to match Russian strength in conventional armament, at least to the point of enforcing containment. There was question whether an adequate defense or warning system could prevent bombers from reaching targets or could give time for a retaliatory attack to become airborne; and this question remained unanswered throughout the 1950–51 debate concerning policy. It had to be assumed, therefore, by those concerned with policy that a bombing attack *could* be delivered and could *not* be prevented by either side.

It was the thesis of Western policy-makers, then, that the risks of atomic war would be greater for the Russians during a certain period and that this period must be utilized to re-establish a position of equality in conventional armaments. There were those who questioned this thesis, among them the tired Europeans. Their land had been so often fought over and their people had made so many sacrifices that the enormous effort of reaching equality seemed too great to be faced. Since Korea they had been arguing that Russia had now the strength to overrun Europe if she desired; that against 175 divisions (30 of them armored) the West could oppose no more than 12 divisions (4 of them armored); and that to re-establish effective potential nonatomic opposition would require at least three years. If Russia meant to attack, they said, she would do it before the West was ready. If she had no hostile intentions—that is, if she did not mean to resort to outright force—rearmament was not necessary and would only hinder the recovery so well begun with Marshall Plan aid.

This argument was not easy to answer, because the amount of time available to the West depended upon unknowns of crucial importance. The faster and more maneuverable tactical planes and the guided missiles now being developed might make defense against land attack more effective. There was even talk of "atomic artillery," supposed to have been tested at Las Vegas during the winter. But that this would be a dangerous resort everyone who heard the rumor realized at once. For the terms of the struggle might very likely turn on tacit agreement not to resort to atomic bombing, and atomic artillery and atomic bombs dropped from planes were perilously similar. Their use might abruptly end any such hidden truce. There might, furthermore, be weapons able to oppose successfully the armor which had been the irresistible force of World War II. It was generally thought—or hoped—that something of the sort existed and was a Western monopoly. Otherwise, the possibility of meeting Russia's hordes on European battlefields seemed a very great risk indeed. Any such improvements, however, were not only secret, they were still untried, and their strategic importance could not be debated with any realism.

This conjectural element in the Great Debate of 1950–51 made it in many ways unreal. Some of the unknowns in the calculations supporting American policy may have been known to the military; but the public had no information. Democracy operated as well as it could, even if a good deal in the dark. The debate resulted, however crippled from lack of fact, in what seemed to be majority agreement to give up dependence on the Bomb and to rebuild the old-style armies. Perhaps the conclusion was reached from lack of alternative. Perhaps the West, unwilling to resort at once to preventive atomic war, had to make the effort or else within a few years face something like surrender.

An alternative might have presented itself at the Paris conference of the spring—negotiation. But Secretary Acheson contended that negotiation must wait until the West had built up a strength to equal that of Russia; only then, he argued, would the Russians give up the idea of world conquest and come to an arrangement.[5] By the spring of 1951, furthermore, the acerbations of the last four years had brought the American public an asperity in dramatic contrast to its immediate postwar mood. Russia had made true at least one

5. The Russians had refused to recognize the strength represented by atomic monopoly when the United States had possessed it, but their actions may have been based on confidence in peaceable intentions that for propaganda purposes they professed not to believe in.

of her propaganda claims. It would now take a great deal of conciliation to stop the progress of the West toward a showdown.

The President and his official entourage still insisted strenuously that they aimed at preventing war. But they had not begun the preparations necessary to the negotiations which must occur at some time and place if there was to be no war. In a democracy the terms would have to be debated, for those who were to negotiate ought not to be inhibited by fear of uncertain reception at home of any arrangements they might arrive at. Yet no discussion had been started. And when the deputy foreign ministers met in Paris on March 5, 1951, Western negotiators had no instructions from their electorates. Those who were suspicious of American intentions, especially in Europe, claimed that negotiations were not what America really wanted. Certainly, the American reluctance to confer seemed marked.

If this reluctance was real, it must have come from strict adherence to the condition that Secretary Acheson had publicly insisted upon: the equalizing of Western and Russian strength. Such a condition must have been based on an undisclosed premise—the confidence evidently felt by Western planners that the Russian power in conventional armaments would be matched or surpassed before Russian atomic bombs could deliver a paralyzing blow. To stand upon such a stipulation was to take a calculated risk that Western confidence might be unjustified. Professor Urey, for instance, ventured the guess—but it was only a guess—that the Russians in the spring of 1951 had as many as fifty atom bombs, enough, if delivered, to paralyze the entire Western industrial complex.

It was crucial to such risk-taking that the Administration overcome the difficulties raised in Congress over the building-up and deployment of conventional American strength. In spite of their growing resoluteness, Americans were evidently not confident that Russia could successfully be opposed in Europe. But the loss of Europe to Russia would double Russia's industrial potential and more than double her strategic power. It would throw America back into a secondary position from which recovery would be next to impossible; no equalizing of strength could be attained. There evidently existed in the American situation an almost insoluble paradox.

Equality of strength might be well in the future—1953 was a

current estimate—but it was late for opening a public debate on the terms for compromise. Despite the horrors of the putative war, Western determination was now hardening dangerously and might interfere with future arrangements for coexistence. Only by extensive discussion could the West become accommodated to the likely conditions. The leaders of such a debate would need a really profound knowledge of democracy as well as a firm global strategy to be implemented—the vision of a Lincoln, a Wilson, or a Franklin D. Roosevelt. Without question, it was very late to begin such a process, which must at best consume a good deal of precious time.

What were the chances that the momentum toward war might thus be checked and turned to the uses of peace? There were at least faint signs that leaders in the West had recognized the deadly danger of provocation. Ambassador Jessup, only a few days before leaving for the futile preparatory talks in Paris, was moved—perhaps officially requested—to make an eloquent address of warning against "preventive war." Preventive war was, of course, a holdover term from the time of American atomic monopoly and inappropriate to the Western weakness of 1951; and there were constant reminders from older and cooler heads in Europe that the risks of aggressive pressure were very great. Yet in the United States a significant public urge to undertake immediate hostilities was apparent. It came of impatience, the increasing tortures of uncertainty, and the suspicion that time ran against the West.

Europeans feared this impatience perhaps even more than Russian aggression. They thought, indeed, that American impetuosity had already led to unwise decisions in the Far East. Their reaction —French and British—to the North Korean attack would preferably have been to stop short of armed intervention; their small contribution to that effort had been a measure of their support for it. But they were especially opposed to the neutralization of Formosa, arguing that the only justification for such an action would lie in an intention to use Formosa as a staging base for an invasion of China. United States involvement in a continental war in Asia they regarded as a commitment which would preclude adequate attention to European defense even if it did not precipitate the third world war on whose brink the nations teetered.

Europeans also feared that American impetuosity might lead to the use of the atomic bomb, either in ending an "intolerable vulnerability" to repeated attacks from the Manchurian "sanctuary," or, in some fit of annoyance, against Russia herself. For no one in America had the slightest remaining doubt that the North Koreans and the Chinese were Russian puppets; and there was strong sentiment for ending the masquerade which allowed the Russians to send one after another of her satellites into conflict while maintaining a sanctimonious neutrality herself. In December a presidential statement construed to mean that the Bomb was a possible resort, brought a hurried visit of protest from Premier Attlee and then from other heads of state. The use of the Bomb, Europeans were clear, would at once precipitate a global conflict in which they would be destroyed.

There thus developed a serious division among the Allies caused not so much by Mr. Truman's statement as by the emotional and intemperate debate then proceeding in every available forum, including the Congress. For those who had an interest in supporting intervention in China—and they were curiously and unaccountably influential—had somehow made a marriage with the always latent isolationists in the United States; and isolationism suddenly and incredibly blossomed out as an active movement for preventive war. Evidently isolationism had all along had its source in a kind of American fascism, which favored the Nazis and Fascists as against the British, French, or German Socialists. But naturally that was not their attitude toward Russians who were Communists, even though they preferred a dictatorship. Every instinct they possessed demanded the suppression of the state which embodied this competing philosophy, and it could not be destroyed without scotching its source in Moscow. To them a number of well-placed atomic bombs seemed ideally suited to the end they had in mind. They reasoned simply that, with the Communists rooted out and the menace of Russian expansionism removed, they could return to the pleasant occupation of developing their businesses.

It was the fear that this vocal, and, as the Europeans feared, majority, opinion in the United States was prevailing and that they might be catapulted precipitously into an atomic conflict as the result of a unilateral decision taken in Washington which brought the heads of Western governments hurrying to the White House.[6] They were evidently to an extent reassured. But there were lingering doubts. Europeans always have great difficulty in distinguishing between the most vociferous and the most fundamental American opinions. They have trouble understanding that a noisy to-do issuing from an activist minority with strong influence on organs of mass communication may be proportionate to a reluctance on the part of most Americans to accept the point of view so spectacularly being touted. They would understand it at home. They give their own people, however, credit for sense and judgment which they can never quite believe that Americans possess.

Nevertheless, behind all the senatorial emotionalism, the editorial threats, and the commentators' exhortations, something of a public policy was taking shape; and European leaders gradually came to understand that it could pretty well be depended on, provided the frightened, the excitable, the self-interested, and the fanatical were not so situated that the people could be committed to more by harassed leaders than they intended. Europeans were still not reconciled to the neutralization of Formosa, were still halfhearted about Korea, and were still fearful that American intentions in Europe would provoke Soviet retaliation. But the comparative calm of the early spring of 1951 was in great contrast with the anxieties of the preceding autumn.

By spring, Americans were coming to a determination that they would reach, if they could, a situation of strength which would not involve reliance on the atomic bomb. They hoped somehow to neutralize that weapon, although there were still military men and armchair strategists who periodically made irresponsible references to its ready availability. But Americans had not gone on to a discussion of the accommodations involved in such a neutralization. Here American leadership, perhaps understandably, yet regrettably, had failed; for the responsible policy-makers were so tormented still by the emotional enemies of communism in the Congress and the press that all their efforts had had to be devoted to shaping and defend-

6. Prime Minister Attlee came early in December and was followed by René Pleven of France. This was the period immediately following the Chinese entry into the Korean War, when, as *Time* put it, "the U.S. and its allies stood at the brink of disaster after the worst defeat the U.S. had ever suffered" (December 11, 1950).

ing a reasoned policy for the first stage of the explosively charged game of power politics now being played with the world as a field. The second stage had not even been outlined.

Consequently, the most intractable element in the whole situation was the quietly shaped and entirely praiseworthy determination of the American people not to be threatened and pushed around by any more dictators of whatever political complexion. Their intentions were simple at bottom, just as they had been simple before— they wanted to end an intolerable menace and then be let alone. Unfortunately, they had not even yet grasped all the implications of the atomic bomb. They hoped to see it banned by international agreement. But the age of atomic weapons and of air power had made obsolete the conventional disarmament which had been a fixed reference in American foreign policy for so long, for the Bomb could be built and dropped by any ambitious industrialized nation which escaped from scrutiny for even a little time and which possessed the means of delivering it at strategic targets. The old, easy continental security could never be again.

It would not be an impossible task for American leaders to persuade the people that Russians had a right to prosper, to have the kind of government they really wanted, and to be secure. The compromises necessary to coexistence, although they ought to be prepared for, would not be at all the sort to which Americans would have fundamental objection. But finding a way out of the present crisis would not solve the problem raised by the atomic bomb. Any peace worth having would henceforth have to be based on a system of unexampled vigilance against political renegades of all sorts—in other words, world government. This solution would be a long jump into the blue for Americans—so long a one, and so unprepared for, that it seemed almost fantastic to suggest it. But was there any other?

Yet the movement for world government now languished in the minds of a few advocates who were strictly excluded from policy-making. Some atomic scientists continued to warn the public ineffectually that no other alternative existed; some social scientists pursued the exploration of such a structure as might be expected to function successfully; a few public men avowed their devotion to the cause; but hardly anyone with responsibility for policy even looked in that direction. Among men of affairs there were only two of prominence and influence whose voices were heard. One of these was the Prime Minister of India, Jawaharlal Nehru; the other was Justice William O. Douglas of the Supreme Court of the United States. But about all either could do was to affirm faith in the ultimate persuasion of mankind to one government for a unified world. During the year Justice Douglas, in an address to the United World Federalists,[7] came close to the exhortation of despair when he cried:

> We who understand the importance of this great task, and who have joined together in this venture, have an obligation to history. Let us return to our homes and carry on the good fight. The road is hard and the obstacles many; but in front of us lies one of the most challenging goals ever set before the eyes of men. If we are to keep the blight of the atomic bomb from the earth and the people, we must be the architects of new instruments of government; we must seek peace through law.

But about Justice Douglas' plea there were only too many who were cold—cold because they could see no progress toward the goal Chancellor Hutchins and his colleagues at the University of Chicago had a few years before defined.[8] Indeed, Mr. Milton Mayer spoke for the discouraged many when he said bitterly that the world government movement would disintegrate as the war movement accelerated. The end is in sight, he said. "War will come faster than world government . . . and at the end of the war there will be a bit of charcoal to constitutionalize."[9] And Pandit Nehru, because of his moderation, was currently very unpopular in the West.

7. In October, 1950; reprinted in *Common Cause*, January, 1951.

8. In *Preliminary Draft of a World Constitution* (Chicago: University of Chicago Press, 1947).

9. *Common Cause*, May, 1950. It is worth notice, as one of the signs of the times, that the world government center of the University of Chicago, begun with such vigor immediately after Hiroshima, and followed in the preceding chapters here, was liquidated at the end of June. The last issue of *Common Cause* was published in that month, and its valiant "maximalist" editors, G. E. and Elisabeth Mann Borgese, were being separated from the University. Mr. Borgese, with a mixture of pride and sorrow—pride in an honest effort and sorrow at the failure of its positive program—wrote in the June issue his last editorial.

"The first two years," he said, "were dedicated to the Preliminary Draft of a World Constitution, a 'proposal to history': not a ready-made world law for the coming World Republic . . . but a plain testing ground where the problems of the present disorder and of a conceivable new order could be concretely probed. Its chief purpose—the exposure of the empty peace slogans which had been silverlining the mushroom of Hiroshima—to a considerable extent has been achieved.

"Maximalism, a government of progressive justice, as against minimalism, a government of security seating the status quo on its bayonets, has been the un-

There remained the United Nations, not by any means a world government, but still a world forum; and it continued, in its limited way, to function. The internationally minded were conscious, however, that interested spectators, watching the building operations on First Avenue in New York, still often inquired of workmen there whether they expected to finish in time for the final dissolution. Evidently men were becoming reconciled to the postponing of world organization until another war had ended. And, taxed with the paradox that if such a war occurred there would be nothing to organize, they said frankly but hopelessly that they knew that very well.

Leading people out of such a despairing dilemma would seem to be the first duty of statesmanship. There were two stages in any American course of action which might lead to peace: the first, to arrive at a negotiable situation; the second, to find the compromises necessary to success in negotiation. The question of 1951 was whether the attainment of the first—momentum of rearming—was not being allowed to make the second—reasonable recognition of Russian claims—impossible. If so, and we went on into war rather than negotiation, we went, it was agreed, to a destruction which no statesmanship could repair.

The Great Debate of 1950–51 seemed by mid-April to have petered out. The Administration had won, but not without one of those gratuitous rebukes to the presidency which senators cannot refrain from administering whenever the opportunity arises. The necessary divisions for General Eisenhower's Western European Army were approved; but the President was told, in effect, not to

---

swerving line of *Common Cause*. . . . Nothing, we have maintained, holds any promise of peace—permanent and worthy of men, not slaves—short of a binding document and pledge apt to win the hearts and minds of a great majority of mankind and to act in due course on our antagonist herself. . . ."

These were noble words from a dedicated mind; but they were spoken to an unlistening nation. Mr. Hutchins was gone from the University of Chicago now, and the world government workers were all dispersed to their individual tasks.

Perhaps it should be noted that a careful statement of the minimalist position was now in print. Mr. Grenville Clark, after submitting it to the Congress, had published it as *A Plan for Peace* (New York: Harper & Bros., 1950). It would keep the institutions of world government "confined to matters clearly and directly related to the prevention of war." But no more attention was paid to the lesser than to the greater proposal.

send more without congressional consent. This attempted coup had been inherent in the debate from the beginning. It had started indeed with the belief of a group of senators that they could force the dismissal of Secretary Acheson and dictate the naming of his successor. This, as Professor Henry Steele Commager said,[10] would have reversed a hundred and fifty years of practice and precedent and would have made the effective conduct of our foreign relations all but impossible. "More is at stake here," he said, "than appears on the surface. What the critics and enemies of Presidential power are doing is clear enough. They are engaged in substituting for the Presidential system a bastard product of Presidential and Parliamentary. . . . If they succeed they will impair and may destroy the constitutional fabric of the Republic."

The President stood firm on the issue of Cabinet integrity; but the frustrated senators found a cheap and dangerous revenge in asserting the right to limit his powers as Commander-in-Chief, an act, as Senator Lodge remarked, which would have made the Senate an executive arm of the Joint Chiefs of Staff. These were old issues thought to have been settled long ago in equally troubled circumstances, particularly when the impeachment of President Johnson had failed. But that the Senate remained unconvinced that it need recognize any constitutional limitations was shown by loud talk of another impeachment, which issued from irresponsible congressional sources. The only real question in these minds was obviously whether the necessary public support could be commanded. If it could, the Senate would defy the clear constitutional right of the President to choose and dismiss his Cabinet, to conduct foreign relations, and to deploy military forces as Commander-in-Chief.

This appalling lack of congressional restraint was able to show itself, and finally to issue in a defiance of the Constitution, because there was undoubtedly a disaffected public opinion upon which extremists could rely. Americans were taking the uncertainties and the inconclusiveness of international events very badly. There was too little of the steadiness and patience which were most of all called for by the circumstances. There was, on the contrary, a pervasive restlessness and impatience; and this supported very poorly the policy of continued and determined containment of Soviet Russia

10. *New York Times Magazine*, April 1, 1951.

to which the Administration was committed. No matter how prudent and realistic the military and civilian policy-makers might be, their constant awareness of public suspicion, heading up into congressional recklessness, had its effect. It tended to bend their judgments in the direction of an aggressive response to provocation, and it limited sharply their consideration of the elements of a possible negotiation for peace. Until mid-April, however, their firmness was remarkable and, considering the pressures upon them, admirable. With MacArthur's summary dismissal in mid-April, however, all the acerbities were sharply intensified. The rising again of popular passion and senatorial insistence resulted in further agitation for aggression and further limitation on negotiation.

When the MacArthur removal occurred, the deputy foreign ministers of the United States, Great Britain, France, and Russia had already been meeting in Paris for several weeks. What might have been expected to be merely a routine task had, because of concurrent events, turned into a fruitless stalemate. It gradually appeared that for once the Soviet representative, Mr. Gromyko, had more freedom of maneuver than had the representatives of the Atlantic Pact powers; and, of these, the most immovable appeared to be Mr. Philip Jessup of the United States. Thus the effect of the Great Debate in America registered itself. Until its course had been run, and the Administration had shaken itself free of its shackles, there was no possibility of attaining the leeway necessary to the striking of the vast bargain for coexistence which was the corollary of Administration policy. This freedom—or a measure of it—might have resulted even from the limited victory represented by legislative approval for sending troops to Europe; but that gain was somewhat more than nullified by the revival of passion caused by MacArthur's defiance of authority. The clamps were rather tightened than loosened, and there was an indefinite postponement of negotiation.

The plain fact of most importance was that Americans had lost faith in their leaders. After his removal, MacArthur was received by many of his countrymen with what amounted almost to idolatry, not because his policies were approved or even fully comprehended, but because they blamed the unlucky officials in power at the moment for not having avoided the crises created by popular insistence. Democracies always need leaders wiser than the people, able to resist even the most powerful pressures toward unwisdom and capable of turning popular sentiment in the direction of support for the policies demanded by the national interest. This is a prescription for a peculiar greatness met with only infrequently, a greatness Mr. Truman lacked.

Yet Mr. Truman, like others before him, had grown in the presidency. Ordinary human material undergoes, in the White House, an amazing transformation. The presidency confers resolution, an awareness of a public interest to be sorted out from many phony representations of it, and the power to manipulate mighty forces so that the public interest is served. A certain wisdom also descends upon the President, along with a new skepticism concerning the motives of those who seek him out. He possesses the sources of information out of which the policies to further the national interest may be made; and he has the freedom to shape an institution about himself which will be more powerful, more intelligent, and more perceptive than any of the individuals who are joined in it. But what the President must have in the great crises, and what the enhancing chemistry of the presidency cannot confer, is that touch of magic which gives him an almost indivisible unity with the people. He must speak their better thoughts; he must utter such a recognizable wisdom as will shame them into compliance with wise policy. Only if he has this indescribable but ineffable quality of the born leader can he beat down the opposition inherent in the Congress, dominate the debates over policy, and carry his country across his years into a new era of triumphant history.

Mr. Truman's opposition, in spite of his growing wisdom, in spite of the realism of his policies, was winning its way to a public he had not had the genius to capture. The Korean War seemed to have little point to many Americans, who could not understand the utility of limited objectives. And negotiations in Paris were fated to come to nothing so long as the diplomats had not the backing from American public opinion that the President had failed to create. The rapport with the people which Mr. Truman had conjured up in his 1948 campaign had dissolved in the atmosphere of doubt, distrust, and opposition which had been so prevalent ever since. This heavy fog seemed impermeable. The bipartisan foreign-policy coalition had shattered; the southern Democrats were disaffected; and only the President's stubborn refusal to yield his last ditches barred the way to premature and reckless aggressions which would most certainly bring on global war.

This might be a temporary condition. The Administration might rise to the challenge of MacArthur as it had not to a gradual decline of confidence and the subsequent crumbling of its congressional support. It had talked about principles, such as punishing aggression. But it had not insisted on the advantages of a limited war. The fact that the Korean conflict was pinning the Chinese "volunteers" to Korea and denying them the far richer prizes of Southeast Asia, that it was demonstrating to Moscow that more bloodless victories could not be won, and that it was yielding precious time for rearmament—none of these points had been carried into the people's minds and hammered home.[11]

The President and his associates would now have to rouse themselves to far greater effort than they had so far expended in justifying Asian policy. And, meanwhile, there could be no end to the fatal armament race. Mr. Edward Murrow on April 26 in his evening broadcast called attention to this. Unless we can get on to a discussion of the peace President Truman insists he is working for, he said, this race will end as all such races have ended. The time approached when, if discussion was further delayed, no end to it could possibly be reached before, as Mr. C. E. Wilson, Director of Defense Mobilization had predicted on the same day, we should have so much armament that it would take all Texas to store it. That, Mr. Wilson had said, would be in 1953. And Mr. Murrow felt justified in wondering whether, when we had it, we would restrain ourselves from throwing it at the Russians. We would not, certainly, unless by then we had reached some clear and acceptable alternatives.

It was the fatal Western weakness that hardly anyone—and no one with responsibility—had tried to visualize and to explain the alternatives to war. Certainly there was not even the shadowy forecast of leadership in this matter from the Truman Administration. Even the word "coexistence" had not been heard in Washington lately,

11. See Mr. James Reston in the *New York Times*, April 26, 1951.

so intense was the fear that it might carry the implication of appeasement. In fact, "appeasement" had become a weapon of domestic
terror used so indiscriminately that exploration of peaceful alternatives had very nearly disappeared. There were a few curious and
undaunted persons, however, who continued to wonder what the
avoided questions were; and there were the perceptible beginnings
here and there of a discussion which, if it were not soured by angry
words, would grow into another great debate. It seemed possible,
even in the post-MacArthur atmosphere, to identify the materials of
this forthcoming discussion.

There was, for instance, a growing suspicion that it had been a
mistake to occupy either Japan or Germany. Traced back, these
doubts had their roots in the controversy over the "unconditional
surrender" formula and, to a lesser degree, the use of the atomic
bomb at Hiroshima and Nagasaki as a military weapon. Mr. George
F. Kennan was suggesting[12] that if, instead of unifying the German
people in 1943 and 1944 by identifying their consent to naziism with
active participation in it, the Allies had attempted to split them by
offering dissenters some hope, the war might not only have ended
sooner but there might have been a government which would have
made occupation unnecessary. The quarrels among the occupying
powers might then have been avoided. The Soviets would have been
excluded from Germany, and a democratic regime might have
succeeded the Third Reich. Similarly, there was much evidence by
1951 that the Japanese had forseen defeat a good while before the
atomic bomb was dropped and that an alternative regime might
have been established without complete occupation.

These mistakes, if mistakes they were, needed to be repaired as
quickly and as thoroughly as possible. Getting out of Japan would
probably prove easier than withdrawal from Germany. The Soviets

12. Walgreen Foundation Lectures, University of Chicago, April, 1951 (afterward published by the University of Chicago Press as *American Diplomacy,
1900–1950* [Chicago, 1951]). Mr. Kennan's thesis rested, however, on the encouragement he felt ought to have been given to the disaffection of the generals
and the *Junker* class generally. President Roosevelt, he believed, had a mistaken
conception of naziism—that it issued from the *Junker* class, whereas actually it
was a middle-class movement. The President could not believe that the plot of
the generals against Hitler offered any hope of an alternative. It is possible that
Mr. Kennan was right; but the question remains whether a residual government
by these reactionaries would have answered the purposes of peace.

were established in East Germany; and, even if they were to with-draw, there seemed to be less and less hope of the reunification necessary for a sound German economy. By setting up the Bonn government, dominated by a clerical-capitalist ideology completely hostile to the Communist regime of East Germany, the Allies had hardened the separation between East and West Germany. These difficulties were enlarged when it was proposed that West Germany should be rearmed and taken into the Atlantic Pact. The proposal stirred the Soviets to an obviously determined protest. Any such step was postponed as General Eisenhower in April took command of the Western European Army; but it stood in the background as the deputy foreign ministers met in Paris and was one of the most serious points of contention in the early weeks of the meeting. It was difficult to see, now, how the problem of unifying and neutral-izing Germany could be solved. Certainly the Soviets would be ada-mant about making sure that Germany for a long time to come would be unable to threaten them again.

If the Soviets cared enough about this, however, they might be willing to make other concessions in order to establish it. If Ger-many were safely disarmed, they might well consent to much more freedom for Austria and for their satellites in eastern Europe— Czechoslovakia, Hungary, Romania, and Albania, none of which constituted a military threat. The Allies had a long retreat to make from their German policy if they were to make any such bargain; but, if diplomats could be freed from constant charges of appease-ment, there was something here for them to exploit.

Nothing else in Europe constituted a problem comparable with the one raised by Germany. The Western countries, with Marshall Plan aid, had beaten down their internal Communistic threats until they no longer could be made use of by Soviet negotiators. The Soviets had given up in Greece, which seemed to indicate that the old Russian dream of access to the Mediterranean, though still a long-run Soviet ambition, need not be considered in the present negotiations for coexistence. The Near East, however, was another matter, for here lay the world's richest reserves of the most desirable present source of industrial energy—oil.

Russia was short of oil, seriously short in a military sense; and close to her borders, in Iran and the other Middle East nations, there was plenty of it, denied to her by her adversaries. If coexistence was to be established, she would be unlikely to consent to a settlement which made this denial absolute and permanent. If negotiations were to fail, the Soviets could subjugate or, at worst, occupy Iran. On the other hand, such a move would be a serious provocation in an already tense world, and the resource would be of doubtful utility to the Russians in the immediate future.

Conditions for coexistence in the Far East were more difficult to determine. With India's example before them, the rising nations in southern Asia would not be satisfied with less than she had gained. Like India, Pakistan had become a Commonwealth; Burma had chosen to remain outside and had been allowed her preference; Indochina was now in rebellion because the French had failed to grant similar terms. It was unlikely that any of these sometime colonies would ever again be useful, as they had been, to the West. The most that the West could hope for would be a free association in which their development might be furthered and their materials and markets made available. The firmness with which the Soviets would oppose such a solution could not be forecast very certainly because of China's special interest in the area. The Russians might have no objection to an arrangement which Communist China would find intolerable. Such a no-man's land on the fringe of the Communist continent would be an uneasy solution. But none of these nations was really needed for a Soviet buffer, as were the states of eastern Europe. It would always be doubtful fighting ground for any attack on the heartland. It seemed possible that mutual forbearance might somehow guarantee the independence of Asiatic neutrals.

Strategically, those lands which lay off the coast of Asia were differently situated and perhaps offered the most difficult problem. The Allies could doubtless hold all offshore areas or guarantee their independence. But, if these islands and peninsulas became the sites of naval and air bases, they would constitute a continuing threat to China. The Soviets would doubtless demand their neutralization. Should the Allies refuse, they would be accused of imperialism; but, should they agree, Communist infiltration would be very likely to transform the weak and backward states from within until they became Chinese-Russian puppets.

Solution of this dilemma evidently required agreement to forbear, on the one hand, from infiltration and, on the other, from military threat and from opposition to Russian notions of internal organization. Stalin had once summarily stopped the operations of his Comintern; the Politburo could similarly disestablish the Cominform. But such a drastic withdrawal, such a grand gesture toward coexistence, could only be paid for by an equally valuable sacrifice. For propaganda and infiltration were weapons against which the Westerners had no equally efficient counter. They were handicapped both by principle and by scruple. They would not infringe seriously on freedom of communication in order to suppress Communist propaganda; and, shamefaced half-alliances with Spain and Yugoslavia notwithstanding, they would not justify unscrupulous means by the prospect of achieving democratic ends. It was a kind of paradox that it was their stricter devotion to principle which left the Allies with no adequate weapon against the Soviets but the threat of force. And this threat had been made more and more ineffective by the advent and development of genocidal weapons.

If the Soviets should give up infiltration, reduce the rigors of puppetization, and allow trade and travel, could the West in return meet the repeated Russian demand for disarmament, including the stockpile of A-bombs? Such a solution might be the center of all future negotiation. How the Russians viewed the rearming of Germany, the establishment of the Atlantic Pact military organization, and the increase in the number of American air bases in the Middle East was made perfectly clear by Mr. Gromyko in Paris. In showing his hand so plainly, he may have been bidding for a bargain. Whether progress toward even opening the debate over such terms could be made before the election of 1952 depended on the American public. The campaign issue might well be war versus peace; for the West would by then be nearly ready for a conventional war, and the choice would have shifted from the Soviets to the West.

There were those who believed that coexistence would be arrived at without any successful negotiations just because neither power group would find sufficient advantage in war over armed peace. But an armed peace would be a hair-trigger situation. Both sides would be forced to maintain a constant alert and to carry an enormous burden of military expense. There would, when the first rearming was completed, be a recurring necessity for the modernization of weapons and defenses. This kind of replanning, retooling, and mass production together with the junking of obsolete guns, planes, electronic devices, tanks, ships—all the paraphernalia of war—would require a permanent allocation of something like one-quarter of the resources of both the Soviets and their satellites and of the Atlantic Pact powers. Whether this burden could and would be carried without hope of relief must be an important part of the calculation to be made. Coexistence on this basis was very nearly as unthinkable as war.

The West could never be certain that, if hostilities should break out, the first stroke would not be an atomic bombing. And this uncertainty would feed on the already serious impatience of the Americans. A greater need for leadership and for public discipline had seldom been known. It was tragic that the circumstances made both so difficult. The difficulties were not all American, either. The British were only too well aware of their peculiar vulnerability to atomic attack and of their lack of defense against it. The Lowlanders and the French recalled the recent destruction of their port cities and trembled for their capitals. All three, furthermore, feared for their empires. If Cominform assistance to dissident nationalist movements did not cease, and if European powers had to preoccupy themselves with Continental rearmament, progress toward the transformation of colonies into Commonwealths would be seriously hampered. These nations could not sustain a long armament race and come out of it with their members intact. Nor could they count on sustaining their developing welfare states. Indeed, in April, Britain's Aneurin Bevan resigned from the Labour government in protest against sacrificing economic and social progress for rearmament.

Since the Soviets admitted to a similar uneasiness in the face of armed coexistence, the climate for negotiation seemed to be established everywhere but in the confused American mind, torn between deepening fear and an impatient desire for release from tension. It was the task of American statesmen to create support in the American public for the settlement of those questions sure to be at issue. In the spring of 1951, however, either the leadership for the task was inadequate or the circumstances were too difficult.

The problems of 1951 were not unique in American diplomatic history. It had always been difficult for diplomats to arrive at any firm bargain even in matters of far less importance than those now in jeopardy. Very frequently long and difficult negotiations had been carried out, compromises arrived at, and treaties signed only to meet repudiation in the process of ratification by the Senate. The problem, John Hay had said after long experience, was "constitutional and irreparable."[13]

And on another occasion, writing to Nicolay, Hay said of his career: "My work has been easy to do, and not worrying. The thing that has aged me and broken me up has been the attitude of the minority of the Senate which bring to naught all the work a State Department can do. In any proper sense of the word, Diplomacy is impossible to us. No fair arrangement between us and another Power will ever be accepted by the Senate. We must get everything and give nothing."[14]

These repeated despairing remarks, made by the Secretary of State who served both McKinley and Theodore Roosevelt in full Republican times when no issues of great significance had to be settled, ought to have resulted a half-century later in such a constitutional change as would allow the compromises to be made which would avert world war. In fact, the opportunities for diplomatic action had steadily narrowed. Wilson had had to deal with that "handful of willful men" who had kept America out of the League of Nations to satisfy their senatorial egos. The later Roosevelt had got his United Nations by a tour de force which cost him his whole domestic program of reform and left his successor with a recalcitrant coalition of Republicans and southern Democrats dangerously powerful and hostile to the presidency.

Only a miracle of leadership could have won the way to compromise in the difficult circumstances of 1951. It was not forthcoming.

13. Hay's remark, on this occasion, was made in a letter to Bellamy Storer, American ambassador to Madrid, in 1901. Being Secretary of State, he was saying, "is a thankless and heartbreaking task. . . . The trouble is, of course, constitutional and irreparable. A controlling influence in public affairs is given by the very structure of our government to men of great energy and force of character, but with no corresponding knowledge of a certain class of affairs. It is impossible for us to deal in diplomatic matters with other countries on a basis of equality. We are so handicapped by the Senate and the House that there is nothing to do but to follow a policy of makeshifts and half measures. I see absolutely no chance of improvement" (quoted in Tyler Dennett, *John Hay* [New York: Dodd, Mead & Co., 1933], p. 412).

14. *Ibid.*, p. 325.

Consequently there was even more demand for American negotiators to get everything and give nothing. Even then coexistence would very likely not be approved. Never had diplomatic tasks been more difficult; it was tragic that war or peace for the entire world and thus the issue of survival or destruction should depend upon them.[15]

When, in mid-April of 1951 General MacArthur was relieved of his commands in the Pacific area, a momentous decision was at least implied. The return to imperialism represented by MacArthur's policies was repudiated, and the current American officials, at least, decided to take up the long effort for leadership rather than domination of the democratic world. Echoes of Theodore Roosevelt's shrill demand for expansion, of Bryan's protesting voice, and of Mahan's geopolitics had been reverberating in the daily and weekly press—in *Life* and *Time,* in the Hearst papers, and in the *Chicago Tribune,* on the one side, and in Administration pronouncements, on the other, ever since the conquest of Japan was completed in 1945.[16]

15. For a full theoretical exposition of the power politics involved in the American-Russian struggle, Professor Hans Morgenthau's *Politics among Nations* (New York: A. A. Knopf, 1950) may be consulted. Professor Morgenthau's skepticism concerning the utility of all attempts to reach world government in advance of establishing world community at least put him in position to argue—perhaps made it necessary for him to argue—that accommodation may be reached if sufficient realism can be counted on. It would be an uneasy equilibrium, but he would argue that the unequal development of various parts of the world will make necessary various challenges to the status quo as time goes on. Uneasy equilibrium would be the rule. Only diplomacy, a rejuvenated diplomacy, always active, can serve to avert future crises as they have sometimes averted past ones. It has to be said that this position was that most generally held among statesmen—which made their responsibility, in the peculiar circumstances of democracy, so much the greater. By this measure the diplomacy of the West in 1950–51 seemed less than adequate.

16. The temptation to explore here at some length the expansionist philosophy of various statesmen and political scientists is almost irresistible but has been resisted for obvious reasons of space. A convenient short chapter summarizing the movement in pursuit of manifest destiny may be found in Professor Julius W. Pratt's study, *The Expansionists of 1898.* The part played in justification of what Mahan had called a "looking outward" by Burgess the political scientist, Fiske the historian, Buckle the geopolitician, and many others is not so well understood as it once was. In view of the momentum acquired by the movement, it is rather remarkable that it died out so completely in succeeding decades. This dying-out is no doubt to be accounted for by absorption in domestic economic expansion, the lack of any real pressure for overseas markets, and the relative self-sufficiency of American resources. Also the role of Britain's navy must be remembered. That manifest destiny, prominent just before the Civil War, and revived in the Harrison, McKinley, and Roosevelt regimes, should not have had a more vigorous revival

The Pacific was to be, in the imperialist conception, an American lake, and all the nations bordering it were to be immobilized, at least, and reduced perhaps to satellites. Others took what was coming to be called "the global view." This view regarded the Pacific as a lesser center of the grand world struggle than the Atlantic. It was in Europe that the Administration saw its best chance to meet and face down the Communist threat. But, more basically, it refused to be drawn into reckless military adventure on the MacArthur terms. It hoped to find the strength and resolution to prevail by other means.

Debate over this decision did not lie down at once; it reached, in fact, a new crescendo when MacArthur returned to make his speech to the joint session of the Congress a week after his dismissal. But it had little to feed on. It was in fact over, unless the MacArthur of the Republican party should some day come into power. The sober judgment imposed on the man in the White House by the responsibility for the nation's future, together with the fortunate fact that there were three civil-minded five-star generals—Marshall, Eisenhower, and Bradley—in the military high command, held the line for leadership rather than domination. This decision did not mean that there would be no third world war; it did not even mean that the setting for peace was being foresightedly prepared; but it might mean that the choice for war would not be forced on the Soviets at once and that time might be given for sober judgment.

The next task was that of reminding the American people that coexistence with the Soviets was the only alternative to the war they seemed to have decided against and of bringing them to an understanding of its implications. It would still be all too easy to insist on terms in negotiation which would be incompatible with coexistence. The public mind, without leadership and wide discussion, would not

---

in the circumstances of America's open plunge into world affairs during and after World War II is most remarkable. That the way of collective security, of defense of status quo, and open opposition to all expansionism was chosen will be said by the cynic to show no more than that it suited American convenience—that it is the way of capitalism to exploit without assuming responsibility. But, at any rate, it is fact. American interests are now world-wide; but they are not, in the old definition at least, imperialistic. If Americans intend to subjugate other peoples, it is by what they can fairly call "neighborliness." Their capitalist fellow-citizens may gain from it; but every day they are paying for it sums which would have seemed utterly fantastic a decade ago.

be likely to lay on one side the items of our irreducible public interest and, on the other, those which it had agreed, in effect, were, even if important and engaged with our emotions, not fundamentally necessary. Unless time and discussion had sieved out the irrelevant and revealed the residue, American negotiators could not feel behind them the security of national decision they would need for the task they now had to undertake.

For this conclusion in the public mind Americans needed a reminder of their history, of their new position in the world and among the nations, and of the future for which most of them hoped. This need be no more than a sharp reminder, because the history could be read (they were a literate people), because the position was clear (there were already-gathered facts), and because the future was one they had spoken for in several elections.

There had been imperialist moments. Americans had always moved out into a wider and wider ambient. The landings on the East Coast of immigrants from Europe had begun three centuries of westward movement. The taking of Texas and California had seemed a logical conclusion to this movement; but, even then, the scouts and advance parties were far out across the Pacific creating an issue for decision as to whether the consolidation of the continent was really a conclusion or after all only a good beginning. At one time or another feints were made northward and southward as well as westward. The crisis in the debate concerning the nature of future expansion can be seen in looking back to have been reached shortly after the beginning of the twentieth century. The last powerful exponent of imperial expansion had been Theodore Roosevelt, backed by Senator Lodge and abetted by Secretary Hay. The issue had rather faded out than come to a clear and sharp decision, but there was, gradually, an acceptance of one method as against another. Expansion was not necessarily abandoned; but weaker peoples were at least not to be brought under military subjugation and then forced into formal unity with the nation. Their doors were to be kept open. There were to be neighborly relations with them, even going to the length sometimes of seeing to it that they behaved in a sufficiently seemly manner to avert interferences from other powers. Americans were to send them the capital for development and sell them their goods; they were even to insist on the sacredness of property and

278

profits. But they were not to add more stars to the flag or to accept colonial responsibilities.

Roosevelt, Beveridge, and Lodge, in the large days after the Spanish war, may have thought the argument not yet ended or not yet ended properly; but in the long run they did not prevail. Canada was not taken, as perhaps it might have been; or Mexico, as it might easily have been. Cuba was given independence at once, after her liberation from Spain; and after a while a kind of protected independence for the Philippines was worked out. The Puerto Ricans were allowed as much loosening of relationships as their wiser leaders really wanted. Those were the days of sea power, and it could be understood that American fleets, ranging out into the bordering oceans, gave an unassailable national security. There arose, in fact, a solid opposition to any formal annexations beyond the continent's shores.

It was perhaps inevitable that the coming of the air age should disturb these settled policies, founded as they were on continental isolation together with a protecting navy. But no one seemed to anticipate an argument over the method of expansion by air which was to be so reminiscent of that other expansion by sea. It was not precisely similar. Presumably even Mr. Luce, Mr. Hearst, or General MacArthur would not have added Japan and China to the list of States. But they had learned from the Soviets the technique of creating satellites. The argument was whether eastern Asia was to become independent or was to be incorporated, one way or another, into an American system of dependencies. To the modern imperialists it seemed a logical extension of air-power logistics that such a system should be created and that the relations and arrangements appropriate to it should be established by force if necessary. The others—President Truman and his advisers—were no less concerned with national security in an air age; but, like Franklin Roosevelt, they looked to another, a wider and deeper, source for it. They believed that subjugation—even if it went under another name—was an unstable and temporary status; they believed that free people with democratic institutions would be our natural and inevitable allies; and they believed that the air age was rapidly creating a situation in which subjugation could not possibly be a sufficient protection without conquest of the whole world. They therefore believed our security required a different kind of system—one which was coming to be called "collective." This was the real alternative to conquest.

This system had already an embodiment—the United Nations. That organization functioned well enough for the agreed purposes among all the nations except the Soviets. The real problem was how to bring the Russian and Chinese people into the system in which the West believed and how to prevent their imposing on others the one in which they believed.

It was undoubtedly part of the judgment of the Truman group that a clear decision in America against MacArthurism would be a disarming influence, a good start. If no one could say, with any show of conviction, that it was the purpose of the United States to subjugate any other nation, the Communists would lose a formidable propaganda weapon. Now not only the President himself but Secretary Acheson and three generals had spoken forcibly and unequivocably. So long as the decisions in Washington were made by present policy-makers, there need be no doubt in anyone's mind. The United States wanted friends and co-workers, not satellites.[17] Also, as must have been well noted, MacArthurism was not even official Republican doctrine. A powerful section of that party espoused it; but it was not certain that it was a dominant view; and, after all, the Republicans had been a minority party for twenty years. What lingering doubt there could be in the mind of friend or enemy that America had abandoned imperialism rested on the chance that it would be officially adopted by the Republican party and that the party would win in 1952.

For five months in the spring of 1951 the events of consequence for the peace of the world deployed themselves about the meeting in Paris. It was a meeting whose sessions ultimately ran into scores. There was a slight flavor of frivolity in the many references commentators made to the proposals and counterproposals, the speeches, the statements, the planted stories, the veiled threats—and sometimes the actual movement of armed forces—as a great game of chess. Yet the analogy was so accurate as to be in itself disturbing. There was

17. See, e.g., President Truman's address to the Civil Defense Conference, May 7, 1951 (*Why We Need Allies* [Department of State Publication 4218 (Washington, D.C., 1951)]).

something devastatingly final about the centering of all the stresses and ambitions of the two straining groups—East and West—in one place.

The Soviet Union had made the first move early in November, 1950, by demanding, in a note to the Western powers, a meeting on "the demilitarization of Germany." The Westerners countered with a proposal for a much more inclusive discussion on "the causes of tension in Europe." The Soviet Union at that time very much wanted a meeting, and it was to resolve the differences about an agenda that the deputies of the foreign ministers met in the Palais Rose early in March. What was bothering the Russians specifically was the evident purpose to include West Germany in the Atlantic Pact and to rebuild the German army. A rearmed Germany, they frankly said, presented to them an intolerable threat.

It became clear at once that the public suggestion for rearming Germany had been a diplomatic blunder, arising from a gross misunderstanding of Soviet sensitivity; for it was with the greatest reluctance, with repeated intimations of Russian "insincerity" and preliminary statements of certain failure, that American diplomats prepared to go to Paris. Presently the Russians did not care to have the meetings succeed either, because it became all too apparent that the Germans would have something to say about rearming and that what they would say, at least for the present, would be an emphatic "No."

The embarrassments of Paris were the worse because President Truman and Secretary Acheson had said so often that the Russians could be talked to effectively only from strength; and strength, in the sense they meant, was several years away at the end of an intensive effort to rearm and to gather up the West's potential into an effective resisting and striking force. German rearmament might be decisive in shaping this force, but, if it involved premature conflict, it was an impossible resource. In the late spring as General Eisenhower took over the command of the embryonic European army, he partly relieved Secretary Acheson of his embarrassment by gently suggesting that Germans for his army were less important than had been insisted by the Secretary. But the Russian desire for a foreign ministers' meeting was thus dissolved, and from then on they merely sparred for any propaganda advantage they could secure from the embarrassments of the Western diplomats. To proceed from a deputies' meeting to a gathering of the ministers themselves was unnecessary.

So far as there could be gain or loss from the unreal discussions, the losses fell to the West. The Communists scored heavily by identifying Americanism with capitalism; and such was the Western need of unity, and so strongly were the capitalists intrenched, that genuine democracy was being driven under cover everywhere except in Britain. In America, especially, dissent from capitalism was being successfully identified with lack of patriotism. To be against "free enterprise"—that is, to criticize the operations of big business—was close to being against the government itself. The crown and glory of democracy, the magnificent Bill of Rights, was its crown and glory no longer. Only at considerable personal risk could men speak and teach the truth as they saw it; they were foreclosed from engaging in public affairs if there was a taint about them of critical appraisal. America under the Communist pressure was well on the way to becoming what the Communists said it was—a center from which capitalist expansion proceeded.

The machinery for thought control was made effective, paradoxically, by freely elected legislators who "investigated" their fellow-citizens for any nonconformance and who seemed not to see that presently legislatures themselves might be destroyed by the narrowing restrictions. It was a time of permanent hysteria, of reaction against the frustrations of a conflict which could not be brought to issue, yet which must be waged in the shadow of the Bomb. If Russians could not be punished for imposing intolerable anxiety on the world, there was some relief in turning against neighbors who were at least like the Russians in having unorthodox views—ones which were not recognizable as simple common sense. It was doubtless with cynical knowingness that the Fascist-minded took advantage of this disease spreading through the public mind, but they were nevertheless effective as no such group had ever been in the past. The year 1950–51 was one not only of danger but of terror.

The truth was that Americans had not been quick enough to modernize the mechanics of representation. Not the whole people, but the narrowest and most rabidly orthodox of local businessmen, were represented in the legislatures. It was they who furnished the funds for increasingly expensive political campaigns and who maintained the lobbies to demand from the legislators the *quid pro quo*. This is to state the complicated system of influences and the interlocking interests far too simply. But it does no violence to the significant underlying fact that representative democracy was in grave danger of committing suicide through the perversion of representation.

How this background of American sickness affected matters at Paris was not hard to see. It made negotiation, already unreal because of the doctrine of equated strength, quite impossible. For any concession, the negotiators were aware, would instantly become "appeasement," and a congressional investigation with all its now-perfected apparatus of character destruction would be brought into play. Mr. Gromyko had the advantage over Mr. Jessup, because, unlike the American government, the Soviet government had complete freedom of action. It was the prisoner of an ideology, but one from which there was no dissent which needed to be considered.

The British and French diplomats also faced disaffected public opinion; but their role in the conference was minor. The Labour government had a very parlous hold on its electorate, and the unforgiving Churchill was still losing no opportunity to embarrass his political opponents. Because of these political difficulties, as well as because of Britain's current economic weakness, the British could hardly be said to play even a secondary part. The French situation was worse. Until late in June, M. Parodi was tormented by a coming election and by the combined attacks of the French Communists and the Gaulists. The French and British representatives sat at the meetings in the Palais Rose, but they might as well not have been there for any effect they had on American policy in the negotiations.

There were, in fact, no negotiations. Nevertheless, there were centered in Paris all the forces, ponderable and imponderable, at work in the world. The deployment, before the end, was complete.

The distribution of real strength at the Paris conference was not easy to assess. The intensive secrecy which to the Soviets seemed so natural had spread now to the West. Each side denounced the other; neither side revealed more about its power than it could help. But behind all the recrimination there was some solid knowledge which not only weighed with the negotiators but seated itself in the public mind. Westerners came to understand at least something not only of the Soviet intentions but of the means they possessed to carry them out—or they came to conclusions based on what they believed to be the situation.

One of these conclusions was that the Soviets would not hesitate to subjugate the West by force if they could but that they knew they could not succeed—not even in the spring of 1951. Thus, if possible, they would avoid the attack. There was evidence for such a conclusion. In Russia there was currently a production of less than 22 million tons of steel, whereas in the United States alone there was a production of more than 100 million tons; and the Western Allies added some 50 million tons in comparison with no more than 6 million tons from the Soviet satellites. The coal and oil comparison was even more unfavorable. The United States alone produced six or seven times as much of both as did the Russian power complex. Straight through the list of strategic materials the situation was the same. Only by an improbable tour de force could the items of basic industrial power be equated. Russia might overrun Europe and so subtract the industrial potential of the Ruhr, the Saar, Luxembourg, and Lorraine from one side and add it to the other. She might occupy the Middle East and capture its enormous oil reserves. But a war would put these facilities out of operation for many years. During these years the Soviets would have little more than they now possessed, and they would be under desperate attack.

Those who knew something of Russia's agricultural problem, furthermore, realized that the boundless productivity of the vast Russian plains was partly myth. For one thing, practically the whole of the Soviet empire lay above the forty-fifth parallel, with a three-month growing season. For another, the black-soil region, which was the most productive, was tormented by drought. Actually Russia had less arable land than the United States and produced only half as much grain with fifty million more people to feed. Nor could the satellites produce substantial surpluses for Russian consumption.

Westerners appreciated the ability of Russians to work and fight on a standard of living far below that of the West. It was known that the Russians could divert, without civilian protests, all kinds of resources to military uses in proportions that would cause revolutions in democracies. Nevertheless, the disproportion of resources appeared to make a sustained war against the West impossible for the Russians to win. It was therefore gradually and cautiously conceded that the Politburo probably did not want one.

What the Politburo would decide under extreme pressure, however, was another matter. It could be argued—and many Europeans, especially, so argued—that in spite of those 175 available divisions casting their shadow over Europe, and in spite of the 15,000 fighter planes and the 300 new submarines, the situation must already seem desperate to the Russians and that the Politburo calculations must be shifting over from the rational to the reckless. A few Westerners were already beginning to believe that it was time now to talk business, that to wait for a situation of equated strength was to accept responsibility for forcing a Russian adventure into world conquest which otherwise would not be considered in the Kremlin. For General Eisenhower had completed the organization of his European command by the end of June. The United States had been mobilizing for a year and had upwards of three million men in various stages of training. Six divisions were battle-hardened in Korea, and one had landed in West Germany and had been deployed, along with the occupation forces already there, on a defense line; and there were more American divisions to come. Elections in France, Italy, and Germany, furthermore, if they had not resulted in any considerable Communist losses, had not registered any loss for the moderates either. Russian penetration by propaganda was not succeeding, and this result was clearly attributable to recovery through Marshall Plan aid. The European Recovery Administration was a more effective agent for the West than was the Cominform for the East.

Furthermore, Russian expansion in the Far East was slowing down. The Korean adventure seemed about to result in a definite check to armed aggression. After a year of advances and retreats the battle line was about where it had been in the beginning. The Allies, moreover, were very much stronger now than they had been before.[18] They had lost men, and they had used precious material; but they

18. There appeared a careful assessment of gains and losses from the Korean War on June 24, 1951, in the *New York Times*, "One Year of War in Korea: A Balance Sheet for the United Nations and the Enemy," by Hanson W. Baldwin.

had learned lessons it would have been too late to learn on European battlefields, and they had been stirred to a mighty effort of rearmament. If the Russian scheme had been to try out the principle of satellite warfare and to weaken the West, it had failed.

On the Russian side of the scale, it is true, there was trouble, serious trouble, for the West in Iran. The oil fields necessary to European strength were being nationalized. Ironically the Soviets had had little or nothing to do with the disturbance; British exploiters had pressed too hard. Their unwillingness to meet Iranian demands for such a share in the profits as would be politically acceptable had fed a reactionary nationalist movement until it had become uncontrollable. The Iranians showed no desire to turn to Russia, but any loss to the West of resources and industrial strength was an advantage to the Soviets. In the Middle East—and in Africa, where nationalist troubles worsened—the Communists undoubtedly gained at the expense of their opponents.

On the whole, however, even optimistic reports which might be flowing into the Kremlin would not lead to the conclusion that the year had enhanced the comparative power of the Soviet imperium. The creation of European and Asiatic satellites, so staggering in its effect, seemed to have come to an end. The Politburo planners had to decide whether to call a halt or to enter on the reckless adventure of a world war. And the West had to decide whether it would settle for coexistence with present Communist nations and in effect guarantee their integrity in a system of collective security or whether such an arrangement would be so dangerously unstable that war was preferable to its continuing risks.

Perhaps—and this was the great imponderable of 1951—the momentum of competitive rearming, the clumsiness of negotiators, or the inability to check a once-aroused combativeness might prevent the carrying-out of rational calculation on either side which would emerge in negotiable positions. This effort for the establishment of coexistence, which was now the only alternative to war, was a very delicate and difficult matter indeed.

The meetings of the deputies in Paris, where the confluence of all the year's tensions and ambitions was visible, failed miserably. After seventy-four fruitless discussions extending from early March to late June, the Western representatives simply went home. There were final recriminations from both camps, but they added nothing to the arguments already made. They had come close to agreement on the subjects about which the Big Four foreign ministers might have talked if they had met; but the crucial issues of the Atlantic Pact army, of American air bases, and of Russian armament had not been resolved. The Russian principal in the Paris meetings was, of course, Andrei Gromyko. He was back in Moscow when, on June 24, he was called on by United States Ambassador Alan Kirk. This visit, at the direction of the Department of State, was to seek clarification of a sensational speech made by Jacob Malik, Soviet representative at the United Nations, over an American radio network just before the first anniversary of the North Koreans' attack.

This speech seemed to offer a cease-fire in Korea on terms acceptable to the nations engaged in the conflict. He did not, at least, seem to require a prior engagement to agree on the terms of a settlement with Communist China. There was evidenced at once a skepticism in America which was offset by an eager optimism among the other nations. But American doubts were modified by Mr. Gromyko's assurance to Ambassador Kirk that what the Russians had in mind was a purely battlefield agreement to stop the fighting and to withdraw from a neutral zone. What would follow would be extremely complicated; but at least there would be an end to the slaughter.

Superficially a cease-fire would be a return to the *status quo ante*. But neither side would be able to ignore what had occurred during the bloody year of fighting. What the Russians had lost was the incorporation of South Korea into the Soviet regime. Perhaps they thought they might sovietize the pitifully prostrate little nation in another way. But that would at the least require years to do. The South Koreans might turn against the West; but, if they did, it would be after a considerable time; and obviously the Soviets had not wanted to let that time elapse. As a western outpost on the Asiatic mainland it was embarrassingly close to Manchurian ports and heavy industries and would undoubtedly be a continuing irritation if not a real block to plans for the conquest or penetration of Japan. By now, however, the Americans had the largest air base in the world on Okinawa; and Japan, Formosa, and the Philippines lay across seas which, though narrow, the mighty navies of the West were entirely capable of protecting from any attack mountable from the mainland for years to come. Korea, therefore, may not have been so vital in strategic terms as it had been a year before when it had seemed possible that Western withdrawal from the borders of the Pacific might be forced. It could only be assumed that the Russians were preparing to use other tactics in the East. That they had not given up the idea of gaining the whole of Asia and of its outlying islands could be taken for granted. Their satellite war had not succeeded. They would resort to other measures, modifying their time schedule and waiting for the opportunities which, in Communist theory, were inevitable. Some day in capitalist confusion and imperial blundering, the West's attention would falter. That would be the Communist opportunity—one well prepared for, no doubt, by careful ideological penetration, especially in Japan and the Philippines, whose economic situation seemed so fundamentally hopeless.

Mr. Gromyko had not made possible a meeting of foreign ministers as he might have by agreeing in Paris to an agenda which no one supposed would, in any case, have been binding. But he was making possible what seemed at first an inconsistent *modus vivendi* in the East. How reconcile the two? They seemed inseparable on the theory that the Russians wanted disturbance everywhere, wanted to bleed the West, wanted to keep pressure everywhere on Western containing forces. But Korea, if it had resulted in some bleeding, had resulted in far more determined strengthening of the West, in valuable experience, and in deepened hostility to Russian designs. After Korea there would be no more taking by default, no more costless expansion. A return to a simulation of co-operation may have been judged necessary to a weakening of the now rapidly growing threat. At Paris the effort to include in the agenda the Atlantic Pact and American air bases on the Russian periphery had failed. That in fact had been the demand which had caused the final breakup of the conference. Perhaps in a more pacific atmosphere there could be negotiation which would relieve the anxiety now urging them toward war. Whatever went on in the Russian mind—whether these were the moving considerations—no one could say. But at the moment there seemed to be no other tenable suggestions.

What must have weighed heavily in Russian calculations was the once-more-repeated miracle of a mounting American strength. No other modern nation except Germany had demonstrated the almost magical ability to concentrate on a mighty national effort of such rising momentum. Germany had, by a narrow margin, been broken. But the United States was at the height of her industrial power and would in another year or two be able to bring to bear in conflict a force such as had never before been gathered and discharged at a political objective. The hard-minded Russians were doubtless less fooled by the superficial bickerings and seeming divisions in the United States than were America's allies, who were so frightened by its various manifestations. Behind the screen furnished by the fruitless MacArthur debate, by the sensational crime investigations of the year, by the dissents of the isolationists and the irresponsible caterwaulings of the isolationist Republicans, it must have been noticed that the billions needed for the armed force build-up flowed easily through the Congress, that new weapons were being blueprinted for mass production, that at Las Vegas and at Eniwetok more tests of atomic weapons were being conducted, that inflation, for all the talk, was being brought under some control, and that the American public was being thoroughly conditioned to a permanent state of jeopardy. These facts must have carried great weight in the Russian calculations.

The divisions among Britons, like those among Americans, cannot have been of a kind to make the Russians happy. They consisted mostly in differences about the means to combat the Soviets, not differences about the end itself. In neither nation did the Communists now have a fifth column of any account at all. And if doctrinaire Communists in Soviet inner circles found this hard to reconcile with their theoretical commitments, trusted Soviet observers familiar with the West from service in the United Nations or in Western embassies must nevertheless have insisted on certain facts. And anyway the theoretical element of greatest elasticity had always been that of time. Before the West collapsed from internal stresses there might be an interlude of sufficient length to accommodate a devastating assault on the Soviet bastion in western Russia. Even those Russians who believed in penetration and satellite warfare must have been reconsidering. Had it been wise to follow policies which had stirred the West to so mighty an effort?

The effort was mighty, however it was looked at. It could not be measured in output of munitions, because the end product of mass industries emerges from a long and involved process of planning, tooling-up, and arrangements for co-ordination, and it was in these preliminary stages that the most remarkable advance had been made. Behind American industrial organization there was the recent experience of preparation for World War II; there were even a good many plants in stand-by condition and a considerable reserve of such necessities as machine tools. But the production of basic materials had also increased, illustrating once again the power of industry, given an unlimited objective and freed from competition, to expand. In the twelve months from Hiroshima Day in 1949 to Hiroshima Day in 1950 the production of steel, for instance, had amounted to less than 80 million tons; during the same period of the next year it amounted to nearly 103 million tons. Such achievements represented the slack inherent in capitalism, with its tendency to restrict, to overcharge consumers, and so to reduce gradually the output of goods; for during the same period the output of consumers' goods continued high. It was not high enough to prevent price-bidding, however, and there was a very noticeable rise in general price levels. This last, although an organization now existed to check it, was sufficient to be the most disquieting feature of the otherwise strengthening economy.

The Administration was doing its best to stop inflation but was obviously severely handicapped. Under the Defense Production Act there had been set up an Office of Price Stabilization; but its grant of power was limited. The act itself, under which the whole mobilization effort was being conducted, expired at the end of June and, because the Congress was lobby-ridden as never before, could not be strengthened. The Administration felt itself lucky to have even a temporary renewal while the argument proceeded as to whether any controls would be continued. The powerful combination furnished by the National Association of Manufacturers, the United States Chamber of Commerce, and the farmers' organizations (the Farm Bureau Federation and the Grange) had been fighting furiously for complete freedom all year. They were opposed by no really effective interests, although some labor organizations, conscious that the wage-price competition would in the long run result in reducing real wages, did what they could. The really exposed groups in the community—those with fixed incomes—had lost, in the last few years, some effective allies. The more powerful labor organizations had succeeded in contracting for wage scales tied to the cost-of-living index; and farmers had a hard-and-fast commitment by law to the parity principle. These groups were therefore exempt from the effects of inflation.

If everyone's income had been correlated with rising costs, there would, of course, have been no advantage in such exemptions. It was only because some groups were powerful enough to seize benefits at others' expense that these inequities could exist. They could be retained only so long as others in the community could be forced to consent. But meanwhile the distorting effect was considerable. An economy could operate by throwing the costs of inflation on its weaker members so long as those members did not revolt. And real resistance would not build up in a short period. The whole system of social security was jeopardized when the real incomes of its beneficiaries fell steadily month by month. But there was as little concern about pensioners as there was about the pressure on salaried personnel throughout the system or about the value of incomes from savings. The weight of influence lay with the expanded business concerns whose profits spiraled satisfactorily as inflation proceeded and who knew how to protect their interests in Washington.

Those who objected to the current procedure or, like the President, had some concern for its long-run effect, had less attention paid to them in the confused and riotous goings-on in Washington than ever before. Members of the Congress shamelessly cut themselves loose from caution and openly espoused those dangerous friends whose company in more normal times they had feared to keep.[19]

19. Mr. Drew Pearson, the well-known columnist, was moved to write in July (various newspapers, July 23, 1951): "Not only has the 82nd Congress failed to pass a single appropriation by the end of the fiscal year but a good many members don't seem to care that they are being called the 'horsemeat' Congress [a reference to the strength of the cattlemen's lobby in opposing controls]. Never in my recollection have both morals and morale been so low. Never in my recollection has there been less idealism, less patriotism, such poor party discipline; never such shameless absenteeism. . . . This is the tail-end of a tired, uninspired administration—probably the end of a long period of Democratic rule . . . and without leader-

The Congress refused to support controls of more than a nominal sort, such as business itself needed to maintain a minimum of co-ordination; and it would not accede to the President's request for such increases in taxation as would establish a pay-as-you-go policy. But there was no hesitation about voting something like a hundred billion dollars of authorizations for expenditures by the armed forces. It was obvious that, if these obligations were incurred on schedule, they could be paid for only by resort to deficits and that these deficits would result in lowering the value of the dollar. The point was made clearly enough, over and over, by an Administration which felt its obligation to the national interest, but without effect. The Congress was more interested—and hoped that the American public would also be interested—in noisy but futile whoopings and hallooings about matters which were none of its business or which were irrelevant to the main issue of mobilization. Never had representative government fallen so low, measured by its faithfulness to the public interest. There had been bad times before; the years just preceding had caused concern for those who thought democracy impossible in other than a representative system; but the majority abandonment of responsibility in 1950–51 brought something like despair to thoughtful men.

Nevertheless, effective planning had prevailed in the mobilization effort itself—favorable to big business, of course, but effective. Judicious use of government loans and tax remissions had made possible a considerable expansion in the production of basic materials. By 1953 there would be new plant capacity for a 20 per cent increase in steel, aluminum, and similar industries and for added power plants. About then the new munitions for war would begin to emerge in overwhelming quantity from redesigned and retooled factories.

There had been some concern over this delay in the production of actual arms. The decision not to freeze designs and begin mass production of planes, tanks, and weapons until the latest models had been tested and proved was risky. But, in all probability, it would

---

ship every Congressman adopts the law of the jungle—every man for himself. Instead of voting what's good for the country, he votes what's good for himself or the lobbyists who helped fill his campaign chest." Similar, but equally critical, comments were made by other Washington correspondents, even those not usually given to acerbity. Many also commented in July on the seriousness of such a situation having arisen at a time of such a dangerous international instability.

create superiority in the field. One of the lessons of Korea had been the costliness of obsolescence. The Russian jet planes had been faster and more maneuverable, the tanks had been superior in firepower, and the artillery—traditionally a Russian specialty—had been more effective than anything being used by the Allies. There had not been enough of these Russian supplies, and what there was had not been used expertly; but it could be understood how these more advanced designs, managed by the Russians themselves, and added to their considerable superiority in manpower, might affect a battle in Europe. Western troops had to be re-equipped; and, if the latest possible designs could be brought into the field at the outbreak of further hostilities, they would in all probability make the difference between success and failure.

No one knew, as one Pentagon spokesman put it, whether the Russians would take advantage of the "spring shooting season" in 1951. There were those who thought they would and who looked for immediate successor incidents to the Korean failure. That they proved to be wrong must have been an enormous relief to General Marshall, who, as Secretary of Defense, bore the most direct responsibility for the decisions about timing and preparation. In 1951 orders were beginning to flow out to prime contractors in considerable volume, and subcontracting was rising. But production engineers were merely beginning to study their problems of plant adaptation, tooling, scheduling, and the assembly of materials. Not until July 1, 1951, did the really effective Controlled Materials Plan of the National Production Authority come into operation. Until then there was not much more than a kind of negative priorities system for withholding materials from "nonessential" industries. From then on estimates of needs for selected productive processes would be made, materials would be regarded as one national supply, and allocations would be made in accordance with a national plan.

The Production Authority did not have an easy task, since it did not know what timing was required, what quantities of materials were needed, and sometimes not even what designs were to be used. It was required to provide for an enormous output of munitions, a few of which were specified as to time and design; beyond that, in 1951, it had to estimate generally the probable needs for materials and unspecific plant capacity. Closer planning would have to be carried on as the situation developed. Meanwhile the Authority could perfect its own organization, provide the machinery for allocation and reallocation, and hope that overhead decisions would be made in time for its machinery to operate.

With these problems, it was remarkable what was actually accomplished during the year toward mobilization. Even more remarkable, however, was the progress made by both sides toward recognizing the hard realities of the strategic situation. There were signs of Russian desire for truce in Korea for several months before Jacob Malik's speech precipitated the cease-fire talks between the field commanders. These negotiations could not be taken by themselves, in the way they were presented to the world, as simple arrangements to stop the small war there. The Paris meeting, it began to be seen, had been adjourned to another forum. The United States was again reluctant; every step was taken with protestations of probable failure; and the President devoted most of his speech answering Mr. Malik to denunciation of the Politburo. The American concept was still that equated strength had not been reached. There was no recognition of the possibility that the Soviets might by now regard rising strength in the West as the onset of that intolerable situation which would call for an immediate choice between coexistence and war; and there was no suggestion that any sacrifice in the interest of accommodation might have to be made.

Yet there had been a careful use of publicity about the tests of new atomic weapons at Eniwetok and Las Vegas. Their import could not have been missed by the Russians, and there could not have been any other purpose in the skilfully released information than its effect on the enemy. Taken together with bases all around the Soviet periphery, the American progress in atomic weapons—artillery, guided missiles, the hydrogen bomb—constituted, it would seem, the kind of threat which the Russians must soon regard as ultimate.[20] The inconsistency of this closing-in with reluctance to negotiate was a strange feature of American policy.

No secret was made of the impending situation. Mr. Wilson set

20. On March 20 General Marshall had reported to the President: "As of tomorrow . . . the strength of our armed forces will be exactly double what it was on June 25, 1950." This would be 2,900,000 men, which had grown to 3,500,000 by June 30, 1951, and was still increasing on Hiroshima Day.

1953 as the year of climax for American strength. Late in January and early in February tests of atomic weapons were made at Las Vegas. As the *New York Times* suggested:

The very fact that the tests were held in Nevada, instead of at the atomic proving grounds at Eniwetok, strongly indicates that the weapons tested are artillery weapons and guided missiles. Such weapons require a large territory for testing, such as is available in the 5,000 square mile gunnery range in Nevada. Eniwetok is much too small for such tests, as the shells, rockets, or guided missiles would all explode over the Pacific, where no detailed study of their range and effects could be made.[21]

There followed the further tests at Eniwetok. These evidently included explosions of improved A-bombs and probably a test that confirmed that the A-bomb could be a trigger mechanism for the H-bomb. Anyone could conclude just from information in the press that progress toward an entirely new set of weapons was rapid. Atomic weapons might be available in the field within a year or two. If the Russians had no other sources of information, what they read in the newspapers could tell them that presently their conventional artillery would be so obsolete as to be worthless; and of what use would be a vast complement of tanks when faced with atomic artillery? As the New York *Herald Tribune* pointed out: "If atomics can be brought into the tactical sphere, the advantage of teeming populations and simple economic structures which Russia and her Asian satellites now enjoy would be neutralized. The whole present picture of world strategy, in fact, would be drastically revised."

Doubtless policy-making Russians had shrewd appraisals of American progress in atomic research available to them, and they could be expected to anticipate, by at least a year or two, the coming equating of strength. Their ability to overrun Europe or, indeed, to challenge the containing powers anywhere would disappear unless they had equally revolutionary developments to unveil when the crisis should come. No one could read in *Pravda*, for instance, what the likelihood of such matching advances might be, but there was very general confidence in the West that they were not being made with sufficient speed. There had not been an atomic explosion in Soviet territory since the one announced in September, 1949. Yet the Russians were exploiting feverishly all the uranium deposits available to them. The most likely explanation was that no more ex-

21. February 7, 1951.

periments were necessary to the production of a single model and that this one type had been frozen for mass production; if so, the Russian bomb would be obsolescent compared to the American. If the Russians had decided in 1946 or 1947 to sacrifice progress to quantity, they had decided unwisely. Their bombs would be sufficiently destructive, if delivered in sufficient quantity, to put European and American industrial centers out of business; but the H-bomb would be immensely more destructive, and a much smaller percentage of those sent would actually need to be delivered. The Soviets could yet move on, however, to new weapons.

The Soviet strategists must also have considered seriously the almost total absence of efforts among Americans in 1951 to turn their government away from preparations for war. Some few organizations, such as the Committee for Peaceful Alternatives, still persisted, and the Quakers still insisted on the possibility of peace. But obviously the hearing given to such suggestions was inconsiderable. Although a resolution passed by the Congress and signed by the President offered friendliness for the Russian people and hope for peace, its hostility to the Russian government, as apart from the people, must have marked it as no more than an attempt to separate the two, a strategy which the Communists with their propaganda against capitalism had themselves relied on with greater success than the West could hope to achieve.

Even the atomic scientists had given up. Their *Bulletin* for the year went in heavily for discussions of civil defense and for technical consideration of the development of atomic energy, but it published no more pleas from the great scientists for conciliation or warnings of impending destruction. In the issue for January, 1951, there was a review of their five-year effort. Said the editor, finally:

> While the present emergency continues—and it may continue for many years—scientists—and others who think in terms of rational reorganization of the world—will have to be patient and humble. For the time being they will have to be content with contributing to the solution of day-to-day problems.[22]

The scientists' present resolve "to be patient and humble" was a resolve the whole West would have to make, however, if the free

22. "Five Years After" (editorial), *Bulletin of the Atomic Scientists*, January, 1951, p. 5.

world was to survive in a long struggle short of war. Miss Barbara
Ward reminded Americans that the containment of Russia was not
a new idea—that for European nations, and especially Britain, it
had been the center of policy for several hundred years.[23] Waiting,
furthermore, was a weapon the Russians had always employed. The
Russian view of the conflict had, she remarked, a perverted but, in
some way, sublime basis. The Politburo could well have convinced
itself that the conflict was already won if events could take their
course and war could be avoided and that the only danger to a
Soviet triumph was a last convulsive attack from the West which
might destroy the Russian center out of which flowed to all the lesser
centers the stream of communism. Containment, as a policy, deliberately undertook to meet this monolithic confidence with a
matching confidence in Western principles. Miss Ward thought the
cause good enough and the resources of resolution sufficient. She
was not in a position of responsibility; but she spoke with one of
the clearest and most widely heard voices of the younger generation.

There were signs, at least, that the excesses of a year of fright
and recklessness had passed into the stage of coalition and organization. The excesses were being identified, and the emotions and interests behind them were being submitted to discussion. The Mac-
Arthur episode had been useful in this respect. McCarthyism, as the
furthest reach of that reckless demagoguery which had been spreading so dangerously for years, was aligned, in the choosing of sides
precipitated by MacArthur, with all its natural allies. It was now
seen to be of one piece with the successive Un-American Activities
committees; it went back to Father Coughlin, to the Liberty League,
to Wirt and Dies, and came down through Hickenlooper, McCarran,
Wherry, and Knowland direct to MacArthur. Senator Taft had now
allowed himself to be identified with it. If, as was generally expected,
he should be the Republican candidate for President in 1952, it
would at last emerge into a national political issue. Americans would
then decide whether they wanted to risk a preventive war with communism or whether they could choose the path of resolution and
patience.

Americans were finding it hard to understand that Russians, after
their experiences since 1917, had a profound fear of invasion. The

23. *New York Times Magazine*, July 8, 1951, pp. 5 ff.

scars left on the Russian mind by the alliance of the Western Allies with the White Russians after World War I and the savage German invasion during World War II they generally ignored. There would doubtless have been sympathy for the sufferings of the Russian people and comprehension of their fears if there had been any available reminders of recent history. It was no part of the official intention, however, that the militant mood should be softened, lest the mobilization effort should be weakened; and the press, having constituted itself the defender of capitalism, was interested only in a jingoism which made no sense unless it issued in preventive war. Very few reminders of Soviet fears were available. The *émigré* Russians of various sorts were intent either on the possibility of overthrowing the Bolshevik regime or on those futile explorations of their wrongs which had characterized the exiles since 1917.[24]

One of the few attempts to explain what must be the Russian attitude toward Western hostility was made by Professor D. F. Fleming of Vanderbilt University, writing in the *Western Political Quarterly*.[25] This was a reminder that, of all the causes of war in the past—population pressures, dynastic ambition, religion, economic rivalry—the oldest and deepest cause of all was fear. It might be fear of jungle neighbors who were different, fear of men who practiced strange rites and held to outlandish customs, or fear of nations that were thought to be hostile. It is natural, said Professor Fleming, for a man or for a nation to dread the recurrence of any awful experience, living as it does in the memory and being so difficult to dispose of rationally. And what fear could be seated more fixedly in the mind than that of invasions still recallable by those still living? The people of the South, although none can now remember its terrors, still react violently to the historic memory of Sherman's march to the sea.

What would the feelings of Americans be if the United States had been ravaged, as Russia was, from the Atlantic to the Mississippi, with 15 millions killed, twice as many made homeless, 60 millions treated to every degrading and brutalizing experience that the fascist mind could invent? Only

24. For an account of these attitudes, at once sympathetic and critical, see Vera Sandomirsky, "The Coming Russian Revolution," *Common Cause*, June, 1951, pp. 565 ff.

25. December, 1950, pp. 528 ff. The title of Professor Fleming's article was "The Rule of Fear and Hindsight in World Politics."

then could we know how the Russians feel about their security from future attack through East Europe. It is easy for us in our continental island to say that of course the Russians know that Germany or the West is not going to invade them again. But every educated Russian knows that this has happened three times since 1914. . . . They would have to be superhuman indeed to put aside the memory of these long-drawn-out agonies of death and destruction. Being human, it is as inevitable as anything can be that they should resolutely determine to close the invasion gates in East Europe, through which all these horrors have come, and keep them closed.

Fear, of course, was not only a Russian trouble. France recalled the German invasions, three of them, each more terrible than the one before, and knew that she would not survive another; Britain recalled her bombings and her utter defenselessness after Dunkirk; even the Germans, who thought themselves a warrior people, must recall the wreck of their cities by British and American bombers and must add this recollection to a fear of Russian occupation. China, too, had been ravished by "foreigners"; and Japan had suffered not only the fire-bombing of Tokyo but the immolation of two of her cities in a bath of atomic fire. The world, indeed, was ridden by fear. The fear might be mostly historic and, in terms of the future, unreal, but it dictated policy nevertheless, even in America; for Americans were just as certain that the Communist states intended their destruction as the Russians were that the Americans intended theirs. There existed, as a result, a classical race for rearmament; "the two giant powers lie on opposite sides of the earth; neither has anything that the other needs, yet their mutual fears promise to lay the world in ruins."[26]

There were some signs, few and faint though they were, that an orderly arrangement of affairs might gradually be hammered out in spite of all the difficulties if the Eastern conflict could be liquidated and if no other overt incidents occurred. In President Truman's speech at the United Nations in October he had suggested that both conventional and atomic weapons be considered by a disarmament commission. This was a departure for the United States, but one which had been asked for nearly a year before by the Federation of American Scientists.[27] Heretofore, American policy had rested immovably on the Baruch proposals of three years be-

26. *Ibid.*, p. 535.
27. *Bulletin of the Atomic Scientists*, January, 1951, p. 23.

fore. And this had been in spite of many new developments, including the decision in 1950 to go forward with H-bomb construction. The scientists were momentarily hopeful at this belated and unacknowledged acceptance of their views; and they were even more encouraged when the Assembly of the United Nations, by a vote of forty-seven to five, with three abstentions, adopted an implementing resolution proposed by Australia, Canada, Ecuador, France, Netherlands, Turkey, the United Kingdom, and the United States.[28] But their hopes were considerably deflated by Russia's failure to recognize that there was any good faith behind the modification of the American position. The Soviets suggested instead that the existing Atomic Energy Commission prepare forthwith conventions for the "unconditional prohibition" of the atomic weapon and for the international control of atomic energy.[29] But Mr. Vishinsky's speech (of an hour and forty minutes) was a rehash of the old charges against the capitalist nations; even he did not take seriously the alternate proposal. It thus appeared that any ideas emerging from the reconstituted commission would be unacceptable to the Kremlin.

The apparent result of this gesture, then, was merely to strengthen the picture which was growing in so many minds of an elite in Russia for whom there are only friends or enemies and for whom the only friend is one under absolute control. In the view of the Politburo the whole of the West was enemy-held and had to be treated as such, because enemies do not merely attempt to maintain their strength; they aim "unceasingly at the annihilation of the party."[30] Nevertheless, Americans, after the year's dangers and tensions, seemed determined to relax after the meetings began at Kaesong. The Administration, seeing its whole policy of containment jeop-

---

28. The resolution read: "*The General Assembly Decides* to establish a committee of twelve, consisting of representatives of the members of the Security Council as of 1 January 1951, together with Canada, to consider and report to the next regular session of the General Assembly on ways and means whereby the work of the Atomic Energy Commission and the Commission for Conventional Armaments may be coordinated and on the advisability of their functions being merged and placed under a new and consolidated disarmament commission."

29. Doc. A/1676/1951.

30. See Nathan Leites, *The Code of the Politburo* (New York: McGraw-Hill Book Co., 1951).

ardized, was frantically opposing a letdown. But it was fruitless. The tensions had been too great to be sustained.[31]

To feed the hope of accommodation, also, there was late in July another indirect suggestion from the same Mr. Malik who had suggested the possibility of the cease-fire in Korea. The occasion was a visit to Moscow—Mr. Malik was now at home—of a group of British Quakers, who, like Quakers everywhere, refused to admit the preponderance of ill will among men. They had suggestions to make, after talking at home with Mr. Herbert Morrison, the Foreign Secretary; and Mr. Malik, for the Russian Foreign Office, appeared to accept them. The most startling of these suggestions proposed that the Russians repudiate Communist agitation in other lands. This at once called up memories, not too old, of the abandonment of Comintern activities during the last war. Mr. Malik rested on a statement Stalin had made as long ago as 1936 that Russia was not interested in fomenting revolutions elsewhere; such changes were a matter for the people themselves in other lands.[32]

If this statement did not comport very well with recent activities of the Cominform, or with recent pronouncements of Mr. Molotov, it did seem, in its devious diplomatic way, to be an offer which the West might exploit if it had the wit and resolution. It occurred to millions of anxious people that such a bargain was what they had been waiting for—an end to Russian aggression by infiltration and revolution in exchange for a release of the Western threat to Soviet integrity. What would come of it no one could say. But there it seemed to lie on the table between the opposing powers. The question was whether public opinion would permit it to be ignored.

31. Mr. Acheson's speech at Detroit on July 24 (reported in the *New York Times*, July 25, 1951) was still another plea for more arms to implement the policy of equated strength and another incitement to belligerence. President Truman's speech in the same city a few days later appeared to have been drafted by the same hand; its theme was similar (*ibid.*, July 29, 1951).

There was no hint that the current Soviet peace moves might be met with any counterproposals; and there was no attempt even to suggest what conditions might be considered necessary to a general settlement. There was only hostile discouragement for the Soviet tentatives, which were becoming by now impossible to ignore and hard to belittle.

32. The Associated Press dispatch of July 28 reported the matter fully, and it was published with considerable prominence in most newspapers, including the *New York Times* of that date. It said not only that the Soviets were not interested in "exporting revolution but that the Soviet Union was ready for negotiations of a business-like character with a view to agreement" on outstanding world issues.

The atomic year ended on a challenging note. On August 6, 1951, President Nikolai Shvernik of Soviet Russia answered President Truman's note transmitting the congressional resolution of friendship for the Russian people. It was conciliatory, even pacific. It conveyed a resolution of the Soviet Presidium. The Russian people, it said, cannot understand why the United States government continues to reject suggestions for the conclusion of peace among the five powers. The State Department and the press received the renewed suggestion coldly. It was an attempt, it was said, to bypass the United Nations. The efforts at Paris had shown how impossible it was, in present circumstances, to deal with the Russians.[33]

But the "peace offensive" was becoming formidable. It was something which could not be met by negatives and objections. Were Americans, behind the scenes, in consultation with their Allies, preparing for negotiation? No more could be said on the darkest of all anniversaries than that no sign of willingness to bargain was yet apparent.

33. *New York Times*, August 7, 1951.

CHAPTER VIII *1952*

THE year that stretched from Hiroshima Day in 1951 to Hiroshima Day in 1952 could be spoken of as the year of the great dilemma—except of course that there were, for the United States, not *one* but *two* dilemmas. (1) Should America adopt a military program costing another fifty-five billion dollars (plus other military costs of twenty billion dollars), thus unbalancing the budget by some fifteen billion dollars and advancing open-eyed into outright inflation, or should these expenditures be adjusted to expected revenue with the risk of continued weakness vis-à-vis Russia? (2) Should a confrontation of Russia in western Europe be prepared for, or should the thesis be accepted that Russia would not attack but would continue peripheral harassment by proxy? Both of these are the kind of irritating questions of great consequence which a democracy can neither settle nor leave to its statesmen. They hung in the air unsolved.

The first—the size of the security budget—was, of course, resolved by the late adoption of appropriation bills. The Congress accepted a certain risk; there was to be a "stretch-out." But no one was happy, and no one regarded the settlement as more than tentative, subject to change at any moment. The second question, what to prepare for in Europe, was only resolved to an extent. Certain estimates were agreed to and then revised downward. The great Lisbon conference of February might almost as well not have met for all the result it had. Yet there was taking shape a European army, and it was said to be reaching "deterrent" strength. What was certainly true was that confusion had grown greater and that sometimes there seemed to be a kind of refuge in indifference. It was an uneasy refuge, out of which each person peered with growing apprehension. Danger, a kind of impersonal, menacing, and unfocused danger, was understood to be growing more and more imminent. There was a lingering hope that it might not actually materialize out of the mists where diplomatics went on, but that there was no real reason to hope each was told by his inner consciousness. For, if there was any materialization, it was the vague but menacing shape of war.

War, however, had lost all visual reality for Americans. What it might be like, when and if it came, could not be conceived, as other wars had been, by any of the ordinary apparatus of understanding. It would not be a soldiers' war in the old sense. Soldiers seemed in prospect likely to be figures moving in a dream, the main characters of which would be civilian masses set wild by panic, rushing from their cities into an unready countryside, and separated from all the civilian mechanisms upon which they had grown so dependent. Left behind would be uncounted dead, stinking in the ruins. Torn from those to whom a personal tie existed, and reduced to struggling for the elements of survival, men would soon reach a state of savagery.

Mankind had grown away from any kind of readiness for such a situation. And there seemed no effective preparation to be made for it. Anything which could be thought of was a denial of civilization itself. It was no wonder that the small conceptions of those charged with civil defense met with complete and universal indifference. They simply seemed unsuited to any circumstances likely to arise.

There was renewed testing of weapons throughout the year at Yucca Flats in Nevada and rumors of new tests at Eniwetok. These tests received considerable publicity. Crowds watched them from afar, and they were covered by the press—a curious reversal of the policy maintained since Bikini in 1946. Was the publicity intended to indoctrinate the public, along with the armed forces, in what an atomic attack would be like? The idea might, of course, be to demonstrate that progress in adapting atomic energy to war was actually being made. The Administration could thus justify the huge expenditures, present and future. Confidence in the conduct of these operations might not be maintained if all of them went on behind an impenetrable curtain of secrecy. These demonstrations might also serve as a warning to Russia; the enemy might be reminded that we were still ahead in the rearmament race.

The fact that this race went on in a mounting crescendo was, however, the main underlying source of anxiety. Nothing had checked or promised to check it. The various meetings and exchanges during the year were futile. The Administration rejected various Russian tentatives, presumably because that "position of strength," about which Secretary Acheson had so often spoken, had not been reached. There was a growing suspicion that such a position was a purely imaginary one which could never be reached. If it meant a position from which force would offer a practicable alternative, it clearly could not be reached in any foreseeable future. That simple concept could not be what the Administration had in mind, as its other policies revealed. The military build-up was even being stretched out, and the hypothetical equality of conventional force, which had in 1951 been planned for in 1952 or 1953, was now put off until 1956 or 1957.

The Russians would not knuckle under to a Western threat which was not clearly overwhelming. If such comparative power was not going to be achieved, what, then, was this "position of strength?" Would it have been reached when western Europe was stabilized through rearmament and could again offer real resistance to the Communist fifth column? And when the Middle East and the Far East had ceased to seem vulnerable to Communist expansion? Perhaps. If Russia came to recognize that, short of war—which she could not win—there was no further possibility of movement outward from her present borders, that might be conceived as a setting in which negotiation could begin.

In these circumstances neither side would negotiate from a position of strength in the sense that it could invoke force. It would thus be very difficult for either to gain any advantage. Negotiations of this sort would be long, frustrating, and impossibly delicate; they would be made difficult (especially for the democratic West) by the practical impossibility of coming away with anything which could be represented as a victory; and they would be tormented by a continuing, costly, and exhausting armaments race which would furnish unremitting incidents and tensions. The prospect at best was not a pleasing one. The Western diplomats contemplated it with obvious reluctance and distaste. But it was getting harder and harder to postpone its undertaking.

At Panmunjom in Korea, indeed, a kind of prologue to negotiation was in progress. Watching its processes, Westerners began to have some realization of the alternative to war. The Communist negotiators were tough, unscrupulous, and conscious that they had an advantage. The representatives of the United Nations had to find a forbearance that previously they would not have believed they possessed; for their activities were shaping the pattern for many other similar trials yet to come. They could not break off altogether, however great the provocation, because to do that was to accept the certain failure of negotiation everywhere. If they could not work things out in Korea, the adjournment would be to a war which would involve the wholes of those masses whose unwilling surrogates they were.

They were not much helped by the society they so patiently represented. It happened that a presidential campaign was coming on. Such contests were subject to unscrupulous eruptions, and there were participants who were not above jeopardizing the national interest for their own benefit. It was certainly an unscrupulous oversimplification to say, as Senator Taft did, that Korea was Truman's war. The inference was that it ought not to have been begun and that alternatives still existed. This was the inference that millions made; and they applauded the suggestion which had enabled them to make it. But it was not true; and to say that it was constituted an abandonment of that leadership which statesmen ought to furnish. It was a kind of betrayal of those on the firing line.

The statesman's duty to be wiser than the people, and to play on their predilection for abandoning responsibility is a very difficult one; but a democracy which is a world power must have such leaders. It sadly lacked them in 1952. Not only Taft but MacArthur, Hoover, and numerous lesser Republicans appealed passionately to the popular revulsion from the hard ordeal of Korea. It was useless for President Truman, Secretary Acheson, and Mutual Security Director Averell Harriman to insist that Korea was a victory of sorts, that it had served to stop Communist expansion, that it had checked aggression. There had been no military victory; there would not be any. The truce talks were being carried on with an enemy which had not been defeated. This was a new kind of experience for Americans, and it was not a pleasant one. It was natural that they should wish to find someone to blame.

While the Korean incident lingered in this unsatisfactory state, preparations went on for other challenges to come. Not only were atomic-manufacturing facilities being expanded but the expansion of capacity to produce all kinds of basic materials was in full swing. There was a good deal of uneconomic forcing about this process; but there was even more in the expansion of the military plant, which was mostly undertaken on a cost-plus basis. Concurrently there was some restriction of civilian production, and there consequently appeared here and there pools of unemployment, the accompaniment of business decline. At the same time there were high taxes and inflation.

The stretch-out of military production was a kind of recognition that conditions had become intolerable. It was deliberately decided to change the end date for maximum military build-up. It relieved the stresses. More materials could be made available for civilian production, and the pools of unemployed could be absorbed. But it soon became apparent that *permission* to produce was not enough. High taxes and inflation had eaten into consumers' capacity to buy. The market for civilian goods was soft. There was news of reduced production in Detroit, Schenectady, New England—many industrial centers. And this raised again the specter of a readjustment when military expenditures should level off. There was question whether another great depression might not occur. This economic dislocation enlarged the disillusion about Korea and reinforced the fear that the United States had undertaken too much. A recurrence of this kind of isolationism was the phenomenon exploited by Senator Taft.

It was undoubtedly this confusion and disaffection of Americans in circumstances of strain and uncertainty which had forced the adoption of a policy calculated to maximize risks and so to create more strain and tension as time went on, at least until the crisis of comparative weakness had passed. The causes of the confusion were to be found in that flabbiness of the Administration which had earlier enabled the opposition to force the adoption of MacArthurism. The American people had not been convinced by a firm and lucid exposition that American policy in Korea or Europe was consistent and necessary. Now that the final steps had been taken at Lisbon to settle on the form and size of the European army (in February), and at Bonn to contract for German participation (in May), following the peace treaty with Japan (in September, 1951), they regarded what had been done with, at best, skeptical tolerance; and the Congress with obvious reluctance voted (in June) a seriously reduced appropriation for mutual security.[1]

None of these steps was undertaken and carried through with the assurance of purpose and unity. To the close observer, it might be clear enough that the rather ponderous maneuvers of the West were intended to attain that position of strength from which bargaining could be begun. But the interim period in which Russian tentatives were being rejected and in which the Korean negotiations were getting nowhere was a trying one. What was needed was a clear exposition of aims and of the steps necessary to attain them.

It was quite possible that the Administration's objectives might not have been very heartily approved even if they had been understood. The policy of containment was being attacked as beyond the ability of the economy to support and was only reluctantly being implemented with congressional appropriations—and this reluctance seemed to be justified by demonstrated military insufficiency in Korea. Probably there had been in many minds a very real, even if unjustified, reliance on miracle weapons or on American superiority of some other sort. It was humiliating to discover, as the first Korean battles developed, that the arms used by the enemy were so effective and that those possessed by Western armies were in many ways so inferior. If we had no novel weapons available, and if the enemy's were quite as good, how, it was asked, could we hope to sustain a policy of pressing in upon him around a global periphery? There was no very satisfactory answer. Those who understood the mechanics of procurement, the necessity of first establishing a firm production of basic materials, and the complicated nature of preparations for mass production might see the strength that was in the making. But the ordinary citizen knew only that at the moment the

1. "Mutual security" was now to be the name for Marshall Plan aid. But the Congress, besides cutting it severely, had forced an almost complete concentration on its strictly military phases. The President's conception of general technical and economic assistance fared worse and worse in successive Congresses.

enemy was too strong everywhere to be subdued by any power available to the West. He did not want to wait. One moment he wanted to attack the enemy "and get it over"; the next he wanted to withdraw from all engagements and "make America strong at home." He was not thinking or acting as the responsible and determined part owner of a vast machine whose effect in the world must be judiciously managed. And the kind of leadership he was getting was not calculated to condition him for patience and resolution. He was scared and defiant, and his reactions were the irresponsible ones to be expected in such circumstances.

American resolution might have been strengthened if the debate about coexistence had broken into the open. But it still remained muted and fugitive.[2] There was no official intimation of the hard demands the United States would make vis-à-vis the Soviet Union if and when negotiation ever began.[3] Inferences could be drawn from developing policies, but it was difficult to separate what was being done to attain a negotiating posture from what would be regarded as essential to the national interest. The interests and reactions of the Western Allies provided further complications. Misgivings over the Japanese peace settlement in Australia, New Zealand, and the Philippines were only less than those over the Bonn contracts in France, Belgium, and Holland.

These contracts were prepared after the Lisbon meeting of the North Atlantic Treaty Council in February, 1952.[4] The decision at Lisbon was to create a European defense community; and included within it were two new members, Greece and Turkey. Estab-

2. Some of the most thoughtful approaches to the problem were made from the relative detachment of Britain. Some of these reached print in the United States; for instance, a hard and realistic article of Edward Crankshaw (author of *Cracks in the Kremlin Wall*), which appeared in the *New York Times Magazine*. "Coexistence between antagonistic powers," said Mr. Crankshaw, "remains an axiom of life on this planet. . . . We coexist now," he said, "and the coexistence can only be ended by a war of annihilation."

3. Except the very general suggestions of Governor Stevenson of Illinois (on May 5 in San Francisco).

4. The North Atlantic Treaty was signed on April 3, 1949, by the foreign ministers of twelve nations. These foreign ministers were constituted the North Atlantic Council. Since then eight meetings had been held—Lisbon was the ninth —successively in Washington (three), London, New York, Brussels, Ottawa, and Rome. Despite formidable opposition, there had been set up a military command in western Europe under General Eisenhower.

lished as the military arm of this community was a European army with contingents from six Continental nations—France, Italy, Belgium, The Netherlands, Luxembourg, and West Germany. The eventual force envisaged was one of forty-three divisions—fourteen French, twelve West German, five Benelux. Added to these would be whatever force Great Britain and the United States should contribute. Both the West Germans and France had made reservations: the West Germans, that they should have an equal voice in the North Atlantic Treaty Organization and that the future of the Saar should be settled to their satisfaction; and the French, that there should be controls on German arms production and that they should have guaranties against further German aggression.

Before these arrangements had gone so far, however, the West's best bargaining issue had seemed to be the often-expressed demand of the Soviet Union that both Germany and Japan be neutralized. It was often pointed out—by Mr. Walter Lippmann, among others—that a neutralized Germany would be a welcome buffer between West and East; and that, rearmed, Germany might hold the balance of power. She could threaten the East or she could threaten to make an arrangement with Russia which would jeopardize the West. These possibilities the Administration ignored in favor of pressing on with the rearmament policy. With the signing of the contracts with Bonn, it remained only to learn whether ratification would follow. There was opposition in France of serious proportions; but there was also opposition in Germany. The Social Democrats, led by the fiery Kurt Schumacher—who was, however, soon to be removed by death—argued that West German participation in the European defense organization would make impossible the unification of the two Germanies. Herr Konrad Adenauer, the West German Chancellor, had, in fact, signed the contracts without the consent of the Bundesrat. He finally got that consent because he still commanded a nominal majority; but there were to be elections in September, 1953, and all the signs pointed to defeat for Adenauer's group.

The warning signs in France were almost equally ominous. Only American pressure, persistently and unremittingly exercised, kept the policy from being abandoned. Even in America there were many who did not think it wise. Obviously the Administration thought— or hoped—that, once the policy had begun to operate, it would be accepted. But the violence of the Russian reaction led those who had felt it wiser to neutralize Germany anyway to argue that the best bargaining issue the West possessed was being thrown away for the doubtful gain of a few German divisions in a European army.[5]

The Lisbon agreements were signed, however, and the process of setting up formal treaties and securing ratification began. The contractual papers for peace with Germany were signed on May 26 in Bonn, and the European Defense Community Agreement, admitting West Germany to the community, was signed on May 29 in Paris. The event was far-reaching, but there was no consensus that the outcome would be favorable. If the treaty shut off negotiation over Germany's future and convinced the Russians that negotiations were not intended by the Western powers, it would force them to seek alternatives; and all the alternatives were ominous. If, however, it was merely a step toward the position of strength from which it was conceived that negotiation might begin, and if that conception was reasonable, it would prove to have been justified.

The Russian concern about the German settlement had been made all too plain. On March 10, again on April 9, and finally on May 25, as the Big Three foreign ministers conferred with Adenauer in Bonn, Soviet proposals had been sent to the Western powers. These were that the Big Three meet immediately with Russia to frame a treaty which would unite Germany and would permit German rearmament but would also forbid the Germans to join the European Defense Community. These proposals had the kind of appeal to Germans which might be expected among a people disunited by force and set against each other by warring ideologies ruthlessly propagated. The one thing all Germans wanted was an end to interference and a return to nationhood. Moreover, the Social Democrats, who had felt themselves forced into an unnatural minority by the predominantly conservative-clerical make-up of South and West Germany, longed to be reunited with the largely Protestant and progressive East. Joined again to the eighteen million Germans in the Russian zone, they would have the political majority to which they felt entitled. Under Schumacher's leadership, they made the

5. Those divisions could not materialize for several years—not until well after another West German election. Even then, the entire European army would still be a long way from matching the Russian force, to say nothing of what the satellite armies of Hungary, Romania, and Czechoslovakia could add.

most of the unity issue, and it was not at all certain that even in the West they were not in a majority. Nevertheless, the Allies pressed their temporary advantage, and the contractual agreements were signed.

The immediate questions were two. Would the Russians now resort to force? Or would they continue to hold out the hope of unity and seek to prevent ratification of the contractual agreements? Perhaps—and this seemed most likely—they would use both methods. The first move was to renew pressure on Berlin. They interfered with Allied patrols and made the Iron Curtain across Germany more impenetrable by clearing and fortifying a three-mile zone. They also prodded the Communist shock troops which formed fifth columns in the European countries. It happened just then that General Matthew B. Ridgway was being substituted for General Eisenhower as Supreme Commander of SHAPE. On the occasion of the new commander's arrival in Paris, the French Communists staged riotous demonstrations which the police put down with savage ruthlessness. The riots were not confined to Paris. They were almost as serious elsewhere in the provinces. They were not even confined to France. Everywhere in Europe the hard-core Communists responded to Moscow's call and protested, rioted recklessly, and affirmed their solidarity with Moscow.

These riots had a prepared background. Two lines of propaganda had been made to sweep through the Communist world, from Peiping to East Berlin. One was the peace offensive, of which the Moscow trade conference of April was one incident; the other was the incredible charge, blown up and endlessly reiterated, that the United Nations forces in Korea had resorted to germ warfare. Westerners might be inclined to laugh off so preposterous a suggestion—not even Communists could be got really to believe such an invention—but this was to overlook the power of convinced hatred and the picture of aggressive intentions which had been so long building up in Asia. Even Western statesmen and generals were at last forced to deny what it revolted them to have even to recognize, and of course their denials were used against them.

The West, in the meantime, had not ignored the Russian tentatives over Germany. The Allies agreed to four-power talks leading to German unification, but under the condition that there must be assurance, by report of a United Nations commission, that the elections to follow would actually be free. Europeans generally felt, however, that this was an issue which ought to have been raised in actual meetings as elections were prepared for. They therefore interpreted it as another excuse for avoiding any negotiations at all, and the effect was unfavorable.

This reaction was much stronger than it might otherwise have been because of the long controversy over rearmament which had been going on throughout the year preceding the Lisbon meeting among the European Allies themselves. The Americans, the Europeans felt and said, were pressing too hard. More was being asked than could be attained without ruining the European economies just now regaining their stability with the assistance of Marshall Plan aid. This attitude was part of a growing anti-American feeling in Europe, which threatened to be more and more embarrassing. So far as it was focused, it seemed to center in a belief that Russian intentions were completely misunderstood in America and that, because they were misunderstood, the strategy for meeting them was irrelevant. The argument ran that Russia did not mean to attack western Europe but rather to subvert its governments, if it could, and to transform the nations one by one into Communist satellites. The way to meet this kind of danger was to go on with the work already begun with Marshall Plan aid to strengthen the economies; to remove the cause of discontent by raising wages, stopping inflation, and increasing productivity; and to work toward better common relations. The forced military build-up, which diverted effort from civilian productivity to the armament race, played directly into the Russians' hands.

This line of argument affected even official Europe, and efforts were intensified to secure American consent to even further postponements of the full armament program—a demand which was the more powerful because it was reflected in the thinking of many Americans as well. The general result was a change of policy which amounted to a softening. And the stretch-out was accepted not only for Britain and the rest of Europe but for America as well.

This softening did not please those who had rested their policy vis-à-vis Russia on attaining the equality they felt essential before bargaining could begin, and Mr. Charles E. Wilson's resignation as head of the mobilization effort in April had as its background continued criticism of the stretch-out. His last report was a defense of the policy. He felt and said that it had been more important to expand basic productivity than to produce "hardware" which could not be used. He admitted that the long series of cutbacks in military production represented a "calculated risk"; but he said also that the unattainable schedules of the military planners had been responsible for the allegations that the defense program had been lagging. The schedules now in effect, he said, were realistic and would be met. By the end of the year (1952), four billion dollars worth of military supplies would be turned out each month, an entirely satisfactory result. He felt that the decisions taken to slow down military production in favor of producing raw materials and enlarging basic plant capacity would give the nation a greater and more lasting strength; and that his assertion was true was generally admitted—if war did not come in the interval.

For at least two years more, then, the West would be inferior in actual military readiness; yet there was no slowdown in provocation along with the stretch-out. True, the provocation was evoking a more moderate reaction than ought to have been expected. There seemed to be some reason to believe that the Kremlin had modified its aggressive policy. During the year there was no repetition of the Korean incident. Even in September, 1951, so acute an observer as Mr. Edward Crankshaw gave it as his opinion that moderation had become a Russian policy. He recalled the fact that, although the Soviet Union had never disarmed after World War II, it had not undertaken a rearmament drive on the scale being undertaken in the West; he even suggested that the Kremlin may not have intended to engender the reaction which had followed Korea.[6] If he and others like him were right, there was a stretch-out in Russia; nevertheless, the State Department was foolhardy to go on devising provocations which might convince the Russians that they were really being threatened. Their deathly fear of German invasion was not a provocation to be lightly used.

In 1950 the United States had put forward, and the Soviet Union had rejected, a new scheme for disarmament. In turn the Soviet

6. *The Listener*, September 27, 1951, p. 491.

Union had made a proposal; and it of course had also been rejected. There was, however, some small progress on agreement as to further procedure. This consisted in the establishment of a United Nations Atomic Energy and Conventional Armaments Commission to be substituted for the two existing commissions, which were so hopelessly deadlocked as to have ceased all practical functioning. The new commission was to go searching for common ground and to report to the Security Council and the General Assembly. It would submit such treaties and conventions as it could devise to a later disarmament conference.

The proceedings that led to the establishment of the commission were marred by vituperative and undignified exchanges between the American and the Russian delegates; but they were graced by an unexpectedly calm and statesman-like speech from Anthony Eden. That Mr. Eden, who was now the British Foreign Minister, in succession to Mr. Herbert Morrison—the Tories having narrowly won over Labour in a fall election—could look at Russians without shuddering and resorting to invective was so welcome a change from American vituperation that the reception it received in the world's press constituted a rebuke to United States representatives. There was noticeable relief that a new and less excitable influence was being brought to bear in Western counsels.

There was no noticeable slackening in the degenerating relations between East and West. Throughout the year the Communists carried on a most illogically combined peace and hate campaign. The peace drive had been building up for a long time with the use of the familiar Communist clichés, endlessly reiterated in every organ of communication. The picture was that of a peaceable Russia working ceaselessly to establish stability in the world, to end the armaments race, and to relieve the tensions of ordinary folk. The drive came to a kind of climax in an international trade conference in Moscow in April. There had been long preparations for this. As long before as October a selected list of Western businessmen and economists—I was one of three at the University of Chicago—had received letters from Oscar Lange of Poland, once a professor at the University, suggesting that they join in such a meeting. The acceptance of Americans was so frigidly frowned on by the Department of State, however, that almost none of any standing went to the meeting. The conference was held, however, and was conducted with a surprising minimum of propaganda. It resulted in few trade arrangements, largely because of American objection, but it undoubtedly was useful to the whole Soviet purpose; for it emphasized the unnatural stoppage of East-West trade, which had once been so important to Europe, and underlined Soviet willingness to remove the existing barriers.

The Kremlin had the best, furthermore, of the exchanges between East and West Germany—the subject of repeated notes. Russia's proposal that a neutralized, unified, and rearmed Germany be achieved in new meetings seemed, on the face of things, to be a much more constructive approach to the most irritating outstanding issue than that offered by the West.

But the peaceableness of the East was sought to be fortified by an accompanying hate campaign so exaggerated and absurd that its effect was to neutralize the peace drive. For a long time the slogans of the Kremlin had included all possible variations on "warmongering," "imperialism," and "capitalist exploitation." But, when the Russians added an accusation of germ-and-gas warfare in Korea, they reached a level of unreality which tried the credulity of the most convinced Communist. They persisted, nevertheless, week in and week out. The charge was introduced into United Nations meetings and even into the Toronto meeting of the Red Cross, where its chilly reception was obvious. Its chief effect in the West was to infuriate Americans and again reduce the already low level of diplomatic interchange. Very possibly it contributed to that undoubtedly hostile background in which disarmament talks rapidly lost all reality.

The commission set up by the Assembly in January got down to business in April in New York. By the middle of the month newspaper headlines rather wearily announced "UN Disarmament Talks Make Little Progress." By the middle of June complete collapse was recorded obscurely on inside pages. During its first meetings the Russians sought to seize the initiative in a fashion by now familiar. They had to repeat the Kremlin formula, and they went through it with energy. This consisted of a repetition of capitalist sins, climaxed in this instance by charges that the United Nations generals in Korea had employed everything from spiders to contaminated pork in their Korean germ warfare. When this time-wasting period was over, a serious working paper submitted by the United States was taken under consideration simultaneously with the Russian submission.[7] Two committees were set up, one for each proposal. The working paper of the United States put forward principles to guide a progressive disclosure of present armaments as the first necessary step to atomic control and general disarmament. The Soviet proposal, however, required the immediate prohibition of atomic weapons and a percentage reduction of armed forces and armaments; census and inspection were to follow.

A percentage reduction would, of course, have fallen most heavily on those nations which had disarmed after the war, and the Russians could not have put it forward seriously. There was, however, some optimism at first, because presently the Soviet Union made certain oblique concessions. These appeared to grant the point that prohibition of atomic weapons should not take place until after controls had been set up and admitted also that a rigorous inspection system would be necessary. If these concessions had been made in 1946 or 1947, they might have enabled negotiation to continue at that time. They were less important now. For one thing, no one believed they would be adhered to. But most important was the firm belief of the United States delegates that the first step should be, not atomic prohibition, but a census of arms to be followed by a disarmament conference.[8]

The West, however, not to be put in the wrong by persistent Soviet pursuit of its proposals for percentage reduction, countered with the offer to agree to ceilings on armed forces and armaments. This suggestion Mr. Malik termed a "false and hypocritical" proposal, designed to allow the United States to increase its armed strength in relation to the Soviet Union. Such was exactly its purpose, in a way; but it had been coupled with a clear statement that it was to be only part of a whole disarmament plan extending to atomic and bacteriological weapons and including armies, navies, and air forces. Mr. Malik fell back on denunciation.

7. This working paper may be found in full in the *Bulletin of the Atomic Scientists*, June, 1952, p. 135.

8. Cf. David R. Inglis, "The New Working Paper and Atomic Policy," *Bulletin of the Atomic Scientists*, June, 1952, p. 132.

An examination of the technical situation by Mr. David F. Cavers, professor of law at Harvard University, did not yield much hope of compromise. No control plan, begun so late, could actually be air-tight. Consequently, the danger of secret operations would remain considerable, even with the best inspection. Neither side, further-more, really showed any disposition to compromise. Mr. Cavers' sug-gestion[9] that perhaps the best hope might be in the negotiation of a standstill agreement, backed by adequate inspection, was, like other such suggestions, ignored. The only possible hope for a rebeginning lay in an inventiveness and a fresh approach which might enable both sides to escape from preconception and get down to earnest study. Yet, as Mr. Cavers said, for four years no new ideas had come from American official sources, in spite of the certain knowledge that only some new approach could possibly break the deadlock. Meanwhile, A-bombs were being stockpiled, and work on the H-bomb was progressing.

It was very important that influential commentators like Mr. James Reston, of the *New York Times,* viewed the proceedings as a battle in the war of propaganda. The harm done by raising hopes certain to be disappointed was thus less than it might otherwise have been. But what was to be said of statesmen who opened themselves to such a cynical view of their intentions? If they had had anything in mind, this interpretation said, it was to persuade people that they had peaceable plans when in fact they had none; or at least none that had the slightest hope of being accepted. These leaders were roughly handled in the world's press; and they deserved to be. Instead of centering discussions at the Assembly on an impossible disarmament, they ought to have been centering attention on settle-ment of the matters which had led to rearmament. This kind of dis-cussion they had avoided from the first.

The Americans played an inglorious part throughout the year in rejecting approaches to negotiation. They were not able any longer to rely securely on the negotiation-from-strength formula. The un-

9. This suggestion was made in an article in the *Bulletin of the Atomic Sci-entists,* March, 1952. Mr. Cavers was not a newcomer to this discussion. He had followed events closely and commented on them brilliantly in other articles, notably in "Atomic Power versus World Security," *ibid.,* October, 1947; in "New Life for the UNAEC," *ibid.,* December, 1948; and in "An Interim Plan for International Control of Atomic Energy," *ibid.,* January, 1952.

easiness and the repeated approaches of the Russians showed plainly that the West had reached a position of potential strength which was, for purposes of negotiation, as good as strength-in-being. The truth was that there were no settled ideas concerning the purpose of negotiation. Doubtless there were those in the Administration who had studied the problem; but in a democracy it is quite as bad not to have backing for ideas as not to have any ideas at all. Negotiators for democratic governments are not given much leeway. They are held closely to agreed purposes and are not allowed to bargain. The American statesmen were now in a position of having approached as weighty a comparative strength as they were likely to have from which to negotiate but of not being able to proceed because they had neglected altogether the necessary preliminary of preparing national opinion for what must happen.

This impasse was frustrating, so much so that in June the French and British, supported by other NATO members, tried to force the United States into acceptance of Russian tentatives for European peace talks before the actual ratification battles concerning the Bonn contractual agreements should take place. Mr. Acheson stubbornly declined to be moved; but he would doubtless have to move before long. Europe was restive, and the Allies were being put in the wrong. There was active opposition to rearming Germany, particularly; and even in the United States, with any encouragement, a unified and neutralized Germany might have proved a more popular goal than a German army that would be a potential threat in Europe. It began to look as though the arming of Germany had become a hard and irreversible American position and not a bargaining gambit as Europeans had assumed.

If nothing else, the adding-up at Lisbon had revealed the true strength of Europe vis-à-vis Russia. And, taken at its best, it did not look favorable. Mr. Walter Lippmann remarked wonderingly that realists of General Eisenhower's experience could hardly regard the prospective force as a really defensive one. It must be regarded, he thought, more as a stabilizing element within Europe itself, calculated to suppress dissent and create unity, and therefore to build up European economic strength and engender a higher morale. No hint of such a recognition came, however, from an official source. But, if the European rearmament was intended instead to convince the

Cominform that no further disruption of European states was possible, where were the signs that this expensive and trying achievement would be brought to bear diplomatically?

The Europeans thought the time had arrived to try out the Russians in negotiation. But the Americans would not.

America's reluctant dragons were, it must be said, tormented by certain difficulties the Europeans could hardly appreciate. Americans felt uncertain still about military strength, not so much in Europe as at home. There was no agreement as to how much armament was needed or what kind—or even how it ought to be disposed.

There was also further controversy as to whether more basic industrial expansion ought to be undertaken, whether stand-by plants should be built, or whether an all-out effort ought to be made at once to set up a military machine. The stretch-out was by no means universally approved.

Taken at its face value, Mr. Charles E. Wilson's last report as Director of Defense Mobilization[10] recorded an amazing achievement. In the light of this report the current criticism might seem almost inexplicable unless it was fully realized that very little of the results in actual military strength had yet appeared. The criticism came mostly from those who wanted less basic expansion of productivity and more concentration on armaments.

The argument ran something like this: If Russia intended to make a military challenge at all, it made no sense for her to delay; her rearmament had begun from a high plateau of war strength and had already reached, or was rapidly reaching, a maximum, especially if considered in relative terms. Why should she grant time for the American effort to extend into future years if she was convinced that the reaching of the maximum would result in challenge and perhaps war? All the information published indicated that the Soviets now had an advantage in air and submarine strength and in conventional arms greater than would be possessed at any future time. They must, furthermore, have accumulated a stockpile of A-bombs large enough to cause vast damage. A plan for reaching maximum

10. It was given the suggestive title *Strength for the Long Run*. Its date was April 1, 1952, and it was issued by the Superintendent of Documents, Washington, D.C.

strength in the West in 1955, or even later, thus left the acknowledged enemy with a known superiority for all the intervening time.

There were only two possible answers to this line of argument. One was that Russia had no hostile intentions of a military sort; the other was that, if Russia had latent intentions of aggression, they would be held in check by American superiority in atomic potential. Neither answer led to public agreement. If there was no actual aggression to meet, what was the reason for so vast a rearmament? Could all the effort and sacrifice be justified for reaching a bargaining strength the use of which was completely undefined? Or were there aims, beyond those anyone had visualized, which would require an overwhelming power to attain? Was it to be American policy, for instance, to force Russian withdrawal from eastern Europe, to separate her from China, or to build a barrier between her and the Middle East?

On the other hand, the deterrent effect of Western atomic superiority had diminished. For a certain number of A-bombs—the quantity had not been agreed on—would constitute an absolute amount, no matter how many an enemy possessed. If one hundred constituted enough, and the Soviet Union had one hundred, the relative superiority of the West did not constitute an effective check.

Clearly American policy-makers were caught in a militaristic momentum from which escape was now impossible, with ends in view which were wholly undefined except in such generalities as derived from fear and revulsion, from lack of understanding and imagination, and from inability to conceive any alternatives. It was not the responsibility of the defense mobilizers—or of the Atomic Energy Commission, producer of the A-bombs—to consider such matters. If this group had any relevant thoughts, they were not exposed for public discussion. But whose business was such policy-making? And what sort of reasoning was employed? There was some suspicion that the important decisions were being made mostly in the Pentagon and on what were vaguely referred to as "military grounds." But in a democracy, sooner or later, the basic questions concerning intentions and the power needed to effect them would have to be argued out.

Meanwhile, however, it was incontestable that a vast transformation of the American economy was taking place. It could be seen in the charts accompanying Mr. Wilson's report; but its existence was amply enough substantiated by every running account of industry's operations. For instance, the chairman of the Council of Economic Advisers, testifying before a subcommittee of the Joint Committee on the Economic Report in March, 1952, used these figures concerning *private* investment:

In 1951, gross private domestic investment was at a rate of approximately 59 billion dollars; contrasted with about 52½ billion in 1950 and about 47½ billion in the previous peak year 1948. (All comparisons are in terms of 1951 prices.) Investment in producers' durable equipment, which is at the heart of our productive strength, was about 27½ billion dollars in 1951, contrasted with about 24½ billion dollars in 1950, and about 23 billion dollars in the previous peak year 1948.

These figures became even more impressive when translated into the growth of capacity in such industries as steel, aluminum, and electric power.

That the economy could thus enlarge itself, supply consumers with their highest-ever total of goods, and *besides* go on with rearmament was a phenomenon without precedent. A more rigorous policy would have sacrificed consumers' goods and basic expansion for conversion of existing plant to military production. There was some bracing for such a sacrifice and some limitation of automobile and electric-appliance production, for instance; but it did not cut deep and, indeed, was abandoned before most consumers were aware of it. So high was the volume of consumers' goods that credit controls were being eased by the spring of 1952, and there was a movement in the Congress, stifled only with some difficulty, to scrap the whole apparatus of control. It was not being used, anyway, it was said, so why keep it? And, in fact, the controls measure was passed in an almost useless form.

All this was evidence of a pattern of policy, not made explicit, but easy enough to visualize by inference from what was happening. If military production was not to be brought to its maximum until July, 1955—the current target date—a decision had been made somewhere and by someone that armament would not be needed until that time. The current controversy concerning this was caused by a complete ignorance concerning the elements of this decision. But it became evident that the policy-makers, whoever they were,

judged that a wider war than that going on was not imminent.[11]
What was to be aimed at was a continuing strength to be used as
weight for enforcing policy. And it was in such terms that the
whole effort had to be appraised, quite apart from the question
whether the decision taken had been a wise one.

If what was aimed at was an expansion of military might appropriate to later bargaining rather than an all-out war effort, the program
seemed not only a sufficient but a politic one for a democracy. A high
flow of consumers' goods guaranteed satisfactory public support. Expanding productivity would create strength for long-run objectives.
Delaying the freeze of design would enable factories to produce armaments of the most effective sorts. Mr. Wilson's explanatory chart
showed a pattern of military expenditure reaching a high point at the
end of 1952, continuing on a "plateau" through 1953 and 1954, and
attaining maximum in 1955. Beyond this gradual rearmament what
was wanted was a "mobilization base"—that is, the facilities needed
for a rapid expansion of military goods such as had not existed in

11. Mr. Thomas D. Cabot, one-time president of the United Fruit Company, was
persuaded to come to the Department of State as Director of International Security
Affairs late in 1950. He stayed ten months. When he left, he wrote an article for
the *Atlantic Monthly* (June, 1952, pp. 75 ff.) in which he described the decision-
making process in which he had taken part.

He found it immensely more complex, and therefore slower, than in business;
but he argued that slowness was infinitely less costly than mistakes. A whole series
of working papers, written and revised at various levels, and endless discussions
concerning them, were involved in every decision. And usually the decision was
that indicated by the resolution pointed to in the discussions.

What Mr. Cabot said about those taking part was very revealing. It indicated
the kind of people being drawn into the shaping of foreign affairs by the Truman
Administration and showed something, perhaps, of why it was that there was a
profound uneasiness among Americans.

The criticism Mr. Cabot heard came from the other side—from businessmen
and generally from his conservative associates in Boston. His defense was against
their criticism rather than that of liberals. This was why his remarks were so
revealing. I quote from two of his paragraphs intended as defense from conservative
critics:

"Perhaps it is fortunate that in recent years a considerable number of businessmen and business lawyers have been brought into the State Department at the
policy-making level. Of the dozen top men in the Department at Washington, over
half were previously highly successful as corporation executives or lawyers. . . .

"The fact that so many of those who determine foreign policy come from the
conservative class is a fair answer to the critics of the State Department who
charge it with mistakes based on leftist prejudices. One who knows the Department can recognize in the top echelon of command three who were high executives
of companies listed on the 'Big Board,' three who came from law firms usually
associated with Wall Street and two who were Wall Street bankers. . . ."

previous national emergencies. There were two reasons for establishing such a base. First, in future emergencies the dangers to national security would be immediate as they never had been in the past. From Pearl Harbor in 1941 to D-Day in 1944 represented an interval never again likely to be granted. Second, what planners called "lead-time" had been significantly lengthened. From drawing board to assembly line was now a matter of years, so complex had modern military equipment become; and there were few possibilities of shortening the stages. They must not be lengthened by delays to provide plant capacity or materials.

In spite of the presentation of a plateau pattern for rearmament —arrived at, as Mr. Wilson cagily said, "for a variety of reasons"— there would be a constant struggle going on between improvement and volume production. There never had been a period in which technological changes had come so rapidly. We were, in fact, in the later stages of a revolution; and in these stages an accumulation of accelerations takes place. Jet engines, electronic devices, nuclear-powered ships, planes, and vehicles, guided missiles—all these were just coming out of the scientific and technological concentrations of past years.[12] Completed models would be obsolete almost before they could be put to use. Choices for delay while new improvements were made, or for going ahead and risking obsolescence, had to be made continuously.

The problems involved in the establishment of the mobilization base were somewhat simpler. They required the stockpiling of materials and the expansion of plants to make them. Oil and other sources of power, steel, aluminum, chemicals, and other materials were notably increased. Steel would reach 120 million tons, and aluminum 1.5 million tons, in 1953. Chemicals would reach a level two and a half times that of 1939. Nitrogen would reach a 70 per cent expansion by 1954. By 1954 power production would be 57 per cent higher than it had been in 1950.

Suppose that, once this base had been established, the economy was called on for some fifty billion dollars a year for military expenditure to maintain the strength then in being. How would the great capacity beyond this, and beyond consumers' needs, be em-

12. President Truman launched the first nuclear-powered submarine in June, 1952. It would have its trial run early in 1955.

ployed? Even at first and casual consideration the imagination was stimulated by the possibilities. Here was the potential necessary to great projects—a rebuilding of cities, road systems, railroads, getting final control over river systems, conquering soil erosion from water and wind. Yet what was feared instead was overproduction and depression.

If there had existed in the United States a collective economy, the curious paradox of overproduction need not have been anticipated. What existed, instead, was a kind of modified capitalism. The modifications were important; but whether they were sufficient to achieve stabilization (full production) in "normal" times was a real question. That was why "normality," or anything approaching it, was dreaded. To understand what it might be like, it was only necessary to recall the conditions before war preparations had begun back in 1938–39. Even with such New Deal stabilizers as the social security system in operation, there had been much unused productive capacity and serious unemployment.

People wanted goods and services; the ability to provide them existed; how, then, enable people to satisfy their wants? If people came anywhere near getting what they wanted, the productive system would be straining with effort instead of half-paralyzed. The root of the problem, according to many economists, lay in "underconsumption" or "oversaving," both individual and corporate. If earnings were put aside for the future, instead of spent—or even if they were distributed by corporations to shareholders who saved them—the demand for goods declined, unemployment resulted, and the downward spiral was well started. Savings might be necessary for capital; but all savings did not go into capital; or perhaps they created too much capital, resulting in unused plant capacity. Various measures had been taken to control this cycle, some effective, some not. But the economy had not seriously tackled the problem of continuous maintenance of high productivity and of full employment.

The difficulty was that those in strategic positions in the capitalist economy resisted the necessary measures—any measures. They wanted to be free to exploit instability. At the same time they tightened and expanded their own organizations and created more and more areas of rigidity. This activity finally presented the kind of problem most difficult to solve in a democracy—one in which special interests would have to submit to the public interest. Freedoms would have to be limited, privileges reduced, and a working whole created out of otherwise warring parts.

There was a kind of alternative, one that had been relied upon now for twenty years: inflation—the creation of purchasing power by the government through expenditures beyond its collections from taxpayers. The resulting cheapening of the currency diminished purchasing power among all those with fixed or semifixed incomes; but it also enlarged the market for the kind of goods bought with government funds. These might be public works; they might be purchases by the recipients of social security payments; they might be loans to other nations; or they might be armaments and military pay. By far the largest out-payments since 1940 had been these last. Military expenditures had kept the economy going for more than a decade, and, so long as it went and only those with fixed incomes were seriously injured, no basic measures for stabilization were even considered.

The kind of equalization needed might have come about through the adoption and implementation of the parity principle of NRA and AAA in early New Deal days. Suitably modified and intelligently administered, and supplemented with the minimums of social security and pension payments, there might have been by now a situation in which everyone could buy from everyone else, each having work and income and therefore the ability to satisfy his needs. That "concert of interests" about which President Roosevelt had often spoken, but had not been able to establish, might have become a saving institution for capitalism.

It had not been established. The economy had become dependent on inflation and a military market. The end or even a diminution of military spending and of its accompanying inflation frightened everyone who contemplated it. Every time a relatively peaceable interlude occurred, the economy trembled. It was no wonder that the Russians had reasoned, in the language of their propaganda, that the capitalist system was inevitably made up of "imperialists" and "warmongers." Exploitation, it seemed to them, was of capitalism's essence. Without "warmongering" it would break down.

But the years, even if they had not seen the establishment of stabilizing institutions—other than wartime controls—had produced a good deal of thought and even of public education. The capitalist economy possessed the knowledge, even if not the organized deter-mination, necessary to a resolution of the paradox which many of them still refused to contemplate. It was time, however, to begin the construction of the necessary implements. There was discussion; but in the Congress, where the carpentry would have to be done, there was a cold aversion even to suggestions for curing the disease of maladjustment. This aversion was perhaps more marked in the Congress than elsewhere and might give way rapidly enough when the controlling special interests had become convinced that only by sinking the interests of each—to the irreducibly necessary extent—in the interest of all could the interests of each be protected. Never-theless, there was a very marked uneasiness everywhere outside the United States over the reluctance of Americans to recognize the na-ture of their economy and the imperatives for its full functioning.

Communist fears of aggression were based on the conviction that the capitalist economy would collapse if militarism and imperial-ism declined or disappeared. Even America's European allies felt that the American economy had come to rely on military expendi-tures and that these would lead to aggressiveness which could end only in war. The Administration's diplomatic behavior lent only too much support to such a view. Disarmament negotiations got no-where. The United States pressed her determination to rearm Ger-many against all opposition. She avoided meetings to relieve the growing tension. Could it be that policy-makers feared collapse if peace should even appear possible? Many Europeans so believed.

Europeans are never knowledgeable about American politics any more than Americans are about European politics. And politics of a peculiarly pervasive sort dominated the presidential election year of 1952. Since 1948 President Truman had faced a Congress almost as hostile as the Eightieth, against which he had so effectively cam-paigned on his "whistle-stop" tours. Almost none of his "Fair Deal" program had been got into legislation. If he should run again in 1952, and should win, he would continue to be ineffective, not only because his party was riddled from infiltration by privilege-seekers and was deeply divided on several large issues, but because its major-ity element—secure *popular majority* though it was and undoubtedly responsible for successive electoral victories—could not gather a congressional majority. Its minority element in the Congress could always rely on the support of the Republicans, and the two groups together formed a nonparty coalition that could not be overcome. The four years since 1948 had thus provided an exhibition of obstruction, emasculation by amendment, and legislative sabotage which must have seemed to a closely watching world the stigmata of a nation so hopelessly divided as to be incapacitated for action.

The attack of the legislative upon the executive branch of the government had continued. The technique of congressional investigation, with obvious intent to embarrass the Administration, had been developed by Senator McCarran even further than it had been by his Republican predecessors. The Senate, for years restless about the publicity so cheaply garnered by the House Un-American Activities Committee, had established one of its own—one that not only had done violence to the rights of the individuals attacked but had tended, with complete irresponsibility, to break down the effective conduct of foreign policy. For the committee had operated on the thesis of the China lobby[13] that the Administration had been responsible for the winning of China by the Communists, and the target of its attacks had been the Department of State. In fact, the China lobby, which had as one of its objectives American support for a Nationalist reconquest of China, had become a weapon in the Republican effort, abetted by like-minded Democrats, to discredit the Truman Administration.

Foreign policy was not the President's only vulnerable spot. Congressional investigations had produced something like scandal in high places. During the previous year White House influence in securing loans for favored individuals from the Reconstruction Finance Corporation had been uncovered; this year serious corruption had been found in the Bureau of Internal Revenue. An unpopular foreign policy, undeniable corruption to take responsibility for, a Congress so out of hand that price controls were all but abandoned, a rising cost of living, unprecedented taxation—all these made election prospects seem unfavorable. Then, too, the President was now sixty-seven years old. He concluded that he had had

13. Thoroughly exposed at last in a blistering series of articles published during the spring in *The Reporter.*

enough; and although he conceded nothing, and kept up an aggressive party front, he resolved to announce that he would not again be a candidate.

There was at once a furor over the succession. The Democrats had a nice problem. True, there were by now more acknowledged Democrats than Republicans; but there were millions of independent votes, and these would be determining. Thus the candidate had to be one who could appeal to progressives, yet be untainted by nearness to the White House, and dissociated from the quarrels engendered by the Truman peculiarities. The Democrats were finally to pick Adlai Stevenson, popular governor of Illinois, an experienced administrator, and an internationalist with a following in the heart of the Middle West.

The Republicans had greater difficulty in finding a candidate. For two years a battle to the death had been shaping up between two individuals who represented different approaches to conservatism: Senator Robert A. Taft and General Dwight D. Eisenhower. Taft was an isolationist, the darling of the *Chicago Tribune.* He stood for everything which had become traditionally Republican: freedom for business but regulation for labor; a minimum of social services; isolation from foreign entanglements but yet active antagonism for China which seemed to contradict it. He had the willing support of the professionals of the party. But he had one handicap. All the indications from the polls of public opinion were that he could not win. In fact, those indications were sadly plain that no "real Republican" could win against a good Democrat. The party stalwarts fought hard; but the polls prevailed. General Eisenhower was nominated. The regular Republican organization was embittered, and there was left a party split which a Democratic candidate might well enlarge.

One thing about the coming campaign was fortunate: The candidates were not likely to expose the nation as deeply divided and vulnerable while the election impended. Both were aware of such dangers; both agreed that allies were necessary and would have to be helped. If Taft had been nominated, one of the rare campaigns fought on issues of foreign policy might have resulted at the worst possible moment. On the other hand, if Mr. Stevenson were to win the election, his having defeated General Eisenhower and not Taft might be disastrous; extremist right-wing Republicans would then be able to point to still another defeat for their own internationalists and would call for a renewed program of obstruction and isolation such as Taft had been shaping for two years past. Taft himself would still be in the Senate, the most powerful of the Republicans, and surely an embittered man. The result might well be a tussle between the President and a group representing more than one-third of the Senate—enough to defeat a treaty.

By Hiroshima Day matters were not very well shaped. Only the preliminary shots had been fired in the developing campaign. Mr. Stevenson was basing himself on his own state capital in Springfield and thus pointedly dissociating himself from recent White House proceedings; and he had chosen a nonprofessional as chairman of the Democratic National Committee. The retiring President was still trying to see to it that the issues should be as he conceived them, thus committing Mr. Stevenson to literal succession; but he was having no success. It was an interesting unacknowledged conflict. As for General Eisenhower, he was fumbling and quite undecided how to treat the Jenners, the Kems, the Capeharts, and the McCarthys in his entourage. If he espoused the Taft Republicans, he would become their prisoner. If he did not, where would he find the organization he needed for his campaign? It was a dilemma.

The American democracy of 1952 was making an awkward accommodation to the position of power so effectively but carelessly achieved in two world wars—it might be said the *usual* awkward accommodation, for decisions on complex courses of action in strange new circumstances cannot be made quickly in a democracy. There were those who questioned whether the democratic system could operate successfully at all in such conditions—whether some disaster might not result from lateness, lethargy, or irrelevance.

The American people had not yet made decisions about the development and military use of atomic energy, or, indeed, about their foreign policy. In consequence the Marshall Plan, running on to the establishment of NATO and the European army guaranteed by American support, the Korean adventure, the Japanese peace, and the setting-up of a separate West Germany were, all of them, commitments of doubtful validity because they had not been fully discussed and agreed to. It was inevitable that all of these should therefore be reviewed with unseemly acrimony as the quadrennial debates of the presidential year came on. Then it could be seen how deeply divided the democracy was and how little unity had actually been achieved, even though the two candidates did not greatly differ as to principle and even though each refused to exploit the division.

Beneath the surface of politics the American people in 1952 were having a difficult debate with themselves. It went on mostly within the mind of each individual, where the loyalties and traditions lay, and where the technological complexities of life were reduced to some kind of meaning. To project into the atomic age the values and morals hitherto accepted as guides to conduct was not proving much easier than in the preceding years. There were, of course, familiar principles. However much they might be ignored, they were accepted as right. They consisted in doing good to others, in being just and tolerant, in using strength with restraint and for the common good. This kind of morality President Wilson, for instance, had taken and shaped to national objectives that had been generally accepted. It had served to justify two world wars and had been the assigned reason for the humanitarian cast of domestic policy through the past several decades.

Within the nation, however, as within its individuals, there existed a whole series of other impulses, continually at war with the humanitarian ones. These counseled hardness, intolerance, and the sharp and persistent pursuit of national objectives; they characterized sympathy and tolerance as soft and unrealistic and regarded a narrow xenophobia as necessary to survival. This kind of policy for the individual was the familiar free competition of economic theory; for the nation it was an exclusive concern with selfish aims. And it was said in defense of it that, if each individual nation pursued exclusively and persistently its own interest, the good of the whole world would result. There was a great deal of moving back and forth among these two sets of moralities and loyalties, and it was in this lack of consistency that the Allies saw the worst fault of the Americans, both as individuals and as a nation.

There were those who believed that single-minded pursuit of national advantage was the only practicable policy. Professor Hans J. Morgenthau in his book *In Defense of the Public Interest* attacked the American tendency to justify foreign policy by moral principles, especially since the morality often seemed a cloak for self-interest. Two world wars had been justified as crusades for democracy and against aggression, when the motivation was the same as had actuated Britain for four hundred years—the redressing of the balance of power in Europe so that no nation or group of nations should constitute a threat. If the United States interfered in South America, it was to re-establish law and order, not to protect American investments. When resistance was organized in Korea, it was against "armed aggression," not to contain the power then threatening American interests in the Pacific. Professor Morgenthau made a passionate statement of the case for expediency, for the sloughing-off of all sentiment, morality, utopian longings, or legalistic encumbrances. But his argument was based on the premise that the formation of such a policy ought not to be dictated by public opinion. Diplomacy ought to be a free-functioning arm of government to be used as intelligence requires. Catering to a public desire for an easy conscience leads, he said, to deceit and demagoguery and perhaps to disaster.

Nevertheless, as Professor Dexter Perkins pointed out,[14] in a very real and permanent sense America's foreign policy does arise out of American opinion; it is not something formulated for the people, imposed on them, or even interpreted for them. It is something the democracy creates in its own slow, awkward, hesitant, and unsatisfactory way by a process of rejecting alternatives—a process which may annoy all others concerned but which must be adhered to as long as the democracy goes on. This process is of course subject to leadership and education. There is reason to think, however, that it cannot be forced very much; that, when forcing is tried, there are very likely to be embarrassing repudiations and reversals. Discussion and debate, prolonged and elaborated, is its very stuff; and, when the policy is arrived at, it commands unity and engenders an almost resistless energy for effectuation.

This process is not foolproof. It has led to disaster in the past, and may in the future. The great depression of the thirties was the

14. His lectures at Uppsala University were published at about the same time as Professor Morgenthau's. They were titled *An Approach to American Foreign Policy*.

result of an unresolved discussion; Pearl Harbor had happened to a nation which ought to have prevented it. Democracy is no guaranty of success. Indeed, a totally wrong answer may in the end emerge. One hundred million or two hundred million people may be wrong, just as one or two may be.

It can be argued, nevertheless, that, even with all its weaknesses, the democratic process is better than any alternative. It may be slow and far from sure; but when its answer arrives, if it does arrive, it represents the conviction of a people who are then determined in implementation, who do not have to be driven or even persuaded. It may be wrong and may bring disaster; but dictators and presidiums can be wrong too. Who could have been more mistaken than Hitler? And, if disaster is to come from a mistake, it is perhaps better to have the responsibility widely shared.

It is not, furthermore, a simple matter to define the national interest. It may be that for nations, as for men, honesty is the best policy in spite of Machiavelli—or Professor Morgenthau—and that the good of all is actually the good of each. Perhaps a recognition that these "moralistic" guides to conduct are the very ones most influential in the shaping of genuinely democratic decision is the key to understanding American policy. Perhaps no other kind of conduct on the part of democracy's representatives is likely, in our time, to achieve public ratification. Indeed, statesmen may be measured by their grasp of these fundamentals of Americanism and democracy and by their skill in shaping them to effective action.

Leadership is essential to the formation of durable public policy. Part of a democratic leader's usefulness is in his knowing what he may not do, but the other, and larger, part is in knowing what he must do, how to prepare for doing it, and how to choose the time. He must, furthermore, have a special rapport with the public that will enable him to create widespread support for his program. President Roosevelt provides the most striking recent example of skill in these arts.

Effective leadership of this sort, however, depends not only on the skill of the leader but on his acceptance, conscious or unconscious, of a whole range of social attitudes. What is to be done must seem to the majority of the people to be right; and they will not judge a nation's conduct in terms very different from the terms by which they would judge an individual's. Thus the counsel of those who advocate a kind of foreign policy for democracies of the same kind as that used by Castlereagh and Canning, or by Hitler and Mussolini, or by the contemporary Soviet Politburo, is irrelevant; such a policy is not available to Western statesmen. What they can do is to formulate a line of conduct which will be supported because it seems "right"; and they must hope that the strength of democracy will be sufficient to effectuate it.

An indispensable preliminary to important negotiation, then, is the precipitation of public debate about the issues to be negotiated. Such a debate was at last going on in 1952 as Hiroshima Day approached. The question was not, it appeared, whether balance-of-power policies should be followed; they could never be followed successfully by a democracy. The question was: What was required of us and of our statesmen by the kind of people we were and the kind of power we possessed? In this debate, either we, as a people, were not getting the leadership necessary to progress toward a settlement, or we were so extraordinarily confused by the application of our principles to the novel situation in which we found ourselves that decision had not yet begun to materialize.

As to American foreign policy, the Department of State made available during the year a clear and concise exposition of how it conceived that policy.[15] There were, without question, differences of opinion about our diplomatic conduct. The liberal internationalist would condemn it as being too inflexible yet not really faithful to democratic morals, and, at the moment, would point to the neglect of Latin America, to alliances with both Franco and Tito, and to unwillingness to bring on negotiations with Russia. The determined isolationist would say that we were helping others before ourselves, actually neglecting the national interest to build up Europe; and he would point to continued Marshall aid, to the Point Four program, and to overgenerous support for the "do-gooding" of the United Nations.[16]

15. *Our Foreign Policy, 1952* (Department of State Publication 4466 [Washington, D.C.: Division of Publications, Office of Public Affairs, March, 1952]).

16. That this opinion was not negligible there was plenty of evidence. Some of it came from the speeches of local politicians, particularly in the Middle West, which became more violently isolationist—and at the same time chauvinist—as the political campaign warmed up; and MacArthur and Hoover were featured keynote

The professionals in the Department of State, when they actually published their version of American foreign policy, were—they must have been—well enough aware of these greatly contrasting views, and well enough aware, also, of the unresolved conflict in American minds which was projecting itself into their special field of social relations. Indeed, a foreword, signed by President Truman, indicated one kind of solution to the moral dilemma. "The purpose," he said, "of American foreign policy is to defend the independence and the integrity of the Republic. To do this we must build peace in the world: not peace at any price, but a peace in which the peoples of all countries—big and little alike—can live free from the fear of aggression."

Several implied principles and attributions were packed into these seemingly simple sentences. They were intended, of course, to appeal to everyone. Our own interest comes first; but it can only be had if a peace is insured in which not only we but others will be free from aggression. Is nothing, then, ever to change? Only, obviously, by peaceful arrangement. What the President said was that independence was precious and that it could be had only if its recognition was universal and if its institutions were "built." Peace and independence were identified. The interest of all was the interest of everyone. How short a step to the necessity for activity in pursuit of this interest! "We are actively at work, every day with our neighbors and friends . . . not only to overcome any threats to world peace but also to strengthen freedom and justice so that, in future, the dangers to peace will be less."

Going on to the body of the exposition, in an extraordinary seventy-eight pages of compact explanation, there was the text for volumes of philosophical comment. Ignoring all the background, and stating the most controversial propositions as though they were axioms, the Department's operating code was simply stated. At least it *seemed* to be exposed, unless the apparent naïveté was intended

---

speakers at the National Republican Convention. But there was deeper and more sinister evidence from a careful survey made by Benjamin Fine of the *New York Times* (June 29, 1952) that responsible school directors over most of the country were under serious pressure from powerful patriotic organizations to abandon study classes and groups whose purpose was better understanding of the United Nations. There was indeed a good deal of right-wing talk about abandoning the United Nations, of which this was only one expression. What had become of historic American good will for others?

to hide rather than reveal what the diplomats were really up to. That was said by some cynics. But it seems unnecessary to believe that it was so. It is much more likely that the summary was actually a statement of the beliefs and propositions which were the basis of action. What were they?

The beliefs were as follows—the interpretation of what we are like and what we approve:

We are an independent nation, and we want to keep our independence.

We attach the highest importance to individual freedom, and we mean to keep our freedom.

We are a peaceful people, and we want to see the time when war and the threat of war are abandoned as instruments of policy by all nations.

We are a friendly people. We have no traditional "enemies." We want to settle our differences with other peoples as good neighbors.

We believe in justice. A peace based on justice is the only peace which can endure.

It could be said—and was—that these statements gave the American people credit for virtues they did not possess or, at least, did not hold so firmly as seemed to be implied; also that they omitted some obvious vices and faults, such, for instance, as impatience, an occasional and spasmodic stretching of the national muscles, and a tendency to be much better neighbors in times of stress when neighbors are needed than in times of calm when they are not. But I think it must be admitted that the picture was the one most Americans hold of themselves; even the slightly inflated assertions that we possess (although there can be no question that we do value) individual freedom, that we are always peaceable and friendly, and that we are invariably devoted to that justice which is the foundation of enduring peace. There is no hint that we are human and therefore fallible and sometimes even downright sinful. And it would perhaps have been better to have said so and merely to have claimed that we aspire to the mentioned virtues and know them to be right. And that, therefore, they are the permanent foundations of our policy.

When the statement went on from these generalities to the specific problem of 1952, it was said that there was one overmastering objective: that was opposition to the expansion of communism. The contrast at the center of the present conflict was stated clearly: "The foreign policies of the United States are designed to promote world conditions that will advance the freedom and security of all free

336

nations. The rulers of the Soviet Union want a different kind of world, one in which they can bring all nations under their control." It might be said that there was some confusion here—Professor Morgenthau would say so—in identifying communism with Russian imperial expansion. But most Americans obviously did not agree. It was quite easy to support the notion that the old Russian ambitions seemed to be the same as the ones controlling the modern Politburo. There was the interest in Asia, the determination to dominate the eastern Mediterranean, and the ruthless holding in fief of the border nations to the west. And it was quite true that modern Communist statesmen had these objectives in common with Peter the Great, Alexander, and all previous Russian statesmen, noble or otherwise. But that the Communists did not go further, because of their fanatic, exclusive, and absolutist beliefs, seemed to me to deny the obvious.

There was a new pope in Moscow with pretension to temporal as well as spiritual power. He was a collective pope; but he stated categorically what could and could not be said, written, and even believed. He insisted on a unification of physical and moral forces, not as they may be worked out through discussion, experiment, and majority control, but through appeal to absolutes in the book of Marx as interpreted by authority. And he believed not in persuasion, individual conviction, and general consent but in force, in violence, and in individual subjection to the doctrine enunciated by authority.

The Politburo happened to be not only the interpreter of this doctrinal absolutism and the controller of the violence which enforced its will but also the master of the Soviet Union which had suddenly and unexpectedly become one of the two most powerful nation-states. As a matter of fact, all that stood in the way of instant extension of Politburo control to the whole planet in 1952 was the United States. But the American seat of power was far removed and for the moment invulnerable. Fifth columns were proving to be ineffective. And there existed that new and monstrous threat, the Bomb, whose unleashing might destroy the Communist center of power as well as the capitalist. It might be that Russia could not have conquered the world if atomic weapons had not existed; but she certainly could not conquer it now that they did exist.

Clearly it was quite justifiable for President Truman's Department of State to say, in 1952, that communism rather than Russian imperialism was most to be distrusted. For the conflict was not one to control the balance of political power, alone, but was one also to possess men's minds and souls. And the Communists understood— and doubtless hoped that their opponents did not—that, once men's minds and souls were occupied, the material strongholds would fall without resort to war. They would probably not draw back from war as an instrument if it appeared to be certain of success; but they would not risk a doubtful one. They would merely intensify their other means of attack, encouraged to do so by their theory of inherent capitalist rot. Perhaps they knew, and perhaps they did not know, that capitalism was not correctly described in their books, that it had possibilities of modification and was actually changing, so that the decay might be checked and might even turn out to be a fruitful upward spiral. Whether or not that was known to Russia, the Department of State was again correct in saying that domestic health was our best armament. So long as Americans and their allies could feel that they had a measure of welfare and of freedom, they would not risk trading a hypothetical welfare for an admitted sacrifice of freedom.

How would the program to combat communism be specifically outlined? There would be the accumulation of sufficient strength to resist any further raids outward from the borders of the Communist heartland; there would be a continuing and enlarging effort to secure the neutral world by friendship and assistance; there would be recognition of the independence and equal status of others, and of the growing need for interdependent relations, by strengthening and supporting the United Nations; and there would be a continuation of work for disarmamant and particularly for the joint and secured use of atomic energy.

Why was this not a good foreign policy? Why was it increasingly rather than decreasingly said that as a course or direction it was weak, mistaken, confused, indecisive, and even cowardly? Perhaps it was because it was not really implemented and could not be implemented until there was general agreement that this was what ought to be done. Such an interpretation seemed possible. Or perhaps it was that the struggle still going on in American minds, dismayed by the new responsibilities of power and still overwhelmed by the uncertainties brought into the world by the Bomb, was far from being resolved. Which would come uppermost, a calm and resolute facing of the long, demanding task required for the working-out of the democratic program, or a convulsive resort to violence in the effort to relieve tension and achieve release from fear? What was not often enough understood by those who ought to have been the helpful leaders of a people trying to find their better selves was that this struggle was actually and relentlessly going on and had by no means as yet approached its end. The "man in the street" was still awfully apt to say, "Let's use the Bomb and get it over with," rather than to ask, "How can we resolve our differences and come to a workable arrangement?"

For a workable arrangement was possible, even with such an unrepentant absolutism as the Politburo. It might be temporary. We might always know that to Soviet leaders it was merely a convenience to be abrogated at any moment. But we could remember also that what was to their interest they would be likely to do. And this was to their interest. They neither wanted to be destroyed nor to go on living in actual danger. So long as they could proceed with their domestic program and feel reasonably secure, they would undoubtedly consent to physical disarmament in the belief that our defenses would some day crumble from within. It was a question of our negotiators having behind them a people who wanted negotiation, and who would allow them the necessary tolerance, which was holding up all approach to something more like peace in 1952. The real trouble was in the Western mind more than anywhere else.

What could be said of this mind? That it was neither empty nor full; that it had some prejudices and rigidities, some adhesions to principle; but that it had also a kind of experimental temper? Any kind of characterization tended, in this way, to become vague and uncertain. Even the oldest and shrewdest observers were cautious about generalizations. What, then, did it mean when Professor Perkins, for instance, said of American foreign policy that it was the product of this mind? Or when Professor Frank Tannenbaum was certain that it had been shaped in accordance with certain principles he could enumerate?[17]

17. "The American Tradition in Foreign Relations," *Foreign Affairs*, XXIX (October, 1951), 31–51.

The difficulties with this kind of attempt at characterization are obvious. Principles are not a biological inheritance; they are socially transmitted. They are shaped by educators and given meaning by specific leadership. A slipshod education or an irresponsible leadership may attenuate them or may pervert their operation. What we obviously have here is a social construct issuing not out of any original differences between Americans and others but out of a consciously built and maintained traditional way of doing. If Americans had a preference for the independence of peoples, for freedom of thought and expression, for neighborliness, and so on, it was not because these traits issued from a peculiar human nature; it was because, over a long period, these had been preferentially selected attitudes, praised by leaders and accepted by the led.

It was also true that Americans had a deep and traditional belief that people were better for being materially well-off. They had always wanted others to share their own prosperity. This was now being interpreted as issuing from a shrewd self-interest. It was even being enlarged—with some holding back—into a new policy. Hungry people become Communists, it was said; misery begets revolution; the best way to meet the challenge of communism, therefore, is to feed the hungry and succor the miserable. Point Four was less a way to save the world than to save the United States.

There was the kind of moral confusion involved in this to which contemporary leaders were prone. It was part of the deprecation they seemed to think necessary. If friendly impulses could be made to seem selfish and shrewd, that was a stronger justification for them than mere friendliness by itself. The difficulty with this kind of thing is that it confuses the sources of social impulse. A foreign policy cannot be founded, for instance, on the appeasements demanded by xenophobes and reactionaries any more than it can on a concept of pure original human impulse.

The truth is that policy—foreign policy or any other—for a people is shaped in their discussions among themselves, discussions which may be very greatly influenced by leadership. Leadership is an intellectual exercise, or ought to be, in the interest of the group as a whole. And, when what we are talking about is the nation, leadership is the shaping of public opinion so that wise action will result. If there did exist an American foreign policy, it was a policy which had grown out of these democratic processes and would go on growing out of them. But it was not helpful to contend that it had a mystic origin or that it was somehow inevitably guided toward wisdom. It had a very complex but not mysterious source; it might very well, because of bad leadership, turn out to be unwise.

The saving grace of democratic decisions would always be that it had been argued out. But there was undoubtedly a kind of contract between leaders and led which, if it was violated, ruined everything. This was not a contract that leaders would be wise; but it did rest on an assumption of honesty; and the worst fault of the modern democracy lay in the corruption of discussion. The powerful admunicating machines—press, radio, television—were, in the first place, not publicly owned. And there was always the danger— and sometimes the fact—that ownership passed to those whose interest in the deliberate perversion of discussion was obvious. This had gone so far with the press as to discredit it seriously as a democratic instrument. The same thing might happen to radio and television.

Given honesty among leaders and free and full discussion, a foreign policy would be arrived at; and it would be one fully implemented with the whole strength of society. It was one of the most disquieting characteristics of the contemporary years that neither honesty of leadership nor full and free discussion could be counted on. Sometimes they existed; sometimes they did not; and there were all degrees of existence. If there was one contribution Western statesmen were under compulsion to work for, it was the purification—it could almost be said the revivification—of democracy. For it was only democracy which could oppose the dreaded rigidities, restrictions, and violences of communism. It had been President Roosevelt's clearest perception that this was true; and one of his greatest contributions had been the implementing of this perception.[18]

18. Mr. Sumner Welles at the end of an article (in *Foreign Affairs*, XXIX [January, 1951], 204) discussing certain Roosevelt decisions had this to say:
"I have known no man in American public life who believed more implicitly than President Roosevelt that the hope of the world lay in the renewal of the people's faith in democracy. He saw more clearly than most of his contemporaries that the power and menace of Communism lay in the fanatical faith of its prophets and its addicts, even more than in the military force and vast potential resources of the Soviet Union. To him, Communism was bloody, stifling, and intolerable. It was revolting to the passion for individual freedom which he had in-

But conversely it could be said in all fairness that it was his successor's greatest shortcoming that he had no conception of this fundamental need and that he not only made no contribution to the purification of democracy but had done it, in the management of his great office, deep and long-lasting injury.

What ought to have been remembered in considering American relations with other nations was much the same thing to be remembered about individuals in their relations with each other. There is always a struggle going on between inward and outward turning, between considerations of self and of others, between kindly and friendly impulses on the one side, and fears, suspicions, and impulses to withdrawal on the other. When these conflicts are partially resolved, or at least sufficiently resolved so that they find expression in institutions—say, a social security act, a public education system, a forest reserve, the Red Cross, or any other of numerous similar institutions which represent social impulses—there may still be a lingering minority objection or, in many individuals, only a half-hearted willingness to support them.

The same observations are relevant in national relations. There are some Americans who have an unreasonable and persistent dislike for some other peoples—the Irish for the British, the Jews for the Germans, "old American stock" for East Europeans, and so on —but these dislikes do not often become institutionalized. There is an exception to prove this, as other, rules—the prohibition against Asiatic immigration. Mostly the international bars and barriers are economic rather than cultural or social.[19] And economic discrimination is regarded as permissible because, in the American book, selfishness in economic matters is supposed to be a virtue. There is maintained a rigid difference between what is allowable in economic intercourse and what is virtuous in other matters.

Economic discriminations aside—tariffs, for instance—there is a

herited from his Dutch and New England forebears. He frankly recognized the appeal which Communism's promise of economic security held for millions of starving and down-trodden men and women in may parts of the world. But he believed Communism would never prevail provided democracy became a living reality here in the United States and in the other free nations, and provided those who cherished democracy were willing to strive for its fulfillment and eventual supremacy with the same self-sacrificing fervor shown by the Marxists in fighting for their ideology."

19. Even in this case, the original exclusion had an economic motivation.

very remarkable likeness between individual relationships and national ones. The inaccuracy involved in putting it this way is obvious—international intercourse is a delegated responsibility. The Department of State may or may not correctly interpret a people's wishes with respect to other peoples. Misinterpretation by those out of touch or sympathy with a wide public, or, what is perhaps just as frequent, a departmental impulse toward appeasing its more vocal critics, may result in the shaping of a policy which is in fact unrepresentative and cannot, if the issue can be made, secure a majority approval. The attempt to maintain such a tour de force leads the Department to defend itself with what are often formidable propaganda efforts. These become conflicting, so that it is difficult to know just what it is the Department intends. Sometimes this whole process results in reversing policies or in defending them from the wrong people.

It was a serious criticism of the foreign policy centering in 1952 that its operators had fallen into some of these confusions. It sometimes seemed to represent the better impulses of Americans, as when the Marshall Plan and when Point Four were put forward. It sometimes seemed to represent their worst ones, as when immoderate attacks on the Soviet Union were allowed to dominate one whole sector of our intercourse. There followed from this the neglect of that exploration of coexistence which must take place if there was not to be active war. For several years now this necessary activity had seemed to be trying to find its way into public discussion. Each time this appeared about to happen, some officer of the Department of State was detailed to belabor and suppress it. The United States was no further along toward an understanding with the other great power in the world in 1952 than had been true in 1945.

The strangest affair of its kind in all history still continued to prolong itself at Panmunjom. Daily—or almost daily—for more than a year the military meetings had taken place. The generals sought an armistice. But they could not agree. They could not agree because even the simple arrangements necessary to the cessation of hostilities were prejudiced by the longer-run arrangements they implied. The latest of a long series of obstacles was a failure to agree on a basis for prisoner exchange. This seemingly simple matter had turned—as everything did—into a matter of principle on which each side had taken such an unyielding position, and taken it so publicly, that compromise was impossible. And, as the November elections in the United States came nearer, the negotiations at Panmunjom became more and more difficult. The Democratic Administration could less and less afford to concede anything, and the Chinese were inclined to demand more because a settlement would be so obviously agreeable to their opponents.

For the Chinese, the "twilight war" was a fairly comfortable arrangement. It provided them with a convenient foreign enemy to belabor; it enabled them to maintain and to train—under battle conditions, but without great losses—a large army, and to keep that army in the north without Russian objection, a military position they were bound to insist upon anyway so long as Japan was a base for United States forces. Since the Americans could concede nothing and since the Chinese preferred to await the election, the strange farce of negotiation went on listlessly.

To the Chinese, the American election was the event on which their future policy must turn—that is, until the nominating conventions had been held. The selection of opposing candidates both of whom were generally favorable to settlement, and not to MacArthurism, had the effect which only the defeat of Taft, if he had been nominated, could have had. After the selection of Eisenhower and Stevenson, the Chinese no longer had political reasons for stalling. They might possibly be more willing to reach a settlement.

Thus, as Hiroshima Day approached, the prospect of a cease-fire seemed somewhat better than it had at any time in the past, although real peace negotiations could hardly start until after election. Not only was MacArthurism fading away, but neither side wanted the alternative to negotiation—war. A return to active fighting would involve attacks on Chinese home territories and reciprocal attacks on bases in Japan and Okinawa, and thus, inevitably, the extension of the war to other allies.

The fact that neither side wanted war was what had kept negotiations going; and what had prolonged them so was the consciousness on both sides that politically embarrassing concessions would have to be made when the peace was approached. Even the signing of an armistice would have political reactions as soon as the Eastern and Western peoples realized that it involved a recession from principle of enormous scope. It would, in fact, imply the partition of Korea—something both sides had vowed not to permit—and the division would be based on the finding of an equilibrium between the powers of East and West. Half of an unhappy people would have been sacrificed to capitalism on the one side and communism on the other. There would have been no self-determination, no consultation of those disposed of. Moreover, this pattern would have been established for settlements all around the Communist periphery.

Partition of Indochina would logically follow the partition of Korea. And other matters would soon be involved. The Formosan question would have to be settled in violation of principle too. China would not get it back; but neither would Chiang get back China. And recognition of the Communist regime and its seating in the United Nations assembly might very well follow the erection of a Republic of Formosa. But how would this necessary trading accord with American or Communist principle? One commentator put it this way:

This sort of peace settlement would be, in fact, a solution on eighteenth-century lines, in which power alone counts, and the wishes of the people are in no way operative. Here, indeed, is the real underlying difficulty of any settlement. The only practicable solutions involve a cynical disregard of the very principles for which both sides claim to have been fighting. The communists abandon the South Koreans to the regime of Syngman Rhee, whom they describe as the running dog of American imperialism. The United Nations consign the North Koreans to the control of the powers whom they stigmatise as harsh and inhuman totalitarian tyrannies. If this sort of bargaining were to be extended to Indo-China and Formosa could the public in the West and the faithful Communist Party comrades in the East be induced to believe that such a program fulfils their aspirations?

The same shrewd commentator who made this observation went on to a concluding paragraph:

Thus before any lasting settlement can be made the West must first resolve the contradictions inherent in the present policies. We may aim to build around China a ring of fortresses and bases by which China's power can be held in check and her ambitions frustrated; in which case we are seeking a military and not a political solution, and accept the probability of ultimate war. Or we may seek to arrive at a settlement which will leave on our side of the line between the two worlds all those peoples who genuinely wish to live in our way, and understand our ideals, renouncing to the communist side those marginal areas where there is no inclination to take our side. These countries, falling naturally into their traditional position within the zone of Chinese power, can only with difficulty be kept beyond it, and if retained by the West, will continually provide a cause of friction and a reason for the abiding hostility of a resurgent China.[20]

It would be politically difficult in the West to come to such an arrangement; but the real question—the one with which statesmen of the future would have to deal—was: Could the Western conscience accommodate itself to a permanent settlement on such a pattern? There was, it seemed obvious, an equally difficult situation in the making elsewhere. What but expediency could account for the alliance of the democracies with Tito and Franco? How justify the rearming of an admittedly unrepentant Germany? Justification was not even attempted except to say that we needed allies and that the German divisions were essential.

It was indeed true that those who would have it that American policy came out of a deep and traditional view of things had much to explain. They might say that the exceptions were temporary and that in the long run they would not prove acceptable. But that was all they could say in explanation. Of course, they could object on moral grounds. This they did; and their case was a strong one in certain respects, especially as it related to Germany, that is, it was consistent with definite moral position. They would have liked to see Germany free but neutral and disarmed; and it did appear that the more stable elements of German society wanted the same solution.

There was a possible way out, but no one spoke of it; and its pursuit seemed more and more remote with the passage of time. That, of course, was the granting by each of the virtues of the other. It would then no longer be wicked to make the practical arrangements which must be made. The populations involved would not be consigned to purgatory, however their boundaries might be settled. There was so little approach to this kind of arrangement, however, that not even a trace of it could be detected in the atmosphere either of Moscow or of Washington.

It seemed to me that such an arrangement was possible. I thought that the Politburo would agree to discontinue Cominform activities

20. C. P. Fitzgerald, "The Powers and the Twilight War," *The Listener*, XLVII, No. 1214 (1952), 7.

in the West in exchange for the border security they felt so deep a need for—including the neutralizing of Germany. But such a bargain would require a reversal of the current mutual fostering of distrust and suspicion. I had an idea, however, that an era of better feeling might very rapidly develop, in reaction from tension and fear, if it were given the least chance. There was a humanity which was common alike to Communists and democrats.

Some such solution—something fresh and new—might develop out of the impending political campaign. Even the candidate of the Democratic party was uncommitted to present policies. There was reason to believe that he understood the duties of leadership as those presently in charge did not. If he were to win—I, at least, thought it possible—the long impasse might be broken. That there was a chance of a solution if America should show more willingness was very generally believed in Britain. Mr. Ernest Davies, Undersecretary of State for Foreign Affairs during 1950–51, commenting on this, said:

If, as I believe, Russia does not want a general war,[21] . . . then it might be willing to negotiate a *modus vivendi*, provided it is convinced of two things; first, that the Atlantic Pact is a genuine defensive alliance, and is not the framework for an aggressive war, and similarly that, in the Far East, there is no intention of engaging in an all-out war. Second, that if Russia is convinced that if it attempts to further its objectives by aggressive action, then it will be faced with a united and determined bloc of democratic countries who will be ready and strong enough to resist. It may well be that of this it is already convinced, but to satisfy it on the first score is difficult. It requires in the first place that the West endeavours to take no action which Russia would interpret as intolerably provocative, and secondly there must be a genuine attempt on both sides to settle the causes of international tension. There must be a readiness to discuss them on merit, and a willingness to engage in reasonable compromise. Unfortunately, heretofore, America has . . . been ready to regard any offer from the U.S.S.R. with extreme suspicion, and the inclination has often been to reject them as being for propaganda purposes only. This is particularly so in the United Nations, where United States action sometimes has given rise to the suspicion that she would favour conversion of the organisation into an anti-communist bloc. The way for cooperation must be kept open and Russian fear and suspicion taken fully into account. It may be that there are signs that Russia is groping for a way out of the present impasse. . . . Its slight advance nearer the West on disarmament and atomic weapons at the recent General Assem-

21. This was also the opinion of General Eisenhower, as he indicated in a famous homecoming interview in Abilene in June. For the Russians to start a war they could not win, he said, would be "silly," and they were not silly.

bly and the truce talks in Korea and the feelers on German unity may be signs that Russia is exploring the situation.

This was the view of a very moderate English critic. There were those—especially the Bevanites—in the British Labour party who went much further and almost accused the United States of provocation to war. On the whole, the dissent to American policy among Europeans was so serious that for a time the Russians seemed to be shaping their diplomatic actions to the widening of the split and to taking advantage of a growing discord. The appointment of Andrei Gromyko as Soviet ambassador to London, taken together with differences among the Allies concerning German rearmament, indicated the Russian view that something could be made of the growing irritation. The Russian suggestion in July for a four-power meeting on Germany, with a limited agenda—a meeting to which the Americans had to agree—carried the strategy further.

It had to be admitted that during the year there had been a startling growth of factions opposed to the United States. They were composed, not of the Communists, who had caused so much trouble before the Marshall Plan had had its reconstructive effect, but of the liberals—those who believed in peace and toleration but who suspected that those in charge of American policy did not. And the truth was that the United States was deliberately persisting in a hard and uncompromising attitude, seemingly on the theory that until she had attained superior power it was a waste of time to communicate with the Russians at all. This attitude the Europeans thought uncivilized and obstructive, and disapproval of it was what lay behind the extraordinary outburst of criticism in the House of Commons when the Yalu River power plants were bombed in June.[22] There were some things said in that debate, indeed, which, if taken seriously, would seem to indicate hopeless differences.

The British attitude, it must be said, was influenced by yet other worries. The expected competition from German and Japanese in-

---

22. The power plants on the Yalu were furnishing electricity to Manchurian factories, airfields, and radar defenses. It was the American view that they were legitimate military targets. The British thought they were overclose to the border and that their destruction definitely risked an extension of the war. Also, as it turned out, many of the annoyed British had been under the impression that no hostilities were going on and that this reopened them. This was a measure of the British interest in the common undertaking in Korea which caused acid comment in America.

dustries was now materializing, and Lancashire textile mills were feeling the pinch. The Tory government had cut food subsidies, and the cost of living was rising. Indeed, not only was the cost rising but food was actually scarcer, and the austerities of the war and postwar periods threatened to go on into an indefinite future. The Tory promises of better times turned into mockeries. In the spring of 1952, for the third time in a few years, there was a financial crisis which demanded still further reductions of imports and expansions of exports; and this time such a requirement was almost impossible to meet, so little leeway was left after other efforts.

It was very hard indeed, in these circumstances, which were only less drastic in France and Italy than in Britain, to see Germany doing so comparatively well. There industry was thriving, the standard of living was well above that of the victorious nations, and a new spirit of enterprise and optimism was taking hold. The Schuman Plan was now all but effective; the last parliamentary ratification had been completed, and the ministers were about to meet to set up the new institutions. This arrangement might do something for Continental nations; but it could only mean more competition for the British, who had refused to join.

Britain's prospect for the future was hardly better than the present reality. Her power was at a very low ebb, and her influence in international affairs corresponded with her decline. Subordination was hard to take and undoubtedly was responsible for a sensitiveness vis-à-vis a powerful and still expanding America which bordered on the neurotic. However far toward recovery other nations in Europe had been brought with Marshall Plan aid, the situation of Britain was chronically bad and even worsening. It began, indeed, to seem hopeless and was recognized to be so by the embarrassing Tory retreat in July from its already lowered arms commitments. This step, said Mr. Aneurin Bevan, was one he had all along insisted must be taken; Mr. Churchill had no adequate answer. The responsibilities of power were very different from the freedoms of opposition. In his old age he was finding himself in a harrowing struggle to salvage a living place for Britain in an otherwise recovering world.[23] Imperial dreams were fading even from the old Prime Minister's ambitions.

23. Cf. an interesting analysis of the situation of the British vis-à-vis Germany by E. H. Carr, "The Puzzle of Anglo-German Relations," *The Listener*, July 3, 1952.

The race in atomic armaments continued. In the autumn of 1951 the Russians set off their second atomic explosion.[24] The President announced it, and all other information concerning it was withheld; but presumably this bomb was not just another of the type used before. Russian progress might be in the direction of tactical weapons, or it might be in the direction of the H-bomb, that superhorror the United States was also preparing to produce. During the year, furthermore, the British completed work on an atomic bomb, and by spring they were sending an expedition out to Australia to set it off. And the operations of the United States Atomic Energy Commission, of course, were vastly expanded.

At the beginning of the atomic year—on September 18—Senator Brien McMahon, chairman of the Joint Congressional Committee on Atomic Energy, made a startling proposal. It seemed to him that the nation was approaching a dilemma. "I can see ahead," he said, "only military safety at the price of economic disaster or economic safety at the price of military disaster." He therefore asked the Congress to increase expenditures for the production of atomic weapons, including those of a tactical nature, by six times the present rate and to reduce correspondingly—or more than correspondingly—expenditures for conventional weapons. Only thus could we escape bankruptcy. At the same time the Senator, always a peace-minded man, not only proposed new attempts to reach an agreement on disarmament but offered a pledge on the part of the Congress "to make available to the United Nations—when an effective system of worldwide disarmament takes effect—a substantial portion of all money saved for a period of five years." These funds would be spent by the United Nations "for peaceful development of atomic energy, technical assistance to underdeveloped areas, and general economic aid to all war-ravaged countries."

It was not these pleas for peace, however, but the Senator's disclosures about progress in atomic armament that attracted most attention. These were summarized by the *Times*, as follows:

1. That an atomic weapon could now produce, at a cost of twenty or thirty dollars, the same explosive force which costs literally thousands of dollars to produce by ordinary means.

2. That havoc equal to all that was caused in the rain of bombs that fell

24. *New York Times*, October 4, 1951.

350

on Germany across the six-year span of World War II could now be wrought by the United States in a single day.

3. That the atomic bomb no longer had to be zealously hoarded, and that thus with the expansion he proposed it was possible to work a revolution in military firepower that could bring us peace power at bearable cost.

The Senator thought that within three years it would be possible to establish mass production of atomic weapons—not only bombs, but shells and guided missiles with atomic war heads—in a volume comparable with the present production of conventional weapons.

The nation was startled. People had not realized that a gradual development had taken place which had turned the A-bomb into a tactical as well as a strategic weapon. Nothing came of Senator McMahon's central proposal to abandon conventional armaments; but there was another vast enlargement of the atomic weapons program, and during the year there were repeated exercises accompanying bomb explosions at Yucca Flats in Nevada which drove home the lesson Senator McMahon had begun to teach.[25] What was going on now, according to almost casual reports in the press, was the adaptation of the Bomb to tactical uses, made possible by an "unexpected development of bombs of small size." A year or two previously a shrinkage in diameter to less than five feet had not been thought possible within a decade; but already the mechanism was being inclosed in even smaller casings. How much smaller was not revealed;

25. There had, by the end of April, been thirty explosions. *Newsweek*, on May 5, tabulated a box score, as follows:

1945: Three, U.S.—July 16 at Alamogordo, N.M.; August 6 at Hiroshima; August 9, at Nagasaki.
1946: Two, U.S.—July at Operation Crossroads, Bikini.
1947: None.
1948: Three, U.S.—April and May at Eniwetok.
1949: None, U.S.; one, Russia—announced by President Truman, September 23.
1950: None, but President Truman ordered hydrogen bomb.
1951: Fifteen, U.S.; two, Russia. In January and February, five of the U.S. blasts at the Nevada testing site; in May, "several," probably three (possibly four), at Operation Greenhouse, Eniwetok; in October and November, seven at Nevada testing site (including two with troops). President Truman announced the second and third Russian bombs in October.
1952: Three, U.S.—April 2, 15, and 22 at the Nevada testing site.
Grand total: 26 or 27, for U.S.; 3 for Russia.

U.S. News and World Report in its issue of February 1, 1952, had also made a summary of progress which it called "The Real Story of New Atom Weapons." Like others, it emphasized tactical developments.

but it was known that such bombs were being adapted for artillery projectiles.

No one seemed interested in the implications of the tactical uses of the Bomb. They were, however, very serious. Much of the hope for an agreement on disarmament had rested on the unique nature of the Bomb. It had a distinctive source; it was made by novel methods; and it was of such a nature that its use would be strategic only. But, if it was to be used on the battlefield and dropped from small planes in quantity, it became something very different. Its prevalence in national armaments would lead to a reliance upon it which would make prohibition of its use as unlikely as the prohibition of the military airplane. I could remember all too well, myself, a period when President Roosevelt's hope of disarmament was centered in the banning of the military plane.

Yet the power of the atomic explosion was still being multiplied. No one not directly involved knew whether the formidable problems involved in H-bomb development had been solved; but only substantial progress could justify the huge expenditures authorized during the year. It was "disclosed," furthermore, by the Alsop brothers, Washington columnists, that the first of these superbombs would be detonated at Eniwetok before the end of summer. This, the Alsops said, would not be the true superbomb, although it would result from hydrogen fusion rather than from the fission of U235:

Until very recently, there was the most widespread doubt among the best-qualified scientists that the true superbomb could or would ever be built. The vital recent development is that this doubt has been resolved.

The character of this weapon which is in prospect goes beyond what the normal human imagination can comprehend. The two-megaton bomb will achieve total destruction in an area just under 100 square miles. It will devastate by blast an area just under 180 square miles. In its single explosion, a whole vast megalopolis, a great modern capital, can be wiped from the face of the earth. . . .

Meanwhile the State Department's Advisory Committee on Disarmament, including such eminent scientists as Vannevar Bush and J. Robert Oppenheimer, has . . . raised its voice. Because of the superbomb, the committee is insisting that a bold new effort must be made to explore the possibility of a disarmament agreement with the Soviet Union.

One reason for this, in turn, is the extreme probability that the Russians will have a superbomb of their own almost as soon as we will. They started with the same knowledge. While our hydrogen bomb development was kept in low gear for several postwar years, theirs was almost surely in high gear. So the fact that this weapon is now in prospect cuts two ways and cuts very deep. Altogether, the development herein reported promises to change the shape of our world and it is time that someone said so.[26]

This was the kind of material available to the American democracy as it entered the new age. The information came, not from authoritative sources, but from journalists who picked up bits of information here and there and pieced them together. If what the Alsops, and others, said was true, the most fateful decisions in the history of mankind were being made, or were about to be made, by a small and largely unrepresentative circle of insiders. Even if the journalists were far from accurate as to the progress of the scientists and engineers, the known facts—appropriations, publicized tests, the construction of facilities, and so on—made it apparent that literally earth-shaking events were impending.

Had democracy, even in America, become a fiction? Had it been permanently confined to those old areas where public discussion did not affect what was now called "security"? And in these new areas, where decision would determine survival, was democratic discussion to be altogether excluded? If decisions concerning the manufacture and the use of these weapons were to be left to so small a group as now controlled them, then the central prerogatives of democracy had been surrendered. Perhaps that was the kind of world into which we were being taken involuntarily. But this matter, too, ought to have had some discussion from other than journalistic sources. Yet the literature of political science could be searched in vain. Even the *Bulletin of the Atomic Scientists*, although it continued to publish useful information, seemed no longer to discuss with its former forthrightness the issues upon which decisions were being made.

The machinery of democracy had not disappeared. The Atomic Energy Act of 1946 was still controlling;[27] and under it a civilian commission was in charge of operations. It was true that the military had charge of the bombs; but only the President could authorize

26. The Alsops were among the most insistent explorers of nuclear probabilities. A warning similar to this had also been given in their column of February 17, 1952.

27. It had been amended only once, in the fall of 1951. This amendment appeared to reduce security restrictions; what it did actually was to reduce them if it appeared to the decision-makers to be in the national interest. A convenient summary and a reprint of the amended act may be found in Byron S. Miller, "Atomic Energy Act: Second Stage," *Bulletin of the Atomic Scientists*, Vol. VIII, No. 1 (January, 1952).

their use. Also a congressional joint committee, of which Senator McMahon was the chairman (until his death in July, 1952), was at least active in keeping track of what was going on. These were democratic agencies; so were the appropriations committees to whom the AEC must come for funds. But the President must rely on advice—largely from the military. The appropriations committees had no information, and even the joint committee of the Congress—the "watchdog committee," as Senator McMahon called it—could effect but a very limited supervision. The role of this group was described in different ways by different observers. Some said that it was a captive of the commission and pointed to the former law-partner relationship between Senator McMahon and Chairman Dean; others thought it extraordinarily diligent and influential. What was known was that the commission reported every policy decision to the committee. Sometimes it consulted the committee before making its decision, and the matter would be argued at length; sometimes initiative even originated in the committee.

As *Time* remarked on January 14, 1952: "Never did so many trust so few so blindly as the people of the United States and the rest of the free world trust the members of the Atomic Energy Commission." To those who were concerned because, in its most vital area, democracy was so circumscribed and restricted as almost not to function at all, the only hope seemed to lie in delegation of function to a competent representative body such as the joint committee. It could not take the place of publicly argued decisions on great matters; but it was at least something on which to rely.

The major development of the atomic year seemed to be progress toward the use of nuclear weapons for tactical purposes. The dangers of this progress produced a warning from the Federation of American Scientists:

> In any decision on the use of such weapons, it is essential to take into account the psychological reactions of the people of friendly, enemy, and neutral countries as well as the immediate military objective. It would be a poor bargain if we won a local engagement at the expense of alienating world public opinion. . . .

It would be a mistake to consider any atomic weapon as "just one more weapon, and to leave consideration of the effect of [its] use to military commanders alone." The only real escape, however, seemed to them to be the current disarmament discussions in the United Nations. It was their hope that "public attitudes and governmental policies will permit flexibility on the part of American representatives." They underlined it: "The awesome prospects of destruction . . . should lead this country, as well as others, to make now the most serious attempt to achieve universal reduction of armaments."

By Hiroshima Day in August it seemed clear that these hopes had been no better based than former ones. The stalemate continued. And time was serving to increase, not to diminish, the fateful tensions of the twilight war.

CHAPTER IX *1953*

THE year from Hiroshima Day in 1952 to the next in 1953 was dominated by three events about which all others seemed to rotate as swollen streams do about the centers of whirlpools. General Eisenhower was elected to the presidency of the United States in November; Marshal Stalin died on an early March day; and the incident in Korea reached the long-delayed, unsatisfactory stages of its liquidation in June.

The truce in Korea might not have happened if Eisenhower had not been elected or Stalin had not died. The accession of Eisenhower probably influenced it less than the disappearance of Stalin. For the new Administration in Washington had even less ability to affect policy than the old one had had; either that, or its inclinations were weaker. Events seemed to happen one after the other without any noticeable reaction on its part, a consequence of the deep division in Republican ranks as well as of the ineptitude of the new strategists. But, when Stalin had gone from the Kremlin, a new Soviet policy had begun to show itself at once. It was just the reverse of that expected by those who ought to have known most about Russian intentions.

For a long time most of the "experts" had pictured Stalin as the most reasonable and least fanatic of the powerful central group— the old Politburo, now become the larger Presidium. He had been a practical politician, it was said, who had understood the utility of compromise; the others around him were not only stiffly doctrinaire but were ignorant about the West. They had no adequate conception of the tradition of democratic liberty; they thought it childish and irresponsible and therefore inimical. They were intent on extin-

356

guishing from the world the institutions which expressed its principles and substituting the reasonable Communist state. Stalin had
said, on occasion, that the two systems, communism and capitalism,
could live together. None of the other Kremlin people had been on
record with such remarks, and none was thought to agree.

There was, therefore, widespread expression of surprise when a
new and softer policy immediately became evident. It was hardly
noticeable at first, and, because of journalists' preconceptions, it was
received with skepticism. None of the first conciliatory gestures, it
was pointed out, affected the central issues between East and West.
A group of American small-town journalists and their wives, it was
learned, were traveling in Russia and being treated with the utmost
courtesy. (It was interesting to see how their factual reports were
regarded when they returned. The nearly unanimous comment was
that they had been hoaxed. Those who had their own ideas of what
Russia was like were not going to be disabused by a few travelers.)
An American journalist who had been jailed in Czechoslovakia for
"spying" was suddenly released; the Russian wives of American
newspapermen in Moscow were allowed to depart with their hus-
bands; and an agreement to open the Danube was suddenly negotiated with Yugoslavia. But there were soon more important concessions. A new attitude of co-operation seemed to develop in the international agencies where East and West met, notably at the United
Nations, where an agreement was reached on Dag Hammarskjöld as
Secretary-General after years of disagreement. And at Panmunjom
the long and apparently insoluble stalemate was suddenly resolved
by new proposals from the Communists. When the Russians consented to a new convention for the Turkish Straits, it was no longer
possible to ignore the change. Stalin had talked of coexistence, but
he had never made the least move in its direction. Now there was
action as well as words.

But there was no answering readiness to move toward negotiation
in Washington. The new President had not yet any policy of his own.
His Secretary of State, John Foster Dulles, had been an author of
the Truman-Acheson policy and was suggesting that it be carried even further—that a policy of *containment* become a policy of
liberation, of developing a spirit of resistance among the peoples
under Soviet rule. A speech approaching definition of this attitude

early in the Administration so thoroughly frightened the Western Allies, and especially the French and British, however, that the President himself awoke to the situation into which he was being drawn. What Mr. Dulles actually said about this on August 8, 1952, at Denver, had been: "We will abandon the policy of mere containment, and will actively develop hope and a resistance spirit within the captive peoples, which, in my opinion, is the alternative to general war." This seemed like a *non sequitur* to Europeans and provocative besides. They liked it no better when, as Secretary of State, he repeated several times during the spring almost the same words, coming finally to "liberation."

Having come fresh from the attempt to organize a European army, which, he saw more and more clearly, depended on the creation of an institutional Europe, President Eisenhower was obviously alarmed by the reaction to Mr. Dulles' more adventurous tentatives. It had sounded to the French, especially, as though the new intention in the United States was not to rest on a defensive alliance for western Europe but to organize a movement for detaching the satellites from Russia. Such a move seemed thoroughly unrealistic in view of the vast power the Russians possessed and the collective weakness of the Atlantic nations.

The French—and others—were inclined to feel lucky, or grateful, that the Russians had not moved down to the Channel while Europe was prostrate. They realized that this forbearance had been the result of a calculated policy, not of an inability to carry through such a project. But it seemed the height of folly to presume on the situation. If the Russians were going to interest themselves in the East, or in home development, and rest content with the present barrier of satellites, nothing could be more foolish than to make such a policy impossible, which "liberation" would certainly do. So the realistic French were horrified. They said so. And the new President awoke. He, in effect, repudiated his Secretary of State; and Europe calmed down.

But Europe did not ratify the conventions which had been drawn up the preceding year. They had, so to speak, lain on the tables of various parliaments. European legislators wanted neither to repudiate nor to adopt them. They did not repudiate because they wanted American aid continued; they did not ratify because they were afraid of the consequences. The treaties had progressed to the formulation and submission stage because of American insistence; but such pressure worked better with members of governments—ministers— than with legislators. The legislators were balky. When, late in April, the Council of the North Atlantic Treaty Organization gathered in the Palais de Chaillot for its eleventh meeting, it not only could report no progress in ratification, but it moved in an unmistakably defeatist atmosphere. The Soviet gestures of conciliation combined with the predominance in the American Congress of the senators who had in the past most loudly favored American withdrawal from Europe produced a climate in which the urgings of the military for larger appropriations were futile. The Lisbon meeting in February, 1952, had tuned its commitments to "a critical year"—1954. At Paris, in 1953, there no longer seemed any reason to think 1954 especially critical. The NATO ministers fell back rather weakly on a "permanent emergency." At the end their communiqué pledged their countries to "broaden co-operation . . . and so to make the Atlantic community a lasting reality." But there remained the hard fact that the European Defense Community Treaty—the treaty which would integrate a rearmed West Germany with the defense forces of five other western European nations—had so far been ratified only by the lower house of the German parliament. No further ratifications were in prospect; and there were elections pending in both Germany and Italy with the outcome very doubtful.

The discouragement was reflected in a retreat toward reality in military planning. The goals set at Lisbon, which had immediately appeared to be beyond reach, were now stepped down to a new level, which again, however, no one appeared to accept as sufficiently low. The Lisbon target in 1952 compared as follows with that of Paris in 1953:

	LISBON TARGETS		PARIS TARGETS	
	Planes	Divisions	Planes	Divisions
1953	6,500	75	5,500	60
1954	9,000	96	7,000	70

A force of such dimensions, vis-à-vis that of Russia and Russia's satellites, might have a deterrent effect; but it was not a base from which to talk of "liberation" or "rollbacks," and every European was anxious to have the new Americans recognize this truth.

What everyone was conscious of, but what was not discussed, was a further question: Had all these planes and divisions any importance? The atomic weapon was the real deterrent to any ideas of conquest the Russians might be disposed to generate. But no one outside a small group in the United States knew what atomic power was available to the West.[1] Even the British, who had contributed well over half the expertise which had resulted in the original A-bomb, had been excluded by the Atomic Energy Act from participation in any future development—an act of congressional hysteria in the face of mysterious power which was harder and harder to justify.[2] Absurd though it was, the commanders of the European army, only a few of whom were Americans, were thus by law excluded from knowledge of the weapon of most consequence to their operations.[3] For the reduction of atomic weapons to tactical size was now known to have been achieved. The atomic cannon had been fired at Yucca Flats; its picture had been in all the newspapers; and it had rolled down Pennsylvania Avenue in an Army Day parade. The hydrogen bomb of incredible power—the strategic weapon to be carried to its target by intercontinental bombers—and the A-bomb small enough to be fitted into an artillery shell: these weapons would make all others obsolescent. The Korean pattern was to be discarded.

But if there were difficult and unsatisfactory problems to be met by General Alfred M. Gruenther—now substituted for General Matthew Ridgway as Supreme Commander[4]—in Europe, those to be

1. By Hiroshima Day, 1953, the United States had set off at least forty-four atomic explosions, including a probable four which were tests of, or which led to, the H-bomb. An entire armory was supposed to have been developed, both of strategic and of tactical weapons. One military critic estimated that the United states stockpile was now well over the thousand mark: he also estimated that the Russian stockpile was in the range of one hundred to three hundred.

2. In his news conference on July 8 President Eisenhower pointed out the outmoded restrictions of the Atomic Energy Act written in the hope that this country could retain the "secret" of the atomic bomb. Representative W. Sterling Cole, chairman, now, of the Joint Congressional Committee on Atomic Energy, favored caution in the releasing of information, he said; and the impression he gave was that nothing would change (cf. *New York Times*, July 9, 1953, p. 1).

3. It was the more absurd because the British had, during the year, exploded a bomb of their own at Montebello, off the western Australian coast. Perhaps the most interesting account of this explosion—much more interesting even than Churchill's announcement in the Commons—was that of Mr. W. G. Penny, who had been the scientist in charge, in *The Listener*, for November 13, 1952.

4. General Ridgway had become the Army member of the new Chiefs of Staff,

met in the Pacific were even more complicated and difficult. In Europe there existed at least a general policy; in Asia there was none. And the discussion which might lead toward one had never been begun. It had seemed for a moment in the presidential campaign as though debate was about to begin. Governor Stevenson had said that coexistence implied the negotiation of conditions; but this had been before the campaign had well begun and while the Governor was not yet an avowed candidate.[5] When the debate materialized, further specification was not forthcoming. There was a discouraging tendency on his part to fall back on mere defense of the position of the Administration. This did not go beyond shoring up the contention that Communist expansion had been stopped by the challenge to aggression in Korea. That in itself was sought to be interpreted as a victory. This, however reasonable, an American majority plainly did not accept. It was a kind of negative result impossible to justify, as they thought, in view of the sacrifice and expense involved. It left things just where they were before, with Korea divided, the Communists still an overwhelming threat, and no assurance against further such incidents. The threat might actually have been just as serious if the United Nations armies had stood on the Yalu instead of on an indeterminate line halfway down the peninsula, but the occupation of all Korea could have been interpreted as a victory of sorts. And there was no chance of pretending that anything like victory was represented by the negotiations in progress. Also, if a simple cease-fire was to require, as it already had, two years of talk, the settlement of larger issues in a peace conference to follow might not reach any conclusion for several years, just as those in Austria had trailed out over more than two hundred meetings and then merely come to a stop.

Yet Governor Stevenson, if he lost the election on any one issue, lost it on this one. General Eisenhower had nothing else to offer, and it was clear enough that he was taking Mr. Dulles' advice on the Eastern issues. But at least he was not in the position of defending failure, frustration, needless sacrifice, and national humiliation. All these terms, as well as many others, were used by the Republicans,

---

as Admiral Robert B. Carney had for the Navy and General Nathan F. Twining for the Air Force. The chairman, in succession to General Omar Bradley, was, for the first time, to be a Navy man, Admiral Arthur W. Radford.

5. In his speech at San Francisco on May 5, 1952.

and, late in the campaign, he did not scruple to capitalize on the discernibly increasing disillusion by promising dramatically to go himself to Korea, once he had been elected, and find a way out of the impasse. This promise was made good in the sense that he actually made such a journey; but it amounted to deception, nevertheless, because he knew well enough before he went that there was no way out of what the command had got into there except by negotiation. He produced no miracle; but by then he had been elected, and the issue had served its purpose. Curiously enough, it was very generally agreed that, if the new President felt that the present hand must be played out, then it must. In this, the Korean issue was like every other major controversy of the campaign. Promises were made; they were not kept; and no public accounting was attempted. But the Eisenhower credit rose rather than sank.

It was obvious that the American people, after years of missing the fatherhood they had projected upon Roosevelt and had never been able to create in Truman, had settled once again on a symbolic protector and champion. The years of tension, of dread, of frustration, and of risk had made the demand for such a symbol irresistible. Somehow they found it in "Ike." He was their man. In the familiar appellation, in the trust and affection they bestowed upon him, there was release from all the besettings of the atomic years.

Those intellectuals, skeptics, and realists who had followed Stevenson and had seen in him possibly the most excellence they had ever seen in a presidential candidate were numbered in the millions. They gave him a loyalty they had never given to Truman and hardly even to Roosevelt. But they were far outnumbered by those who felt in the Eisenhower familiarity with God a reassurance that complex things were simple. The General's unintellectual faith in principle, his very vagueness about every difficult matter, furnished a kind of relief, an escape from intolerable decision. To the Stevenson sort, this escape seemed tragic, a betrayal of people's best instincts and besides a dangerous trusting to ignorance and fumbling. The new President showed no comprehension of his responsibilities; he repeated the old folly of neophytes in the White House about "co-operation with the Congress," which meant, if it meant anything, complete irresponsibility in the formulation of policy and the frank abandonment of leadership. Yet there was no doubt that, in spite of everything, "the legend" was growing and would continue to grow without consideration of competence. The American people had found a champion and would not let him go.

General Dwight D. Eisenhower, the new President, was the product of an Army career and came to public notice as commander of the Allied expeditionary force which defeated the Axis powers. He had been selected for this duty by General Marshall and President Roosevelt. His public reputation was owed to their support, and the victory of the forces he commanded was owed, not to his talents, but to the productivity of Western industry, a skill in organization which was characteristic of Western culture, and the inevitable cracking of the brittle German machine under Hitler's insane direction. General Eisenhower had presided over the victory, however, and so had attained the place in public regard such military chieftains often achieve—Grant, for instance, after the Civil War. He had said once that soldiers ought to keep out of civilian affairs. This had been in 1948, when even Democrats were tempted to cash in on his notoriety. In 1952, when it appeared likely that he could be elected as a Republican, he had a change of mind. He not only consented to run; he fought strenuously for the privilege.

His nomination over the dead bodies of old-time party regulars who had supported Senator Taft left wounds. These regulars were the worst threat to the ticket. They might just not have got down to the necessary hard work of getting contributions and getting out the vote. In this matter the General showed such eagerness that there were many who felt that he had badly overdone it. To close the breach, he blandly accepted Taft's rather harsh terms. It was called a sellout, and the scorn implied must have smarted, If it did, the General did not show it. He exhibited even greater tolerances. For such senatorial candidates as Jenner in Indiana and McCarthy in Wisconsin—to mention only two of a representative breed—he displayed a public approval that his conscience must have questioned; and to win something in the solid South—as it appeared he might well do—he accepted the worst compromise of all: He promised support for a tidelands oil bill, several times vetoed by Truman, rejected by Stevenson, and denounced as outrageous by conservationists. It was worth billions to the oil interests. They bought their privilege cheaply. When the bill was passed, even the most conservative newspapers wondered aloud whether the principle might not result in the giving away of many more resources won in the long struggle for conservation—the range lands, the forests, the water-power sites, and the minerals. The Republican President seemed eager to divest the public of its riches for the benefit of predatory interests: shades of Theodore Roosevelt! The gains of fifty years seemed to be lost. The conservationists were appalled.[6]

General Eisenhower's had been a strange victory. Throughout his campaign, however pressed by the intelligent Stevenson, he had refused to grapple with any issue more realistic than sin, atheism, communism, bungling, bureaucracy, and public corruption. He was against all of them. By implication, the Democrats favored all of them; and, in fact, many voters thought so too. These voters and the Eisenhower hero-worshipers turned out to be a majority. Aside from the Republican regulars, this majority proved, on analysis, to be made up of the younger members of the electorate and the women. The younger people were by now a generation without any recollection of depression or of the kind of predepression conditions which had precipitated the debacle of 1929. They could give way to their annoyance with the Democrats without any worry about reversion to the Republicanism of Harding, Coolidge, and Hoover. There was very general approval of the outrageous demagoguery involved in Eisenhower's saying in the western country, which had so benefited for three decades from federal enterprise, that he intended to see to it that the long nose of the federal government was kept out of the people's business. The housewives blamed Democrats at once for the high cost of living and for the bureaucracy which might have

6. For an interesting account of the Republicans' "give-away" policy and its implications, the article by W. M. Blair in the *New York Times* ("News of the Week in Review"), May 3, 1953, might be consulted. Mr. Blair reported the conservationists' consternation. Involved, he said, were water-power sites, grazing lands, mineral rights, and timber. He could point, already, to bills "liberalizing" grazing rights, turning over forest lands to the states, etc., which had been introduced in one or the other House. Official policy, as defined by the new Secretary of the Interior, Douglas McKay, gave some reason to believe that further gifts would be made even if with some caution. He spoke, for instance, in the field of water power, of public and private interests "moving along together." This meant, the conservationists were sure, that everything would be given away that could be without creating too big a row. They intended to furnish the row and to keep all the resources they could in federal ownership.

checked it except for Republican emasculations; and Eisenhower accepted and confounded the confusion. It was good politics.

It was remarkable what Governor Stevenson did with what he had. He was a most attractive figure. He was witty, serene, wise, and candid. His speeches, more largely written by himself than those of any recent candidate, were of a quality touched only by those of the genuinely great figures in American history. Of course, he had help. It came from many sources—all progressive, but all gifted.[7] Altogether he outlined a moderate, progressive, and tolerant policy the nation would have done well to approve. But the Republicans had most of the money, most of the organs of admunication, and a monopoly of that curious large-scale genius for manufacturing phony issues and stirring up tempests about them which had been developing in American society for some time.

Mr. Stevenson, with so enlightened an approach, was vulnerable in many irritating and unnecessary ways. There had been corruption. True, it had been Democrats who had exposed it, but no one gave that kind of credit. They had allowed a vast and unusually slothful bureaucracy to grow up about the basic social services which had been the gift of the early New Deal. They had allowed cheap patriots to convey the suspicion to a basically frightened people that disloyal persons were involved even in the atomic weapons projects;

7. Speaking of Stevenson, Mr. James Reston (in the *New York Times Magazine*, November 9, 1952) said: "The idea persisted that he was writing all of his own speeches, but it wasn't true. The soaring speech in the Mormon Tabernacle—probably the noblest document of the campaign—was almost entirely the work of Herbert Agar. . . . The shrewd and moving address in Richmond was almost entirely the work of David Cohn. . . . And throughout the campaign he drew upon memoranda from probably the most brilliant stable of writers ever gathered together in a Presidential campaign: Arthur Schlesinger, Jr., Archibald MacLeish, Bernard DeVoto and Kenneth Galbraith; Robert E. Sherwood, and Judge Samuel Rosenman, formerly on the speech-writing staff of President Roosevelt; James Wechsler, editor of the *New York Post*; and David Bell and Clayton Fritchey, who headed the White House staff working in Springfield.

"General Eisenhower did not even attempt to write his own speeches or contribute much to them, even at the beginning. He relied, not on the Harvard faculty, but on the staffs of the big Eastern magazines for his scripts—Stanley High from *The Reader's Digest*, Gabriel Hauge from *Business Week*, C. D. Jackson from *Time*, and Emmett Hughes from *Life* for almost all his prepared addresses."

A completely unprecedented thing happened after the election: a collection of Stevenson's speeches became a best-seller. They were indeed an impressive statement of moderate liberalism: *Major Campaign Speeches of Adlai E. Stevenson, 1952* (New York, 1953).

the Republicans capitalized heavily on the Hiss, Fuchs, and Rosenberg cases. And the middle-income groups, who had achieved middle incomes because of Democratic policies, were annoyed at all the corollaries of their prosperity—taxes, strengthened labor unions, regulations of all sorts—and were willing to separate themselves from a generous percentage of their gains to support a Republican candidate.

Eisenhower more closely resembled the father-image desired by a majority of Americans than any other public person. He represented victory, success, the overcoming of troubles. He promised security—at low cost; he promised that the restraints and limitations of mobilization would be eased; he promised little government with large results. It was cheering to have a man of experience in organization say that government was swollen and could be reduced, that the budget could be cut and taxes lowered. But especially it was good to hear that the tasks ahead for the United States were not solely characterized by sacrifice, and restraint, and danger; and it was cheering to hear from a military man that security had become too costly, that our Allies were shirking, and that we need no longer carry the whole burden of Western defense.

The entire campaign of the General, who had until May been directing the forced cohesion of western Europe and the shaping of its army, was based on this kind of appeal. Mostly he emphasized freeing the domestic economy, abolishing controls, returning to stability. He appealed for the return of the conditions everyone wants—until the results are apparent. As one old trade-unionist said to me: "My damn-fool boy don't remember the depression. He's always had a job. He thinks a balanced budget will bring paradise. He don't like his taxes. Steak costs too much, his wife says—even if they have it every day. Nothing I can say convinces him. I guess we have to go through it all again. I hope I die first."

There were not enough old unionists, enough farmers who remembered six-cent cotton and thirty-cent wheat. Stevenson talked sense; he appealed to people's intelligences and to their consciences. He warned the electorate that Republican policy had not changed. It meant weak government but strong business; and strong business would create the anarchy out of which depression comes as destruction from a storm. Republicans would weaken the securities built into social life. They would value sound dollars above sound people. But they were, he said, making utterly reckless promises. They could not stop the expansion of communism at lower rates. Such an undertaking was a costly business, and they would have to do it precisely as it had been being done. What they could and would do would be to turn over governmental functions to private business, to rifle the nation's riches for the benefit of a few. These Republicans had learned nothing. They never would. And, when they had brought on another debacle, the repair work would be enormously expensive.

Nearly twenty-seven million Americans voted for Stevenson, but more than thirty-three millions—many with an apologetic air— voted for the symbol of retreat to safety, for the leader who had no doubts. Stevenson's vote was greater than any Democrat had ever had before, except Roosevelt in 1936 and 1940. It was far more than any Republican had ever had until 1952. Perhaps it was more than any *Republican* had had even now, for Eisenhower had run far ahead of his ticket. The party had a bare control of the two houses of the Congress—so slim a control that the traditional biennial falling-off might well erase the majority. There was a good prospect that presently Eisenhower and the southern reactionary Democrats would be, in effect, governing the nation.

When the campaign was over, the estimates of its costs reached fantastic amounts. Mr. James Reston estimated eighty-two million dollars.[8] Mr. Reston thought this too large a sum; and theoretically everyone agreed. They also agreed, however, that nothing was likely to be done. For money had won an election and a position of dominance. Its advantage was unlikely to be given up.

Salesmanship and money had played a vital role in electing Eisenhower, and they were well represented in his Administration. When Stevenson looked over Eisenhower's Cabinet list, he offered a characteristic comment: "The President," he said, "has substituted cardealers for New Dealers." Not only the Cabinet, but all the thousand or so top policy-makers, and the ten thousand or so makers of plans, composers of memorandums, liaison men, and advisers, all were businessmen or businessmen's sychophants, many of them automobile executives and publicity men. It did not look like a crowd which would betray the national interest for a mink coat or a refrigerator,

8. *New York Times Magazine,* November 9, 1952.

as some of Truman's little men had done; but anyone who thought protection of the public domain, benefits for workers or farmers, or provision against depression would be any part of their concern was more innocent than any of the Washington commentators, even those who worked for the most reactionary publishers. They could not conceal their deep concern for the national honor.

This revulsion was not, however, felt by the people—at least not by many of them. Steady giving-in to the demands of the rapacious lobbies, whose representatives had been hanging about Washington corridors for years waiting for this opportunity, seemed to be a way to people's hearts. There was ample evidence from the familiar polls that the new President was rapidly gaining more public approval. Even while the tidelands bill was being fought over in the Senate, and the White House was waiting benevolently to make it finally into law, the index of approval rose. It rose, also, as the President and Secretary of the Treasury Humphrey discovered that all the campaign about economy, reduced budgets, tax relief, and an honest dollar was the product of sheer ignorance and must be repudiated. All the withdrawals, the taking-backs, the face-savings, so fearfully undertaken by those newly responsible for national affairs, did not in the least diminish public affection for the President.

This rise of popularity in spite of compromise, refusal to give leadership, and withdrawal from responsibility—which were certainly the most marked character of the Eisenhower presidency up to Hiroshima Day in 1953—raised some real questions about democracy. It was quite clear that thirty-three million voters could be wrong about their own interest. They could persist in being wrong. They could refuse to make any connection between qualification and responsibility; they could reject the plainest evidence of incompetence. It was no wonder that the cynical view, secretly held by so many professional politicians about majorities and elections, should have spread even more widely.

The Stevenson followers watched with an amazement which gradually turned to cynicism. Only Mr. Stevenson himself kept his sense of humor and his faith that presently the tide would turn toward reason. He departed on a six-month exploratory tour of the East. He was heard of from time to time, doing something wherever he went to restore an American credit which had been about exhausted. Perhaps when he returned American fatuousness might wither a bit in the heat of his wit. Meanwhile the Eisenhower sun rose and shone, bright and beneficent on a confused Republic.

There seemed in Washington in the first months of 1953 to be no President at all, except as a kind of empty symbol to be adjured daily by the press to come to life and take control. It was only after several fatal months that there began to be signs of life in the White House. By then, the President had to cope with well-intrenched opposition within his own party in the Congress. Chairman Daniel Reed of the House Ways and Means Committee, for instance, stood pat for tax reductions, despite the foolhardiness of such a policy in the face of defense expenditures. The bill extending the excess-profits tax for six months (which would at best reduce the anticipated deficit for fiscal year 1954 to some five and a half billion dollars) finally passed only after the President had demonstrated his prestige by "going to the country," late and with reluctance.

In the Senate, presidential difficulties were even worse. Senator Taft, honestly anxious for Republican success, did his best to collaborate with the Eisenhower people, but he had serious reservations about foreign affairs. It seemed to him and his followers that the country was attempting the impossible in both East and West. The burden of such allies as France was heavy; it was also useless. France could not support the war in Indochina; but she would not give it up. She maneuvered to shift its burden to the United States, yet refused to compromise on the issue of independence. She even reduced expenditures for defense in mainland France in the belief that the United States would shoulder them. Britain, moreover, was preoccupied with the Commonwealth, and Italy was paralyzed by political conflict. It was clear that no time could be bought by support of such pusillanimous partners. In the East, furthermore, the policy, unaltered since Truman's Administration, and less skilfully pursued, was resulting in the sinkhole of expenditures—not to mention the loss of life—which the Senator had forecast.

Ultimately Taft made his opposition formal. On May 26 in Cincinnati, his son Robert A. Taft, Jr., read a speech for his father, who was in the hospital with a mysterious illness:

I think we might as well forget the United Nations as far as the Korean war is concerned. . . . We should do our best now to negotiate this truce, and if we fail, then let England and our other Allies know that we are withdrawing from all further peace negotiations. . . . I believe we might as well abandon any idea of working with the UN in the East and reserve to ourselves a completely free hand.[9]

And on Europe:

I have always been a skeptic on the military practicability of NATO. . . . [I have never understood how] United States troops could effectively defend Europe. . . . That defense must be undertaken by those who occupy Western Europe.[10]

In spite of the President's sacrifices for the sake of harmony[11] the split among the Republicans had now forced its way to the surface. It caused a good deal of consternation, especially among the Western Allies. Their awareness of the divergence had undoubtedly been responsible for their reluctance to ratify the Bonn Conventions as well as for the slowdown in all the NATO developments; but now reluctance became paralysis. They felt a renewed concern, furthermore, about the continuance of the Mutual Aid program. Would the isolationists kill it off entirely? Or would the President use his latent but undoubted power and insist on its preservation? As time went on, he still confined himself to the soft and indirect "lectures" of the press conference. Compromise ate deeply into the policies opposed by the isolationists; but battle on the Roosevelt or Truman scale he refused.

Presently tragedy intervened. Senator Taft's disease was recognized to have incapacitated him indefinitely. He passed the Senate leadership to a younger man, Knowland, the Californian, often referred to as "the senator from Formosa." The President would be far less well served now; his problem had become doubly difficult. It was an opportunity for the Democrats. With tongue in cheek they represented themselves, in issue after issue, as "the President's friends," supporting him when the isolationists of his own party were castigating his policy as "copying the Truman-Acheson appeasement." It really was Democratic policy, the Democrats said, and they were glad that it was recognized to be so.

9. *New York Times*, May 31, 1953.   10. *Ibid.*

11. It was obvious that he thought compromise as necessary to presidential method as it had been to that of a supreme commander. Contrasting and divergent personalities and groups had to be molded into an army.

The President had other troubles. McCarthyism flourished in the climate of conciliation until it threatened to exclude all other blooms from the governmental garden. The senator from Wisconsin was riding a wave. He competed for linage and place with the President himself and on equal terms. He had now succeeded to the chairmanship of the Senate Committee on Government Operations (the parent-committee for investigations) and had assumed the chairmanship of a subcommittee which had by August 6 got more publicity, perhaps, than any such group in history. His versatility was amazing. He ranged over the whole of American social life and stabbed everywhere at government operations. He had an unequaled facility for finding spots which yielded the greatest returns. His sense of timing was excellent. He always had a reserve of sensations useful for smothering any attack on himself. And he made commitment without reserve, something hardly any politician is willing to do, and got away with it. He seldom produced facts, but he was never taunted with the failure. There had been others of this sort, of course—Huey Long had been the beau ideal, and there had been many lesser figures—but there had been none so effective. He was very soon—say by March of 1953—in a position of such strength that to challenge him was a major risk.

During the early months McCarthy's favorite target was the Department of State. When he had finished with it, he had wrecked "The Voice of America" and undermined the Mutual Security program (there had been an incredible to-do about some fringe trading still being done by Allied ships with Communist China). He had also made sorties—mostly of the one-shot variety—into many fields of private affairs. When the session had ended, it had to be said that investigation had become the major activity of the Congress, highly profitable politically, because the costs were so low. There were no rules which protected individuals mentioned, no attempts to be fair or just, and no yielding of allowances. In 1953 this contest in unscrupulousness reached fantastic proportions even to minds accustomed to outrage by the mounting hysteria of recent years.

The senator from Wisconsin, looming so large, resembled somehow one of those gargantuan balloon figures which are led by guide ropes every Thanksgiving Day along Broadway in New York City. Those five- and ten-story blowups, lighter than air, dance and billow down the city canyons to the delight of onlookers and to the profit of Macy's store. They are capable, however, of haunting the dreams of susceptible children, who find it somehow unreasonable that domesticated dolls should take on elephantiasis and bound irresponsibly through the November streets.

The President had allowed compromise to become an expected rule, and thus he was inflating little by little the McCarthy ambitions. Presently the Senator attempted to prevent the confirmation of the Eisenhower nominee as ambassador to Russia, Charles ("Chip") E. Bohlen. This opposition must have been something of a surprise to Mr. Bohlen, who long had been regarded by progressives as an extreme conservative, one of a typical lot in the career service, of whom they were profoundly distrustful. The Senator can hardly have considered Mr. Bohlen to be a real security risk, but he was ready by now to challenge this Republican President as he had challenged the Democratic one. His position was strengthened when the President allowed him to humiliate Mr. Harold Stassen, now Mutual Security Administrator, who was compelled to apologize to the Senator for suggesting that the subject of Allied trading with Communist China was something the Department of State's experts might handle more profitably than a congressional committee. Such successes were food to McCarthy's ballooning ambition. He felt confident, obviously, of his fanatical and obscurantist following; they might well make him President if he could undermine the Eisenhower fortress.

The President finally came to understand at least something of what was going on. The Senator had by now given up the retail harassing of movie actors, authors, schoolteachers, and so on—these were left to the amateurs, Velde and Jenner—and had emerged into the wholesale field. He was now challenging entire policy systems of the Administration and so of the President himself. Before the atomic year closed the President had obliquely met the challenge on several issues—Mr. Bohlen was finally confirmed—among which the most conspicuous were those of "book-burning" and the Communist infiltration of the Protestant ministry. McCarthy's charge that Communist writings were kept in the libraries of the Department of State abroad had led to panic, and the actual burning of books by their custodians in an excess of fear and abnegation was reported—one among unsavory incidents of a similar sort, becoming all too familiar. The President finally took a half-step. He advised the students at Dartmouth College "not to join the book-burners" but to find their knowledge where they liked. He followed this step with another when McCarthy hired Mr. J. B. Mathews as chief investigator of his subcommittee just after Mathews had accused the clergy in print of being riddled with Communists. The President assured the spokesmen of the Conference of Christian and Jews that he had no doubts about the loyalty of the American clergy. It was McCarthy's aim to make the issue one between himself and the President, and he was beginning to succeed—but only beginning; the President was a hard man to corner.

The most serious danger—and the one which really came closest to arousing the President—presented by McCarthyism was its interference with the conduct of foreign policy, its promise of imposing on the Administration all the limitations favored by the middle-western isolationists whose representative the Senator was. There was desire for peace at Panmunjom, there was rising unrest among the satellites, and in Russia there was a bitter struggle for power, following Stalin's death. All these offered opportunities. But they were the sort which only careful, patient, and determined diplomacy could enlarge. That kind of diplomacy was made impossible by McCarthy and his kind.[12] If not McCarthy, then Knowland, if not

12. There was a disconcerting analogy to be drawn between the irresponsible attacks on the American executive, which seemed in recent years to have increased in fury, and the unfocused parliamentary anger which Charles I had been utterly unable to appease. Students of government wondered sometimes, as especially angry outbursts occurred, whether there was any stopping place short of the abolition of the executive and the assumption of power by congressional oligarchs, just as in the English case. Perhaps only after such a complete victory could the possession of power be made responsible. Certainly the senators had no policy except that of destroying the President, whoever he was. They were driven by those whose creatures they were—the interests who wanted no general overriding public interest represented in so powerful a place as the presidency. For the presidency was inimical to them, even though its occupant was in theory agreeable to their claims. This only made him more vulnerable, as appeasement always does.

That this conflict was inherent in American institutions was by now evident. It was McCarthy and McCarran today; yesterday it was Borah, or Lodge, or, in Lincoln's time, Wade or Stephens or Sumner—a long roll. Today it was Eisenhower —yesterday, Roosevelt, Wilson, or Lincoln. It was the same conflict which had existed in Britain so long as the powers were separated—Parliament representing diffuse interests and the king the one interest of the people. The interests could not and would not tolerate the threat to their freedom. Then their champions were Sir

Knowland, then McCarran, or others of their group, carried their war on reason, compromise, and coexistence into successful sorties whenever any suggestion of arrangement seemed to be in the air. The American people were farther from, rather than closer to, peace year by year. They were, on the one hand, unnerved by dread of atomic attack and, on the other, driven by some irresistible compulsion to support provocations of the power from which the attack might come. The fomenting center of this American disease was the Senate. The isolationists now represented quite perfectly the boiling frustration which had seized on so many Americans. A fear and hatred they were powerless to suppress drove them to gestures and actions calculated to unleash the very forces they most dreaded.

The President, a temperate and calculating man, if neither a notably wise nor even a moderately learned one, gradually began to establish the principles of his policy. They were military principles. He figured to get the maximum effect with a minimum of expenditures. He saw that a stronger and more united Europe was worth a whole army to the West. He saw that a well-oiled and freely running United Nations, even if hopelessly susceptible to sabotage, was still vitally necessary unless all contact among competitors was to be broken off. He saw that cessation of fighting in Korea was essential if a swollen flood of spending for defense was ever to be checked. He therefore wanted generous aid to Europe (and incidentally a continuing build-up of the European army); he wanted strong support for the United Nations; and he wanted a Korean truce. Beyond these points, it was hardly possible to say what his policy did involve. Yet if the pronouncements of the President and Secretary of State Dulles were studied with some care, it was possible to think that, vis-à-vis Russia, they had at least defined the starting points for negotiation.

John Eliot and Mr. Pym, and Oliver Cromwell. They overthrew the executive even though he was a king and killed him in their fury.

There was real question what the senators would do, if their intentions were unmasked and their desires implemented, with the President. Would the executive be made, as in Britain, a committee of the Congress? If so, would the Senate be emasculated as the House of Lords had been?

The time was approaching when the latent crisis of government would be precipitated by this conflict between the Congress and the President—between those who demanded freedom for interests and those who united their interests in the Chief of State. It would be precipitated by the necessity for achieving and maintaining a policy vis-à-vis a power which might annihilate a government which could not function with the necessary freedom.

There was no reason to suppose that the intransigents, merely because they were Republicans, would allow the same policy they had been denouncing all along to proceed toward realization if they could help it. And the struggle became an open one when Senator Taft spoke in Cincinnati. Eisenhower and Dulles might propose, but the senators intended to dispose. They were warning the world that they could kill policies and that these were the kind they meant to kill.

The logic of the senatorial demand, a few commentators said, was war with Russia. No other outcome of the fulminations, projected into practice, was possible. They did not dare to say so. Yet their irresponsible forays into policy obviously had an enormous—and probably growing—support. It seemed to come especially from veterans who felt the frustrations of unwon wars and had no patience with diplomacy. That it had to be dealt with it was belatedly discovered.

On April 16 the President made an admirable speech, one that obviously had been worked over and over by all those in the White House and the Department of State who were responsible for formulating policy. It was handled in the grand manner—delivered in advance to seventy foreign governments, broadcast over and over in many languages to all the world, and followed up by a complete campaign of explanation. It came at an opportune moment. The Russian "peace offensive" after Stalin's death in March had had a successful opening. It was clearly up to the United States to make response.

The President began by putting the blame for world tension on the Soviets. He welcomed an apparent change. Then he went on to define the evidence which would prove to him that there was actually good faith behind the new tentatives: There had to be a truce in Korea (but he made no mention of Communist membership in the United Nations or of the status of Formosa); there had to be an end to the pressures on Indochina and Malaya (which neither Russia nor China had admitted to exerting); there had to be a settlement in Germany which would include unification and freedom; there had to be a conclusion to the tedious bargaining in Austria; and there had to be more "independence" for the eastern European nations—

the satellites.[13] The President then made a suggestion which he obviously hoped would prove to be the attractive alternative to the xenophobia of his party's isolationists: "As progress in all these areas strengthens world trust, we could proceed concurrently with the next great work—the reduction of the burdens of armament." He specified the reduction of armed forces, the limitation of resources used for military purposes, the international control of atomic energy and the prohibition of atomic weapons, the restriction of other weapons of "great destructiveness," and international inspection to guarantee compliance with all these agreements. He went even further and embraced the positive program adumbrated by his predecessor—which had been so maddening to the reactionaries of both parties—technical assistance to backward areas. "This Government is ready," he said, "to ask its people to join with all nations in devoting a substantial percentage of any savings achieved by real disarmament . . . to develop the undeveloped areas of the world, to stimulate profitable and fair world trade, to assist all peoples. . . ."

This program, as the atomic year ended, stood as the foreign policy of the United States. It was as good and as sufficient as it had been when Truman and Acheson had formulated and defined it. And it was no better. It left many questions unanswered; but many of those were ones which had to be unanswered because they were, and had to be, subject to negotiation. Negotiation, however, was proving as impossible for the new Administration as it had for the old.

The President obviously was up against something he did not know how to handle. He was frustrated, as his predecessor had been frustrated, in the implementation of policies which were as American as Main Street. It might be that, because what he wanted to do was thus indigenous, basically acceptable to the national conscience, he would find a way to do it. But the objectors were stubborn and well fortified. They rested on fear, suspicion, the longing for rest from responsibility; but they also relied on the peculiar toadying to demagoguery inherent in a system of large-scale admunications. Senator McCarthy had more headlines and a greater lineage in the press, his face was oftener seen on television, and his voice heard on the radio, than was true of any other American—except, doubtfully,

13. Passages concerning the satellites were obscure and were interpreted as softening former unfortunate pronouncements of Mr. Dulles about "liberation."

the face and voice of the President himself. Because of this, if for no other reason, he could dictate, at least negatively, foreign policy. He could, and did, keep discussion of coexistence from occurring.

When, in the middle of May, the *New York Times* found the President's press conference worthy of a four-column headline, it had to be equally shared with the Senator. The President was saying that he was willing to sit down with Sir Winston Churchill (as he had now become), Georgi Malenkov, and other world leaders to explore anew the possibilities of peace. But sharing the headline was McCarthy's attack on Attlee.[14]

Under the circumstances the most the President was prepared to do, actually, was to arrange for a meeting at Bermuda. Nor would he admit that this was to be preparatory to a further meeting with the Russians. Churchill had openly hoped that it would be; but the President by now had his head cramped over his shoulder, as Truman's had been cramped for years, watching for treacherous attacks from the rear. He simply did not dare undertake negotiations in which he might reasonably be expected to yield as well as to gain something. The violence of the storm in the Senate, reflected in the press, on the radio, and over the television networks at the least hint of compromise, could be anticipated. This anticipation was paralyzing Republican, as it had paralyzed Democratic, policy.

The Bermuda conference was postponed. Sir Winston had to rest; after the labors of the coronation of Elizabeth II and its corollary Commonwealth conference, he had a stroke; and anyway France's Chamber of Deputies chose this time to deprive the nation of a government for more than a month. Later, three foreign ministers— Great Britain's Lord Salisbury, France's Bidault, and the United States' Dulles—met in Washington. By then it was July, the Beria crisis was on in Russia, and the moment had obviously passed for the kind of spectacular seizure of opportunity Churchill had had in mind. Things were left to follow the distressingly downhill course of the past years.

The Russians continued to coo softly. But they rejected a suggestion that Austrian talks be resumed, and, when the Allies addressed

14. Said the *Times* (May 15, 1953) : "Speaking from the floor of the Senate, and thus with immunity from any possible action for libel or slander, Senator McCarthy called Mr. Attlee 'Comrade Attlee' and accused him of having joined Dean Acheson, the former Secretary of State, in past compromises 'with treason.' "

another note to them about German unification, making the identical suggestions so often rejected before, it was clear that the same old meaningless dance for appearances' sake had been resumed. The only exception was at Panmunjom.

Hardly ever in history had the death of a man presented the whole world with such a riddle as immediately materialized when Stalin died on March 6, 1953. In spite of long anticipation, no one seemed to have any adequate preparation for it. Such intelligence as was available to the Western public had not been informative about recent struggles for power within the ruling group in Russia. There was no clue to the effect on external relations the readjustments sure to take place might have. The whole world waited for some sign. After a few weeks it came. Beria was purged from the Presidium, and the inner volcano erupted into the Eastern skies.

The face and figure of Stalin had been for more than two decades the sign and symbol of Soviet power throughout the world. His image was clear on a billion minds to whom it stood for fatherhood; it was equally clear on another billion to whom it represented the bloated and sinister face of revolution. But, if the image was clear enough in the one and the other half of the world, what it actually stood for was understood only in the vaguest way. The Stalin myth, indeed, was a vessel which thousands of demagogues had filled with their own elixirs and sold to the particular people they had hoped to impress. The responsible statesmen of the nations were not altogether innocent of the same abuses. That Stalin moved in the shadows behind the Kremlin walls had been convenient to some of the most reputable leaders of a long generation.

What Stalin was and stood for, however, there was not much excuse for not knowing at any time after the shakedown following World War II. He was a latter-day Russian imperialist. He intended, as the great Russians had always intended, that the heartland of the world should all of it come under the administration of Moscow. The impulse to expand over a "logical" space, to have *Lebensraum*, and to make the national holdings secure was, of course, one which had dominated the minds of most imperial statesmen from Caesar to Churchill. Stalin, however, had followed the classic impulse with skill, with absolute ruthlessness, and with a single, unclouded end in view. The nervousness of his contemporaries in the West came from not understanding what the logic followed by Stalin called for. They exaggerated his aims and were in process of exhausting themselves in frantic preparation for defense against blows which Stalin would never have thought of delivering. It was not that they misunderstood imperialism—that all national politicians understood—but they had an unreasoning fear of the devices at his disposal: communism, with its drive to world conversion, and the Bomb, with its potentialities for world destruction.

Those who knew Russia and Stalin best—Mr. George Kennan, for instance, who knew Russia so well that the Soviet foreign office had seized an excuse for keeping him outside[15]—held that there was an explicable and understandable plan in the Russian mind, that it was being executed coldly and with calculation, and that no diversion would be allowed to take place. The plan called for a solid Russian core, for a surrounding area of affiliate-nations ranging outward to safe allies on all sides, and for agreement of sorts with all other countries in the world with power to attack or to put pressure on inner Russia. The first line of defense was the agreements; the second was the satellites; the third was a disciplined people; the last was a trained army. All Stalin's life had gone into the perfection of this system. He never for an instant had been diverted.

This interpretation was of course known to Churchill and to Roosevelt. It was inherited by Truman and Eisenhower, but neither seemed to understand it very well; or, if they did, they were not prepared to recognize the conditions it determined for coexistence.

As the truce ground toward its conclusion, Korea appeared more and more as an unfortunately violent outbreak in a long diplomatic conflict. It was as if two antagonists had, in a sudden unreasonable temper, come to quickly regretted blows and then had had a hard time finding ways to stop the fighting and get back to manageable argument.

It can be imagined that Stalin had from the first regretted the Korean incident. He had nodded, and it had begun. Then he had had for a long and difficult period to find ways to control the unwanted violence. Of course, it was not entirely unfortunate. It had

15. He had been declared *persona non grata* by the Kremlin after a press interview which was chosen to be interpreted as insulting.

involved the United States in a war on the Asian mainland and so had shattered the most elementary rule in the staff book. But it had supported occurrences in the West which were not to Russia's interest —the NATO build-up, an access of independence in the satellites, and a vast rearmament effort in the United States. So on the whole he must have regretted it. Once started, the war had to be accepted as a fact; but the thing to do was to liquidate it and get back to the *status quo ante*. The Chinese, feeling their revolutionary oats, might be hard to control. They were young in the common faith; but, since that faith was communism, they were amenable to a certain discipline from the seat of the mother-church.

Discipline had come to be the chief usefulness of communism in the Stalin book, for there was evidence that communism as a dynamic social force had succeeded too well—that it had threatened to become unmanageable. In recent years it seemed to have been played down. An inflated patriotism, almost like the old imperial glory, seemed to have displaced the theory of determinism and proletarian equalism. The achievements of Russia in later decades had been magnificent—economic transformation, victory in war, expansion, the adhesion of satellites in the West, the alliance with China. But it had ceased to be clear that the achievement was merely the unrolling of a predestined historical scroll as the philosophy of communism seized on men's minds. Stalin appeared to feel that he deserved the credit; he and Lenin—with Lenin a shade less prominent, and old Marx nowhere any more—were just next to deified. The Red Army came in for a lot of praise too—not surprisingly, considering its performance during the war, but still not too logically if it was only the servant of historical forces. And it should not be forgotten that Stalin was a marshal or that his party apparatus infiltrated the army's organization.

The extent to which the later members of the Presidium of the Central Committee, along with Stalin, had their tongues in cheek about communism was one of the imponderables which Western statesmen were unable to assess. It was obviously, as a fifth column, the source of an intense dread to those in Europe; and that it was not negligible even in the United States was evidenced by the success of McCarthyism. In the United States, however, the responsible statesmen of successive administrations had feared the unreasoning popular disturbances of McCarthyites more than communism itself. They knew that agitation for revolution was a negligible threat to a middle-class economy such as the whole of North America had now become, with small exceptions south of the Mexican border. What was more anxiously watched was the uncontrollable passion aroused by the suggestion of disloyalty constantly reimplanted and cleverly enlarged by the demagogues. For there did continue to be an annoying public response to the most fantastic innuendoes. It showed how vulnerable Americans believed themselves to be and to what savagery some were prepared to resort for their own protection. The less likelihood there was of revolution, the more its imagined advent alarmed the timid and excited the ignorant.

There were those who said that this was a direct result of prosperity. And it was true that the transformation of America into a high-energy, high-income society was well along. Every year's advance, at this stage, added appreciably to a national product already unprecedented in all the annals of mankind. It was so distributed also —and the New Deal could be thanked for this—that nearly one-third of the population had moved into the luxury groups, another one-third had reached well-being, and even the remaining one-third were secure in a far-from-miserable minimum. An economy of this sort was bound to feel its contrast with much of the rest of the world. Envy is so prevalent a failing among middle-class people—it seems to intensify as the reason for it attenuates—that Americans were sure the rest of the world was jealous and resentful. Some envy was reported from Western outposts in the East. In India, for instance, it seemed to be almost endemic, although Ambassador Chester Bowles had by his modest behavior and sincere sympathy succeeded in dissipating a good deal of it.[16] In China envy was an article of faith, but not under that name. There it was transformed into a whooping cult. Westerners were magnified, even beyond the Russian enlargement, into monsters—capitalist exploiters of the poor, bloody imperialists, warmongers—unfit for association with selfless and co-operative Communists. This kind of thing, reported to Americans so often and so bitterly, had worked them into a state of resent-

16. He was rewarded by dismissal, one of the less lovely trucklings of the new Administration to its chauvinists.

ment which tended to stifle their naturally generous impulses. What was the use of helping people who only abused you in return?

This was material for the merchants of hate. It helped them to incite suspicion of others and to make a policy of isolation. For-eign-aid programs, as a result, fared very badly in the new Congress. The President asked for a modest amount in the first place, but what was granted was a very nearly useless percentage of what was asked for. The Point Four work which had promised so well, and which the President himself had proposed in his foreign policy speech to enlarge, almost disappeared; and even the military aid for allies, which had now supplanted economic aid entirely, was cut about in half.

The death of Stalin, curiously enough, reinforced isolationism in the United States. It might have been supposed that because Stalin's was a known hand on the controls, and because his policy could be understood to be one of penetration but not unbearable provocation, his death might be taken as removing a restraining influence in Rus-sia, or even as precipitating further danger, since it was likely that Russia would find active quarrels with other nations necessary to smother quarrels at home. In was fact, nevertheless, that, as time went on, the President's policy of support for Europe lost ground and that isolationism gained it.[17] Even the NATO army into which Eisen-hower had poured so much energy and had seemed to believe in so sincerely promised now to be weakened by malnourishment. There were those, however, to whom this reaction seemed, even if curious, perhaps unwittingly wise. Their hopes centered in the current Rus-sian "peace offensive," whose most impressive reinforcement was the actual signing of an armistice in the Korean War on July 27, and on the dismissal of Beria from the Presidium. Beria's downfall, they argued, showed that a fierce struggle had taken place after Stalin's death; but it had been settled quickly and effectively, thus removing any necessity for concealing conflict at home by belligerence abroad.

It seemed clear, indeed, that those hard reasoners like Mr. Kennan, who had been saying all along that Russian policy was understand-able because cast in a historical tradition which had and would de-

---

17. This gain may have occurred partly because another—and not very con-sistent—part of contemporary Republicanism was a return to financial normalcy, and a balanced budget was only to be reached by reducing foreign aid and military expenditures.

termine its course, were more than justified. If Stalin's death had any effect, it was to remove an influence which tended, even if usually checked, toward the unpredictable, the whimsical, which men of power will always indulge in. The collectivity had been important even in Stalin's time. It was supreme now. This view was reinforced by the remarkable editorial statement published in *Pravda* on July 26. This document got the usual treatment in Washington; it was brushed aside. There was nevertheless a hint, in the official reaction, that its significance was understood.

Stalin was gone, the statement seemed to say, and tradition could now be administered with complete dispassion. But "there is at present a greater need than ever for the alleviation of a dogmatic approach to Marxist-Leninist theory. . . . The party demands an understanding of the creative nature of Marxist-Leninism." This, to Americans, had a familiar sound. It was what they were used to hearing about their Constitution. The governing body of dogma would not be allowed to be interpreted in such a way as to prevent the doing of what must be done. And what must be done would be determined by the "collectivity." "The normal activity of party organizations and the entire party as a whole—as taught by Lenin— is possible only under the strict observance of the collective leadership principle, which guarantees the party against unforeseen events and one-sided-ness in the adoption of decisions."

Concerning this *Pravda* statement, Mr. Harrison E. Salisbury noted:

> The principles are restated in terms almost identical with those of pronouncements . . . spoken over Stalin's bier by Georgi M. Malenkov and Vyacheslav M. Molotov. Mr. Malenkov's words are repeated at several points without formal attribution. His criticism of dogmatism . . . in the approach to Marxist-Leninist theory, which is described as "not dogma but leadership in action," is also quoted without attribution.[18]

Evidently the Presidium was now "a collectivity"; it renounced personal dictatorship; it declared against the dogma which would prevent practical action.

As to this practical action, there were two sufficiently clear passages; one on foreign policy, and one on domestic matters. That on domestic matters said:

18. *New York Times* of July 27, 1953. The excerpts quoted here from *Pravda* were printed in the same issue of the *Times*.

In internal policy the party considers one of its most important tasks is to go on showing untiring concern for the maximum satisfaction of the constantly rising demands of the Soviet people. On the basis of the expansion of the national economy, the standard of living of workers of the socialist community will steadily rise, while their material and cultural demands will be met with increasing abundance and on a wider range.

This, to American ears, had a familiar ring too. With the change of no more than a word or two, it could be mistaken for a plank in any of the recent party platforms. In Russia its significance was that it promised the end of sacrifice in the interest of the future. During all the years since 1928, when the first five-year plan had begun, consumers had been asked to defer their demands. Resources and effort had gone into building heavy industry, to laying the "broad base" which would make greater consumption possible at a later time. Now there was to be an end of waiting.

For outsiders, the significance of this unequivocal declaration was that it was inconsistent with war. Vivid recollections of the interventions following World War I had made the army important in the 1920's. Military preparation against the possible aggression of Hitler, Mussolini, or even a "capitalist" army had been vital in the 1930's. While these threats existed, it was possible to argue reasonably for austerity in the interest of basic strength or even of military production. But even Russians, in the course of two-and-a-half decades of abstinence, could tire of it. Obviously now there was a demand for the fruits of that productive machine for which so much sacrifice had been made. Some appeasement was necessary; and it meant turning from military to peacetime production.

The declarations in the same *Pravda* statement concerning foreign policy were consistent with this domestic intention:

In foreign policy the main concern of the Communist party goes to insuring the peaceful toil of the Soviet people, to maintaining peace and preventing a new war. The party holds that the policy of peace is the only right one, being in conformity with the vital interests of the Soviet people and all other peace-loving nations. In all its foreign policy our party bases itself on Lenin's directives on the possibility of a lasting coexistence and peaceful competition of two systems—socialism and capitalism. . . . In foreign policy the party will continue the policy of safeguarding and stabilizing peace, of collaborating with all countries and developing businesslike relations with them on the principles of the observance of mutual interests. Only a stable and lasting peace between peoples creates the essential conditions for the further constant developments of socialist economy, for insuring a happy and abundant life of the workers of our country.

This series of clear defining statements may have seemed unimportant to the Department of State, but British observers saw its significance. They had, in fact, anticipated it with remarkable accuracy even before the downfall of Beria. The *Times* (London) had said on June 18, for instance:

> There is as yet no overt sign of departure from Stalin's fundamental policies. . . . Yet there is beyond all doubt a departure from many of his practices and tactics. There is a revulsion against the autocratic rule that characterized him, against the bleakness and harshness of a regime that stifled initiative within the Soviet Union, and against the rigidities and dangers of a foreign policy that aroused a free world to stand in arms against the Soviet Union. It is as if the new leaders of Russia proclaimed that, much as Russia owes to Stalin, he became too set in his ways, too suspicious, too heavy-handed. . . . Hardly a day passes without the Soviet newspapers declaring that no single man but the party—or a committee within the party —are supreme. No attempt is made to proclaim Mr. Malenkov as the sole inheritor of Stalin's mantle; and though the memory of Stalin is praised from time to time there is none of the old fulsome adulation. . . . A recent writer in *Pravda*, almost in tones of apology, admitted that individual leadership might be necessary in time of war but at other times "collectivity" must be respected as "the highest principle of party leadership. . . ."

It was undoubtedly the same perception, spreading through a Europe sensitive to changes in atmosphere, more realistic and less wedded to dogma than Americans, which was responsible for the growing resistance to forced-draft military preparations. They slowed down even more than in 1952. It was even harder now to convince Europeans that the Russian menace was as real as the Americans insisted, and it was not made easier by reductions in the funds for assistance. Even General Gruenther, appearing before congressional committees, could not stem the retreat. It was possible, he said, repeating a familiar thesis, to prevent the looming war by keeping on with the build-up. At one point in his testimony he cried: "We are going to stop this war from ever starting." At another time he said, "I do not think this war is ever going to come."[19]

It may have been that both sides in the potential war judged that the time for negotiation had come. The Americans had a certain deterrent power. They must by now have been realistic enough to

19. *New York Times*, July 26, 1953. The testimony quoted was from a heavily censored release of Senate proceedings on July 18.

conclude that this was all they could expect to have—that is to say, the "position of strength" which Mr. Acheson had talked about would not become such an overwhelming one that negotiation could be forced and terms imposed. Yet current statesmen were as remiss as their predecessors had been in making preparations for give-and-take negotiation. If anything, American opinion had hardened, and bargaining which involved any sacrifice of American interests would be very difficult indeed. The first proof promised to come almost at once following the truce at Panmunjom, for there a political conference had been promised within ninety days. It may well have been prophetic that, on the same day that the *New York Times* announced the first falling-back of troops, an editorial column by Mr. Arthur Krock dwelt fearsomely on the horrors of the war that might follow the failure of the negotiators to reach a peace.

The truce was signed for the Communists by a Korean general and a general of the Chinese Volunteer Army; but everyone saw behind these persons the whole of the Communist empire. One question which hung fatefully in the air was whether that contiguous half-world had achieved, as a whole, the "collectivity" the Russians spoke of for themselves.[20] If they had, the political meeting following Panmunjom would be a fateful one indeed and had better be approached in a more co-operative mood than the controlling body of American opinion seemed to have assumed.

As Americans looked back over the three years of intervention in Korea and the two years of negotiation for a cease-fire, their expressed sentiment was mostly one of relief. The "little war" was over, and they could breathe again; for, so long as it was going on, they had been at a stretch of apprehension for fear it might spread. Why it had not been extended and become a world war no one yet could say. There had been repeated opportunities, and even a good

20. So far as was known there was no formal policy-making body on which both Russian and Chinese Communists were represented. But perhaps the perception of some such development had been prevented by the strong hope in the West that differences between the Chinese and the Russians would appear and could be enlarged. If the Russians and Chinese, on the contrary, were developing a joint "collectivity," its immense significance was apparent. And, since its development was so clearly indicated as a matter of strategy, it would be stranger if it was not happening than if it was.

In an anticipatory discussion, Mr. A. J. Muste in *The Progressive* for June, 1953, argued that such a collectivity was very likely.

deal of loose threatening talk—mostly from the Chinese propagandists on the one side and from senators in the United States on the other. The Chinese, as they had sought to convict the United Nations command of using germ warfare and so of being moral outlaws, had been peculiarly stupid and provocative. This psychological sortie had had a formidable mounting and had been pursued *ad nauseum* without any noticeable effect. But the irresponsible frequent bursting-out of United States senators had gone some way toward supporting the enemy propaganda. The senators were savage. They wanted China, or at least Manchuria, invaded or bombed; they wanted an expeditionary force from Formosa supported; they wanted the atom bomb used on the enemy. Germ warfare did not seem alien to their mood.

Many other Americans had said, during the two years of negotiation, "Thank God for the generals." They referred mostly to General Bradley, chairman of the Joint Chiefs of Staff, that wise, serene, and stubbornly honest man, who was just now ending his service. During the whole incident he had stood between the shouters for action and the policy-makers, wringing from reluctant statesmen adherence to what now could be seen was the only possible policy. Following the advice of MacArthur and his fellow-thinkers it could be seen, even at this short distance, would have been fatal. The United States would have been embroiled for a generation on the continent of Asia with no gain in the end; or she would have used the atomic weapon in a desperate attempt at conclusion and have thus precipitated open world conflict. The end of this no man dared contemplate any more since the H-bomb had become a reality. Indeed, as General Bradley saw so clearly, MacArthurism rested on a concept of military victory as obsolete as the mastodon. There had not been a paying military victory since before the American Civil War. It was demonstrable that negotiation, before every one of them, however much sacrifice might have been called for, would have been, on balance, more favorable to the national interest than the results of victory. Even in the worst case, that of Hitler, it was doubtful whether he might not have been checked by negotiation. It was fashionable now to say that war with the dictators had been inevitable; and perhaps it had. But the costs had been terrific and were still mounting. General Bradley and the others who stuck to negotiation, even with the endlessly irritating Chinese Communists, had in mind not only the costs of the little war but the prospect of evading the large one. They deserved well of their people.

Time and the Germans might have taken care of Hitler. Time had taken care of Stalin; and it appeared that the "collectivity" succeeding him might be easier to negotiate with because it would be guided by understood principles from which there would be no deviation. Those principles might allow enough flexibility for the world accommodation which the *Pravda* statement had said was to be itself a leading principle.

Whether the Soviet flexibility would be sufficient depended more largely on Western flexibility than was generally recognized. Diplomats must make the bargain, and in circumstances in which a vast population on either side waits anxiously to hear the terms the difficulties are immense. For each side has somewhere in its social consciousness a limit to concession beyond which negotiators cannot go. Yet the negotiators have few guides to this tolerance. They are therefore apt to be more unyielding than their reason dictates, lest they be repudiated.

The effect on diplomatic proceedings of demagogues, of political quacks, of the self-interested, of the fanatics, of the xenophobes, is—in a modern democracy, especially—sure to be considerable. It was the special quality of General Bradley that, in his homely way, he could absorb such ugly abuse and keep talk with the enemy going. It was tragic that in the forthcoming peace conference his courage and wisdom would be lacking. That conference would be conducted, on the United Nations side, by John Foster Dulles, whose capacity for either courage or wisdom was, on the record, fairly limited. It was to be feared that the voice of the demagogue would be loud in the land and that the "toughness" of American bargainers might threaten the whole procedure.

At the time of the truce there had still been almost no discussion in the United States of possible peace terms. There had been very little, indeed, in other countries. Discussion, as a matter of fact, had been limited pretty much to periodic warnings from the China lobby that the Communists must not be substituted for the Formosan Nationalists as members of the United Nations. Since this was certainly the first and most harmless of the demands to be made, the firmness with which Dulles and Eisenhower repudiated any such intention was not a hopeful sign. Actually, as was now and again obscure-ly pointed out, it would be advantageous to have the Chinese Communists in the United Nations. Up to now the Russians had been their representatives, a situation which encouraged consolidation. Yet the lobbyists pictured the displacement of Chiang Kai-shek from his absurd position as a base betrayal; and the Administration seemed to assent. This gross sacrifice of the national interest for a tenuous private one actually threatened to stifle any chance for peace in the coming talks.

As for the other probable subjects for discussion, they had hardly been listed. Korean unification had been forced on public attention by President Rhee's curious conduct in the last days of truce negotiation. Until then this issue had been lost sight of in the year-long controversy as to whether repatriation of prisoners should be voluntary. The Allies were taken by surprise when Rhee began to denounce the almost-completed agreement. He was not satisfied with leaving Korean unification to a political conference. He wanted North Korea conquered and held by his government before negotiations began. In the last days of the war he gave the Allies more worry than did the enemy. He was conciliated by various promises, among them generous rehabilitation funds and an agreement that the United States would abandon the peace conference if it turned out to be sham.

This was a strange and doubtful commitment. Even the loosest interpretation of sham would have ended the negotiations, just concluded, for a cease-fire; yet in the end it had been won. The way to it had been a daily test of patience, but the military men had finally agreed, in spite of irritations, because it was to the interest of their principals to agree. It was grossly untrue to say that Americans had been outtraded, or to say that, because the South Koreans were dissatisfied, the agreement was a failure. There had been a time—in the fall of 1950 before the invasion of North Korea had brought in the Chinese—when the war might have been ended with less loss of face. If a joint-control plan for both North and South Korea had been offered then, and if the Chinese had been admitted to the United Nations, the worst of the struggle might have been prevented. Now, almost three years later, the cease-fire line was about where the battle line had been then; there had been three years of war for nothing. Its costs made the concessions necessary for a truce far less acceptable to the American public than they might have been earlier. And the forthcoming approach to peace would have to take place in an atmosphere much less favorable to a settlement.

The upcoming political conference would be confronted with all the issues latent in the attainment of a coexistence in the East. Some of them might be excluded from discussion. The Americans were anxious to keep the issues confined; and, since the cease-fire was a halt in the Korean War, the explicit terms of reference mentioned in the truce document were in fact narrow. But the meeting was to "settle through negotiation the question of the withdrawal of all foreign forces from Korea, the peaceful settlement of the Korean question, etc."; and, since "peaceful settlement of the Korean question" involved the attitudes and behavior of the world's great powers, the "etc." would be likely to require the demarcation of spheres of interest throughout the East. China would demand that when foreign troops left Korea they should move farther away than Japan, Okinawa, and Formosa, whence they could threaten the Manchurian industrial center. She would request trade with Japan, pressing the reciprocal advantages to both. The Western negotiators would indicate their belief that the wars in Indochina and Malaya were part of the same disturbance that war in Korea had been part of; they would want to know that the Chinese armies were not going to be transferred to these points when they left Korea. Pressure to admit the Chinese to the United Nations would be very great, especially since the negotiations themselves would, in a sense, constitute recognition.

On none of these questions had the American public—or the Allied public, for that matter—been prepared except by the specious China-lobby arguments, so unaccountably enlarged and reinforced by the slick-paper press. If the Eisenhower representatives were to make any concessions at all, as, of course, they would have to do, public acceptance would have to be argued for as the negotiations proceeded. This procedure had been difficult enough in the Panmunjom meetings. Adjournments there had been not so much for lack of agreement as to discover what the tolerances were within which the negotiators operated. This kind of uncertainty would be many times worse in the political conference. The Panmunjom agreement had required two years. The political agreement might well require far longer; it might, indeed, run on into the years after another presidential election. If it lasted so long, the credit generally felt to be due the Eisenhower Administration for the truce—very great credit, in spite of inexcusable blundering—would be dissipated in the controversies over the peace.

The Republicans had gained something from the Korean promises of 1952—it had then been "Truman's war." They figured the truce an asset for the congressional elections of 1954; but the peace might turn out quite otherwise for 1956. By then, unless the negotiations had been abandoned, they would have become the center of controversies almost unprecedented in their bitterness. It would be to the Administration's advantage to get them over quickly, and they could be got over quickly only by withdrawal in a high storm of patriotic indignation and abuse of the enemy. It would require a devotion to peace and a high-minded party selflessness to avoid some such issue. And the Republicans were not credited generally with any such virtues.

The prospect, in spite of the truce, was not a favorable one for peace. But assuming that pessimists about Republican abnegation were wrong, and that time and the necessary long debate would be suffered, there were reasons for thinking that agreement could be reached. The advantages to both sides were obvious. It only required that negotiators should represent their own nations' plain interests. True, the way of negotiation between equals, or at least between sides resolved not to appeal to force, is hard—how hard had been seen even in the relatively minor dealings at Panmunjom. But, however hard, it was now the only way open. The Korean War had ended where it had begun. Another would be likely to do the same. It would not pay.

The end had come at Panmunjom, in all probability, because the Chinese saw that, unless they stopped dissipating their energies in Korea, they could not fulfil their commitments to transform their economy. When the truce was reached, they at once began a conspicuous to-do about their first five-year plan. Perhaps the need to go on with this would be the best guaranty that something would come of the peace conference. They might give a good deal for peace just at the moment. If this was so, the West had an opportunity it ought not to miss.

Wars ended in stalemate now because neither side dared use the weapons which might end them in victory. This lesson was learned from Korea; and it would be true, henceforth, of every war except the final one. And of that one everyone now said it would end in worse defeat for the victor than for the vanquished; the victor would have to repair the damage and succor the victims. One man who had said this urgently and insistently in other years had been Mr. Leo Szilard, chief author of that memorandum, just before Hiroshima in 1945, which had been intended to prevent the use of the first A-bomb. It was perhaps a measure of the corrosion of Americans' minds and the corruption of their hearts that his voice was no longer heard. He, along with Mr. Harold Urey, and many others, had gone in pursuit of other enterprises. His moral sensitivity was unwelcome.

The compulsion to bury the Bomb somewhere below the level of consciousness afflicted nearly all Americans; even those engaged, in one way or another, in the bomb-making enterprises seemed almost to work in a kind of coma. It would not bear thinking about. As a social phenomenon this was nothing new. It had been this way ever since Hiroshima, except that now the neurosis had grown much worse. A whole people now began to seem quite capable of sleep-walking to disaster. Since the undertaking to manufacture the H-bomb in January, 1950, the democracy had suspended its decision-making processes; its moral sensibilities were numbed; and progress toward fatality was accepted, much as a man accepts progress through life toward death. Death must come to all men; so the H-bomb was part of a future toward which humanity moved inexorably.

There were stirrings of conscience, signs of resistance, mention of alternatives, even suggestions for defense. They seemed to begin, then always to wither away. No one paid attention in the prevailing heavy lethargic atmosphere. Once in a while a raucous shout disturbed the viscous air. It died away as the ripples disappear when a stone is thrown into a pond. The stone sinks to the bottom, the water lies above it, and no hint remains of any disturbance.

On November 11—historic date in Western annals—the Atomic Energy Commission issued a release which said of still another Eniwetok test that it "included experiments contributing to thermonuclear weapons research." Some few correspondents thought this form of words reminiscent; and, sure enough, they found, when they looked it up, that exactly the same words had announced the tests at Eniwetok in May, 1951. These two identical sentences were literally all that the American public had heard from official sources since President Truman's announcement in January, 1950, that he had "directed the Atomic Energy Commission to continue to work on all forms of atomic weapons, including the super-bomb."

"I have directed. . . ." A decision had been made, a democratic decision, in the sense that his people had delegated to Harry Truman the power to make it; not a democratic decision, however, in any real sense of wide, much less majority, consent, either active or passive. This is not a criticism of what was done or the way it was done by Mr. Truman. It is a criticism of the pretense that there had been participation. There had been none. Besides being frightened into coma, the sovereign people had had no material for judgment and no machinery for referendums if they had had the material. Other representatives of theirs had decided when they had passed the Atomic Energy Act that nuclear knowledge should be secret. Keeping information from Russia was more important than making it available for democratic decision. This was partly—but only partly—the hysterical reaction of profoundly ignorant men, politicians faced with the mysterious product of the intelligence they feared and hated. They would doubtless have suppressed all intellectualism if they could; but this was one bit of it, at least, which could be stamped into the ground out of which it had come. The other influence, out of which they acted, was that genuine distrust of democratic processes which is so characteristic of the politicians. This is natural. These processes are ones they have found that they can manipulate with ease. If they can manipulate them, there can be nothing very valid about their results. Why not admit the truth— and professional politicians are nothing if not realists—decisions in a democracy are made by demagogues and worth as much as demagogues' decisions ought to be worth. Why all this mystic talk about validity? If a really good and useful decision is to be made, it ought to be made by a businessman or a general. These are the stable and trusted persons of our society.

So the atomic weapons were to go on being developed as a result of decisions taken by the powerful few in and around the White House with whom the President consulted. And the excuse—but not the reason—for thus limiting the decision was that, if there should be release of information and open discussion, the Russians would overhear. That this was nonsense, everyone knew who knew anything at all about it. But there was a conspiracy to pretend that it was so. It was a conspiracy to which "the public" in its temporary paralysis did not seem to object. At least there was no outcry.

I have remarked before on the political naïveté of the atomic scientists. Not being politicians, and not even understanding the methods of politicians, even when they were observably at work, scientists were still capable of exhibiting indignation. So far as they were concerned, such words and phrases as "democracy" and "sovereignty of the people" were still filled with their original, sacred, and exciting content. They meant what they seemed to mean. It followed that in this instance, about which they knew, the scientists were indignant with that righteous indignation only the pure and unsophisticated can find in their hearts. They knew, and insisted on saying, that secrecy was nonsense and that it was being used as a cover for preventing democratic processes from working.

If to a sophisticated observer, the picture was one of sheep rushing toward a precipice led by a few terrified old rams, and if the same picture was apparent to the scientists, the difference was that the scientists occasionally broke out, even if the original breakers-out, Szilard, Urey, and their company, had retreated, bruised and wary, from the fray. There was, for instance, an indignant article in the *Bulletin of the Atomic Scientists*, the burden of which was that the scientists' forecasts had now come true but that the corollary precautionary measures had not been taken by responsible officials.[21] There was some satisfaction taken in the comparing to be made between the discretion of the scientists and the indiscretions of others in past years. If secrets had escaped, it was by way of official "leaks." But the basic fact was that *any* scientist in *any* country could have

21. "The 'Hydrogen Bomb' Story," *Bulletin of the Atomic Scientists*, December, 1952, pp. 297 ff.

deduced the H-bomb's existence; and the only purpose served by secrecy had been to prevent and confuse the discussions concerning policy which ought to have been by now at their height. The bland obfuscation of the AEC announcements actually had done no more than keep the lid on a furiously boiling pot. No scientist anywhere in the world was fooled, and certainly not Russian ones. But what the editors wanted to get to was the urgent necessity for official disclosure which would permit democratic processes to function.

The influence of the advent of these weapons on the course of political and military history is a subject that was anxiously discussed in 1950. It is time to renew this discussion—even though the general reaction to the long anticipated event has been one of exhilaration about a new American "first," and complacent hope that now, finally, we have reached an extreme in terror weapons that will serve as effective deterrent to anybody intent on starting a war.

If there was the "exhilaration" noted by the *Bulletin,* it was a rather strange afflatus. The considerable number of comments which I took pains to gather and analyze did not seem to me to exhibit nearly the congratulatory fervor I had expected. Most of them, in fact, took an extremely dubious view of such a weapon's use. Typical of most of the newspapers, omitting the more ebullient chauvinist sheets, were comments in the nation's two largest cities, presumably the ranking targets for enemy attack. The *Chicago Sun-Times* said (on November 18, 1952):

The overwhelming majority of Americans, whether they like it or not, calmly and soberly accept the fact that we have no alternative to survival except as a leader of the free world forces rallying against an implacable Communist enemy.

It is possible—and most probable—that we are viewing the development of the H-bomb with the same soberness and calmness. As horrifying as the new weapon may be, its development was inevitable. It was in our own enlightened self-interest that we were the first to devise and explode the weapon. But we must realize, too, that it has increased our burdens and responsibility.

We must do everything possible as a nation to try to prevent the use of either the A-bomb or the H-bomb in actual warfare. We can best accomplish this by devoting most of our energies toward the building of permanent world peace. . . .

It was that weighty representative of Eastern conservatism, the *New York Times* (November 18, 1952), however, which was most stirred by the event and most eloquent in reaction:

We move toward the supreme crisis of our generation and perhaps of all the generations of man. Whether the hydrogen bomb is now available for military purposes or whether it is not, we can now be fairly sure that such a bomb is practicable. We can also be fairly sure that if such a destructive force as this is let loose the consequences will be fearful beyond all possibility to imagine them. . . .

The *Times* editorialist had no doubts about the proximate Russian success in achieving a similar H-bomb explosion: "No physicist doubts that, if a hydrogen bomb can be developed here, Soviet Russia will eventually develop a hydrogen bomb of her own. Thus we come face to face with a situation in which a world war might literally wipe civilization from the face of the globe."

If this was clear to a lay editorial writer, it must be equally clear to everyone in a better position to know. Yet, when the Russian explosion did take place, some nine months later, no further progress was visible in the adjustment of men or nations to its imperatives. That announcement came as one atomic year closed and another opened. Georgi Malenkov made it to "1,300 cheering members of the Supreme Soviet in the Great Hall of the Kremlin." When the United States, he said, had long ago lost the monopoly of the atomic bomb, she had begun to comfort herself by talking about a monopoly of the hydrogen bomb. "This is no longer so; the Government of the Soviet Union must inform the Supreme Soviet that the United States no longer possesses a monopoly of the hydrogen bomb." The very announcement of the Russian progress was cast in the language of threat and counterthreat. Was it true of both the Soviet and the American governments that they did not recognize what the sober *Times* had so fearfully reported: that mankind moved "toward the supreme crisis of our generation, and perhaps of all the generations of man?"

There was one group of men on whom the weight of crisis rested heavily. On a raw and chill Chicago day—December 2, 1952—the original group of bomb-makers had met to celebrate the tenth anniversary of their triumph over all the obstacles of nature. If "to celebrate" connotes rejoicing of any degree, however, it is the wrong word. They were there to recall a historic event; but there were more regrets than rejoicings, and there was not much hope.

Enrico Fermi was there to point out where he had stood on a balcony overlooking the pile. He had waited in the cold until the instruments told him of success. He had announced quietly: "The reaction is self-sustaining." As much as any single event can separate periods in men's affairs, that announcement had ended one and opened another era. The scientists now recalled how Mr. Arthur Compton had presently sent Mr. J. B. Conant a telegram for President Roosevelt's eyes: "The Italian navigator has landed in the new world. The natives were very friendly." An unusual illumination had lit some scientist's mind when he conceived this analogy. Fermi was indeed a new Columbus; and atomic energy was a new world. The landing had even been toasted in Chianti, that noble Italian wine. This last had been an inspiration of Mr. Eugene Wigner, one of Fermi's collaborators. Besides Fermi, there was also present Leo Szilard, the Hungarian who had enriched then, and on every day since, the empire of mankind.[22]

Ten years later the hinterland of that new world in which Fermi and his colleagues had landed was yielding to exploration. Nuclear energy, in spite of preoccupation with its uses for war, was opening out infinite prospects of betterment in man's condition.

This tenth year of the new age would have been rich indeed with promise if its skies had not been so heavy with the threat of storm. Lay watchers like myself had already understood that some "breeding" process had to be mastered before real potentialities of peacetime energy could open out. Our initial visions of power so cheap that an era of abundance might soon arrive had been shattered by scientific caution. There was not much fissionable material, scientists pointed out, and even if all of it should be used to produce power, the supply would not last long. Furthermore, fuel was only a minor element in power costs. Heat exchangers, generators, transmission lines, and other installations made up most of the cost anyway. Recently, however, there had been progress that only those who had kept careful watch on such developments would have noted. Mr. Gordon Dean, chairman of the Atomic Energy Commission, had pointed out the chief milestones in a speech on June 4, 1953.

1. The first successful operation of a nuclear chain reactor—the accomplishment of Enrico Fermi, Leo Szilard, and others in 1942.

22. The *Bulletin of the Atomic Scientists* published in its February, 1953, issue reminiscent articles by two of those who had participated in the events of 1942: Samuel K. Allison and A. H. Compton.

2. The first production of atomic power in an "experimental breeder reactor" at the Reactor Testing Station in Idaho.

3. The production of power by the more efficient "homogeneous breeder reactor" at Oak Ridge.

4. The conclusion by four "industrial study teams" in 1952, after studying the reactor development program, that atomic power would be "ultimately practical."

5. The beginning in 1953 of operation of the prototype power plant for submarine propulsion.[23]

He then announced exciting news: "Dr. Zinn, Dr. Lichtenberger and their Argonne colleagues" had demonstrated the principle of breeding. It now appeared that breeding would so stretch out the supply that it might equal at least all the world's oil reserves, and perhaps exceed them. By burning U235 in the presence of U238, as much as or more new fuel would be produced as was used up. U235, being less than 1 per cent of natural uranium, and U238 being the rest, this procedure appeared to increase greatly the useful supply.

Dr. Zinn himself had explained the process in an article in the *Bulletin of the Atomic Scientists* for June, 1953. The fuel produced heat, the heat produced steam, the steam produced electricity. As a kind of by-product, more fuel was produced than was used. There were difficult engineering and chemical problems still unsolved; but their solutions seemed so much less formidable than the obstacles already overcome that it seemed incredible that they would stand permanently in the way.

News of these breeder reactors was now breaking into print everywhere. During late 1952 and into 1953 they were a major topic of discussion not only in the *Bulletin,* but also in the *Atomic Scientists News,* its British counterpart,[24] and in the general press. The Canadian effort was summarized in the *London Times Weekly Review* in November, 1952. Chalk River, it seemed, was to have "the world's most powerful reactor."

Nuclear fuel was practically certain now to be of immense economic importance within a decade, and its possibilities for smaller nations were first recognized during the year with the announcement of an agreement among several European countries to establish a

23. Speech at Atlantic City, June 4, 1953. Atomic Energy Commission release.

24. E.g., "Industry and Atomic Power," by Sir Claude Gibbs, November, 1952; and a whole symposium in the issue for September, 1952; some further references were made in nearly every issue thereafter.

joint laboratory. It had been in Europe, indeed, that the successive discoveries had emerged during the early years of the century. It had, in fact, been Italian and French genius which had prepared the way in pure theory and in the first experiments. Only later had the northerners added their contributions; Lord Rutherford and the other Britishers had built on much solid work already done. By comparison, Americans were neophytes and upstarts. Even so late as a decade after the first pile had succeeded in Chicago there were many Europeans in the list of nuclear workers in America—in spite of McCarran and McCarthy. How foolish, to the scientists, the policy of secrecy and exclusion seemed!

The question now became: Who was going to control production of power? Had the Eisenhower victory in 1952 settled that "the long nose of the federal government" was from now on to be kept out of the business of producing power, even nuclear power? It looked to many vigilant progressives as though this vast developing resource might very well fall completely into the control of big business, not only because the Republicans frankly supported such a policy, but also because almost everyone seemed to agree. If so, the public interest would come out about where it usually did—strictly subordinate to the profit and convenience of the private exploiters.

The turn to reaction throughout the world—an obvious phenomenon of 1953—was likely in the United States, it seemed, to cause a reversion to the policies of fifty years ago. General Eisenhower resembled no other President so much as McKinley: McKinley had been a convinced compromiser too; he had let business into Washington; he had presided blandly over the rape of the nation's resources. And, because he would not become a mobilizer of the American conscience, he had allowed himself, against his judgment and desires, to condone the most useless, and even disgraceful, of all our national adventures—the Spanish-American War. The analogy was a dismaying one. Big business of 1953 was not sufficiently different from that of 1900 to be trustworthy. It had fifty years of growth behind it; and the resource it wished now to monopolize and exploit was even more valuable than had been the prospective fuels of that time. But the significance of business influence in Washington lay, not in what it might do to the domestic economy, but in what its unrelieved blindness might lead to vis-à-vis the world. It was the deepest tragedy in a series of tragedies that irresponsible adventurers should be so influential at a time when genocidal weapons made their first appearance on mankind's agenda.

The suppression of protest, reform, and constructive movements was not a solely American phenomenon: There was hardly a government left in the West that had not turned far toward the right. The most moderate of them was the British; but even in Britain denationalization was going forward, the equivalent of American isolationism had a firm hold (its manifestations were mostly enthusiastic anti-American outbreaks), and Churchill was again confidently talking like an eighteenth-century adventurer.

Britain did not exactly draw closer to Europe; she showed no increasing willingness to join any formal Continental organization. But she did show an increasing tendency to share with France, Italy, and other Continental nations their active and resentful resistance to American pressure, which had not lessened as American generosity had withered. President Eisenhower's effort to maintain this generosity could not be very vigorous, for he seemed determined to sacrifice, or fatally modify, every policy, foreign or domestic, that threatened the unity of the Republican party. The consequence of his evident desire to conciliate the increasingly isolationist Republican senators was a mounting wave of anti-Americanism in Europe such as American foreign correspondents unanimously testified they had never seen in their lifetimes.

For the Europeans were now convinced of what they had all along suspected—that the United States was committed to war with the Soviets; that she had no desire for conciliation, much less arrangements out of which a more secure peace might eventually emerge. It followed that the American directives for European conduct were calculated to serve a policy of aggression that would lead to the preliminary immolation of Europe in the holocaust of war. The best way to insure the Russian occupation of the whole continent was to avoid renewed Russian trade and other mutual exchanges and arrangements; it was to continue the policy of provocation—now called "liberation."

Part of the trouble in Europe—but naturally a minor part—arose out of differences in the Near East and the Far East. Britishers believed the United States intended an aggression not only in eastern

Europe but on the continent of Asia, whereas British policy was to conciliate the Chinese Communists and to encourage their independence of Russia. There would presently be an acrimonious difference of opinion, which could hardly be stifled, about the admission of the Chinese Communists to the United Nations. For the United States Senate had added to the flaring distrust by passing a resolution out of hand declaring unanimously against the admission. The French, furthermore, resented the United States role in Indochina, where a revolution was in process, and in French North Africa, where revolution was incipient, especially in Morocco, site of heavy American investment in bomber bases. The United States was torn between a traditional anticolonial policy and her desire to hold the line against communism in Indochina and protect her investments in Morocco. To the French, her aid seemed insufficient and her demands overdomineering. They were having no further American advice. They were deliberately stalling about European unity and even about NATO and the joint army with its German divisions. Seldom had so mutually important a co-operation had to exist in so hostile an atmosphere.

The most important questions to be settled, once the Korean disengagement had been made, concerned Germany and Japan. Those nations had been bombed unmercifully. Their factories had been destroyed; their cities had been demolished; and millions of their citizens had been killed or incapacitated. Moreover, their trade with others had been ended and their territory divided. But they were great nations still. What had made them strong before would make them strong again. And it was of enormous importance what choice they made of affiliation, whether the world of communism or the world of capitalism.

It might seem very strange, but it was a fact becoming every day more bizarre, that those enemies so recently intent on the destruction of Germany and Japan should now be in so incontinent a hurry not only for their reconstruction but for their rearming. The United States might be pressing Britain, France, and the other Europeans to rearm; but this effort was nothing compared with the urgency of her pressures on Germany and Japan. She doubtless hoped that the rather superficial democracy imposed on them would take root and grow; but she more than hoped, she determinedly planned, that their rearming should be prompt. Both, it must be said, were reluctant—Japan more so. But even in Germany it was obvious that relief from the enormous burden of military expenditure was an efficient cause of a return to prosperity which well outstripped that of Britain and France. German rearmament was still a source of bitter contention in France, where fear of Germany was increased by the contrast between French economic stagnation and German economic growth. This issue was creating the reluctance in France which was bringing the American push for European defense to a dead stop.

German unification presented a further troubling problem. It got no nearer in spite of being advocated by both sides in the contest, because, as time passed, attitudes hardened. There had been a moment while Russia's soft post-Stalin policies were being formulated when negotiation had seemed about to begin. But American reluctance, or lack of intention to find a way, had resulted in an answer to a Russian bid that seemed to Europeans evidence of American determination not to negotiate at all. The reply had insisted that no issue should be discussed in any first meeting or series of meetings except that of "free elections." Since the Russians were on record as opposing these, such a reply left no alternative except rejection.

It could be pointed out that British and French signatures were also attached to these Allied communications. There was an obvious reason: The Americans had been insistent; and, when they were insistent, they spoke with dollars. All three governments, furthermore, may have taken into consideration the fact that Adenauer was less than enthusiastic about unification. His was a reactionary-clerical government, about to go to the polls. Its chances were not too good, apparently, as things were, even in West Germany; but it could not hope to win an election in a unified Germany. There were very few Catholics among the eighteen millions in East Germany.

It was official policy in the West that Germany should be unified, but only if it should be safely non-Communist. It had been for this reason that in all exchanges with the Russians the Western Allies had insisted upon a free election as the preliminary. It had seemed, until the troubles in July, that even this condition might be agreed to by the conciliatory Russians. But in July there occurred a series of serious riots throughout East Germany. The hand of the conquerors had laid too heavily on the land. It had been plundered of everything not destroyed by war; its puppet government was even more contemptible than such governments usually are; and its poverty was beginning to seem intolerable in contrast with the recurring prosperity in the West. Russian tanks stifled the revolt at once. That army intervention had been necessary, however, was an admission it was hard to make after all the pretense about a "people's democracy." The riots hardened the Russians against any arrangement. At the atomic year's end it was impossible to feel that any solution was in sight.

It was so, also, with the Austrian treaty. In some two hundred and sixty meetings, representatives of the four powers had agreed on all but four or five clauses out of a couple of hundred; but for two years meetings had been suspended for lack of further progress. Then, in their soft interval—the three months between Stalin's death and the purge of Beria—the Russians had done what the Americans had preceded them in doing: they had assumed the costs of occupation. This $8,500,000 was a cheap way of putting the French and British on the defensive for still requiring the Austrians to bear the costs in their sectors; but it also led to a resumption of communications. After the East German riots, however, any willingness the Soviets may have felt to conclude the treaty disappeared. The Allies had submitted a "short" treaty in the hope of compromise. The Russians now suddenly asked for the withdrawal of this draft "so that negotiations could be resumed," a step that seemed to be another evasion rather than a genuine approach. Negotiation about specific matters either in Germany or Austria—or for that matter elsewhere—was going to have to wait on more general settlements.

American diplomats preferred to raise specific matters one by one on the assumption that agreement on these would finally add up to a better situation. They were severely handicapped by senatorial critics backed by a chauvinist press, and they preferred small issues to keep the criticisms small. The President's power to negotiate was under fire anyway. The American Bar Association at its August meeting reaffirmed its two previous indorsements of the "Bricker Amendment" to the Constitution, which would have destroyed that power; and the strain of giving anything in trade even in a most favorable bargain might well have set off a movement to put the amendment through. There was a reason of deeper significance, however. The American government had no program for negotiation, especially if it should be—as it would in the end have to be—global. There had been no attempt to weigh the value of alternate concessions; Mr. Dulles and his colleagues still talked as though there were only American claims, no Russian ones. In such an atmosphere it was unthinkable that any general meetings should be held.

The contrary view that a general settlement should precede discussion of specific issues was represented with some reservations by Churchill and the British. Sir Winston hoped that the Bermuda conference of the three Western powers, to which Eisenhower had given reluctant consent, would be the beginning of that realistic global trading which must take place if war was to be avoided. President Eisenhower would have to face the Russian claims, assess realistically the gains and losses to America from any settlement he might make, and begin to prepare opinion in the United States for its acceptance. But Sir Winston had a stroke, and President Eisenhower was all too obviously relieved when the conference was called off.

It was amply apparent to all but the blindest partisan that the American attitude was preventing any negotiation at all and was perpetuating the dangerous explosiveness which might detonate at any one of half-a-dozen places at any time. It was useless to say that it was the Russians' fault and that holding out for general conferences was as wilful as the American reluctance to enter them. What had to come was a global arrangement in which Russian necessities were entertained and weighed against American interests. Talking about specific issues first was futile, because the United States insisted that they be settled on principle as interpreted by herself. American stiffness and unwillingness were preventing negotiations. These were responsible for the progressive defection of Europe. There would have to be a change, and soon, or Europeans would become antagonists rather than allies.

Senator McCarthy and the atomic bomb were an effective combination in the world in 1953. The one created fear, and the other exploited it. Never had a demagogue had so mighty an ally; but never also had a demagogue been more clever in managing an alliance.[25] In spite of all reason, he continued to persuade Americans that a few thousand unhappy Communists menaced their institutions and that the Russians were a danger because spies in our government had passed them secrets. The significance of this was not only that it prevented the Administration from negotiating but that it stifled before it began any organization of what Hans Thirring called an "anti-Communist peace movement."

Professor Thirring has been mentioned before in this chronicle, as one of the significant contributors to contemporary science. He was moved in 1953, as other scientists before him had been, to speak out about the hardening impasse between East and West. He could do it, being Viennese, with a better chance of a hearing than any of those already ticketed by Senator McCarthy as doubtfully anti-Russian. The body of his article was directed to the knotty problem of defining aggression. But he was tormented by the larger issue to which such a definition was by way of being the key. He asked:

Why has not that vast majority of peace-loving people on both sides of the Iron Curtain not been able to choke, by its sheer mass, the fire of hatred and suspicions nourishing the cold war? How is it possible for a one per cent minority of "fire-brands and warmongers" to impose on the world economy the burden of a two-hundred to three-hundred million dollars of daily expenditure, which at best is totally wasted, and, if not wasted, will serve to annihilate the better part of mankind![26]

The answer to this seemed obvious to Professor Thirring. Generally speaking it was because the 99 per cent majority was unable to exert any influence on politics. It was too disorganized. He suggested that unity could only be found in the organization of mass movements among non-Communists whose avowed object would be resistance to aggression—with aggression so clearly defined that there could be no mistake about its occurrence.

Another scientist, Dr. J. R. Michiels, general secretary of the British Atomic Scientists Association, was more pessimistic.[27] And

---

25. Senator McCarthy had, during the year, been the subject of close examination. A Senate committee had made some revelations concerning his finances which were embarrassing; but no one expected Mr. Herbert Brownell, the Attorney-General, to find anything actionable in them. Messrs. J. Anderson and R. W. May had written a book, also, about the Senator: *McCarthy: The Man, the Senator, the Ism* (Boston, 1952). It was widely read, at least, whether or not the lesson learned from it would be salutary.

26. *Bulletin of the Atomic Scientists,* April, 1953.

27. *Atomic Scientists News,* January, 1953.

it must be said that he reflected more faithfully the mood of most of those who were informed and interested but who had no part in the contemporary proceedings. Discussing the impasse which, in 1953, supervened in the atomic disarmament discussions, he said that what existed did not seem to be a "genuine deadlock." The trouble was that the arguments of both sides seemed justified if the mutual fears of both sides were accepted as valid. He thought it possible that Russia might accept the continued existence of stocks of bombs during the transition period now that she had stocks of her own; still, she would be making a sacrifice in doing so. If, however, the transition period could be reduced by careful and detailed organization of the process of disclosure and verification, something might be done. It was, on the other hand, not reasonable to expect the United States to dispose of her stock of bombs until an adequate inspection system was in operation. But there might be some value in a declaration that atomic weapons would only be resorted to if they were first used against the Western Allies. The trouble with this was that only on such an occasion would a democracy resort to them anyway. The whole thing really did seem to be an impasse.

The basic trouble was that "a deadlock occurs because neither side believes in the good faith of the other. . . . It will only be possible to reach agreement when there is some reasonable degree of trust in the other man's good faith. It is manifestly evident that there is no trend in this direction at the present time." And this was as true on Hiroshima Day, 1953, as it had been six months earlier when the Michiels article had been written.

Americans were proving unable to locate the causes of their neurosis—not an unusual condition with the mentally ill. As with an individual, however, it could lead to self-destruction. The trouble in the world—the special, added, and identifiable trouble—was the existence of nuclear weapons. It was this which created fear and held it close in the social unconscious. It was dangerous, but not strange, that personification of the felt threat should be sought in another national entity. Individual identification with national groups was, after centuries of immolation in war, very nearly complete. And another nation to be held guilty was a necessity. It was the part of prosecutor in this cause that McCarthy played so well.

Russia corresponded classically with the wicked antagonist. But there was frustration. Russia could not be punished, actually, for frightening Americans. Americans had not the absolute superiority necessary to successful punishment. But neither could the necessary indignation be withdrawn from. And this was why basically there could be no negotiation until America and Americans had recovered the health in which normal functioning could be resumed.

THE decennial year of the atom—from August 6, 1953, to August 6, 1954—seemed, at least until April, to be just more of the same. Each year of the ten had had its incidents, which had built up a more and more widely diffused sense of insecurity; and this one had had its incidents too. Measured by those of other years, they had not had much impact, except for a short-lived access of fear following an H-bomb explosion in the Pacific. But not until late spring did there seem to be a renewal of danger that war might break out; and, indeed, a very sizable war dwindled toward a kind of uncertain conclusion, not in peace, but at least in armistice. A cease-fire stopped the blood-letting in Korea; but it still kept troops in the field, prepared any minute to resume, while discussions—about the repatriation of prisoners, mostly—went on. But argument never got around to the real issues which must sometime be approached. Even a meeting to set a date for these discussions broke up in angry exchanges.

The Republicans had now been in full charge for a year and a half. President Eisenhower and Secretary Dulles were substituted as policy-makers for President Truman and Secretary Acheson. The fighting had been brought to an end, as Eisenhower the candidate had promised it would. "Truman's war" was, in this sense, over. But absolutely nothing else was changed. There were no credits to be awarded except cessation of battle, which, in the terms of diplomatics, was no credit at all because it settled nothing and produced no leverage for a future settlement. On the contrary, it relieved a pressure which might have brought the Chinese to the conference table.

But the truth was, much as an American historian might deplore it, that this achievement was enough for domestic political purposes. Those in charge were not required to produce the elements of a settlement, to use military strength so that it counted for national purposes—whatever their definition of purposes might be. They were required only to disengage from a conflict Americans had tired of. For all most people cared, they could ship the men, the guns, and all the matériel back home and let the Koreans go hang.

But there is no profit in indicting a whole people, as has been noted by a good many observers. If Americans were to be rescued from their situation, leadership had to be found and people had to be persuaded to accept the disciplines necessary to their responsibilities. They could not abandon themselves to complete self-interest and maintain any national interests. There were very few signs, however, that this axiom was at all widely understood. And, without much question, the atomic year 1953–54 was one of the worst periods through which the democracy had ever passed. Still, there were faint signs of regeneration and courage; a few voices were raised in protest—in spite of the public bludgeoning which such protests immediately brought—and, most important of all, there was a widespread recoil from the now-evident results of Republican victory in 1952. The year 1954 looked, indeed, like a Democratic one.

Considering the general disorganization of the country and the evidences there were that people did not know what they wanted, it had to be set down as pure good fortune that most of the year was one of comparative peace. The final crisis which had been so dreaded all these ten years was not necessarily made any less likely to happen sometime; it had not even been postponed beyond whatever its maturing time might be; but at no juncture, until spring brought the Indochina defeat, had it seemed likely that a premature explosion would take place which would precipitate a third world war. The very fact that such a year had passed into history might be very significant. It began to be suspected by some observers that the crisis was going to be a permanent one or a series of recurrent ones. There was not going to be a settlement; there was not going to be a showdown between irreconcilable systems; there was simply going to be this everlasting tension, rising and falling but never ceasing.

This theory, indeed, seemed to be the only one which could explain the events of the year in contrast with the events of the years just past. There had been just as much friction, just as many differences, a complete absence of conciliation. Yet war had been less thought of than for a long time past. Few even of the Senate jingoes had talked of hostilities as an immediate possibility, and it was they as much as anybody who rejected Mr. Dulles' proposals in the Indochina crisis. Was the world becoming reconciled to division, to a perpetual quarrel, to straining for advantage in the ideological struggle? Was it possible that war was coming to be recognized as an outlawed resort? It was a year when meetings took place about dangerously irritating issues—Korea and Germany, for instance. There were no results because there were no real negotiations. But no one suggested that the failure of the diplomats preceded inevitable fighting. On the contrary, there was a kind of settling-down to acceptance.

The cause of the change, if change it really was, could be located at or near the same locus which had caused all the disturbances of the decade since Hiroshima—or if not *caused* them, then *shaped* them. The ideological differences between the Communists and the capitalists would have existed even if nuclear progress had not been so rapid; but the differences would not have held the potential of genocidal destruction. The Soviets on their continent and the Westerners on theirs might have gestured and shouted, but not even intercontinental bombers armed with the bombs of the second World War would have held the threat of total destruction. It was that ever present and monstrously enlarged threat which made the difference between the old kind of relations and the new. Each nation now had its bombers poised for instant action—retaliatory action, each claimed—and those bombers were prepared to carry to designated targets the now-perfected H-bomb.

So quickly had the scientists passed through the age of the A-bomb into that of the far more terrible H-bomb that there had never been time for military accommodation to the lesser weapon.[1] Such a thing had never before happened. Military men had never before seen a revolutionary weapon decline into obsolescence before there had been any opportunity to use it.[2] The Army had developed

1. Cf. the knowledgeable discussion of this by General Thomas R. Phillips, "The Atomic Revolution in Warfare," *Bulletin of the Atomic Scientists*, X (October, 1954), 315–17. This was one of several such analyses. General Phillips wrote regularly for the *St. Louis Post-Dispatch*.

2. The explosions of the first, crude bombs at Hiroshima and Nagasaki had not enabled strategists to assess the effect of such a weapon.

410

A-bomb artillery shells, and the Navy had announced that it could fly bomb-carrying planes from its new carriers. Atomic artillery and carrier-borne planes supposedly formed the front opposed to an advancing enemy. But what would become of their rear echelons under the impact of vast bomber fleets carrying genocidal loads of improved A-bombs?

This question was not much discussed; but it was not overlooked. It was the elemental question; and even the most ardent Army or Navy partisan knew it well enough. There was therefore study and discussion of an absolute system of defense. An amply leaked investigation by a group of scientists, which was never wholly acknowledged but never quite repudiated, held that such a defense was possible.[3] Those well-known columnists, the Alsop brothers, were evidently its chosen sponsors. What the system was, they, of course, could only hint; but the hints were broad. The project was for a radar network, it seemed, and for a perfected system of unmanned missiles homing on distant targets as they approached. The defense was to be set at such a distance that not only would warning time be lengthened—it had by now become a matter of minutes with the existing defenses—but the net would be so tight as to be completely effective. There was only one difficulty. The net would cost as much as, or more than, all present military expenditures put together. It was not possible to make a very close estimate; but this was the approximation. Installation, furthermore, would require something like five years. From what the Alsops seemed to know—and from other hints—it was apparent that the Security Council had deliberated over this program, and probably modifications of similar ones, for a long time. But what the public knew was not really very much. And, whatever went on in secret, the project as a whole was not adopted by the Administration.

Thus, while the nation continued to be vulnerable to H-bombing by the admittedly capable Soviet air force, the services continued to manufacture their own versions of A-bomb weapons, and the Atomic Energy Commission proceeded with the development of the super H-bomb. The Soviets were equally vulnerable and equally committed to the armaments race. Perhaps for this reason each side would avoid military trial. Sending out bombers was, in the circumstances,

3. About which more will be said.

tantamount to national suicide and so presumably was beyond the limits of recourse.[4]

It was against this background of developments and decisions that a most curious pronouncement was made by Secretary Dulles, speaking for the Administration. There would, he said, be no more small wars of the Korea kind. If there was any aggression anywhere that originated in the Communist world, it would be accepted as an invitation to, and a beginning of, World War III. What he seemed to say was that if anywhere along the Communist-capitalist frontier—in Germany, in Turkey, in India, for instance—there was begun another invasion of "Western" territory, America's bombers would be released to strike at the Soviet heartland. This intention was seen by so many people to be incredibly foolish and provocative that the reservations and explanations, now become almost habitual with the Secretary, began at once.

The matter was never to be entirely cleared up, but Mr. Dulles would be pressed; what he seemed to have meant was that any aggression anywhere would be met by massive retaliation and that this intention had better be understood. It was evidently his theory that, if retaliation had been certain, South Korea, for instance, would not have been attacked, although it was he who, only a few days before the attack, speaking to the South Korean legislature, had assured them of military support. Fact and theory seemed to have no connection in the secretarial mind.

More moderate people hoped that the Soviets were not on notice that a border incident anywhere, especially some Chinese aggression, would set the bombers flying. The take-off of those bombers would mean the literal end of industrial civilization. This eventuality ought not to be at the disposal of a set of Chinese megalomaniacs. Nor ought Mr. Dulles to suppose that Soviet discipline extended, in any absolute sense, to the Chinese. They worked together; but the Chinese were far from puppets. So strange, indeed, were the ideas and acts of that overturned anthill, Communist China, that it seemed not at all impossible that some newly made statesman there might conceive the notion of causing Russia and the United States to destroy each other. It was foolhardy of Mr. Dulles to suggest the possibility.

4. On this, see the comments of Lord Salisbury in the House of Lords, in the *Manchester Guardian*'s "Review of Parliament," April 1, 1954; also Hansard.

Even if the Secretary, in his characteristically left-handed way, had said more than he meant or not what he meant at all, he must nevertheless have been close enough to Administration policy to understand the dilemma, the contradiction, into which it had been plunged. Either the new weapons, the bombs, were to be strategic reliances, or they were not. If they were, it was hard to see how little ones—artillery shells, tactical bombers—were of the slightest use. Only on the assumption that big ones would not be used could little ones be considered operational. Such a tacit abstaining had governed gas and germ warfare through a decade which had strained all moral bonds to the breaking point. The Allies knew enough about Hitler to be quite certain that he would have resorted to both weapons if he had seen any possibility of getting away clean. He always knew that he could not; and it was this certainty which had prevented their use. It was obvious that the same stand-off had now developed with respect to the H-bomb. It could not be used because retaliation was certain. The last war had developed and had been carried on without the use of, or any threat of using, either germ or gas warfare. But now Mr. Dulles was saying, or appearing to say, what no responsible statesman all through the crises of the forties had even suggested— that the tacit restraint which must govern suicidal weapons would not be honored by the United States.[5]

The provocations and the risks inherent in this doctrine of massive retaliation were increased greatly by the Army and Navy adaptations of atomic weapons. Just what size must a bomb be reduced to if it was not to be classed as among those which would loose the whole armory of atomic weapons on the world? There was no obvious dividing line. The Army could not use its atomic artillery shells,[6] and the Navy could not loose its small carrier bombers, without also asking for the retaliation of intercontinental air attack. Or so it seemed to most students.

Yet the Administration appeared to be very proud of what it called the "New Look" in military planning.[7] This look was not

5. Sir John Slessor commanded much attention in Britain during the year with argument from the premise that the Bomb was no longer available as a weapon, thus adding a soldier to the statesmen who were arguing this way.

6. By late spring the Army in Germany had several units of atomic guns in position on its German front. They were in rapid production.

7. The phrase was actually Admiral Radford's, and perhaps the policy was largely his. As chairman of the Joint Chiefs of Staff, he was very influential.

more and not less than the acceptance and adaptation of atomic weapons to ordinary military uses. The next Korea, if there should be one, was to call into action, not the "conventional" arms of 1950, but the atomic arms from the new laboratories, and this step was actually proposed for Indochina. How it could be taken without causing general involvement in atomic warfare was not made clear. This military ambiguity, linked to the larger ambiguity of Mr. Dulles' doctrine of total reprisal, left matters in as strange a state of indecision and confusion as ever tormented American policy.

The tortuous process by which a mighty nation had arrived at a situation of apparent commitment to total war over any minor incident among thousands of incipient and likely ones was an excellent illustration of the effect of the atomic explosion at Hiroshima on men's minds and their social institutions. The sequence ran thus: The Bomb arrived and made obsolete old weapons; the Bomb, however, was a genocidal weapon, and its overwhelming potency was suitable only to major conflicts; but nations customarily resorted to force for the settlement even of questions not worth a world war; a war was fought—in Korea—in which resort to atomic weapons was avoided; nevertheless, the great powers were forced into a race to develop and "improve" the first crude bombs, a race which took on horrible proportions when the H-bomb supervened; bombing weapons were now so necessary and so costly that it seemed impossible to go on providing full conventional armaments for adequate armies *as well as atomic weapons;* engineering developments, however, had reduced the A-bomb to manageable units—that is, those which were only somewhat more powerful than the conventional weapons of armies in the field and navies at sea; it was thus possible to abandon conventional weapons for these lesser—and cheaper—atomic arms; the Republican victory in the United States came just at the time when such a choice could be made, and its promises of reduced governmental costs, lower taxes, and business freedom could only be made good to any degree by reducing military costs, since these constituted so large a percentage of the national budget.

The final step in this fatal sequence, which President Truman had avoided, was taken by General Eisenhower, who was now President and who was completely trusted in one field above all others—military planning. If he said the New Look was adequate to the needs of national security, there were many who felt that it must necessarily *be* adequate. There was almost no questioning of the decision, almost no realization, as a matter of fact, that a decision had been made. Only gradually did it seep into people's consciousnesses that they were being committed beyond recall to atomic warfare no matter what the size or nature of the dispute in which there was resort to force and that they were thus placing in the hands of irresponsible third parties the power to trigger a conflict between the Soviet Union and the United States.

Governor Stevenson, spokesman for the loyal opposition, was one person who was not in the least fooled. He conceived it to be his duty, if he could, to awaken a bemused people to the peril into which they had so unwittingly and trustingly fallen. He spoke out at a Miami Beach meeting early in March, when the New Look was by way of being accepted without discussion, partly because national attention was being diverted by the most recent excesses of McCarthy:

. . . The Administration has recently unveiled . . . a program of more for our money, "a bigger bang for a buck," national security in the large economy size. . . .

We are told, and I am quoting the words of Secretary Dulles, that we have rejected the "traditional" policy of meeting aggression by direct and local opposition. We have taken the decision "to depend primarily upon a great capacity to retaliate instantly, by means and place of our choosing." . . .

All this means, if it means anything, that if the Communists try another Korea we will retaliate by dropping atom bombs on **Moscow or Peiping.** . . .

Is this a "New Look" or is it a return to the pre-1950 atomic deterrent strategy which made some sense as long as we had a monopoly of atomic weapons? Yet even then it didn't deter attack and brought us to the brink of disaster in Korea. . . .[8]

A few days later, in his weekly press conference, President Eisenhower suggested that this speech was a "demagogic" attack and called attention to his own presumable expertness in things military. This was no very worthy answer to what had been a careful statement concerning the most serious of all contemporary issues. The matter was not one in which a general was better qualified to speak than another kind of citizen. The New Look was not just a military commitment, and the decision to adopt it had not been made by the military alone. In the character of those who helped in the decision-

8. Quoted from the *New York Times*, March 7, 1954.

making process lay the nub of the matter Mr. Stevenson had been getting at. He was afraid that business interests had shared too prominently in the deliberations leading up to decision. He was afraid that they had told the President that the economy would not carry the burden it was being asked to assume. And why? Because heavy taxes and industrial discipline would be required, and these they were determined—as the Republican party was pledged—to end.[9]

This issue was entitled to be called a great and vital one. It was one, moreover, so intimately concerned with the national security that a democratic decision concerning it was essential. It was not one which ought to be "slipped over" in the confusions and alarms of McCarthy diversionary storms, or one which Americans ought to be asked to accept because the President was also a general. The President was obliged to abandon the untenable position he had taken offhand, even if he himself decided not to answer Mr. Stevenson. The Vice-President, Mr. Richard Nixon, was officially designated for that task. He spoke on March 13 after full and acknowledged consultation with the President.

First, he stressed the care with which the revised policy had been formulated in weekly meetings of the National Security Council. He claimed expertness for the President, but he quite noticeably stressed the collective nature of the decision. He came then to the argument. This, as Mr. Stevenson had suspected, had proceeded from two standards. Mr. Nixon did not hide it:

We found that in the seven years of the Truman-Acheson policy 600,000,-000 people had been lost to the Communists and not a single Russian soldier had been lost in combat.

We found . . . we were still involved in a war in Korea; that it cost us 125,000 American boys. And again not a single Russian soldier lost in that war.

We found that we inherited a budget—a policy which if continued as recommended by the Truman Administration through the four years of the Eisenhower Administration would have added $40,000,000,000 to the national debt. . . .

Russian strategy called for starting numerous small wars all over the world which we could not win because our superiority on the sea

9. The full report of this press conference is to be found in the *New York Times*, March 11, 1954.

and in the air could not be brought to bear. Russian economic strategy was to force the United States to stay armed to the teeth, ready to fight anywhere in the world that the enemy chose; for such a state of preparation would force the nation into bankruptcy and destroy its freedoms. It was because of these judgments, and after those long Security Council discussions, that what Secretary Dulles had called the "New Look" had been adopted as a principle: "Rather than let the Communists nibble us to death all over the world in little wars, we would rely in future primarily on our massive mobile retaliatory power which we could use in our discretion against the major source of aggression at times and places that we chose."[10]

Following this sufficiently clear statement of the reasons for arriving at the policy, Mr. Nixon went on to the claims for it. These were: first, that the Korean War had been brought to an end; second, that two American divisions had been brought home; third, that the budget was approaching a balance; and, fourth, that the ideological offensive had been seized.

These claims were weak. The Korean War had been ending in stalemate anyway; the budget was in fact far from balanced; and the "ideological offensive" was a wholly subjective matter. It was hard to see how the argument had been advanced by Mr. Nixon's effort. Could it be that the Eisenhower plan was merely to rest without discussion on the warning to the Communists that all future wars were to be total—even the Korean War, if it should be started again? Such a policy seemed incredible, considering the existence of those bombers armed with the latest "thermonuclear devices." Evidently the implications of H-bomb warfare were to be ignored.

Surprisingly enough, however, the debate was suddenly made world-wide. Almost at the same time that Mr. Nixon was speaking, a voice was heard from Moscow. Premier Malenkov, in a speech which seemed to reverse the Soviet propaganda line, warned his own people of the dangers inherent in atomic war. He was speaking to the local Soviets just before the "elections" in Russia. Heretofore it had been customary to dwell only on the world's hostility and the necessity for Soviet defense. This new warning seemed at once a gesture of conciliation to other nations and preparation at home for a reduc-

10. The quotations are from the *New York Times*, March 15, 1954.

tion in emphasis on military preparation. It seemed to be part of a whole, considerably changed Russian attitude.

That attitude had already been defined as a result of the first great international event of the year—the meeting of the Big Four foreign ministers in January in Berlin, the first meeting in several years.[11] When it was over, the general consensus seemed to be that "nothing had been accomplished." On the other hand, although no agreements had resulted, it was certainly of considerable importance that policies had been defined. It was clear now, if it had not been before, that what Russia wanted was a reduction of the threat to her security from the gradually shaping NATO army.

The development of the European army had gone very slowly. Ratification was stalled, perhaps permanently, in France and Italy; and it was after the conference that Belgium ratified. What the Soviets offered was an alternative which looked remarkably like the Monroe Doctrine of the Americas. They offered security to western Europe in exchange for liquidation of the military threat to themselves; and they would not settle for less. They would not, as the Allies proposed, withdraw from East Germany and allow free elections preparatory to unification; they would not even withdraw from Austria. They would not, in fact, do anything until a whole bargain was on the table.

Before the conference closed in an agreement to disagree, arrangement was made for an April meeting in Geneva on Far Eastern questions. At this meeting Communist China would be present. This recognition of Peiping's claims enraged the China lobby in the United States and put Secretary Dulles on notice that he could not bargain, making it certain that nothing would be done at Geneva, as nothing had been done at Berlin. But at least meetings were being held; diplomacy had been resumed. And perhaps in time the China lobby would soften or disperse, and some bargain could be struck.

Corollary with the meeting in Berlin, but not part of it, Secretary Dulles and Foreign Minister Molotov had an unannounced number of meetings on another subject, possible co-operation in peacetime uses of atomic energy. This President Eisenhower had proposed in a

11. The conference of the Big Four foreign ministers met on January 25. It ended twenty-four days later. Discussions occupied more than 91 hours; 15 hours of these were secret.

much-advertised address at the United Nations, immediately following the Bermuda Conference of the Big Three in December.[12] His terms had been vague, but what he evidently had in mind was the possibility that there might be some mutual development of the vast stores of energy involved. Each might contribute raw materials and technical expertise; what resulted would be of benefit to all the world.

In the light of several years of frustration, it seemed possible that the Acheson-Lilienthal proposals and the stubborn American insistence had failed because they had been too bold and firm, even if essentially right; perhaps a much more modest rebeginning would draw the Russians into a relationship which could be enlarged. True, this approach would yield results noticeable only when measured by decades, whereas the destructive potentialities of the H-bomb were an immediate threat. On the other hand, in the United Nations the disarmament negotiations were paralyzed, and all the old proposals were lying unreconciled on the table.

The President's scheme was small or narrow, if those adjectives are appropriate; but it did seem to escape from the antagonisms and hard commitments which nearly a decade of bargaining and name-calling had worked up. The approach to the new proposal was to be quite outside the framework of the old negotiations. It was also to be secret—that is to say, it would escape from all that "talking out of the window" for propaganda purposes which had ruined every other postwar negotiation. At Berlin, Dulles and Molotov and the other ministers were talking about the possibilities. There was no information about the progress of the various talks. There could not and should not be; but many a prayerful hope centered in them.

Sadly, there were no results. The Russians never mentioned the matter at all. In May, Mr. Dulles remarked offhand that negotiations had reached an impasse. No one knew any more. Apparently this

12. This conference had been advertised as preparatory to a Big Four meeting. The French, however, were immobilized, as so often under the constitution of the Fourth Republic, by not having a stable government. It was impossible for anyone to speak for the nation. Nothing came from the meeting because the great question among the Big Three was whether France was to ratify the pending treaties which would establish the European army; and no one was able to say. France was the inventor of the EDC; but now her fears of Germany had grown at least as weighty as her fears of Russia. And ratification seemed as far off as ever. Until the Big Three had a policy, they could hardly deal with Russia.

road too had proved not to be a way to a reconciliation of differences. Toward year's end a finis of sorts was written to the effort. The United States, the President said, would proceed without the Soviet Union; but no one expected that, without the incentive of peaceable co-operation in which the Russians shared, much would come of the proposal.

It was an illustration of the strange state into which American affairs had fallen that neither Mr. Stevenson nor Mr. Nixon in their exchange appeared to dwell *primarily* on the central question of national security—that is, security against outside aggression. Both of them dwelt mostly on the diversionary question of *internal* security raised by McCarthyism, which had now achieved such national publicity that no unrelated question could be discussed with any amplitude or brought to any conclusion. Seldom had a democracy allowed itself such an orgy of sound about so miniscule an issue.

The debate about Communists in government had long since reached an unprofitable stage, if, indeed, it had ever been more than the "red herring" President Truman had once called it. It had grown like a parasite, however, on the obsessive dread lest the atomic weapon should "fall into Communist hands"—meaning those of the Soviet Union. And when Soviet scientific and engineering development had broken the American monopoly, there had supervened a kind of rage that the United States should be forced to acknowledge another nation as an implacable equal. This anger expressed itself by an in-turning obsession. It could not be that another people could equal Americans in resources, intelligence, or energy. It must be that those among the citizenry who had always been suspect for other reasons—intellectual deviates—had betrayed it. On everyone who could be suspected of not accepting what was orthodox—"the American way"—there was turned a fury which gradually undermined the long and carefully defended bulwarks of civil liberty. The danger was no longer merely that honest and inquiring minds were liable to siege from wild-running congressional committees. Sanctions were now being seized and administered by every sort of public or private official. The search for victims had really begun, in principle, to follow the pattern of the revolutionary French terror. To be denounced

420

was to be condemned. To be suspected was to lose position, opportunity, and even the claim to employment.[13]

There had been previous and similar know-nothing movements, but they had died out when, like physical diseases, they had exhausted the number of susceptible victims in the community and had made each sick for a time. Now the disease was not only virulent and prevalent but had begun to be chronic. Those infected did not recover, because the Bomb fed and maintained their sickness like a cancer in the minds of otherwise sane and serious men. The Bomb could not be disposed of; it could not even be kept for American use alone. All this tearing at vitals and spewing-out of hate was a kind of rage at the fate which had at last brought a superior people to the common level of mankind. The destiny of America, so clear for generations to every American, had vanished in a mushroom cloud of smoke—sent up by Americans themselves—which had turned out to require of men new attitudes, new disciplines, new concepts, which they found themselves too stiffly resistant to adopt. It was the paradox of atomic progress that it compelled men to progress socially and politically as they had been conditioned not to do. McCarthy was the agent of refusal. He was the exposer and executor of those who would not confess and comply—confess that the Bomb had changed nothing and comply with tradition rather than the imperatives of progress.

McCarthy was unrestrained. He was a member now of a majority party, but he did not accept any direction from fellow-partisans. He assumed to do the directing. He was the issue, he said, about which the next political campaign would swirl. The big question for the nation was whether his detractors or he were to be accepted by the electorate. President Eisenhower was obviously reluctant to recognize this challenge to his leadership. He deplored and hesitated, sent emissaries to plead for party unity, and on occasion said that issues of real importance were being confused; Republicans ought to be

13. It was obvious that the atmosphere permeating the whole governmental service was one of fear and withdrawal. But seldom has the peculiar degeneration of the American conscience been better documented than in the story of Bernard Goldsmith, carefully told by Anthony Lewis ("Victim of Nameless Accusers") in *The Reporter* for March 2, 1954. The atrocity of his immolation was participated in by so many of his colleagues and tacitly condoned by so many others that his experience illustrated the peculiar social leukemia which seemed to have affected a whole people.

approved or rejected on their merits as organizers of policy. Suddenly he found that his Secretary of the Army was defying McCarthy over a clear issue: whether a general could be made to testify against the orders of his superior. The President refused battle once more and fell back on his formerly announced theory that congressional committees could not be prevented from investigating. He apparently did not see that on his theory the executive establishment could not run at all; it could be given orders by congressional committees about literally everything. He had to learn in the ensuing debate what he had taken longer than any President in history to learn—that, in a government of separated powers, separation is essential and that, when investigation became merely a method of seizing and maintaining direction, it had passed the constitutional limits.

The constitutional issue was the subject of much soul-searching debate. For example, on March 8 in the *New York Times* William C. Chanler pointed out that "the Constitution places the power to determine what information it is proper for Congress to obtain from the Executive in the President. If it were otherwise, as Jackson so clearly pointed out, Congress could quickly usurp the Executive power."[14] There was entered a strong negative by those who believed that the Congress was meant to be supreme and could be checked only by its own sense of discretion. But while the debate went on—and it seemed a strange difference to arise after a hundred and fifty years—McCarthy continued to operate. It was doubtful if he knew or cared anything about the issues. He had got to the stage at which demagogues always, sooner or later, arrive. It was McCarthy against any and all opposition. But, because the President was timid and seemed not to understand the significance of his avoidances, the Republicans were split by them into McCarthyites and followers of Eisenhower. The Democrats could sit back and watch.

This, for the Democrats, was one of those classic situations every political party hopes for. The enemy divided is an enemy weakened. Yet, as Adlai Stevenson pointed out in his March speech, the nation could not afford to have one of its two great parties divided by such an issue. It not only made the party irresponsible; it allowed policies to escape discussion on which McCarthy did not happen to focus.

14. Cf. also Mr. Chanler's further discussion of the separation of powers on March 14 in the *Times*.

One of these neglected issues was that New Look which seemed to Mr. Stevenson so dangerous. That he was right no Democrat could deny, and none did; but he was tacitly rebuked by congressional Democrats nonetheless. They were not so easily convinced that they ought openly to support the President against McCarthy and become, in effect, a wing of the Republican party. Nevertheless, Mr. Stevenson's bold assessment of the situation had an effect as months passed. It began indeed to look as though the reign of blackmail was passing. McCarthy was not so large a figure as the President.

There was, of course, a legislative session in progress, and a program of sorts had been put before it, the first to come out of the Eisenhower Administration. For some time the President had rather plaintively been asking the country in general to give less attention to the McCarthy campaign and more to the real business which had to be got through. For all its numerous specific items—196 by March[15]—the program had a simple orientation. A good deal of it looked like a reversal of New Deal attitudes. For instance, specific state aids of various kinds—for housing, hospitals, roads, etc.—were sought to be either reduced or abandoned. Evidently in the first-flush enthusiasm for states' rights far more drastic measures had been considered, but practically all the structure for this aid was after all to be retained. Some of the "creeping socialism" of the Democrats, furthermore, was to be kept and expanded—for instance, old age and unemployment insurance.

This program was, on the whole, one of compromise which seemed to have got under way but then to have been stopped and turned back. Obviously there had been a severe intraparty struggle over which the President had presided and in each case made up his mind what must or must not be done. He had checked a headlong rush to abandon the New Deal, because, evidently, he had had advice against such a course. But he favored business encouragement wherever he could, sought to reduce government commitments, and hoped that a gradual sloughing-off of responsibilities would be possible. He did not come out of the year-long struggle with a clear and comprehensible policy. The program was not what the right-wingers wanted; but it was far from having a progressive orientation, and many spe-

15. See Cabell Phillips in the *New York Times*, "News of the Week," March 14, 1954.

cial interests were allowed their respective claims. It constituted, on the whole, that "freeing of the economy" to which the party was basically devoted.

There had been some quarreling about principle and some mixing of principle and expediency. For instance, it was no longer certain that the protective tariff was majority Republican doctrine. Even more important, despite the good many reductions in excises, there was doubt whether the new tax structure would after all conform to the "trickle" theory that had been party doctrine since the days when Andrew W. Mellon had presided over the Treasury. Secretary Humphrey and the President believed in it; but they were defeated by the sheer strength of those who believed that first relief ought to go to "the little fellows." For it began to seem, late in 1953 and early in 1954, as though the Republicans might possibly have a depression to explain in the presidential year 1956, just as they had in 1932. What they had to do was prevent a depression from recurring, or at least to lessen its impact and get it over with before 1956 arrived. And among the available means, as everyone could now see, taxes were important. They could multiply or decrease spending and so affect business activity.

It was amazing to note how these ideas, so ridiculed in the early days of the New Deal, and so bitterly challenged by Republicans all along, had now diffused themselves into economic thinking. They were, in 1954, accepted doctrine. Hardly anyone any more said about depressions that they "had to happen" or that, having begun, they "had to run their course." It would be an exaggeration to say that this change was unanimous. But in these Republican days the argument was mostly about how much should be done, not about whether anything at all should be done; and, though there was sharp difference about means to be used, there was hardly any, as there had been in Hoover's time, about whether it was allowable for the government to interfere.

The most critical question, and one which the Democrats had never settled, was whether what had to be done was to bolster businesses and encourage them to expand or to enlarge consumer incomes directly, thus starting activity at its source. Hoover had foundered on the policy of encouraging business. Roosevelt had given way to some consumer support, but, as later appeared, never enough; and he had financed it with government deficits and so a steady inflation. The Republicans, like Hoover before them, were committed to a balanced budget and "an honest dollar"—which meant no inflation. Whether they could check the sinking spell now coming on the economy without inflationary measures was questionable. In the confusions of Washington it was far from certain that any clear line would be followed. Long since, however, the credit-restricting policies of their first days in office had been abandoned—with some awkwardness, since so much had been said about the matter. And the kind of talk issuing from the White House in 1954 was obviously preparatory propaganda for meeting further economic decline by any and all means, regardless of previous commitment.

There was one advantage in having a President with no theory of his own. He was free to chose among what seemed to him practical measures. Hoover had been a man of unyielding conceptualism. Since the concepts in his mind had been unrelated to facts and movements in economic life, they had not furnished remedial deductions. He had failed because of his principles. That General Eisenhower would never do. He believed in the effectiveness of businessmen; he thought government ought to be diminished rather than enlarged; but these were not the kinds of thoughts and attitudes that would prevent his adopting measures the people around him had concluded were necessary. A depression might not be fought very intelligently or with a consistent ideological strategy; but it would be fought.

The New Look in strategic planning not only threatened the national interest; it deeply disturbed the Western Allies. In Secretary Dulles' words, the United States had decided *"to depend principally upon a great capacity to retaliate instantly by means, and at places of our own choosing."* After waiting two months in hope of further explanation, Mr. Lester Pearson, Canadian Foreign Minister, went so far as to question publicly what was meant by the words "instantly," "means," and "our." By then it was well known to all Washington that most of the nations in the "free world" had similarly asked for clarification, if not publicly, as insistently as was diplomatically possible and had got no satisfaction. There was, in fact, a diplomatic uproar.

Did the Dulles "instantly" mean exactly that? If so, it was notice that, if a crisis arose, there would be no waiting for explanation or—what upset the other nations—consultation. Did the Dulles "our" mean the United States exclusively? If so, it deliberately left out of account all her allies. Yet the European army was made up of joined elements from many nations, and part of it could not be committed to movement without the rest of it. And did the Dulles "means" indicate that the H-bomb was among the available weapons? It must; otherwise the whole policy made no "retaliatory" sense—it would not be "overwhelming." Yet, if it did, the United States Strategic Air Force ready at its bases—which now, as one general said, had Russia locked in alligator jaws reaching out on either side to Alaska and Morocco—was asserting an intention to commit the world to atomic warfare on its own judgment and responsibility, if the need arose.[16]

What the historian had to do, if he could, was to explain how such a situation could have been allowed to develop. The key evidently lay in the two Administration standards—security and the ability to pay for it, preparedness and the burdens to which it gave rise. The judgment had been that only the "disengagement overseas and the creation of a central strategic reserve" offered both security and economy. These words of President Eisenhower's expressed the same thought as those of Secretary Dulles. And the Vice-President had stated the concept again in answer to Mr. Stevenson.

If, in contradistinction to what the Vice-President offered blandly in reply to the Stevenson challenge, the real sources of the policy decisions now being defended were searched for, they seemed to lie in a titanic hidden struggle which had gone on for several years

16. The former Secretary of State, Mr. Acheson, in the *New York Times* of March 28, analyzed in some detail the significance of "mobile, massive retaliation, in places of our own choosing":

"America's allies would rightly believe that their very existence was being recklessly exposed to unnecessary risks. Their consent to such a coalition policy could not be expected; their consent to the use by us of bases in their territories could likewise not be expected. . . . In short it would be difficult to violate more completely the principles on which successful coalition policy must be founded." His reference to the theory, held even by Churchill, that the H-bomb was a kind of shield was devastating:

"Strategic bombing is not our first, but our last, resort, reserved for the dread occasion when we must meet an all-out attack with the full attendant horrors of atomic war. No responsible, certainly no democratic, government would use it on any lesser occasion. Indeed the very suggestion that it be so used implies the prior end of democratic government."

before the Eisenhower Administration had come into being at all. One version of the story had reached print in *Fortune*'s issue for May, 1953.[17] It was a struggle, as *Fortune* pictured it, between a group of scientists, centering in J. R. Oppenheimer on one side, and the military—meaning the Strategic Air Force—on the other, the military being reinforced by Admiral Strauss, now chairman of the AEC, and General Nichols, now its general manager.

The Oppenheimer position was summarized as being skeptical of the deterrent effectiveness of intercontinental bombers armed with nuclear weapons and as judging that the existence of a readied Strategic Air Command was goading the Soviets into counter-measures. By 1953 it seemed to Mr. Oppenheimer and his supporters that the only possibility of reducing world tension lay in mutual renunciation of atomic war. The military, on the other hand, believed that the only check to Russian aggression rested on the threat posed by the SAC bombers, which should carry the most destructive load possible.

The quarrel went back to late 1949, when it was first certain that the Russians possessed nuclear weapons. In January, 1950, President Truman reversed a previous decision to postpone work on the H-bomb because of its doubtful feasibility. For Truman's action Mr. Strauss—who was then a member of AEC of which Mr. Lilienthal was still chairman—was largely responsible. He had succeeded against the opposition of an AEC majority, who relied on the support of Oppenheimer, Conant, and other scientists.[18]

The technical feasibility of the H-bomb rested on the judgment of Mr. Edward Teller, who, working at Los Alamos, had satisfied himself of ultimate success. There ensued another battle, so the story went. Mr. Teller demanded a completely new environment. At Los Alamos he felt that the AEC was trying to hamper him—this being

17. It was also reprinted in the *Atomic Scientists Journal* for January, 1954. It was extended and elaborated in *The Hydrogen Bomb: The Men, the Menace, the Mechanism* (New York: David McKay Co., 1954), by James Shepley and Clay Blair, Jr., both of the Washington Bureau of *Time* and *Life*. This account was denounced by Mr. Gordan Jean as wholly inaccurate, and even as "vicious." "It was," he said, "a horrifying combination of little knowledge, outright untruths, and questionable motives." It was also, "to put it mildly, a case of very bad reporting."

18. But not of Fermi, who agreed with Strauss.

the strong Oppenheimer influence. He turned to Secretary T. K. Finletter of the Air Force, who forced the hand of the AEC by offering to set up Mr. Teller in a laboratory under the Air Force. The AEC then capitulated and established the Livermore (California) laboratory. The thermonuclear device detonated at Eniwetok in 1952 was the product of Mr. Teller's efforts.[19]

Meanwhile the Air Force entered on two great survey projects. One was Project Charles, established to discover whether it was true—as Air Force people generally contended—that there was no real defense against mass-destruction weapons and that retaliation was therefore the only possible policy for national safety. Project Charles was implemented at the Lincoln Air Defense Laboratory at Bedford under the direction of the Massachusetts Institute of Technology.

Simultaneously the Air Force had awakened to the prospect that atomic weapons might be adapted to the support of ground troops. With the Army, the Air Force asked the California Institute of Technology to undertake an evaluation. This work, begun early in 1951, became Project Vista.

Later that year Vista prepared to report. Its central proposition was that short-range tactical air forces could check the Russians in Europe. The corollaries of this proposition were that the SAC would no longer be the central and essential strategic reliance that it claimed to be and that, if it gave way to tactical defense forces, the heavy burden of fear weighing down the world would be lifted. The report was said to have been influenced—partly written—by Mr. Oppenheimer. Naturally it did not suit the Air Force; and after a sharp, bitter struggle the SAC won out over the Oppenheimer group. Tactical defense was abandoned as a basis for policy; retaliation was upheld; the SAC was supreme.

Mr. Oppenheimer did not stop, it was said, with these attempts to bring about the neutralization of genocidal weapons. He tried to prevent the tests of 1952 at Eniwetok. As a member of the State

19. This version of the story was especially resented by the scientists, particularly Director Norris E. Bradbury at Los Alamos, because it was well known that the solid preliminary work, as well as the later technical accomplishments necessary to the perfection of the bomb, had been done at Los Alamos. Even Teller resented this oversimplification and let it be known that scientific achievements of this sort were not to be attributed to any one worker.

Department's Disarmament Committee, he tried to persuade President Truman to announce that the United States had decided, on humanitarian grounds, not to make the test. The President was not persuaded.

Still Mr. Oppenheimer did not give up. He formed, in 1952, what was later called ZORC (for the initials of the scientists who were involved). Its object was to prove the feasibility of a perfect air defense; for a complete defense would destroy the cogency of the deterrent-retaliatory theory. ZORC, and another Oppenheimer disciple, Mr. Lloyd Berkner, it was said, worked out and tested at the Lincoln Laboratory the necessary elements for such a defense. The proposed system had two parts—an early warning system of interlocking radar stations far out on the arctic rim and a deep air-defense system using guided missiles and supersonic aircraft. It would cost a fantastic sum without any doubt; but it would work.

ZORC may have been convinced, but the SAC was enraged. In spite of military opposition, however, Mr. Oppenheimer actually got the plan considered in the National Security Council—it was moved for acceptance by the then chairman of National Security Resources Board, Mr. Jack Gorrie. It was rejected; but there must have been a behind-the-scenes struggle of epic bitterness. There the matter rested when the Eisenhower Administration took over and the deliberations of the new Security Council began.

On April 12, 1954, the press all over the country carried on front pages a sensational story concerning Mr. Oppenheimer. He was charged with being a security risk and had been suspended from privileged access to the classified material available to him as a member of AEC's Scientific Advisory Board. This event was a stunning reversal for the American scientists who had generally assisted in the perfection of the Bomb but had had reservations concerning its use. In the person of Mr. Oppenheimer they felt themselves being coerced into conformity with military judgment. He had not agreed with the Air Force and with Admiral Strauss, suddenly risen to a position of power. The charge against Mr. Oppenheimer seemed to the dissident scientists of his persuasion to be in the familiar totalitarian tradition of charging with treason all those who differed in judgment with those who turned out to possess the power of the state.

There was one good thing about the proceedings. The action of the AEC had forestalled a McCarthy persecution. It had been known for some time that the Senator had in reserve an attack on the scientists as a handy diversion to be used when needed. He was in a hot controversy with the Army for "coddling Communists"; if it went against him, he would follow his usual tactics and obscure his defeat by the production of a blanketing sensation. But this consideration cannot have given Mr. Oppenheimer much relief. Those who knew him best comforted him somewhat by telling him that he was now to defend an inner fortress of democracy the capture of which by the enemies of freedom would have sinister consequences for all men and women of liberal views.

Mr. Oppenheimer had been the most prominent of all the scientists engaged in the nuclear program. He had organized the Los Alamos laboratory; he had been one of those present at Alamogordo; and in every decision since he had taken an important part. He had left the government to become the head of the Institute for Advanced Study at Princeton University several years since; but he had continued to be a principal consultant. He had also, in 1953, been appointed a member of the Science Advisory Committee of the Office of Defense Mobilization; and he was a member, by appointment of the Secretary of State, of a panel to advise the State Department on armaments and their regulation. He had, in a real sense, presided over and guided the whole development of nuclear weapons. He was the very center of the work. And in the course of these activities he had been investigated again and again and certified to be loyal. To say, after eleven years of such service, to a man of his attainments and position that he was disloyal was to make a monstrous accusation.

There were extensive hearings;[20] and there was a determination by an AEC Review Board, and a final one by the Atomic Energy Commission itself. Neither decision was unanimous; from each there was one dissent. The Review Board appointed by General Nichols consisted of Messrs. Gordon Gray, president of the University of North Carolina, Thomas Morgan, former chairman of the Sperry

20. They were published as a government document, *In the Matter of J. Robert Oppenheimer: Transcript of Hearing before Personnel Security Board, April 12, 1954, through May 6, 1954* (Washington D.C., 1954).

Gyroscope Company, and Ward V. Evans, professor of chemistry at Loyola University. This board found unequivocally that Mr. Oppenheimer was "loyal"; it said, moreover, that he was possessed of a high degree of discretion in dealing with classified materials. It was his opposition to the H-bomb program that led the majority to recommend that his clearance be suspended.

The case then went to the Commission. This group appears to have paid little attention to the Review Board's report and to have acted mostly on General Nichols' summary.[21] Its chairman was now Admiral Strauss; its other members were Messrs. Henry D. Smyth (author of the famous Smyth Report), Thomas E. Murray, Joseph Campbell, and Eugene M. Zuchert. The majority opinion held that, on grounds of character and associations, Mr. Oppenheimer was a security risk. All the incidents on which it rested had happened years before and had been reviewed again and again. In 1947 Admiral Strauss himself had voted, after a serious study of these same materials, in favor of an Oppenheimer clearance. The opinion disallowed the relevance of the H-bomb issue. It said nothing about loyalty.[22]

Clearly Mr. Oppenheimer was found to be unworthy of future trust because he disagreed with the Strategic Air Force about strategy and with Admiral Strauss and General Nichols about the H-bomb. After opposing the Bomb's manufacture in every way open to him, he had lost his argument in the complexities and machinations of Washington officialdom. He was being punished for having held and defended an opinion against which the decision had gone. His appointment as consultant was to have ended anyway in June, 1954, and the decision of the commission in his case was not made until the day before it expired. He was the victim of the vindictiveness of the victorious individuals and of their determination that he should never again turn up to plague them.[23]

---

21. This was the opinion of Professor Harry Kalven, Jr., who reviewed the whole case for the *Bulletin of the Atomic Scientists*, X (September, 1954), 259 ff.

22. Professor Kalven found this silence disturbing. He also analyzed dispassionately the incidents on which the "defects of character" allegations rested and found them so absurd as to engender a "sense of incredulity" (*ibid.*, p. 269).

23. Substantiating evidence was supplied by such journalists as Roland Sawyer and Nat S. Finney. A condensation of their accounts, which appeared originally in the *Christian Science Monitor* and the *Buffalo Evening News*, respectively, was printed in the *Bulletin of the Atomic Scientists*, September, 1954, pp. 284 and 285.

No occurrence could have illustrated more vividly the disruption of the moral judgment of men than the Oppenheimer case. In the face of supreme destructive potential no dissent to official opinion was allowable. Man was drawn totally into the orbit of the weapon. He might not discuss the thing itself for security reasons; he might not argue against its use lest he weaken the will to destroy if, in the judgment of the military, destruction proved necessary to the national security. Not even to a distinguished participant in the invention and development of the weapon was dissent or questioning allowed. The decision had been made and had passed into the care of the military for execution.[24]

What the deliberations of the Security Council concerning the fundamentals of national strategy came to we have seen reported by the Vice-President with appropriate solemnity. Naturally, however, the burden of exposition was on the Secretary of State. During March he was very voluble. By then the qualifications and modifications of the New Look made necessary by protests from other nations and from Mr. Stevenson were in. A Dulles article that appeared in *Foreign Affairs* was offered as a fuller explanation.[25] In this article Secretary Dulles explained that the "means" which had so worried Mr. Pearson of Canada was the creation of both local and central mobile defenses and that commitment to particular retaliation was not to be made in advance. The enemy was to be kept guessing, but also to be left in no doubt of the potential strength and the ready will to retaliate.

The "ours" of the original Dulles declaration he defined as "collective" action; and "instantly" by inference meant as quickly as

24. Mr. James Reston, in the *New York Times*, June 6, 1954, summarized the scientists' reaction to the Gray Board's recommendations:

1. They suggest that a scientist, like a soldier, is expected not only to obey but also to show enthusiasm for government policies, regardless of his own convictions.

2. They suggest that a scientific adviser can be punished by a security board for holding opinions contrary to government policies.

3. They imply that the scientist's advice must conform to the Strategic Air Command's doctrine that the best defense of the United States is a paralyzing offense.

Mr. Reston ended his extended comment by remarking: "Dr. Oppenheimer may be expendable as the Gray Board suggests, but the confidence of the other scientists is not."

25. It was considered to be of such importance that it was reprinted in full in the *New York Times*, March 17, 1954.

agreement could be had, but without having to wait for actual military preparations. He cited NATO as an example of collective defense for western Europe and the security treaties that linked Australia, New Zealand, the Philippines, Japan, and Korea as an equally good example in the western Pacific. A similar collective arrangement, Mr. Dulles said, was in the making in the Near East with Turkey and Pakistan as the nucleus.

The transcript of a press conference was published on the same day in the *New York Times* in which further explanations were elicited by questioning. Mr. Dulles pointed out that in his speech "what I advocated was 'capacity' to retaliate instantly. In no place did I say that we would retaliate instantly, though indeed we might retaliate instantly in conditions which called for that." He thought he had made it clear that "our" referred to the "free world."

If there were an attack upon the United States and if we had the capacity to respond from our own bases, we would certainly do that. It is, I think, well known that the bases which we have in foreign countries are in general not usable as a matter of law, and as a practical matter, except with the consent of the countries where the bases are. . . . It is implicit in our security system that it operates with the consent of the other partners who have helped to provide the facilities which create a sort of international police system. . . .

The Secretary denied that the capacity to retaliate instantly would mean that a limited challenge in some remote area would have to be met by either an all-out war or no resistance at all.

Let us take, for example, the declaration made by the sixteen powers in relation to Korea, which is one of the illustrations I made in my speech. It was stated there that if aggression should be resumed that the reaction would not necessarily be confined to Korea. Now what does that mean? That does not mean that there will be an effort made to drop atomic bombs on Peiping or upon Moscow. It does mean that there are areas of importance to the aggressors in that vicinity which may have an industrial or strategic relationship to the operation which would no longer be what General MacArthur called "a privileged sanctuary."

Thus, under pressure from allies and political opponents, was the New Look worn down toward a close resemblance to the Taft-Hoover doctrine of other years. None of the words of the announcement meant what they seemed to mean. Secretary Dulles had promised by inference that the Administration would not meet any situation, except attack on the United States, unilaterally; that it would not act instantly; and that it would not use means not agreed on by all.

What remained was the implication that economies were to be made in the interest of "long-run endurance," and economies meant centering upon H-bombs and tactical atomic armament at the expense of conventional weapons. Yet the contradiction involved in developing both kinds of atomic weapons remained unexplained. If a Strategic Air Force was to drop H-bombs on any and all aggressors, why stockpile tactical atomic weapons? And if, by tacit agreement with the enemy, H-bombs were to be last rather than first resorts, so that lesser weapons would after all be necessary, what then became of the "freedom of action" spoken of by Mr. Dulles? Either there was freedom to retaliate at will with the Bomb, or there was not. If there was not, aggression would be met as it had been met before. Wars would be limited; "privileged sanctuaries" would be attacked only if the attack promised to "pay," and it would not promise to pay if it threatened to precipitate a world war.

Mr. Stevenson was now fully entitled to say to Mr. Dulles that the Secretary had been declaiming irresponsible threats in order to please domestic patrioteers, mostly Republicans; but that he had not meant what he said and had had, in fact, to take most of it back or lose the allies who would not be bound to the unilateral judgment of an Administration they did not trust anyway.

The residue from this stripping-down of the New Look, sifted in subsequent congressional queries, was that the Security Council and the President had determined on a concentration of massive and mobile strength within the secure boundaries of North America. However it might be concealed or sought to be explained away, this concentration involved withdrawal from contact with the potential enemy both on the east and on the west. This contact would be maintained by those nations which adjoined China and the Soviet Union. For this purpose the United States would give assistance and promise help in time of need. But the truth was that her posture was one not primarily of giving aid to allies but of readiness to strike out in reprisal when and where military judgment determined that it would pay in strictly practical terms. That such a judgment could only in essence be unilateral—though other opinions would be consulted if time allowed—was perfectly clear. Sir Winston Churchill spoke of it in the Commons, where he had a first-class revolt to deal with; and the French and British press found it a subject for repeated discussion.

Mr. Dulles was called on to defend the policy before congressional committees, and, although he made a clumsy job of it, the opposition was unable to force any retractions—possibly because the opposition itself had no clear policy. The Congress was extremely happy about a seven-and-a-half-billion-dollar tax-reduction bill, and any alternate defense policy would require higher rather than lower taxes. Few were willing to advocate such a sacrifice even if it was necessary to better defenses.

The partial commitment to massive reprisal, even if it lay camouflaged in a surrounding thicket of explanations, reservations, and protestations of mutuality, made a difficult problem for Secretary Dulles in the conduct of foreign relations. The truth was that the adoption of the Taft-Hoover concept of American security had been precisely what the shrewdest politicians in other nations had anticipated would happen as the result of Republican victory in 1952. They had hoped that President Eisenhower, as an experienced world strategist, would resist; but they had had hopes, not confidence, mostly because they had had an almost pathological fear of American isolationism, besides some experience with Mr. Dulles. This doubt, indeed, was not new; it had created a skepticism about the sincerity and permanence of the Truman Doctrine, the Marshall Plan, and, finally, the European Defense Community, which had tormented all of Mr. Acheson's negotiations.

What the United States intended—that part of the United States which in the long run, Europeans thought, would come uppermost and prevail—was what could be read daily in the *Chicago Tribune* and had been expressed with such frankness by the late Senator Taft. The United States of industry and commerce intended to reduce and consolidate her commitments to a burden which could be carried as capitalist insurance; and at the same time she intended to create a situation in which the decision to use her massive concentration of retaliatory power would be safely deposited at the heart of the concentration. Allies would be encouraged, assisted, and advised; but they would not be allowed to commit the retaliation potential to action. This commitment, however the fact might be concealed, would be a decision to be made by the United States—and, moreover, by the right people in the United States. Such was the New Look. Mr. Dulles had given away the intention when he had made that unfortunate speech which, in one sentence, had used the three equivocal words—"instantly," "means," and "ours." Not just Mr. Lester Pearson from near-by Canada knew what they meant; when the explanations were all over, everyone knew.

Everyone knew; but nearly everyone in the United States, it seemed, approved! An almost audible sigh of relief went up as the American people themselves understood, in spite of all the protestations to the contrary, what it was that the Administration was up to. Here was a foreign policy, combined with a strategy for national security, in which they actually believed. It seemed to them realistic in terms they could understand. It brought back, they thought at first, their power to control their own actions; it ended the loose mutuality they disliked; it took from foreigners the right and ability to control American destinies.

Doubts drifted in, however, to blacken the June-clear skies. True, France, for instance, or some other third-class nation could not now determine American action; but the Chinese, by starting more Korea incidents, could. The Soviet menace had not actually been relieved. The Bomb had not been subdued; the H-bomb, indeed, now at full maturity, bloomed thrice in the Pacific skies during the spring, and its destructive power was so wide that it proved impossible to quiet the alarm which followed. And, as if these uncertainties were not enough, scientists began to talk of competition for "space bases."[26]

While the H-bomb tests were still in progress and fresh alarm was spreading throughout the world, new crises arose in the Middle East; and, before there had been time to assess the importance of these disturbances, the Indochina situation degenerated disastrously. In January, Bidault at Berlin had made plain to the other Allies how sick France was of the eight-year-old war in Indochina and had

26. E.g., anyone could read in the newspapers of March 22 the Associated Press dispatch which quoted the director of New Mexico's Institute of Meteoritics, as saying that "the nation first establishing a station in space will win absolute control of the earth. If the Russians do it first, we and the rest of the world will become just as tractable as they want us to be." The quotation here is from the *New York Times*.

said frankly that France would escape by negotiation if she could. If negotiation involved recognition of the Communists and admission to the United Nations, she was willing. Not only that, she saw no reason why, if the Korean fighting could be ended by splitting Korea in two, the same solution might not do for Indochina. This indication of withdrawal had infuriated Mr. Dulles, who had responded by enlarging American aid and beginning the preparation of opinion—he had been joined in this by the President himself— for intervention. By April the military position of the French had so deteriorated that he began to threaten the use of that retaliatory power he had until then spoken of only generally. At this point, however, the European Allies balked, and Mr. Dulles had to undertake a frantic unexpected visit in mid-April to see whether he could not persuade them to join in a specific warning to the Chinese that if they sent in "volunteer" armies, as they had done in Korea, they would be attacked at home. Since this attack would have enabled the Chinese to invoke their mutual defense treaty with Russia, World War III might then have begun. The most he could get from the Allies was a kind of tentative agreement that, if the meeting at Geneva on April 26 failed altogether, then some warning might be given to China.

Yet the meeting was bound to fail. The renewed Communist pressure on the French in Indochina was clearly a preliminary to the Geneva meeting, where, for the first time, the Chinese would come face to face with the Western powers and consideration of the questions surrounding coexistence would be impossible to put off any longer. But the senators of the China lobby—Knowland leading— were issuing blast after blast of threats warning against any arrangement at all with the Chinese Communists, especially their recognition by the United States or their admission to the United Nations. Mr. Dulles responded by protesting that neither of these actions had been contemplated. He thus abjured in advance the bargaining points he might have used to best advantage without the sacrifice of any American interest. What, then, was the use of the Geneva meeting?

American foreign policy seemed hopelessly inept and amateurish; there was reason to be grateful now for the cool sense of the British, who set to work to repair as much of the damage as they could and to try, in spite of Mr. Dulles' wild talk, to make something of the Geneva opportunity. Sir Anthony Eden, and his superior, Sir Winston Churchill, were old hands at mediating; but it did seem unlikely that they could salvage anything from the wreck Mr. Dulles had made of the Allies' case.

Disarmament had not entirely dropped out of public view, but little hope of it remained, even though there was a sudden revival in April of discussions in the United Nations. The truth was that disarmament, in spite of people's hopes, was understood by everyone not to be possible until East and West had met the imperative of coexistence: that they should come to a stable situation, agreed to by both, which was not likely to be disturbed by an aggression which would invoke atomic retaliation. This was the coexistence about which statesmen would not talk, and which Mr. Dulles appeared now to have pushed back behind the barriers to bargaining raised in his pre-Geneva speeches. His situation was the same as Mr. Acheson's had been. But it did seem as though experience might have been a better teacher.

It was in a climactic two-week period at the end of April and the beginning of May that the confusions and contradictions of American policy produced their inevitable consequence. In that short time the loud talk about retaliation, the policy of accepting dependence on nuclear weapons, and the complete inability to negotiate were all revealed as absurdly inadequate to the situation and desperately unrealistic as guides to the conduct of our foreign affairs.

When Communist pressure on Dien Bien Phu increased in April, Secretary Dulles again began making provocative speeches, saying that Viet Nam was the key to Southeast Asia and that, if it fell, all the neighboring nations would fall as well. President Eisenhower, backing him up at first, spoke of Eastern nations collapsing "like dominoes." First, Vice-President Nixon, then others, began to hint that military measures might not be far off; and it was widely suspected that the Security Council, at the urging of Secretary Dulles and Admiral Radford, chairman of the Joint Chiefs of Staff, was seriously considering immediate atomic intervention. What seems actually to have been most seriously considered at first was, not the landing of troops, but the use of tactical atom bombs dropped from planes stationed on American aircraft carriers at that moment in near-by waters. But the situation worsened so rapidly that the practicality of simple bombing vanished before a decision could be reached. The Chinese came to Ho Chi-minh's support so massively, and Dien Bien Phu was almost at once so closely besieged, that nuclear bombs could not be dropped on the enemy without risk of injuring the French forces themselves.

Whatever Mr. Dulles had had in mind, or the Security Council had intended, the public reaction to the hints of unilateral intervention was so violent that all those who had started out as its advocates were, within a two-week period, trying to pretend that nothing of the sort had ever been contemplated. And at the same time the President finally saw where his Secretary of State was taking him. He was, after all, the same President who sometime before had observed that "there was no longer any alternative to peace."

The dismal defeat of the Indochina tour de force brought American diplomacy to practical paralysis. When a week before the Geneva conference Mr. Dulles suddenly made a trip to Europe to persuade the French not to negotiate and the British to adopt some sort of joint support for the French position, the British ministers pointed out that what Mr. Dulles proposed to settle by force was precisely what the Geneva conference had been called to talk about. Its prospects might not be very bright for the West; but they were no different from what they had been when Mr. Dulles himself had been pressing for the meeting. Britain therefore rejected outright the suggestions for violent action. His visit to France during the next few days was even more disastrous. The French, having listened to his speeches for the last month, not unnaturally had the impression that the United States was about to throw in troops or, at the least, immediate air support. He had to retreat. American public opinion would not allow such an intervention; and the President had let him down.

Mr. Dulles was in a tighter dilemma than any Secretary of State had been caught in for a long time. The United States could not intervene; yet defeat in Southeast Asia had been made to seem a disaster. The British would not join an adventure of intervention; and the French were so thoroughly beaten as to be ready to negotiate on any terms. And how could they be persuaded to hold on when an offer of actual military assistance was out of the question?

The French had moved so slowly toward independence for Indochina in the postwar years as to lose any advantage from granting it. The truth was that what was going on there was insurrection, not an attempt at conquest. The American scheme for training a Vietnamese army like the South Korean army was based on a false premise. The Asians were more fearful still of Western colonialism than of Communist domination, in Burma and India, where American had replaced British imperialism as the object of successful Communist propaganda. Neither the United States nor any other Western power could intervene successfully in any nation which resented the assistance to the point of joining the Communists in opposition. Yet through the spring months the Security Council's decision to prevent Communist expansion had stood without presidential veto; and the United States had come closer and closer to the incredible decision that unilateral invasion, if necessary, would be undertaken.

The Communists at Geneva were aggressive and unreasonable. They were winning everywhere in the East, and, after the fashion of their kind, they preferred the diplomacy of toughness. They obviously thought that the United States contemplated intervention. And, if she had acted, what they had always wanted would have happened. The American armies would have been bogged down in Asian jungles fighting satellite powers; and the Russians would have been quite clear of any involvement.

American policy was collapsing not only in the Far East but in Europe. Germany, rising like a phoenix from the ashes of war, had thoroughly frightened France and, in fact, had caused serious differences in Britain. The Labour party was nearly disrupted by argument pro and con. The specter of a German-Russian *rapprochement* haunted all European foreign offices. The memory of the Molotov-Ribbentrop business in the first stages of the last war was still sharp. And it was obvious that Chancellor Adenauer, as France dithered about ratification of the European pacts, was having difficulty preventing his own people from proceeding to negotiation with the Russians. If West Germany was not to be taken into the European Community on an equal basis—which included rearming—then her future might lie, as Germans had always seemed to feel it lay—in using her great energies and talents to organize the peoples to the east of her. Thus Germany, in spite of American objections and in spite of Adenauer's best efforts, was flirting with the Communists who controlled the area—or most of it—involved in the historic *Drang nach Osten.*

It had been in anticipation of this eastward look that Mr. Acheson, as Secretary of State, had advocated the European Community in which there would be scope for German genius. He had not invented this idea. It had, in fact, come from France. Schuman, as foreign minister, and Monnet, as planner, had conceived of a Europe knit together into economic union which would have the size and variety of a continental economy and would thus give scope for German genius. At the same time it would increase productivity and raise the levels of living everywhere. The first steps in this scheme had been taken. The European Coal and Steel Community was now in existence, with its administrative center in Luxembourg and with Monnet at its head. It had not yet come into full effect, and the old cartelists were still struggling to keep their prerogatives; but it seemed likely to prevail over all difficulties in the end. There was this much of clear gain in Europe.

There had been suggestions, many of them, for going further in economic matters. The most likely of these centered in agriculture; and this might come next. But the political concomitants, being prevented by fears and prejudices, did not progress. The continuing attempt to build the Strasbourg institution (European Union) into a European government, or, indeed, to give it any appurtenances of sovereignty, had failed completely. Statesmen still met at intervals and addressed each other; but their situation of unreality was unmistakable.

The proposal for a European army had from the first been the kind of tour de force which could succeed only in circumstances of crisis. Normally, such a development, without the prior organization of political institutions, would be unthinkable. How could there be one army responsible to separate sovereign states? The answer was: Only in time of military necessity such as had existed during the Napoleonic Wars and two world wars of the twentieth century. Nevertheless, it was hoped that the treaties creating the European Defense Community would set up an even closer alliance than had joined the United Nations in World War II.

France's historic position vis-à-vis Britain and the United States had been that she wanted guaranties of support. She was in Europe and would receive the first blows from the East. Of old the enemy had been Germany; and the theory was that Germany had attacked because it was her judgment that perhaps Britain, and certainly the United States, would not intervene. This theory extended now to Soviet aggression. It assumed that there would be less chance of attack if it was certain that both Britain and the United States would intervene. Such intention to intervene could be made absolutely plain by the incorporation of British and American forces in an army which also included those of France and the smaller countries. Furthermore, it was clear that the immense Russian power could not be opposed with any show of equality without incorporating German strength.

The French understood this theory well enough; but, when sober consideration followed the first logical thought, most Frenchmen were not so sure that they did not fear Germany more than Russia. They thought of an army in which French soldiers served under German commanders, and their revulsion was more than logic could overcome. They began to find reasons for not ratifying the treaties which had been their own idea. And the structure of the Fourth Republic was such that so far no French government had even dared bring the treaties into the Chamber of Deputies for consideration.[27]

The French attitude was proving almost equally unco-operative toward the American plan for a Far Eastern defense organization now being pushed by Secretary Dulles. The defeats and humiliations in Indochina had hurt French pride; and being forced to agree to division and independence in Indochina had left resentments. In spite of the fact that the war there had for a long time been mostly paid for by the United States, Premier Laniel, in announcing to the deputies the defeat at Dein Bien Phu, said sullenly that it had happened because France had had to fight alone. If Indochina could not be held as a colony, most Frenchmen were unmoved by the suggestion of fighting for its salvation from communism.

So soon, also, as Mr. Dulles began to feel this resistance in France, and outright opposition in Britain, there appeared a countermove-

---

27. The deputies could repudiate a government without themselves dissolving. For the year's most interesting discussion of the French decline see Ronald Matthews, *The Death of the French Republic* (New York: Frederick A. Praeger, Inc., 1954).

ment in Asia itself. The Indonesians suggested a movement among themselves, the Indians and Ceylonese, whose purpose would be to negotiate an anti-aggression pact with the Chinese Communists. It seemed that the effort of the United States to isolate and ostracize the Chinese Communists was going to fail.

In the midst of his crumbling policy, when he was just home from the humiliation of Geneva and being bitterly assailed on all sides as a diplomatic failure, Mr. Dulles reaffirmed in the now familiar language of the Republican isolationists that

it would be intolerable for us to concede hundreds of millions of souls to despotic rule. . . . The Soviet rulers tell us occasionally that there could be "coexistence" between their society and ourselves. We must beware of these professions. Coexistence is not part of a Soviet Communist creed, except in the sense that non-Communists are allowed, in a physical sense, to exist. It can never be satisfactory to the Soviet Communists that freedom is suppressed only within what is presently the area they dominate. Freedom anywhere is a constant peril to them. . . . Thus Soviet Communist rulers are driven not merely by their own lusts but by their own doctrine to seek constantly to expand their own control.[28]

It was discouraging to have the American Secretary of State in 1954 so immobilized in the web of his own words. He was no further advanced than Acheson had been. It was not that what he said was not true. The Communists hated freedom and would always try to suppress it. But to an operating statesman in 1954 this fact was an irrelevancy. No matter what the Communists' ideas were, they had either to be dealt with or conquered by force. A way of living together was possible if the hard-core interests of each could be brought into balance. The arrangement might be precarious; but surely it would be better than scrambling on the slippery slopes of continual denunciation, meanwhile going on with an armaments race on the scale of the present one. Such an arrangement would have to be made soon; there was no time for the slow accommodations of American opinion such as might bring a change in Administration that would create a new policy. Before then the train of events might end in that war of holocaust so dreaded by everyone of imagination.

The truth was that by the end of the atomic year the United States was very nearly alone, with the wreck of impossible endeavors

28. The text of this speech at the College of William and Mary was printed in the *New York Times*, May 16, 1954.

lying all about. Everything had gone awry. On every issue Secretary Dulles had been on the side which the Allies did not approve; and every issue had been settled against his opposition. Once leader of the postwar world, the nation had become merely a bad-tempered on-looker at events which it disapproved but could do nothing about.

France changed premiers once again in crisis as the Geneva meet-ings came on. But this time a more determined man was found, one who set out to escape from the impasse of reactionary colonialism which had come to its logical end in the humiliations of Indochina, of Tunisia, and of Morocco. Pierre Mendès-France met the crisis by dealing at Geneva with the representatives of the Soviet Union and of China. It was Molotov and Chou En-lai who worked out with him the partition arrangement which was so economically absurd as to be patently temporary, but which did follow the pattern of Korea. France did not escape without humiliation, but she escaped. Eden of Britain played an active part in the mediatory proceedings; Sec-retary Dulles refused even to be present. In spite of the injury to their pride, Frenchmen were so delighted to escape the strategic sinkhole in the East that Mendès-France became the most popular politician since the war. The time for realism had come.

Feeling behind him the strength of popularity, the Premier next tackled the hot issue of the European Defense Community. It had long been strongly suspected that France was likely to repudiate the treaties which owed their origin to her statesmen of the polit-ical center—men like Schuman and Bidault, who had been thrown up during the years of chaos. Frenchmen could not find it in their hearts to approve German rearming if that involved the merging of all French and German forces in the same army. For two years no premier had dared risk a vote. Mendès-France asked for a decision; and the treaties were defeated.

American policy had been so completely bound to these treaties that paralysis set in. The commitments to Chancellor Adenauer's group in Germany now began to display their unwisdom. Alcide de Gasperi, in Italy, an old and dying man, now out of power, but still strong in his Catholic party, wept when he heard the news from France and presently died—of a broken heart, it was said. Ade-nauer, De Gasperi, and Schuman had hoped for an anti-Communist Catholic Europe. Their scheme had failed. Adenauer was seventy-eight, De Gasperi was dead, and Schuman was out of power. Americans might well ask themselves, as many did, how their policy had come to be tied to such an adventure in negative reaction. The answer, of course, was that it was a desperate bulwark—part of a whole series—thrown up against the Communist threat to Europe. It was of a piece with the Spanish alliance and, in a reverse way, with the *rapprochement* with Communist Yugoslavia.

The British Socialists had dissented all along, and latterly Churchill and Eden had seen where the policy was carrying them and had also drawn back. Britain had never been willing to merge her forces with those of Europe, and she was obviously relieved at the definitive defeat of what had been an American policy which they had felt obligated to support. There would be a return now to realism. There would be difficulties. The West German government, which ought never to have been activated until the German issues had been settled, was now in being and could not be disestablished. It made all the other issues infinitely harder to deal with.

Besides the Catholic bloc, there was another group which was bitterly disappointed when the French defeated the treaties—the pan-Europeans, for whom Carl Henri Spaak was a kind of spokesman.[29] The statesmen of the smaller nations had hoped for an economic merging which would create a viable economy. Theirs was not an aggressive thesis, directed toward communism. It was more a positive desire for a modernized area in which there could be the possibilities for prosperity only to be had in a wide and various producing and trading area. The embarrassment to Mendès-France in dealing with Spaak and his colleagues, as he had to do at once when ratification failed, was far greater than any other he encountered. His own suggestions for alternatives were sharply rejected. In the end it seemed likely that the moderating British, Eden leading, would work out the most acceptable substitute. Germany, the truth was, could not be prevented from rearming. Her sovereignty would now be recognized; and she could go pretty much her own way.

We had now come full circle from prewar days. Now both Germany and Japan would not only be freed of restriction; they would be urged to rearm. Probably, as the French knew very well, the

29. This constituted the "Brussels Treaty Group," formally the European Treaty Organization which activated the EDC.

Germans would be rearmed by the Americans. For the truth was that American fear of the Soviet Union allowed no alternatives to implacable and oversimple opposition. Instead of looking, with a view to enterprise, at a world which was shared with a Soviet Union, armed and economically powerful, Americans—at least official Americans—could think only of futile opposition which had as its basis, obviously, the hope of extermination. They could not look at communism, argue with it, deal with it. They had to scream at it, denounce it, shudder away from it.

The new crowd in Russia—Malenkov-Molotov-Khrushchev, often called the "junta"—and their military allies were making this treatment difficult. It was agreed that they had no objectives different from those of Stalin, at least in the long run, but they had very different manners. There was a strange flexibility to be dealt with; and consequently the Communists were winning friends, even among the Western Allies, at the same time that frightened and inflexible Americans were alienating them.

Furthermore, just at the time when France was finally ending the pretense of the EDC, Secretary Dulles insisted on going through with a similar treaty affiliation in Southeast Asia. It was dead long before its birth. No authentic and important Asiatic nation[30] even attended the Philippine meeting except Siam, whose regime was so notoriously corrupt and fatuous as to offer the most tempting bait since Korea to Communist infiltration. American sponsorship of a southeast Asia defense system which India, Burma, and Indonesia not only refused to join but denounced as inimical to Asian peace was not easy to explain. Suppose, it was suggested, Siam should succumb to inner corruption and the Communists should take over? The United States was now committed to regard such an outcome as a cause for war. To such a pact, the British only with great reluctance agreed; it was worthless. General Eisenhower's good sense would not allow the nation to become involved in another Korea, if only for political reasons. Why he allowed his Secretary of State to set up another similar obligation so likely to be embarrassing went entirely unexplained.

It was frequently remarked by the critics, who became more

30. Unless South Korea, Formosa, and the Philippines ranked as "important."

voluble as the failures multiplied, that the old adage about speaking softly and carrying a big stick had been reversed. Now there was plenty of bluster; but there was no big stick. The concentration on atomic armament had provided the military with a whole new set of weapons which they could not use. For the hard decision which had to be taken at the time of the Indochina defeat demonstrated that responsible statesmen could not accept the risk involved in starting an atomic war for fringe benefits or even to uphold the principle of opposition to aggression.

The President might not think clearly on domestic issues. His was said, with some truth, to be a "give-away" administration. He had the familiar, easy, additive philosophy which held that, if businesses were prosperous, the country would be prosperous. It followed that anything the government could do to make any business prosperous contributed to the national good. This fallacious, antiquated, and often-exposed attitude was obviously one he had picked up from his business and military friends; he could never really have thought about it. But in military matters he was accustomed to think; and he finally saw, when the decision came up to him through all the layers of preliminary planning, and with all the notations attached, that dropping atomic bombs, flown from those carriers off the Indochina coast, as Admiral Radford urged, as Vice-President Nixon hinted, and as Secretary Dulles threatened, was to risk more than any responsible statesman aware of the H-bomb had a right to risk.

It remained to be seen whether the President would be able to pursue into policy the logic of his inability to authorize atomic attack in Indochina. If it was impossible to resort to the adopted weapon in punishing satellite aggressions, some other way of meeting them must be found. To resort to conventional weapons, it had been said, was to yield the advantage to the Communists, especially the Chinese, who had no scruples about the expenditure of men, and who would sacrifice any number for any cause. The Korean War, after the Chinese had come in, had not been a victorious adventure. There must not be such another, so everyone said. Yet what alternatives were there?

The answer, of course, was to furnish an ideological alternative to communism by eliminating the conditions on which communism grew. There were broad areas—Africa, the Middle East, Southeast

Asia, even South America[31]—where the Communists were making appeals with obvious effect. President Truman had understood the need. In putting forward his famous Fourth Point, he had said that it must be the first business of America to rescue other peoples from poverty; that their well-being was not only a condition of maintaining American prosperity but a necessity in the ideological struggle. If the West succeeded in raising levels of living among other peoples, it would sterilize the ground in which Communist ideas were sown.

These were courageous words. The Fourth Point was a genuine alternative. But it fell into hostile hands. President Truman himself, under pressure, modified his vague proposals for helpfulness by indicating that governmental efforts would merely prepare the way for private investments. Given this emphasis, the program already sounded like imperialism, even if a new sort, to most underdeveloped peoples; and presently, after the Korean crisis arose with its insatiable demands for armament, the funds for peaceful penetration grew smaller and smaller. Before President Truman gave way to his successor, the Fourth Point was dead in all but talk. An appropriation was still made to the United Nations Technical Assistance Administration; but it was made grudgingly and with such conditions attached as to make it far less useful than it might have been.

President Eisenhower had, on a number of occasions, seemed quite clear that such a program was essential. Yet the truth was that, by 1954, few funds were available for uses which were not really military, because the Fourth Point program was not agreed to by those who could prevent entry on any serious attempt to implement it. The power of the negative is very considerable in any democracy and is only to be overcome by determined leadership, which will marshal a strong supporting opinion. Neither President Truman nor his successor had created such support for a program they professed to believe was fundamental. They had allowed the military— especially the Navy—to expand to the point of monopolizing all the funds to be got from tolerable taxation. They had taken no steps to

31. The substitution of an American-supported dictatorship for a Communist regime—such as occurred in Guatemala in 1954—was not to win the ideological battle; it was to lose it. The Guatemalan interference was an embarrassment everywhere in the world where the struggle with communism was joined.

relieve, but had rather exacerbated, all the fears and xenophobic emotions which would support military enlargement. In the circumstances, there could be no immediate change.

Meanwhile, of course, the battle went badly. It went badly in Southeast Asia, in the Middle East—everywhere in the poverty-stricken areas of the world. Any change now might come too late. American policy was floundering in the futilities of its own illogic, and the positive policy which might have saved the situation was dead of inanition.

American policy concerning the rest of the world had polarized that world with frightening success. Americans claimed, of course, that the aggressive intriguing of the Soviet Union, not American attitudes, were the cause. But such was not the conclusion of the important third parties who had developed the "neutralism" of the past few years. India, led by Nehru, was inclined to blame the United States rather more than Russia; so were the Burmese; and it was by no means certain that a majority of Europeans did not feel the same way.

The efforts of the neutrals to lend their good offices met with rebuffs from the American side which were at least as rough as those which came from Russia. The demand that friends should show friendship by subservience was one of the characteristics of the time. It had, I believed, to be set down as another of those consequences of the advent of the Bomb. Those who were not with us—and enthusiastically so—were against us. There was no longer any freedom of choice, any middle way, any tolerance or compromise. And what hints there were of flexibility came, it must be admitted, from the other side. These were denounced, almost before they could be made manifest, in the American press as sly attempts to undermine the morale of the "free world." And, uniformly, within a few days, each such suggestion was equally bitterly denounced by a "spokesman" for the Department of State.

Sir Winston Churchill continued to hope for, and on occasion to press for, renewed high-level talks. What he wanted, obviously, before he finally stepped down from the prime ministership into the shadows of age, which seemed to creep around him now day by day, was a chance to sit in conference with President Eisenhower and

Premier Malenkov. His faith in accommodation was never lost. He often said that to lose that faith was to lose everything, because, when it was gone, all hope for the future would be gone.

That time was running out, regardless of statesmen and competing ideologies, was brought sharply to the world's attention when the British Association for the Advancement of Science met at Oxford in summer. The presidential address at that meeting said flatly that, unless the competition in weaponeering stopped, there must be one or another kind of disaster. Either the weapons would be used in war, which would result in the sudden destruction of civilization, or, if war did not come but rearmament continued, with its improvement and testing of nuclear devices, the experimental explosions incident to this progress would gradually raise the level of radiation in the atmosphere until inevitable genetic results occurred. The explosion of a few thousand bombs, even if only in uninhabited areas, would jeopardize effectively the biological future of the race.

This warning had no reference to the admitted policy of the United States military to adapt nuclear weapons for tactical uses, but the implication was not lost on anyone who heard the solemn words. There was no comment from any official American source. There was no hint of a changed policy. General Gruenther of NATO said publicly that nuclear weapons, along with German divisions, were necessary to European defense; and a beginning had been made, it was announced, in equipping the army there with atomic artillery. It seemed that tactical atomic development had become so institutionalized, had gained such momentum, that nothing now could halt it.

President Eisenhower had at least made an effort toward deflection. His proposal to set up an international agency for the peaceable exploitation of nuclear possibilities had been timely enough. There were many efforts in progress to develop power plants. A large one was proceeding at Harwell; its current would be turned into the British grid before many years had passed. The Russians said, without furnishing details, that they had such a plant already in operation. The United States was regrettably behind because it was Administration policy not to go forward with government power plants; the statesmen now in charge were passionately determined that development should be turned over to private industry. Nevertheless, a good deal of research had at least been kept up. The breeder reactor had been devised, for instance, which promised an almost miraculous multiplication of potential from fissionable material. And, in April, Admiral Strauss had announced that the AEC was turning more of its efforts toward peacetime uses for atomic energy.

The whole question of public versus private development of atomic energy was the center of a controversy which went on all year in the Congress. The Atomic Energy Act had reserved to government a monopoly of atomic developments, and, if private industry was to build nuclear power plants, the act would have to be revised. The Republicans, said the Democrats, had given the oil interests the tidelands reserves; they had removed the stringent regulations on the sale of natural gas; they were giving private interests the remaining hydroelectric sites; they had closed down both the synthetic rubber and the synthetic oil plants; they were even discontinuing the experimental extraction of oil from shale in Colorado. They now wanted to present a few large concerns with the government's rights to nuclear power, together with all the billions invested in research and development. There was a very evident belief among the Republicans, however, that Americans approved this kind of approach; and, in the end, they succeeded in amending the Atomic Energy Act so that private concerns could have much of what they had asked.

Whether or not this policy was the infamous betrayal of the public interest that progressives among the Democrats said it was, it was now official that the few existing power concerns would be allowed to exploit nuclear resources, and several announced plans for building plants. It was a fact, however, that both Britain and Russia were going forward faster than the United States.[32] The private interests blamed the Atomic Energy Act of 1946; it remained to be seen whether the "give-away" revisions would make any difference. Democrats, approaching the congressional elections of 1954, found here a useful issue. Private power companies, they said, were now in a position to accommodate the pace of atomic power development to their own interests. They would be slow to make their existing in-

32. The one American power plant of more than pilot-plant size, being developed in the Pittsburgh area by the Duquesne Power Company, was the result of AEC initiative, not that of private power concerns. This fact was a matter for sharp comment by the director of the division of AEC devoted to civilian uses of nuclear energy (officially director of reactor development), Mr. Laurence Hafstad.

vestments worthless by obsolescence. They would be in no hurry to bring the new resources into general use.

How this determination of the Republicans to reserve for private interests the profitable exploitation of nuclear energy, while going on with governmental research and concurrent additions to the stockpiles of bombs, would affect the scheme for an international agency for peacetime development was not very clear. But evidently such an agency was not, in the American mind, to be an action agency. It was not, for instance, to own or operate power facilities. It was said that an exchange of information was to be set up, that foreign scientists and students were to be invited to study American methods in an organized way (a kind of school was hinted at), and that there would be some contribution of fissionable materials for common uses. None of this activity was likely to annoy private power producers.

It would have been thought so innocuous as not to annoy the Russians either. But they were taking the same standoffish attitude about this project as they had in 1946 about the Marshall Plan. They evidently felt that, with rising strength, they could afford not to give any hostages whatever to a capitalist society they believed to be incorrigibly and actively hostile. They did not quite refuse; but all during the first months of negotiation they continued to put up the same block they had used to obstruct the approaches to disarmament. They would not even discuss the matter, they said, unless there was a prior commitment not to use atomic weapons in war. Yet they refused to accept any suggestion for an inspection system which would guarantee that the sequestration of bombs was actual.

Thus there was an apparently unbreakable impasse. The stockpiles grew until even the problem of their disposal began to seem insoluble. The attempt to deflect the march toward destruction was no more successful than the attempt to meet the problem head-on by disarmament.

The curious confusions in American policy probably reflected rather faithfully the divisions among Americans themselves and, in the current year specifically, the divisions among Republicans. It was not possible to say from how secure a base Senator Knowland spoke; but it was very thoroughly respected by the Administration, because the loud-voiced Senator was allowed to check any tentatives toward discussion. A kind of persistent illustration was furnished by the evident desire of many nations to admit the Chinese Communists to the United Nations. Every once in a while some suggestion of weakening on this issue would be made. A trumpet blast from the California Senator would follow; and the Secretary of State and the United States representative at the United Nations would issue passionate denials of any such intention. Usually the Senator was not appeased until the President himself humbly promised that the existence of Red China would never be acknowledged.

Supported by American funds, and staffed by American military and civilan experts, Chiang Kai-shek's little island kingdom off the coast of China continued to threaten loudly the invasion of the mainland. And the China lobby continued to create the impression that it was the American intention to see that the invasion succeeded. Obviously those responsible for foreign policy hoped for a change; but, so long as the President would not face the problem, they were unable to suggest a new approach.

Yet the President was the moderating and reasonable influence in the Administration. It was well known that it was he who curbed the adventurers around him. He seemed to have more grasp of strategy in a nuclear age, more sense of the national peril, and was, it was widely believed, more earnest in the search for alternatives than they. He even spoke, as President Truman had, of coexistence as a necessary fact, to be recognized as the sole alternative to destruction. But he did not implement his tolerance, his caution, and his concern for the national interest.

He acquiesced in further progress toward nuclear weaponeering; he allowed the insistence on German rearmament to go on regardless of unification; he made no moves whatever toward securing the moderating influence of the "neutrals"; he treated the Communist government of China as an outlaw in the society of nations; he allowed budgetary considerations to determine policy not only of defense but of inroads on Communist influence in backward places. There was, indeed, a long list to be made of decisions which would be reversed if what seemed to be in the President's mind were allowed to shape policy. The profound gratitude many citizens felt that their President was devoted to the national interest and their trust in him as leader was invaded by the wish that he would exert himself. They wondered whether he would not sometime give way in crisis to those around him who were so insistent on the general policy of "liberation." This apprehensiveness was hard to measure; but it existed.

Americans, it might be said, were used to uneasiness about their affairs—used to it but not accommodated to it. They were not secure in the sanity of their policy or in their own adjustment to a world in which the atomic bomb was an ever present reality. Nor could it honestly be said that, as the years passed, their excitement subsided. They showed all too evident signs of reacting to recurrent disturbances, real or fancied, in ways typical of hysteria-driven people. They knew—and their sensible public men often said—that this phenomenon in itself was the most dangerous of all. But control over it seemed impossible to achieve.

The worst of these manifestations were those which obviously had their source in the more primitive impulses. The desire to destroy communism—and, along with communism, the guardians of its citadel—was an almost uncontrollable impulse. However unwise, however dangerous, it was apt to break out at the most inappropriate times. It made the life of those whose professions required them to function in contact areas with the enemy completely futile. Any attempt at understanding, much less any sympathy, was marked down as appeasement. It was political death to any politician to have his name even remotely connected with a policy of accommodation. Even Adlai Stevenson no longer dared insist on reason in such matters. As a party of opposition the Democrats took the line instead of insisting that the Republicans were softer toward Communists than they. McCarthy's "twenty years of treason" had frightened them into complete irresponsibility. It was the liberal Democrats who felt impelled to pass the act, advised against by all those who had to handle the problem, suppressing the Communist party. They knew it to be unwise as a matter of defense against the conspiracy to overthrow the government. They were told so by J. Edgar Hoover himself. They nevertheless felt impelled to reflect the impulse of those who would strike out blindly at the people who seemed to personalize American fears.

The time had not come when wise decisions had any chance of acceptance in the United States. What was worse, the responsible statesmen, the chosen leaders, Eisenhower and Stevenson at their head, made no attempt to establish leadership looking to the policy both had said was necessary—coexistence. Americans seemed to move in a fog of peril from which they could find no escape.

Nevertheless, one perennial suggestion came up again and again, a suggestion which, if it did nothing else, indicated a deep-running wish. This was disarmament. Disarmament was well enough known to historians as a recurrent will-o'-the-wisp. For 1954 was far from being the first time in history when military momentum had become so formidable that war seemed inevitable. There was scarcely one of these gathering conflicts that enlightened diplomats had not sought to deflect or interrupt, either by compromising the controversies which might result in actual hostilities or by reducing tension through disarmament. Statesmen and diplomats had averted the outbreak which finally occurred in 1914 several times in the preceding few years; and, looking back, there seemed to be no reason why the issues of 1914 might not also have been compromised. The ensuing war settled nothing. When it was over, there still remained unsettled all the differences there had been before. There were even new ones arising out of the vindictive treaties of 1919. If there was a lesson, it was the one everyone had already known in his heart: Everyone loses in war, the victor with the vanquished.

Statesmen may learn such lessons; but they are not in power when the next crisis arises. Their successors can only have learned by hearing or by reading of the experiences of the past. The sharpness of lessons inevitably dulls in such transmission. But it is not so much the inexperience or the blunted emotions of statesmen which suffer time change. It is the apprehension of peoples. Successor generations have little respect for the tales of old men; they are bored by the wisdom of the past; they are apt to rely on a priori judgments of their own. They are just as susceptible to xenophobia and to national pride as were their fathers or grandfathers who felt themselves driven to fight.

The application of these obvious truths to the situation of 1954 was that all was as it had been before—except for nuclear weapons. The xenophobia and the pride were present. Many Americans were in a mood to destroy the devil communism which hid in Russian bodies; if it was necessary to destroy the bodies to get at the devil, they were prepared to do so. They fully believed that Russian fanatics were intending to attack, to destroy, and to sow with salt the citadels of capitalism. They were not clear what capitalism as the Russians meant it was, but they were told by their favorite demagogues that it was "the American way of life." This meant to them, home, job, and all they loved most in their land. For this they were prepared to fight as the Russians were prepared to fight.

Few times in history had there been more explosive ideological materials than in 1954. The fanaticism of both sides was intense. It ran not only to outrageous misrepresentation of the enemy in repeated whipping-up exercises but to turning on friends, neighbors, and fellow-citizens who would not join the frenzy too. The depth and intensity of the hysteria made a situation so delicately balanced that only the slightest provocation was needed now to precipitate a savage conflict.

On the other hand, even as these emotions seethed in people's minds, as fear and hatred crept in and smothered reason and sympathy, the knowledge of the Bomb's destructive power spread too. There was no one who did not know the awful fact that now a whole city could be engulfed in a holocaust by placing above or on it one bomb; and there was no one who did not know that both Americans and Russians possessed the transporting facilities for the delivery of those bombs.

The plainest of all plain facts was the military standoff of 1954.

When people are possessed by a demon they cannot exorcise, they are not responsible. Their judgment is defective. Their prejudices are exaggerated. Their ability to absorb facts is warped. Regardless of the original rights of the existing controversies, such people need a reduction of tension, a calming leadership, a hope of escape. They cannot explode into rage and destruction; they must, unless they are to end as suicides or as maniacs, find their way back to some sort of serenity, tolerance, and confidence in the future.

Could Americans and Russians, after all that had been said and done, re-establish any belief in each other's decency? Could either go back to a time when each people would have seen the other as human with human hopes and needs?

The only hope for such a reversal of the recent drift toward disaster lay in leadership on both sides able to rise above the easy resorts of demagoguery. The American politics of 1954 seemed still to rely on exacerbation of people's most dangerous phobias. Vice-President Nixon, whatever President Eisenhower did, was sowing fear and hatred as campaign stuff; and the Democrats seemed to be trying to prove that they were more virulently anti-Communist than the Republicans. There was thus little real reason to believe that an access of reason was about to seize on contemporary leaders in America. But there were hints of some change in Russia. There was a diminution of invective; there were hints that some modification of the stubborn attitudes of ten years might be in the making. These changes were not definite enough to build on; but to the sensitive onlooker the atmosphere could be seen to have cleared just the slightest bit.

The anxious neutrals began to speculate once more in ways which showed some renewal of hope that compromise might be possible. They recalled to themselves once more where the issues stood. They even began to whisper again that disarmament might revive. They might only be thinking these thoughts because they must; but they were thinking them. It was true that the referral group set up by the United Nations Assembly in 1953 had got nowhere. But in June, as the latest disarmament meetings came to a dismal close, France and Britain made a new suggestion.[33]

With some faint hope of opening a new door, the French and British proposed that all United Nations members agree to ban nuclear weapons except in defense against aggression and that, after this agreement, atomic control should enter on a stage-by-stage progress toward complete disarmament. Each stage would begin only

---

33. The position of the United States, as the decennial anniversary approached, had not changed except to adapt itself to the new situation of the broken monopoly. The first proposal—the Acheson-Lilienthal plan—had had two principal provisions: public international ownership and operation of nuclear facilities and abolition of the veto in respect of the punishment of violators. These were supplemented by the demand for a rigid inspection system and by the working-out of a system of stages through which the actual giving-up of nuclear weapons would only take place when international control became effective. This last demand became obsolete when the Russians achieved the manufacture of bombs. The position of the United States now was that atomic disarmament must be part of a general program which would include conventional weapons and armed forces.

Opposed to this the Russians had reiterated again and again their unwillingness to entertain any scheme unless it began with the prohibition of atomic weapons. Time after time their representatives had proposed a one-third reduction in all armed forces except atomic armaments and a complete prohibition of these.

after the international agency had decided that it would be carried out. Further than this, atomic control would be deferred until the agency had effected half the agreed reductions in nonatomic armaments. The other half would go into effect simultaneously with the atomic reduction.

The Anglo-French proposals were made public when the Assembly's subcommittee made public its proceedings. The Soviet Union rejected them, reiterating yet again its demand for a prior absolute ban on atomic weapons. But the United States accepted the suggestion as the basis for a new start. And there were faint hints that the Russians might reconsider. These hints were so faint that no one found much hope in them up to the atomic year's end. But there was unmistakable hope that something new would happen when the Assembly met again in September. If the post-Stalin regime had any intention of moving toward the reduction of tension, this was the opportunity. A glimmer of new light seemed to flicker over the gloomy international scene as the decennial year of the Bomb came to its end.

As THE second decade of the atomic age opened out, the conviction began to fasten itself in people's minds that the Bomb was something they would be forced to live with permanently even if it did not destroy them. Their attitude toward it in 1955 was one of growing familiarity, not an easy relationship—the respect it commanded was too overwhelming for that—but one whose every calculation admitted the potentiality of sudden eruption into violence. It was evident that the fearsome thing was not going to be exorcised by the magic of pretense; and mutual avoidance of its use was a very thin reliance. Yet the most that could be hoped for was some uneasy agreement to refrain. And the way of approach even to that was not yet cleared. High-level conferences were constantly talked about; and, like a miracle, the prospect of one finally materialized late in spring. It arose out of a concurrence of circumstances, but basically its acceptance was forced upon the United States by a Russian *détente* in Austria which promised to be a precedent for German negotiations. Nothing might come of it, but hope bloomed suddenly in the air of spring. Perhaps the Bomb might yet be circumvented.

The announcement in the House of Commons in February, 1955, that the "secret" of H-bomb manufacture had been discovered by British scientific workers suggested that within a few years other nations would also penetrate what mystery was left and declare themselves in on the armaments race. There were at least five nations whose scientific competence and natural resources might bring them into the company of Bomb possessors within the second decade. These were Germany, Japan, India, France, and Argentina. And others might not be far behind: Canada, Italy, and Sweden, for instance. And there was always China, where the Communist pressure might, as it had in Russia, force an unnatural technical progress out of unlikely materials in a period shorter than seemed possible at the moment. Meanwhile, it was said, China already had A-bombs, loaned by the Soviet ally.

This prospect that a multination ownership of the Bomb must be expected would again upset all the strategic calculations of American planners. The containment policy of the Truman Administration, and the liberation intentions of the Eisenhower succession, had called for the locking of the Communist world in the "alligator jaws" of widely spread bases equipped with intercontinental bombers—and, later, missiles directed from the ground—capable of delivering H-bombs on demand anywhere in the Soviet Union and in paralyzing quantity. Would those bases remain safe? It did not require too long a memory to recall that not the Soviets but Germany and Japan had set out to conquer the world in the thirties. This was only the fifties. And it would be unrealistic to a fantastic degree to suppose that the impulses to aggression in those nations had been sterilized by defeat in war and the passage of two decades. Give them the possibility of destroying without notice the retaliatory potential of those who in future might oppose their ambitions, and the results of the two world wars might well not be repeated. Next time the aggressors might succeed.

Besides, the multiplication of possessors increased the likelihood that the genocidal threat might be developed by other irresponsible powers. There had been ample demonstration in the Nazi and Fascist instances that even peoples in the Western tradition, liberal democracies, could be corrupted and dominated by small and ruthless cliques. How quickly democracy had been transformed into dictatorship, it was sobering to recall. Imagine what might have happened if Hitler's scientists had been as successful as had been feared by their American opposite numbers in 1944!

Because of the Russian tentatives, the prospect was more favorable for the establishment of a stabilized tension having at least the possibility of preventing or delaying resorts to force implemented with the Bomb. But how delicately the balance swung between peace and war Americans were being at the moment reminded almost constantly by the fulminations of the Chinese. Mao Tse-tung and Chou

En-lai exhibited the same reckless lack of restraint that had marked Russian diatribes a few years earlier. They threatened "complete annihilation" to the "capitalist dogs" led by Dulles and Eisenhower and reminded everyone—including the Soviet hierarchy—that in case of embroilment there existed a mutual defense treaty which pledged the Soviets to come to their aid. This talk had much more the empty character of bluster before certain changes took place in the high command of the Soviet Union.

During the winter and spring there were replacements in the top echelon at the Kremlin which, whatever else they implied, meant increased difficulty for the West. They did not mean that the Chinese would find it easier to influence Soviet actions or that the mutual defense treaties would be any more readily implemented, but they did mean that efforts for accommodation with the West would take some new turn which would require assessment. Malenkov, who was now purged, had been conciliatory. He had also had a sense of responsibility to humanity. His policy was now discredited; and those who had decided against it could be guessed to have decided in favor of its opposite. There was a return to stern and unwavering hostility. These were the reports from Moscow. Whether they were correct would soon develop; meanwhile there were some regrets.

The Western powers, it could now be seen, had made a colossal mistake in not encouraging Malenkov's tentatives toward negotiation. Their coldness had frozen him out of his premiership. If he had succeeded in even the most modest beginnings of agreement with the West, he could not have been replaced by Khrushchev, Bulganin, *et al.*, who took power in January. When the NATO agreements were ratified, his credit was exhausted. The impermeable surface presented by Mr. Dulles had been the same as that maintained by Mr. Acheson. Republicans in the United States and Tories in Britain had convinced the Russians all over again that Western intentions were hostile to conciliation. So far as public opinion was concerned, they were wrong, and even in official policy there were faint, reluctant signs of giving way in response to deep democratic fears—if to no more laudable impulses. These signs had been visible to anyone but totalitarians, who, in the absence of official notification, were unable to discern lesser erosions of intransigence. They simply could not understand where to look in a democracy for evidences of change. Both sides had made a tragic error.

That this overturn in Russia intensified the risk of actual hostilities no one needed to be told. It stood out plainly. The Chinese could now presume on the Russian need for one great friend. Those small immediate occasions which so often in the past had set off vast conflicts were constantly occurring on the Chinese borders. There was no spring day on which it was unthinkable that the trigger might be pulled which would precipitate the atomic war. Two deliberate actions taken by the United States multiplied the immediate danger: the Southeast Asia Treaty Organization was set up, with Secretary Dulles declaring the United States pledged to the defense of all its members;[1] and a mutual defense pact was, with amazing solemnity, considering the relative size of the signatories, concluded with Chiang Kai-shek on Formosa. These were fantastic commitments, so prejudicial to the national interest as to seem incredible. How far their consequences might run only time would tell.

The first of these policies might at any moment involve the armed forces of the nation in endless jungle warfare on the opposite side of the world from their home bases. Until now this had been supposed to be the most elementary lesson of Korea if it had not been known before; and, if Korea had not been enough, the seven-year ordeal of the French army in Indochina should have made it clear. Both these small wars had ended in divided nations; and the salvaged halves were viable only with constant support. They would collapse instantly if the streams of aid should diminish; and the probabilities were that they would not last long anyway.

The second commitment—the mutual-aid treaty with Chiang Kai-shek—in effect set up two Chinas to match the two Germanies, the two Koreas, and the two Indochinas already in existence as a result of American postwar diplomacy. These halves of states were unstable, distant, and demanding. Their statesmen existed by blackmailing their sponsors; and the price would increase as time passed.

The constant threat of involvement in war had again and again to be actively countered. It had come to be one of the chief activi-

1. Cf. the Dulles speech at Bangkok, reported in the *New York Times* of February 24, 1955.

ties of American diplomats. It was, moreover, a worry to the Allies, especially Britain; and the neutrals—India leading—were openly denunciatory. The president of India said, in February, that Formosa ought to be returned to the legitimate Chinese government. That was the position, also, of the Labourite minority in Britain; it much preferred turning toward neutrality. If that should happen, the liaison between the United States and the Kuomintang would be opposed by every other friendly power.

The tour de force by which throughout years of turmoil the China lobby had succeeded in maintaining Chiang Kai-shek in command of a second China was certainly one of the marvels of modern politics. Every interest of the Western nations ran against it. There was not—and from his first expelling had not been—the slightest chance that he might mount a successful invasion of the mainland. And, even if so fantastic a possibility was argued for, why would Chiang in China be better than Mao? Was a dictatorship, strictly comparable with those which had so recently been disestablished in a world war, more desirable than communism? Both were totalitarian; and they were equally antidemocratic. The sole argument for Chiang was that his rule of China would be friendly to the West. But would it? Given real control of a sovereign nation, he would think of China's interests first. And in time he might well find liberal democracy less congenial than the communism which would be the neighboring alternative.

It was indeed difficult to find one argument from the national interest for the support of Chiang. It was sometimes said that Formosa was one of a chain of offshore Asian bases which did and must constitute the outer ring of American defense. But a glance at the map revealed that, not defense, but offense was the only reasonable strategic argument. And offense from Formosa had, it must be supposed, been given up long ago. Its relationship to Japanese defense was suggested. This was remote and psychological. Okinawa and the Philippines, perhaps; but not Formosa. On the contrary, Japan could hardly tolerate an atomic threat to China from Formosa; she herself was too vulnerable to attack from the mainland.

All this had the importance of constant danger. The thunderings back and forth across the seventy miles of sea between the Chinese mainland and Formosa were bombast. But bombast has a powerful effect on a nation of notorious face-savers. And the Communists had been shouting too loudly and specifically about the conquest of Formosa to retreat happily into silence. They must make the attempt or incur a psychological reverse. And the smaller islands just offshore must be a temptation to begin.

But the Seventh Fleet was covering the seventy miles of sea in the strait; and it was said officially to be the most powerful naval force ever assembled. A Chinese attack would start a small war. The question was whether that small one would develop into the big one for which the world had been waiting with dread. That would depend on the Kremlin's honoring or not honoring a pledge; and the unknown policy of Khrushchev and his colleagues was cause for worry. If Russia did intervene seriously, judging that the time for a showdown had come, the many submarines now supposed to be completed would furnish formidable opposition to the fleet. Resort to atomic weapons would be almost certain if the conflict developed into anything of importance.

This possibility of a clash in Formosan waters engaged anxious attention everywhere. It caused flurried intervention by the British. Sir Anthony Eden was not so forthright in his warnings to Mr. Dulles as was Mr. Attlee in the House of Commons, speaking for Labour. He did not say, as Mr. Attlee did, and as the president and prime minister of India did, that support of Chiang constituted aggression on the part of the United States; he took the line that a cease-fire must be arranged, during which more permanent arrangements could be reached. The first thing to do was to reduce the risk that small clashes would grow into big ones. But what he thought the settlement ought to be was obvious. Everyone but American officials wanted to hear the last of Chiang.

Sir Anthony's difficulties were not lessened by the strange and unprecedented American warning to the Communists that an attack on Formosa would be a cause of war. President Eisenhower was persuaded in February to ask the Congress for authority to defend Formosa and, if necessary, to carry the fighting into surrounding areas. This was supposed to mean that, if an attack was mounted, the islands of Quemoy and Matsu still held by the Nationalists, about five miles offshore, and directly between Formosa and the mainland, would be defended; but it could mean retaliatory attacks on mainland bases. There were to be no more of the safe sanctuaries against which General MacArthur had inveighed in Korea. The Congress almost unanimously passed the requested resolution. It did seem that the Dulles-Radford policy had prevailed and that President Eisenhower's many refusals to be drawn into aggression during the last two years had been reversed.

The tension grew. During the week when the Seventh Fleet was covering the evacuation of the Tachen islands—now judged to be indefensible, although Chiang had been encouraged only a year ago to occupy them—the holding of breath was universal. When the task was completed without incident, the relief was enormous. But almost daily Nationalist planes were attacking Communist shipping—blockading the small ports of Amoy and Foochow—and even mainland targets. The planes and the munitions they used were American; the training of their pilots had been American; and American military advisers were actively assisting. These facts, known to all, were the basis for India's protests and for British concern.[2]

No one could predict what the Communists intended. The puzzle was classically Chinese in the idiom of the West; it had elements of paradox and inscrutability but none of ease or tolerance. It had been thought, after the Korean truce, that there might be a lessening of animosity and that, given some time for cooling off, the Communists might be admitted to the United Nations. But this possibility was deliberately destroyed by an outbreak—apparently at the worst possible moment—of villification and provocation calculated to anger even the most reluctant Americans. This seemed the stranger because the experts had been quite certain that the Soviet Union did not at the moment want war.[3]

The Chinese might have got all they wanted by conciliation— entry to the United Nations, gradual reduction of Chiang's power, and perhaps eventual reintegration of Formosa with the mainland government. But they had chosen to scream epithets and threats, specifically to forecast early invasion and to defy the Americans to

2. Cf. General T. R. Phillips, "Quemoy and Formosa as I Saw Them," *The Reporter*, April 21, 1955. This is an exceptionally clear account of our involvement in the Formosa Straits.

3. One reason for this supposition was that *rapprochement* with the Japanese was ponderously being developed and obviously, although it worried the Americans, was in a fair way to succeed. Also the wooing of India and the subversion of Indonesia were not going too badly.

465

stop it. The Congress—and even the President—were only human. If the Chinese came looking for trouble, they were given warning that they would find it.

This was the sore spot now being rubbed. But, if the new crowd in the Kremlin wanted to create more irritations to keep the United States off balance, there were plenty of other opportunities—in Southeast Asia, where the British were worried anew about Malaysia after the fall of Dien Bien Phu and the partition of Indochina; in the Near East, where Arab resentments mounted; and in Germany. This last was the most dangerous of all, as it had been in most years of this chronicle.

The Russians were still trying to persuade the Bonn government, playing on the desire for unification and the widespread hostility to rearmament, that the hegemony of the West would permanently prevent unification and start a new era of militarism. The truth was that for months, as the debate on the implementing treaties went on, there was more civic disorder than at any time since the close of the war. The truncated Reich was deeply disturbed and divided. The West stood on its demand that ratification be completed before any talks with the Russians were initiated. This Western policy was faithfully defended by Chancellor Adenauer. But there was determined and widespread opposition which did not subside even when the treaties had been ratified.

Into this situation the Russians injected a surprising gambit; after ten years of obstruction they cleared the way for an Austrian evacuation—which meant withdrawal in Hungary and Czechoslovakia too. This may have been intended to check German rearmament and open anew hopes for reunification; it would thus overweight the ratification of the treaties, now completed. Perhaps they were preparing withdrawal from Germany too. But also it may have had implications for the Far East. Russia may have been anticipating a United States–Chinese embroilment and have been wanting to reduce tension in Europe. It was good strategy for both problems. Excitement on two fronts is never good policy. The reluctance in West Germany, taken together with the near-chaos in France and a new resurgence of Communist strength in Italy, greatly weakened all the plans for European defense. The situation of the British and American forces on the Continent was one of immediate peril if there should be a

Russian attack—which was what they were there to meet. There would be no German forces for years; and the French and Italians could not be counted on for resolution.

There seemed to be no change of policy in view of these realities. So much attention was being given to the Far East that Europe tended to be neglected. But the situation there had deteriorated alarmingly. Moreover, the rethinking of strategy called for by the development of the H-bomb, although it had not yet begun, would be certain to affect the concept of European defense. It had made the whole postwar strategy obsolete.

Occasionally in the press there was mention of the arrival in Europe of "atomic weapons"—the artillery adapted to nuclear war heads. Momentum is a formidable and unwieldy factor in strategic planning. It did not require military expertness to ask embarrassing questions as soon as the H-bomb was perfected; and critics had been asking them with increasing insistence for some time now. These centered in doubt whether, if the great Bomb existed, the little bombs—and other weapons—were useful. If they were not, then commitment to them fatally weakened the national defense.

The H-bomb and the intercontinental bomber existed. They could not be ignored. They possessed the capability of obliterating entire metropolitan areas. Why would there be fighting on a "front"? Back of that front there would be an empty shell—a devastated countryside. War had moved into a new dimension, and the strategists had not yet caught up. Or, if they had, the military bureaucracy still dominated operations. For the American and British divisions were in Europe, and pressure for the rearming of Germany had not been diminished. Of what use would this force be when it was overleaped by the bombers? The generals seemed to feel that they had done very well to have remade their plans to accord with A-bomb requirements. But the A-bomb was now as obsolete as elephants, crossbows, tanks, or dynamite. Probably the Russians had not advanced any faster; but their armies were at least on their own continent in contiguous territory.

The exercise of adapting military operations to the now-superseded A-bomb was harmful in two ways: it diverted energies from the real problem and it blurred the distinction, once so clear, be-

467

tween nuclear and other weapons. The real problem was to consider what might happen if one or both of the present-day antagonists should resort to the H-bomb which both now possessed. The evidence was that the area of explosion would be immensely increased by the wind-borne fall-out of radioactive materials. A report released by the Atomic Energy Commission served to confirm what had been long supposed—that the downwind reach of this lethal mist would be hundreds of miles. There was no longer any excuse for not facing the fact that to use the H-bomb was to inflict punishment of genocidal extent. The United States or the Soviet Union could be injured irreparably by even a moderately successful bomber strike.

But it was worse than this. That neither nation could make a bomber strike without precipitating retaliation had now been plain for years. To loose destruction on either was to loose it on both. This was the hard fact which all the playing-about with lesser weapons tended to obscure. The Bomb as a weapon had become an untenable resort. It could not be used. Yet the American armies, and presumably those of the Soviet Union, were being very rapidly equipped with atomic weapons of all sorts. They were being tested again in Nevada, to the accompaniment of vast publicity, in the spring. That they were unavailable there seemed to be no realization. But, if it was not realized, then there must be, in the military mind, a distinction between A-bombs and H-bombs. The A-bomb had been brought down to tactical size. Armies could use it. Both President Eisenhower and Secretary Dulles said, in March, that in the next "brush fire" war, A-bombs would be used.

There was not the slightest reason to think that the distinction between A- and H-bombs had any tacit international recognition. Suppose, for instance, A-weapons should be resorted to as a result of Chinese provocation, could the enemy be trusted not to feel that this freed them to use the H-bomb in retaliation? It was much more likely that the first resort to a nuclear weapon would bring the whole range of those weapons into play. Any other expectation rested on a distinction far too slight to justify the deep risk involved. Retaliation was not a limited principle. It was total.

The larger truth was that, as the second decade of the atomic age opened, war had lost its usefulness even to aggressors willing to risk everything except their own extinction. It was open now only to

468

those fanatics who were willing to destroy themselves in order to destroy their enemies. There have always been such individuals; perhaps there were such nations. But if there were, they were not truly democratic ones. They could only be ones disciplined to the control of fanatics. Or, perhaps, a democracy deprived of its right to discussion and to the making of uncorrupted majority decisions.

It was the perception of something like this which had created the fears of recent years. Communists had been regarded in America as terrorists and conspirators with no restraints understood by ordinary people. And perhaps the "capitalists" spoken of in the Soviet Union were as much distrusted. Yet now it was not so much the Russians who were feared in this way. There had been a change. It had been concluded in the decade since Yalta that the Russians intended to conduct a cold and rational campaign, of glacial momentum, and costly to satellites, but without great risk to themselves. It would not include provocation to retaliation. No, it was the Chinese whom the terrorist picture now seemed to fit. And, judging from what was known of their propaganda at home, the Chinese leaders were painting the same picture of Americans for their own people. The Russians would allow themselves to be brought in only if they had judged that they could destroy without being destroyed.

Luckily the Chinese had no H-bombs unless they were loaned by the Russians—a very unlikely loan. But, not so luckily, the Seventh Fleet might well have A-bombs. And their use in defense of Formosa was not ruled out by any instructions known to the public. Quite the contrary. It had been said that A-bombs were now standard equipment. Also it required an A-bomb to detonate the vaster H-bomb. It was an uneasy thought to harbor that an A-war might similarly trigger an H-war. But the restraints such a thought might have been expected to impose were not apparent in American planning.

If there was not coexistence, there was at least a stalemate, however uneasy and however fragile. The likeliest immediate chance of its being ruptured in 1955 lay in the Formosa Strait. And the fact was that withdrawal from contact there would be in the American interest. There were many who thought it ought to be done before the consequences of unjustified extension had to be met. But the reverse of this was the declared policy. Chiang was to be supported in his occupation of Formosa at any cost in American lives or money and at any risk to the national security. Having won an election on a promise to disengage in Korea, General Eisenhower seemed to be in danger of a worse engagement over Formosa. For this he was taken to task in an effective speech by Mr. Stevenson in April. And soon thereafter he seemed to be moving toward withdrawal from the shoreward islands. Mr. Stevenson had wakened the criticism the Democrats had hitherto withheld. They constituted an altogether too loyal opposition.

The best that could be said for the situation, then, in the beginning of the new decade, was that a tense stasis had imposed itself on the nations. It was not something they had wanted; it was something they had worked and maneuvered desperately to avoid. It could hardly be called "coexistence," because coexistence implied a kind of willingness. It was merely an agonizing standoff with no agreement, even a tacit one, to respect any conditions of armistice. No arrangement had been reached, and there was no security implied.

To make it worse, the knowledge each imperium had about the other was defective in several critical aspects. Unless the respective intelligence services knew much more than they seemed to know— judging from the policy of each nation—neither had any accurate knowledge of the other's military readiness; and this lack of knowledge was worst in the most important field. That, of course, was the field of nuclear weaponeering. It was generally said, in the West —Sir Winston Churchill, for instance, kept repeating it—that the United States was far ahead, that the Soviet Union could not catch up for years, and even then would not be ahead. But, as has been pointed out, these comparisons had but slight meaning. If the Soviet Union's small stock of bombs was still enough to destroy the American potential, what difference did it make that the Americans had more? There was a technical term for this: it was called "saturation." Each side had reached the power to inflict this ultimate punishment on the other.[4]

This was what stalemate meant: that sovereign powers—two of

4. President Eisenhower spoke of this at his press conference on March 2 showing that he, at least, recognized the condition of stalemate: "There comes a time . . . when a lead is not significant in the defensive arrangements of a country. If you get enough of a particular type of weapon, I doubt that it is particularly important to get a lot more of it. . . ."

them at the moment, more to be added presently—possessed the capability of destroying each other, that they were implacably antagonistic, and that they were almost out of communication.

This last was not quite true. The United Nations forum still existed, and its Disarmament Commission was still in existence. It was, in fact, meeting in London in spring. But what Russians and Americans alike thought of its likely success in reaching any agreement was easily seen by noting that no important policy-makers on either side were assigned to the meeting. Late in March, President Eisenhower, seized with impatience, and openly convinced that disarmament efforts by present methods were futile, appointed Mr. Harold Stassen to make new efforts and underlined the action by giving him Cabinet rank. "Secretary of Peace," the press called him. But what he could do was far from clear unless it was to arrange high-level conferences. It was now evident that accommodation was not to be reached by a tour de force. The giving-up of weapons would follow and not precede an agreement to coexist. Only when it was no longer needed would the H-bomb be withdrawn from national armories and dismantled. Conferences of chiefs of state, avoided by American wish during all the years since Potsdam, seemed the only hope. This last resort was perhaps the meaning of the Stassen mission. And he seemed to be given some scope by the stirring in diplomatic circles after Russia's Austrian concession. Negotiations might at last be beginning.

The reader who has followed my argument knows that all along I have found it necessary to stress the peculiar nature of the nuclear threat. If armies with conventional arms now faced each other in western Europe, there might be concern; but the situation would not be different in kind from others in the past. There might be conflict, a conquest, an occupation, and a gradual resumption of activity. Lives might be sacrificed, productive facilities destroyed, and liberties lost. Some changes, comparable with those, say, in England after the Norman conquest, might occur. But the existence of the Bomb relegated these considerations and comparisons to the attics of civilization. Barring a final and fatal one, there could be no major move now on either side. The status was fixed. Mr. Dulles' liberation was as fatuous a dream as the Politburo's hope for a Communist world governed from Moscow. The first move toward either objective—except, of course, by way of subversion and internal strife—would invoke a "massive retaliation"; and this would defeat the purpose of the first mover.

If it had already seemed to some of us that, as soon as the A-bomb had been perfected, there was no alternative to coexistence, it was many times more evident that there was no alternative now that the H-bomb had succeeded its less destructive predecessor. We had thought then—some of us—that world government of one or another sort might settle out of the mists from the first explosions at Hiroshima and Nagasaki. It had not. As that hope faded, co-existence in some kind of fair and secure agreement had seemed the least humanity could expect of the statesmen.

It was apparent now—in 1955—that this also was a fast-fading hope. The least tolerable of three alternatives, one not even entertained in the first years of the new age, was what we were likely to have and what we might have to learn to live with—that is if destruction continued to be staved off. The nations were condemned to stalemate—and a hard, hostile, and menacing one at that, with neither side making the slightest concession to reason, with the slanging match still going on, with exposed borders threatened by each, and with third parties licensed to cause incidents any one of which might escape from control. This was the conclusion about our affairs of many a hardheaded analyst. It was what General T. R. Phillips, for instance, foresaw.

Referring to these matters, the most eloquent and the most durable—he alone of the wartime leaders had lasted until now—of the statesmen who had been in power when the A-bomb had first been put to use, spoke in the House of Commons. In his last great speech on a day in March Sir Winston Churchill wondered aloud at the strange paradoxical situation of the world's affairs:

There is an immense gulf between the atomic and the hydrogen bomb. The atomic bomb, with all its terror, did not carry us outside the scope of human control or manageable events in thought or action, in peace or war. . . .

But when the H-bomb was announced . . . the entire foundation of human events was revolutionized and mankind placed in a situation both measureless and laden with doom. . . .

However, a curious paradox has emerged. . . . After a certain point has been passed, it may be said, the worse things get the better. . . . It may well be that we shall, by a process of sublime irony, have reached a stage in this story where safety will be the sturdy child of terror and survival the twin brother of annihilation.[5]

If this sounded like Mr. Robert Maynard Hutchins' "good news of damnation," the reference was only slightly different. Mr. Hutchins had thought in 1945 that mankind would be compelled to form a world government; Sir Winston hoped only for the mutual sense which would sustain a stalemate. He had hoped for more. In age he had hoped to be called a peacemaker; he was forced to forego that ambition. Peace was to be deferred beyond the time given to him to participate in its arranging.

It was true—and to dwell on its implications was a relief—that the "twin brother of annihilation" was reaching adolescence. The protestations of economists who continually called attention to the high cost of power produced by nuclear reactors were being silenced —as so often happens when revolutionary resources are in their developmental stages—by steady reductions. One after another bottlenecks were broken, engineering advances made, and designs improved. By 1955 power from fission was so nearly competitive with fossil fuels that several ventures beyond the pilot-plant stage were being undertaken. In the Pittsburgh area a full-scale plant was being built; in New York and in Chicago others were announced; also the "Nautilus" had joined the submarine fleet. It was obvious that the crust was about to crack. There was some reluctance. The revisions in 1954 of the Atomic Energy Act had not altogether suited the power industry. Its lobbyists had hoped for more generous developmental subsidies than the Congress had granted. They were not too certain either, after the bitter debates, that a change of policy might not yet take place. The admission of corporate entrepreneurs to the power field developed at vast public expense had not been authorized without misgivings on the part of some conscientious legislators. It was not certain but that this might be regarded as another of the Republican "give-away" policies. It might well be reversed when Democrats came back to power—and that might be no further away than in 1956.

5. This speech was reported in full in the *New York Times*, March 2, 1955. A few weeks later Sir Winston finally succumbed to age. He retired and was succeeded by Sir Anthony Eden.

On the other hand, if active work on nuclear power should be resisted, either for these reasons or because of fear that conventional plants might too quickly be made obsolete, the likelihood that public development might take place would be increased. The Americans were not the only power producers in the world; and, as it was, they were behind others in this particular technology. True, the "Nautilus" was a complete operational success, and Navy resistance to similar applications on other ships was breaking down; but, if a real welcoming of the entry of nuclear power to the industrial scene was looked for, it was to be found not in America but in Britain.[6]

There were calm but confident British announcements that within ten years nuclear power would be developing some 2,000,000 kilowatts and that by 1975 this would have grown to 15,000,000 kilowatts. These figures were not firm. But what was firm was the forecast that presently nuclear plants would be the only ones being built. The Fuel Ministry, which was to carry out this program, was quite separate from the Atomic Energy Commission, under whose jurisdiction research was done, and from the military, whose efforts were concentrated on weaponeering. It was a serious peacetime effort to attain greater productivity.

It was obvious that the confidence displayed by the British planners must have sources not only in recent technical advances but in the opening-up of new fuel reserves. And it could be inferred that these were of two kinds. New uranium discoveries had already increased many times what had but recently been supposed to be a very limited supply. Also, even more prevalent thorium was growing easier to turn into fissionable U-235. Moreover, the breeder reactor was multiplying the usefulness of every pound of natural ore.

The conclusion to be drawn from the British program could have been reached by studying the reports of the American Atomic Energy Commission and drawing inferences. But under its present direction it was still a withdrawn and mysterious agency. Chairman Strauss was determined at any cost to civilian developments that secrecy must be maintained, so much so that the policy came under more and more severe criticism and especially by many of the scientists who thought that it prevented developments which ought

6. Perhaps in the Soviet Union too; but the extent of development there was unknown, except for an occasional high-level boast.

long ago to have been undertaken. The trouble—or part of the trouble—was that in the United States all atomic-energy matters were in the Chairman's nervous grasp. In Britain there was a Ministry of Fuel, quite apart from the Atomic Energy Commission, whose purpose was to find a substitute for the dwindling, high-cost, coal supply; and atomic energy obviously offered itself as a ready alternative.

The determination that, if any development at all was to take place in the United States, it must be private development seemed to legislators, as to Mr. Strauss, a matter almost as important as that the most rapid possible entry to the atomic age should be pushed. Considering the investment of taxpayers' money, scientists' genius, and engineering skills made in the first decade of the atomic age, it seemed very strange that the first consideration of the second decade should be to present the benefits to private industry. Yet so demanding was the ideological commitment of bankers and businessmen—who so obviously set the policies of the current Congress and the present Administration—that this actually was the controlling consideration. This might be changed; but, if it were not changed, the United States might well find after a time that others had taken the lead. This had happened in other instances from the same cause;[7] and it could happen again. Indeed it seemed that it would.

Whether the United States or some other nation led the way into the "five thousand years of atomic energy,"[8] it was apparent that the new era had already opened. Worry lest the fuels depended on for power production since the beginning of the age of steam should become exhausted and bring prime movers to a stop could now be relieved. Man did not face a future of diminishing, but one of increasing, energy, and one whose resources were obviously not as

7. Instances with grave consequences can be found in quantity; but consider Europe's three-decade lead in the development of social security; or the British lead in the development of jet engines for flying; or, yet again, atomic energy itself, which only the wartime abandonment of private development and the bringing-in of foreign experts brought to an early and successful conclusion.

8. Mr. W. L. Lawrence, the *New York Times*' scientific correspondent, ventured this estimate of the possible extent of atomic-energy resources in the issue of March 3, 1955. This had the value of any guess, educated or otherwise; but it showed how the earlier pessimism concerning reserves of fissionable materials had given way to new and far more optimistic expectations.

yet all known. About this unknown, speculation was only beginning; but scientists knew in what direction to look. Logic had already told them.

The energy falling on earth from the sun had been looked to for some time; but ways to use it, except for small heating installations, had not been found. Now that fission had been brought under control and fusion had been used for weaponeering, there was every reason to hope that fusion as well as fission would become a source of energy for production as well as destruction. There were hints that developments of this sort might even be imminent. Who would dare predict, after what had happened in one decade of atomic energy, that five hundred succeeding decades would pass without new resources being discovered?

It was not likely that the generosity of nature had been exhausted when fission had made new power sources available. But there still remained the limitations within which men allowed themselves to be confined. To the mythical individual from Mars, it would certainly seem fantastic that the offer of energy from the atom should be accepted in a large area of earth only if it could be exploited for the benefit of a few. Yet the behavior of everyone concerned with the institutionalization of nuclear energy seemed to support the conclusion that Americans would rather not have it than have it owned in common. Since the apportionment of the free air over the earth to private transportation and communication corporations, no stranger disposition had been made of a natural gift. It seemed a kind of effrontery which nature might find it hard to forgive.

Nature's tolerance of man's vagaries could not be supposed to be limitless. And surely the limits of that tolerance grew narrower as richer and richer sources of energy were opened to exploitation. The inappropriateness of bargaining, of setting conditions, of using an offered largesse in private deals must somehow be fundamentally offensive. Perhaps the penalties would be only those of lower standards of life than otherwise might be attained. Those people who persisted in bargaining would be given a bad bargain. If the obvious imperative of collectivization was rejected, those who rejected it might merely be deprived of something they might have had if their society had been better ordered.

On the other hand, rejectors and bargainers might suffer ultimate penalties. To inject the obsolete ideologies of laissez faire into the development of so vast and overwhelming a resource as nuclear energy might bring the productive system to destruction in that twin alternate phase spoken of by Sir Winston Churchill. Obsolete competitive nationalism lasting on into an age of one-world technology might well exact the penalty for absolute incompatibility.

The competitive struggles of the great combines now seizing the potentials of atomic energy might result in bringing on a destruction prepared by nationalism. Nationalism was, in its more aggressive and exclusive aspects, a front for the cartelists, now reaching out for the new resources. It was their ideology which infused "capitalism" and refused to give way to the indicated collectivism of the nuclear age. The threat of the H-bomb in such hands was the threat of forcing the acceptance of an ideology. Man in the decades ahead was required by the logic of his own scientific discoveries to adopt the social institutions which could contain and use them. Neither nationalism of the xenophobic sort nor capitalism of the exploitative sort were appropriate to the new age. The attempt to fill the old jars with the new explosive might well be fatal.

Those who had, during the first decade, tried to discover and bring into use the new institutions required by the new resources could at least have the consolation of having worked with and not against nature. Their efforts had apparently come to very little. Nations still armed themselves and refused to recognize the impossibility of winning a war. The determined effort was still being made to force the vast energies of fission—with those of fusion yet to come —into the profit-making devices they preferred. Neither world government nor collectivism were much further ahead than at the beginning of the decade.

The men of good will in the West were none of them in positions of power. Conciliation was out of fashion, and intolerance was in favor. This was not true in all other places. In India and Burma, and perhaps elsewhere, there were those who were still hopeful. Pandit Nehru spoke at Bandoeng, and his voice was loud. But, if it carried to Washington and to Moscow, there was no ready response. There was a stirring in the diplomatic world when Chou En-lai offered negotiation. Next day, however, the Department of State slammed the door in his face. He reacted by making another claim to Formosa. But the slammed door had reopened a crack at the combined pushing of Asiatic statesmen. Their weight might in time open it further. Bulganin, at the same time, was, he said, waiting for the United States to accept his offer for "broad talks about European problems." The Department of State, as so many times, was again on the defensive. It was under this compulsion—and to assist the Tories in Britain, facing an election without Sir Winston—that a conference was finally agreed to by the United States. Secretary Dulles, introduced as a televised hero by President Eisenhower, claimed that the Russians had bowed to American strength—a claim Mr. Walter Lippmann was prompt to question. It was, he said, much more likely that the reverse was true. The Soviets felt strong in the possession of retaliatory capability. The diplomats, even if they had clear objectives, had at any rate won no tolerance. They professed an understandable pessimism concerning negotiations for which they had made no preparation.

It was not a very valuable credit to have been right when others had been wrong, yet it had always been the consolation of dedicated men; and it remained a consolation even when the new genocidal possibility had to be faced. That threat may have removed the one most sustaining satisfaction of the short individual lives granted to men—that their works would be perpetuated for their successors. But, until the H-day arrived, they could work and contrive and not be afraid just as such men always had. Their motives and their hopes were purer, and so perhaps of heightened value, because even the expectation of succession had been taken from them. They were, in the words of the old abolitionist hymn, "in the right with two or three." In that company of dedicated fellows, however small it might be, they went toward possible holocaust undiminished by fear.

After the passing of a decade of total jeopardy, I understood better the significance of the dream I had had at its beginning. Pushing through the rank hampering growth of dangers and oppositions toward a towered city bathed in ineffable light, I typified man, struggling out of his institutional swathings toward a future of infinite rewards. I seem, however, to have come to a full stop within sight of the city but far short of it. So man in our time!

ACKNOWLEDGMENTS

To E. C. Banfield and Lois Clark, I am indebted for the reduction of my manuscript from the unwieldy size it had attained during ten years to practical book length; Mrs. Clark, besides, was my copy-reader. To General Thomas R. Phillips (U.S.A. ret.), to several among the atomic scientists, and to other friends and colleagues, many of them Unitarian ministers, I owe the debt of one who has been sustained and counseled when they were most needed; but all the responsibility is mine for interpretation and opinion—and this is a book, very largely, of opinion.

Acheson, Dean, 148, 174 n., 176, 197, 246, 252, 266, 280, 301 n., 306, 319, 377 n., 408, 426 n., 441; attacked by McCarthy, 200, 233–36; and Far Eastern crisis, 203–5, 207, 209; and position of strength, 258, 259, 281, 305, 308, 311, 318–19, 386; Dulles facing same problems as, 435, 438, 443, 461
Acheson-Lilienthal Report, 52, 57, 58 n., 94, 96, 97, 99, 107, 185, 419, 457 n.
Adenauer, Konrad, 310, 311, 440–41, 444–45, 446
Advisory Committee on Disarmament, Department of State, 352
Agar, Herbert, 365 n.
Agricultural Adjustment Act, 326
Allison, Samuel K., 397 n.
Alsop, Joseph, 230–31, 352–53, 411
Alsop, Stewart, 230–31, 352–53, 411
America First Committee, 92
American attitudes: dilemmas, 303; traditions and preferences, 340; desire to destroy communism, 454–56
American Bar Association, 403
American economy: and discontent, 52–54; state of, 1946–47, 82–85; economic recession, 1949, 166–69; productive capacity, 214–15, 290, 307; prosperity and business profits, 219–21, 223, 381; measures of control, stability, and mobilization, 284–85, 286, 324–26; and inflation, 290–91, 303, 307, 326–27; transformation, 321–24
American Farm Bureau Federation, 290
American Federation of Labor, 86
American foreign policy: East-West power struggle, 72–73, 242–43; opposition to, 73–74, 348, 445; containment, 74–75, 119, 252, 297, 300–301, 308, 335, 337–38, 357–58, 460; and German rearmament, 150–52, 310–11,

401–2, 445–46; and colonialism, 174, 217; and Korea, 200–202; military control and lack of formulation, 321, 327; statement of policy, 1952, 334–38; and liberation, 357–58, 359, 376 n., 400, 471; Formosa and defense, 462–64; see also Great Debate, 1950–51
American Friends Service Committee, 197; see also Quakers
American Legion, 32
American schools and the United Nations, 335 n.
Americans for Democratic Action, 79 n.
Anderson, Clinton P., 79, 88
Arvey, Jacob, 119, 132
Atlantic Monthly, 113
Atlantic Pact, 154, 226, 281; see also North Atlantic Treaty Organization
Atomic bomb: dangers, 1–2, 4, 15–16, 24, 238; stockpiling, 2, 320; creation of, 12–15, 43; alternatives, 39, 54–55, 263, 457–58; and defense, 57, 257; and military strategy, 176–77, 191, 213, 295–96, 351–52, 360; exploded by the Russians, 225; see also Atomic energy; H-bomb
Atomic energy: peacetime uses, 27–29, 34–35, 418–20, 450–51, 452, 473–76; and military control, 44, 46–47, 100; chronology of development, 178–84; and private business, 451, 475; institutionalization as new resource, 476–78
Atomic Energy Act of 1946, 70, 100–101, 104–5, 106, 114, 353, 360; revisions, 451, 473; see also McMahon Act of 1946
Atomic scientists: against military control, 46–47, 70–71; compromise, 125–28, 296; on Russian atomic program, 176–77; and alternative proposals, 225–27, 300; and secrecy, 225, 394–

485

United Nations Technical Assistance Program, 218, 448

United States Atomic Energy Act, 1946; *see* Atomic Energy Act of 1946

United States Atomic Energy Commission, 70, 94, 95, 100, 101, 113, 130, 177, 225, 230, 236, 237, 321, 350, 354, 393, 395, 397, 411, 468; origins and functions of, 103–6; General Advisory Committee, 104; Military Liaison Committee, 104; and secrecy, 121, 122, 474; presidential summary of operations, July, 1948, 121 n.; and H-bomb, 427–28; Scientific Advisory Board, 429; and Oppenheimer case, 429–31; peacetime uses of atomic energy, 451

United States Chamber of Commerce, 290

United States government: wartime machinery of, 26; relation of legislature to executive, 101–2

United World Federalists, 264

Urey, Harold, 128, 180, 226 n., 259, 292, 294

Utopian thought, role of, 65–66

Vandenburg, General Hoyt, 175

Vatican, 123, 125

Veblen, Thorstein, 38

Velde, Harold H., 372

Vinson, Carl, 202

Vishinsky, Andrei, 110, 255, 300

"Voice of America," 242, 371

Wagner Act, 79

Wallace, Henry A., 74, 93, 132, 161, 162, 164, 174 n., 183, 185–86; influence on foreign policy, 76–77; as leader of dissenters, 78–79; on a balanced abundance, 85; on United States atomic control position, 97–99, 100; as presidential candidate, 120, 131, 133, 160; and the atomic bomb, 180–81

War Manpower Commission, 53

War Production Board, 53

Ward, Barbara, 297

Warfare, as limited by chivalry, 54–56

Wartime machinery of government, 26

Waymack, William W., 100

Weapon limitation, history of concept of, 54–55

Wedemeyer, General George, 201

Welles, Sumner, 142 n., 341 n.

Wherry, Kenneth S., 108, 233, 297

Wigner, Eugene, 179, 397

Wilson, Carroll L., 232

Wilson, Charles E., director of Defense Mobilization, 294–95, 313–14, 320, 322, 323–24

Wilson, Woodrow, 52, 275, 331

Winne, Harry A., 125

Wirt, William A., 297

Wisconsin Public Service Commission, 107

Witch hunts, 229–30

World constitution, 64–65, 134; first draft, 135–37; problems and proposals, 137–41; committee to frame (*see* Committee To Frame a World Constitution); preliminary draft, 264 n.

World Food Council, 249

World government: resistances, 66–69; and Einstein, 128–29; for preservation of peace, 134–35, 264; and the world community, 135–37, 145; and Hutchins, 473

World Health Organization, 158, 249

Yalta Conference, 148, 151, 183, 207, 246, 459, 469

Yucca Flats tests; *see* Atomic weapons tests

Zacharias, Admiral Ellis M., 190

Zilliacus, Konni, 174 n.

Zinn, Walter H., 398

ZORC, 429

Zuckert, Eugene M., 431